# Between Mussolini and Hitler

# DANIEL CARPI

# Between Mussolini and Hitler

The Jews and the Italian Authorities

in France and Tunisia

**Brandeis University Press**
Published by University Press of New England
Hanover and London

Brandeis University Press

Published by University Press of New England, Hanover, NH 03755

© 1994 by the Trustees of Brandeis University

Printed in the United States of America

5　4　3　2　1

CIP data appear at the end of the book

THE TAUBER INSTITUTE FOR THE STUDY OF
EUROPEAN JEWRY SERIES

Jehuda Reinharz, General Editor

The Tauber Institute for the Study of European Jewry, established by a
gift to Brandeis University from Dr. Laszlo N. Tauber, is dedicated to
the memory of the victims of Nazi persecutions between 1933 and 1945.
The Institute seeks to study the history and culture of European Jewry
in the modern period. The Institute has a special interest in studying
the causes, nature, and consequences of the European Jewish catastrophe and seeks to explore them within the contexts of modern European
diplomatic, intellectual, political, and social history. The Tauber Institute for the Study of European Jewry is organized on a multidisciplinary
basis, with the participation of scholars in history, Judaic studies, political
science, sociology, comparative literature, and other disciplines.

# CONTENTS

# ACKNOWLEDGMENTS

This work is mainly based on documentation kept in three archives: the Archives of the Italian Foreign Ministry (Archivio Storico, Ministero Affari Esteri), the Archives of the Italian Army—Ground Forces (Archivio Storico, Stato Maggiore Esercito), and the Archives of Contemporary Jewish Documentation (Centre de Documentation Juive Contemporaine). The first two are located in Rome and the third in Paris. In the Foreign Ministry archives, most of the material I used in preparing this book comes from the "Political Affairs" section (Affari Politici). In the archives of the army, I used mainly the files of the Armistice Commission with France (Commissione Italiana di Armistizio con la Francia). Preserved at the Jewish Documentation Center (CDJC) are the documents, although incomplete, of the Italian Consulate in Paris for the years 1940–1943, as well as documents of the German security forces in Paris.

My thanks are due to the directorate and the staff of these Institutes, who allowed me to view their material and provided me with the photocopies I needed. My thanks are also due to the directorate and the staff of Tel Aviv University Library, of the Yad Vashem Archives (Jerusalem), and of St. Antony's College Library (Oxford) for their kind assistance and to Mr. Marzell Kay, who translated the work from Hebrew into English.

This book has been written with the framework of The Chaya and Binyamin Schapelski Chair of Holocaust Studies at Tel Aviv University, and I owe a special debt of gratitude to Mr. Nathan and Mr. David Shapel from Los Angeles, who established this chair in memory of their late parents, Binyamin and Chaya Schapelski.

D.C.

# INTRODUCTION

In the course of 1937, or in the beginning of 1938 at the latest, Mussolini reached the conclusion that an all-out war between the Great Powers was not only inevitable—this he had vaguely believed for years—but also imminent. Nevertheless, based on the information available to him and the assurances he received from time to time from his allies, he estimated that war would not break out—that is, that Germany would not start it—for another four or five years, and in any case not before the close of 1942 or the beginning of 1943.[1] By that time, the process of rearmament of the Italian Army ought to have been brought to completion—according to plans prepared under his direction—together with the transition of industry to a full war production scale. At the impending hour of trial, the fascist state was to be able to enter the battle outfitted with the same weaponry and equipment as its enemies. Moreover—no less important to the Italian leaders—the country would stand beside the German ally equally in military and economic strength, thereby ensuring commensurate political weight to negotiate peace terms and define the nature of the world "New Order" that was due to arise.

The surprising moves made by Nazi Germany in the years preceding the outbreak of war, without consulting its fascist ally and often in total contradiction to its views and expectations—particularly the annexation of Austria in March 1938, the cancellation of the Munich Agreement and the dismemberment of Czechoslovakia a year later, the signing of the non-aggression pact with the Soviet Union in August 1939, and finally the invasion into Poland on 1 September 1939—all these cast a dark shadow on the nature of the partnership that the German leadership had in mind. For the first time the suspicion arose in the hearts of many people, including inside the fascist leadership, that Germany was planning its steps exclusively on the grounds of its own interests, without any consideration whatsoever for the political plans and aspirations of its ally. Germany would drag Italy into a war not only without consulting the latter's opinion on the starting date, but also and principally without conferring on the tactical moves and the long-term strategic aim. This meant, they began to fear, that Italy would end up fighting a war that was not its own and, at its conclusion, as in World War I, would once more be unable to harvest the fruits of victory.

Indeed, when on 1 September 1939 the news reached Rome of the German attack on Poland, which everyone understood would spark an all-out war in Europe, the Italian government and the Fascist Grand Council[2] hurriedly declared a state of "nonbelligerence," meaning that Italy would continue to keep its obligations toward Nazi Germany in accordance to the Steel Pact despite its refraining for the present from entering the battlefield. From that moment onward, however, Mussolini had no doubt—notwithstanding his occasional emotional and theatrical condemnation of Germany in private circles—that, if Italy wished to retain its status as a first-rank power and not lose its "true independence," then the entry of the country into the war alongside Nazi Germany was an inevitable step. "The question is not whether Italy will or will not enter the war, because Italy cannot avoid entering the war," wrote Mussolini in a top secret memorandum of 31 March 1940 intended for the king, the foreign minister, the chief of the General Staff, and the commanders of the army, the navy, and the air force. "What we must know is only when and how. Our interest lies in delaying our entry into the war as long as possible, until that time beyond which delaying any longer will hurt our honor and our position." With that, Mussolini stated in the same document, Italy would not go to war in order to assist Germany in their war. Italy would fight her own war, in order to fulfill her own goals, and would do so in the framework of a "parallel war" to that of the Germans.[3] Or, as he said in an address to high-ranking officers in April 1940, according to the testimony of one of the generals: "Not for Germany, not with Germany, but by Germany's side."[4]

The notion of conducting a "parallel war"—he also coined the term—that Mussolini conceived toward the end of 1939, became a central component in his outlook and affected many of the political and military steps the Italians took in the course of the war, especially at the beginning.[5] Accordingly, the Italian government decided to attack Greece in October 1940, without first consulting their ally and knowing all too well Germany's opposition to this step.[6] It conducted an independent policy toward countries that were allies or satellites of the Axis in order to create a concentration of forces that would in the future counterbalance the overwhelming might of Germany. It allowed its military and civilian representatives in the occupied countries to make political decisions separate from those made by the Germans; for example, in Croatia the Italians supported the Chetnik fighters led by General Draža Mihailović, while the German Army fought intensely against them. Above all, the notion of a parallel war allowed the

Italians to conduct independent policies toward the civilian populations in the occupied countries and toward national and religious minorities among those, such as the Serbs in the independent Croatian state and the Jews in Croatia, in Greece, and in Vichy France. This was done despite the fact that it was obvious that their policy on this matter would be interpreted as undermining a most basic German principle.

It seems that Mussolini finally decided on the date of Italy's entry into the war only on 27 or 28 May 1940; that is, as he had intended from the outset, at a time when the results of the military operations on French soil were already a certainty and the end of operations, in his estimation, still not so close that it would cast discredit on the Italian intervention or reduce the importance of their military contribution. To his great disappointment, events unfolded differently and, above all, not according to the schedule he had expected.

The speed with which the German armies overran France, which had been considered one of the greatest powers in the world, surprised Mussolini. On 17 June 1940, when the French asked to open negotiations over the terms of the armistice, the Italian contribution to the war effort was still so modest that even Mussolini, who had led Italy to war in order to gain leverage in the peace talks, had to accept the fact that his role in the negotiations about to be opened could not be more than secondary. "The war was won by Hitler without any active military participation on the part of Italy," he commented with obvious dissatisfaction to his son-in-law, Foreign Minister Ciano, "and it is Hitler who will have the last word."[7] In Munich on 18 and 19 June, when the two leaders met to discuss the conditions of armistice to be imposed on France, it became clear that Hitler did indeed have the last word and that German policy goals, at least in the short range, were quite different from those of his ally.

Following the great victories across the European continent, and in preparation for the next stage of the campaign—against Britain, should that country not agree to disarm, or on the eastern front, should such a front be opened—Hitler was interested in not deepening the hostility between his country and France. He believed, as did many in the German Foreign Office and armed forces, that "generous" armistice terms and a policy of "cooperation" in limited, defined areas could bring the Vichy government closer to the Axis powers and might even, under certain conditions, persuade Vichy to join forces with them.[8] Moreover, defeated and humiliated France still possessed two real assets in the global, strategic balance of power: a large, effective navy that had suffered no damage whatsoever in the fighting, and "the empire beyond the sea," with its mighty air and naval bases. The Axis powers felt that it was vital that these be immediately taken out of action and not be allowed to go on assisting the British war effort. The trend of German policy, as expressed in the armistice agreement, was to make the Vichy government responsible for implementing those two missions. In order to strengthen that government, the Germans even agreed to leave a fairly large army (hundreds of thousands of soldiers, plus naval and air units) at its disposal in the lands beyond the sea, enabling Vichy France to protect its colonies "from any invader"—that is, in June 1940, from takeover attempts by the British and their allies, the Gaullists.

Most, if not all, of these political considerations were completely opposite to those held by Italy. The Italians doubted the ability of the Vichy government to impose its authority over the military and civilian functionaries in charge of the navy and the colonies. Moreover, they believed that the risks inherent in that policy exceeded its chances of success, as the former enemy, now in charge of Europe's frontline strongholds in Africa and Asia, might one day abandon them to invaders, instead of defending them. Most of all, the Italians were convinced that that policy ran counter to their own traditional colonialist ambitions and might stand in their way in the long run.[9] These fears, in fact, were far from groundless: both armistice agreements signed by the Vichy government, on 22 June with Germany, and on 24 June with Italy, were founded on the Axis powers' recognition of France's continued sovereignty over all its colonies, at least until the opening of peace negotiations, because otherwise Vichy could not be held responsible for their defense.

Even the temporary agreements made with France for the duration of the war according to the armistice conditions did not fulfill any of Italy's demands. As a result of these agreements, France was divided into two zones, with a "demarcation line" separating them. The one, occupied by the German Army,[10] included the departments north of the Loire River as well as a wide strip along the Atlantic coast to the Spanish border. The other included the departments in the center and south of the country, where the government of Marshal Philip Pétain ruled—in theory and to a limited degree, mainly on internal matters. Within that framework, only a small area on the Mediterranean coast, around the township of Menton, remained in the hands of the Italians, their army having physically occupied

FRANCE, 1940–1942

Zone attached to the German Command at Brussels

Annexed zone

BELGIUM

LUX.

GERMANY

SWITZER-LAND

L. Geneva

ITALY

SPAIN

Demarcation line between Occupied France and Vichy France, 1940–1942

Pithiviers  Internment camps

LINCOLN GRAPHICS, INC.

The "demarcation line" between the German zone of occupation and the zone under the control of the Vichy government.
Based on Serge Klarsfeld, *Vichy-Auschwitz*, vol. I, pp. 16–17. Used with permission.

it during the few days of fighting that preceded the surrender of France.[11] Despite their failure to achieve territorial advantages, the Italians managed to include a clause in the armistice agreement that along the border with Italy a strip of territory extending 50 kilometers into France would be demilitarized and that an Italian-French Armistice Commission,[12] whose headquarters were in Turin, would supervise the execution of demilitarization with the help of observers. They would be entitled to visit the zone without restriction and could even stay there on a permanent basis.[13]

Later on this clause served a very important purpose for the Italians that had nothing whatsoever to do with its original military objective. In June 1940, with the entry of Italy into the war, all her diplomatic and consular representative offices in France had been closed. These offices, more than twelve scattered throughout France, dealt with a wide variety of economic and social interests, as on the eve of the war over 720,000 Italian citizens were living in France as permanent residents (in addition to large numbers of seasonal workers). The signing of the armistice agreement did not put an end to the state of war between the two countries from the juridical aspect, and it contained nothing that would allow the Italians to reopen their delegations, unless the French authorities agreed to this. The Italians therefore made use of their right to send observer teams into the demilitarized zone, and already in July 1940 they opened consular offices, in the guise of offices of the Armistice Commission,[14] in Nice, Cannes, Toulon, Marseilles, Chambéry, and Lyon.

Negotiations on this matter with the Vichy government ended only on 4 February 1941, when the Italians were permitted once more to open consular offices outside the 50 kilometer belt, in Toulouse, Montpellier, Nice, and Hagen. Within the Occupied Zone, on the other hand, after agreement with the German Military Government in July 1940 the Italians opened consulates in Paris, Bordeaux, Dijon, Nancy, Nantes, and Reims. As a unique gesture of good will, the Germans also allowed their allies to open diplomatic offices in Paris, which on 1 January 1942, after long and wearying negotiations, were granted full embassy status.[15] This diplomatic delegation—and later embassy—had a liaison office in Vichy that negotiated with the government of Marshal Pétain on topics of a general diplomatic character concerning the two countries. At the same time, and quite loosely coordinated with the diplomatic representative in Paris, the implementation of clauses in the armistice agreement was discussed within the framework of the joint armistice commission that met in Turin. The consular offices, on the other hand, dealt with the whole complex of Italian economic interests in France, including those of Italian residents. In this context, the affairs of Italian Jews residing in France fell into their hands from the start.

The attitude of the Italian authorities to the large Italian community in France was not unambiguous, and, alongside the desire to preserve national solidarity, there were displays of suspicion, dissociation, and even profound political hostility. This diaspora as a whole was not a source of pride to the mother-country. Among them were many people on the fringe of society, emigrants lacking education and with no professional skills, barely making a living from casual labor. Some even engaged in illicit activities, bordering on crime. In addition, according to an internal Italian diplomatic source, "this colony did not shine either in their past history, their way of life, or in civil obedience."[16] The educated among them, as well as those of the second generation who had acquired an education and a trade, were inclined to mingle with the society around them, and most of them already regarded themselves for all purposes as French. On the outbreak of war they joined the French Army in their thousands or volunteered for the Foreign Legion, fought in its ranks, and sided unreservedly with their country of residence. Even worse were those few intellectuals who continued to regard themselves as Italian patriots and as people whose future was irrevocably bound up with the events in Italian society. They were for the most part political refugees, active in the ranks of the anti-fascist émigrés—*fuorusciti* according to the official term of those days— leaders of the Giustizia e Libertà movement,[17] activists of the left-wing parties, people of the liberal intelligentsia.[18] Because of their educational and intellectual stature, such personalities as Filippo Turati, Luigi Campolonghi, Pietro Nenni, Giorgio Amendola, Ignazio Silone, Aldo Garosci, and others were certainly above the rest of the Italian colony in France and would endow it with both honor and status. It is however doubtful whether the official representatives of the fascist government were prepared to bask in the glory of such men as these.

The confrontation with the small community of Jews bearing Italian citizenship was also problematic. At the outbreak of the war there were about 1,500 Italian Jews in France,[19] the largest group of whom, some 500 individuals, was concentrated in Paris and its surroundings.[20] For the most part, this group was composed of people from eastern Mediterranean countries, mainly Greece and Turkey. They were primarily Jews who had inherited their Italian citizenship from their parents,[21] without ever having permanently resided in Italy. When they moved their homes to France, they retained their Italian citizenship, either out of convenience or commercial expedience, often for a limited period until they could replace it with French citizenship. If one is to judge from the many letters that they showered on the consulate in Paris in the years 1941 and 1942, Italian was for all intents and purposes a foreign language. A few of them were even unable to express themselves in broken Italian and wrote their letters in French. In that language they tried to persuade their correspondents that they were in every way Italians and that they were entitled to Italian consular protection from the laws of discrimination and dispossession decreed by the Vichy government and the German Military Command. Another group, who could be singled out by their special political and social background, was made up of antifascist émigrés, such as Carlo Rosselli (who together with his brother Nello was murdered in June 1937 at the hands of French fascist mercenaries acting as emissaries of Italian intelligence),[22] Claudio Treves, Giuseppe Emanuele Modigliani, Emilio Sereni (brother of Chayim Enzo[23]), and Leo Valiani, who were all among the outstanding personalities of this "emigration." In 1939 and the beginning of 1940, these two groups were joined by a third: Jews, mostly members of well-to-do families, who had settled on the French Riviera after becoming disgusted with the racial laws and the oppressive and repellent atmosphere prevailing in their country, in the belief that within the borders of the great French democracy they would be beyond the reach of the long and menacing arm of fascist antisemitism (not to speak of Nazi antisemitism). They had not imagined that they would be among the first to face these dangers and that, in seeking protection from the degrading antisemitic policy of the Vichy government, they would be forced to turn to the representatives of the same fascist government that had been so abhorrent to them. In any event, there is no doubt that these Jews, regardless of the group to which they belonged, were not the class of citizens whom the Italian representatives in France were interested in attracting or in employing. On the contrary, in the consciousness of these representatives, this combination of elements—cosmopolitanism, capitalism, and leftist antifascism—that seemed to arise from the social and political composition of the Italian Jewish community in France easily combined with the stereotype of the Jew that the fascist government had nurtured since the beginning of the racial campaign of 1938: the Jew as a symbol of the corruption that had attacked democratic society and as the origin of the seething hostility toward the totalitarian regimes.

Political relations between fascist Italy and the Third Republic of France were extremely unstable during the interwar years. Despite several attempts at rapprochement, particularly in the mid-1930s when Laval served as foreign minister and as prime minister, political and ideological dissensions surfaced more and more frequently, troubling relations between the two countries and more than once bringing them to a point of crisis.

In their own views the fascist leaders had quite a number of good reasons to harbor hostility toward its "Latin neighbor." France with its democratic traditions had been from the 1920s the main country of asylum for political émigrés from Italy and the center of antifascist activity abroad.[24] Radical France during the 1930s, in the days of the Popular Front and the friendship treaty with the Soviet Union, was the principal basis for enlisting support for the Spanish "Reds" and one of the main, if not the most effective, obstacles to the expansion of fascism across the European continent. Above all, France with her Mediterranean districts and rich overseas colonies was the country at which most of the unfulfilled Italian territorial claims were directed. It must therefore be added that Mussolini—who from the beginning did not discount the possibility of creating a joint front with France as a counterbalance to the political might of Great Britain or Germany—bore a deep personal grudge from the mid-1930s against the governments that rose in France after the fall of Laval. He accused them of "betraying" him in reneging on the promises that Laval had made to him (that, when the time came, France would not join the opposition to Italy's invasion into Ethiopia, or at least would not be active in opposing the invasion).[25] Within this context, animosity toward France increased, and among the fascist leadership there was growing recognition that the idea of a rapprochement between the two countries in the foreseeable future became impracticable, as it seemed doubtful that it would be capable of serving the objectives of Italian policy in the Mediterranean.

The position taken on the French side was far less homogenous, at least until the second half of the 1930s, and, as might be expected in a democratic society, opinions differed over the question of relations with Italy and its totalitarian fascist regime. The attitude of the left-wing circles was on principle most hostile. Nevertheless, opinions varied even among these between total rejection of any kind of cooperation with "the murderers of Matteotti"—according to Léon Blum's definition—and reserved readiness to cooperate with the Italian government in order to create a joint front against the main enemy, Nazi Germany. Even among the liberals, who in general were not supporters of the fascist regime, there were those who considered it would be unwise to burn all bridges to the neighboring state and believed that it would be preferable to search for some kind of understanding with it, at least at the tactical level of foreign policy. Finally the right-wing circles were used to praise in unison Mussolini's personality, his leadership, and his achievements inside the country and in the international arena. However, even from them were heard from the mid-1930s words both of mild criticism of the Italian foreign policy, for not sufficiently allowing France's senior international position, and of clear disagreement with Italian territorial claims. This broad spectrum of opinions shrank toward the end of 1938, and it gradually disappeared in the course of 1939, when it became clear to everyone that fascist Italy had chosen to join the enemies of France and that it should be treated as a potential enemy (who alongside Germany was liable to represent a real threat).[26]

Of course, Italy's entry into the war in June 1940 deepened the enmity between the two countries. The Italians, as previously mentioned, did not trust the French government that emerged from the ruins of the Third Republic in the south of the country, while Marshal Pétain's government did not look with great favor on the "Latin sister." Italy had gone to war against France whose armies had just been defeated on the battlefield by the Germans and had become a partner in a victory in the achievement of which, in the opinion of many, it had had no part of any kind. In fact, despite the armistice agreement that France signed with Italy on 24 June 1940, the Vichy government did not conceal the fact that, although they recognized the defeat that France had suffered and were prepared to bear the consequences of it, they were not ready to recognize the Italians as partners in the victory over France. Furthermore, they did not consider themselves obliged to meet any Italian economic or territorial demands, neither during the war nor in any future peace conference. "Italy did in fact declare war on us," the French representative said to his German colleague at one of the first sessions of the Franco-German Armistice Commission, "but they did not make war against us."[27] Why, therefore, should they regard themselves as victors and even present victors' demands? Despite the ideological affinity between the two totalitarian regimes (and there are grounds to believe that the men of Vichy who strove to create a new French state out of the "national revolution," inclined more to the model of Italian fascism than to German Nazism), hostility continued to reign between the two governments.[28] In fact, until the beginning of November 1942, diplomatic contacts between them were confined to discussions on matters of a mainly technical nature, concerned with the implementation of some clause or other in the armistice agreement or dealing with the daily economic interests of the Italian citizens living in France.

Within this general political framework, the presence and influence of the Italians in both parts of France until November 1942 were extremely limited, and in any case their ability to intervene on the matter of the Jews were equally very restricted. In the northern zone occupied by the Germans, the Italians could intervene only in the affairs of the Jews who held Italian citizenship. Even to this the Germans agreed only reluctantly, and no one dared expect that they would be ready to grant their allies broader authority. Therefore, negotiations concerning the Jews in that zone focused either on specific subjects relating to the nature and range of consular protection that the Italians would be permitted to extend to their citizens or on formal questions of who could be considered an Italian citizen (where for some reason or other the matter was in any doubt, such as in the case of wives of Italian citizens or of one-time Italian citizens who at some time in the past renounced their citizenship). This situation did not change in the German-occupied zone until the beginning of 1943, when, under heavy German pressure, the Italian authorities decided to evacuate all their Jewish citizens and return them to Italy.

Even in the Unoccupied Zone under the control of the Vichy government, the Italians, until the beginning of November 1942, had no kind of formal position enabling them to intervene in the affairs of the Jews, apart from granting the usual consular protection to all their own citizens, including Jews. These very same Jews, however, just a few hundred in number, were until then in practice exempt from most of the discriminatory measures taken by the Vichy government against Jews,[29] and thus the Italian representatives did not need to intervene on their behalf, except in a few individual cases.[30] During this period the Italians were eyewitnesses not only to the introduction of a policy of social discrimination and of economic dispossession—the like of which had already been enforced in their own country—but also of the arrest and deportation of tens of thousands of Jews from French soil. For the first time, they saw with their own eyes, closely and directly, the true meaning and some of the frightening consequences of German racial policy. After the Axis forces took control over part of the southern districts, this knowledge, together with the additional information coming from other occupied countries, was in fact one of the factors that contributed to determine the Italian attitude on the matter.

The invasion of the Axis forces into the Vichy government zone on 10 November 1942 and the creation of the Italian Occupation Zone comprising ten districts in southeastern France, placed the Italian authorities face to face with a new reality in their handling of the Jewish question. For the first time, they became responsible for the fate of some 30,000 Jews, for the most part registered as "aliens," over whose heads the danger of deportation to the "eastern territories" hung. At the same time the Italian authorities, both in France and in Rome, no longer harbored any doubts whatsoever about the nature and tragic consequences of these deportations, and, although details about what was happening in the lands of exile were not yet known, they certainly did not intend to have their army become an active partner in the implementation of this policy. This was not their policy, and its aims, as had become evident to them, were fundamentally different from those of the racial policy (miserable as it was in itself) that had been introduced in their country in 1938. Furthermore, it quickly became clear to both Italian diplomats and military personnel that for political reasons of their own they could not agree that French police or German security forces should perform the work in their place and carry out the deportations in areas that were under their military control. They believed that any such action would seriously harm their political standing, would be interpreted as relinquishing their sovereign authority in the area to the Vichy government, and would present them in the eyes of the residents as junior partners dragged by the Great German Reich, following in everything the latter's policies. This, after all, concerned a geographical area over which the Italians had notorious territorial claims and where they were particularly interested in appearing as a power standing alongside their ally, yet implementing a consistent and independent policy. For these reasons, officials of the Foreign Ministry and officers of the General Staff in Rome decided, from the outset of their rule in southern France, that all matters concerning the Jews in their Occupation Zone—"alien," French, and Italian—would be subjected to the exclusive authority of the Italian military forces on the spot (and later, under the Italian police situated there). As a result of this decision, the Italians prevented from the beginning any interference, both from the Vichy police and the German security forces—despite loud protests from the Vichy authorities and intense German diplomatic pressure from the uppermost echelons in Paris, Berlin, and Rome—and succeeded in avoiding the deportation of the Jews from their zone of occupation until their withdrawal from France in September 1943.

The number of Jews in France on the eve of the German occupation was estimated at 350,000. Most of them, however, were immigrants from Eastern Europe or refugees from Germany and Austria, who were considered aliens according to the French laws and were not yet eligible for French citizenship. About 200,000 Jews resided in Paris and its environs, and a little over 100,000 were in the northern and western districts of the country that would be included in the Occupied Zone. It seems that only about 40,000 Jews were in the districts included in the zone ruled by the Vichy government. This picture changed dramatically during the war years, at first primarily because of the general events engulfing the country and then because of the social and economic measures taken against the Jews. Many preferred to abandon their homes and request asylum—a precarious one—in the Unoccupied Zone before, of course, the German and Italian armies invaded there in the beginning of November 1942.

The number of Jews in Vichy France between summer 1940 and summer 1942 (i.e., before the great deportations also started there) is not known with any certainty and has been the subject of a number of different and even strange estimates.[31] The truth is that for several reasons an accurate determination of this figure would involve great objective difficulties. Masses of refugees had already entered the region during the fights of May–June 1940. Among these were many Jews who could not, or perhaps did not want, to return to their homes in the German-occupied zone when the fighting had ended.[32] Furthermore, even after the armistice agreements were signed, Jews continued to stream into the region from northern France, Belgium, and Holland. At the same time many Jews were also being transferred there after their expulsion by the German authorities from Alsace (July 1940), from Bordeaux and its surroundings (August 1940), and from the regions of Baden and Saarpfalz (October 1940). On the other hand, during the same period many Jews were leaving the region, either equipped with legal emigration permits or illegally crossing the borders into Switzerland or Spain. The Jewish population in Vichy France was thus constantly in flux, making an accurate count very difficult; no matter how accurate any estimate might be, it can only reflect reality for only the briefest time.

The only reliable piece of information available on this subject is that under the Vichy government law of 2 June 1941,[33] 139,938 Jews were reported in the Unoccupied Zone during the second half of 1941 (and this in a region, where, as stated, the prewar Jewish population probably did not exceed 40,000 individuals). Of these, 73,079 Jews were registered as aliens. In that period, close to 40,000 foreign Jews were already confined in concentration camps in southern France,[34] and it may be assumed that at least part of the internees were in fact not included in the count.[35] It also appears that some Jews did not comply with the law and did not report, on the assumption—which was not entirely illogical in view of the conditions of those days—that nothing good would come to them from registering in the books of the Ministry of Interior (and police). It may therefore be said that the number of Jews within the borders of the Vichy regime during the second half of 1941 exceeded 140,000 and apparently fluctuated between 140,000 and 180,000.

Another country where the Italian authorities were faced with problems similar to those of France over the status of the Jews was Tunisia. This country had also been under the rule of the Vichy government since the signing of the armistice agreements of June 1940. From the middle of November 1942 until the middle of May 1943, it was ruled jointly by the Axis forces who had landed on its soil, allegedly to protect the country from an invasion by the Allied armies. In Tunisia, too, on the initiative of the Vichy government, laws similar to those in force at that time in France had been enacted, discriminating against and financially dispossessing Jews. As soon as the Germans took control, the Jews of Tunisia faced the same dangers as those of Jews in all the other occupied countries of Europe. In both periods, the Italian consular representatives in Tunisia protected their Jewish citizens there, a little more than 5,000 souls, with the full knowledge and support of the Roman authorities. Until November 1942, the Italian Consulate insisted that the Vichy laws against the Jews should not be applied to their citizens, and for the most part they achieved this, in practice if not in principle; during the six months of the Axis rule, they succeeded in preventing all harm to their persons and property.

The attitude of the Italian authorities in Tunisia was also special in one way. In addition to most of the motives that determined their actions in France, the Italians regarded the protection of their Jewish citizens in Tunisia as a part, even an important part, of their efforts to preserve the entire Italian colony living there. The existence of this large, long-established colony, which never fell in numbers much below its French counterpart, had always been one of the central arguments that the Italians used to substantiate their claim for rule over Tunisia. In view of this, the French endeavored in various ways to prevent its development, and the Italians did everything in their power to protect it and to preserve the economic and social positions they held. However, everyone knew that many of these key positions—in fact the majority of them—were in the hands of the small Jewish-Italian community's members. By implementing the discriminatory laws of the Vichy government against the Jews and by transferring their property into the hands of "Aryan" French citizens, not only would the Italian Jews be harmed, but also great damage would be done to the whole Italian colony, even perhaps causing its total collapse. The Italian authorities were therefore most vitally interested in preserving the social position of their Jewish citizens, and in preventing their property from being expropriated and transferred into French hands; they did, in fact, energetically insist on this, in general successfully. It should also be noted that in Tunisia, unlike in France, the Italians protected only their own Jewish citizens. Nevertheless, it seems that in some cases French and Tunisian Jews also benefited indirectly from this action, because the French authorities in Tunisia sometimes refrained from publishing a decree if they realized that the Italian Jews were to be exempted from it, in order not to discriminate against Jews holding French citizenship.

The attitude of the Italian authorities toward the Jews in France and in Tunisia—as in Croatia and Greece—was therefore linked with general political and economic factors, along with local ones peculiar to each country. Beyond this, however, this episode touches directly on some historical issues of deep significance in the history of the Jewish people in modern times. One issue relates to the attitude of the Fascist party toward Jews in general, in Italy and abroad, in both its ideological principles and its practical policies. Another issue relates to the position of individuals and entire communities concerning the fate of the Jews during the Holocaust period. In this aspect, the subject goes beyond the limits of political and economic considerations and enters the sphere of personal and general norms of human ethics. In this work I try to make a contribution on these different levels, as humble as it may be, and to provide answers based as much as possible on documents, evidence, and facts.

# Part I

Northern France: The Occupied Zone

(JUNE 1940–SEPTEMBER 1943)

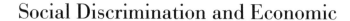

# Social Discrimination and Economic Restrictions

## (JUNE 1940–JUNE 1942)

On 20 May 1940, while the military operation in northern France was going full blast and at a time when millions of French people were abandoning their homes, filling the highways of their country in their flight to the south, the supreme commander of the German forces issued an order concerning the continued orderly conduct of economic, agricultural, and industrial concerns in the occupied areas—in Holland, Belgium, Luxembourg, and France. The order referred to the appointment of managers over the concerns abandoned by their owners and consequently in danger of closure. Some months later, on 27 September, when life was beginning to return to normal, the commander-in-chief of the Military Government in France published an "Order Concerning Proceedings Against Jews,"[1] the foundation for most of the economic and social measures later imposed on the Jews in the Occupied Zone. The order determined that anyone whose religion was Jewish or had more than two Jewish grandparents by religion would be considered a Jew. Those considered Jews according to this definition were forbidden to return to the Occupied Zone if they had fled during the fighting. If they had remained there, they were obliged to report to the *préfectures* (offices of the French district governor) and place a sign in German and in French at the entrance to their business, warning that this was a Jewish business. A second order, also "concerning measures against the Jews," was published on 18 October 1940 and dealt in great detail with the definition of the term *Jewish business*. It appears that this term was not unambiguous, because in practice there was a wide range of "mixed" businesses, such as partnerships between Jews and Aryans, part owner-ships, and ownership of shares. The order determined that the owners of businesses defined as Jewish would be obliged to register them at the *pré-fectures* and that "a commissioned manager might be appointed,"[2] who would act in accordance with the provisions of 20 May concerning abandoned businesses. This clause, which for some reason was phrased in a nonmandatory form, was from the outset understood to be mandatory in all respects, as it seems had been the intention of the legislator, and thus the principle of confiscation of Jewish property in the Occupied Zone was established in theory and in practice.

The question remaining open was who would benefit from this property: the Germans who had initiated the act of confiscation, or the French to whom its execution had been entrusted (they were in charge of both the registration of the property and the appointment of the commissioners). It appears that both parties were interested in the same prize, and both hurried to create facts favorable to themselves. On 27 October and 5 November, General de la Laurencie, the general representative of the Vichy government in the Occupied Zone, contacted the *préfets* and instructed them on how to appoint the commissioners and what procedures to adopt to ensure that the operation was conducted efficiently, without delay, and without allowing anyone to evade the obligations of the German order.[3] The French general thereby served not only the interests of the Vichy government, in whose name he was acting, but also and principally the German policy of expropriation enacted against Jews in the Occupied Zone. A few days later, on 12 November 1940, General von Stülpnagel,[4] commander-in-chief of the German Military Government in France, directly addressed the French commissioners and issued his own instructions on how to act in the performance of their task. The general also informed them that their appointment fulfilled "first and foremost the task once and for all to eliminate Jewish influence in the French economy"; that they alone were responsible for the management of the businesses, as the Jewish owners "were henceforth stripped of all authority"; and that they would have to report on their actions to the authority who had appointed them. In the last paragraph of the instructions, the general added that the Germans and the French would establish "organs," fully authorized and professionally capable of supervising the activities of the commissioners.[5]

While Germans and French were competing for their share of Jewish property in the Occupied Zone, there arose the incidental matter of the fate of the property of Jews, resident in that area, holding Italian citizenship. The orders that had been published, as well as the instructions issued by both sides, spoke in general terms of Jews according to the religio-racial definition defined by the Military Government. The orders did not refer to the question of nationality, despite the fact that in France "alien Jews" represented a considerable percentage of the total Jewish population (in the Seine district alone, out of a total of 149,734 Jews who had reported in October 1940, 64,070 were of foreign nationality or stateless). The legislator apparently believed there would be no one coming forward to protect these Jews, who for the most part were either nationals of conquered countries such as Poland and later Greece, of satellite countries such as Hungary or Romania, or stateless. Therefore, at the time of publication of the order, the German Foreign Ministry confined itself to issuing secret internal instructions to the Military Government in France that American nationals were to be exempt from its implementation,[6] apparently believing they had thereby fulfilled their obligations concerning the problem of foreign nationals. They had not anticipated that these steps would be challenged by Nazi Germany's closest military ally, the Italian fascist government.

Involvement of the Italian Consulate in Paris in the matter of their Jewish citizens began at the initiative of the Jews themselves. They approached the consulate immediately after publication of the first German order of 27 September, wanting to know what their status would be and what would befall their property; some even went so far as to request assistance in returning to Italy. Gustavo Orlandini,[7] the Italian consul in Paris who reported on this to Rome on 6 October 1940, wanted to know "whether and to what extent the Royal Consulate could intervene in the affairs of Italian Jews and their property in occupied France."[8] Although the reply of the Foreign Ministry was sent only with a considerable delay, it was exhaustive and clearly reflected the position of the Italian authorities in those days. On 29 November 1940, Attilio de Cicco, head of the Department for Italians Abroad,[9] wrote to the consul general in Paris:

> You are empowered to inform the German authorities that the Royal Government would show no interest in steps that might possibly be taken against individuals. This lack of interest is to be especially stressed in connection with Jews who had settled in France after publication in Italy of the well-known racial laws. . . . Nevertheless, our lack of interest is restricted to treatment of a personal nature. If steps of an economic nature should be taken . . . the interests of the Italian State are to be protected, in order to prevent exploitation of the situation by others to the detriment of Italian interests as a whole.[10]

At this stage, therefore, the sole concern of the Italian authorities was that the property of their nationals would not be delivered into the hands of the French. As for the laws of social and racial discrimination that had been published or were about to be published against the Jews in France and that evidently would also affect Italian citizens, similar laws had already been in force in Italy for about two years, so what could motivate the directorate of the Foreign Ministry to oppose their enactment in France?

In accordance with these instructions the staff of the consulate in Paris began to prepare themselves for the protection of Italian property. In brief negotiations conducted in December 1940 with the staff of the economic section of the German Military Government, it was agreed that Italian (Aryan Italian, of course) commissioners would be appointed to oversee the businesses of Jews holding Italian citizenship and that the Italian Consulate, not the French authorities, would be responsible for these appointments. Apart from this, all the restrictions in the German orders would be enforced with no exception made for the Italian Jews.[11]

It would therefore seem that the problem had been solved with no difficulty and to the mutual satisfaction of both parties. The Germans achieved their main goal—a free hand in implementing their policy against Jews holding Italian citizenship. The Italians had obtained the little they desired: their share in the property of the Jews (a minute part, as in metropolitan France, unlike Tunisia,[12] the property of Italian Jews represented a small, almost nonexistent percentage of all Jewish property) and the recognition of their right to handle the confiscation of this property, without depending on the French authorities. In fact, the agreement concluded was to a large extent based on misunderstanding, and the positions of the two sides were still widely different. The Italians believed that from that moment they possessed the right to appoint commissioners, according to their own judgment and as they saw fit, over the property of their Jewish citizens. The Germans on the other hand intended, also in the future, that supervision of the operation as a whole would remain in their hands. They demanded that every case be brought to their attention and examined by their own experts, who would be entitled to decide, on the basis of the documentation presented, whether the individual could be considered an "Italian Jew" and what really constituted his or her property. They even intended to screen the proposed commissioners and determine whether they had the personal and professional abilities to serve in this capacity.

It is unclear why the Germans saw fit to act so harshly toward their ally on this matter, more so as at that time they had no reason to doubt Italy's readiness to collaborate with them in the implementation of their policies toward Jews. Perhaps it was simply bureaucratic stubbornness, or perhaps they thereby wanted to demonstrate that they were the real masters and sole arbiters over affairs in the Occupied Zone. In either case, the result was that they drastically overburdened the staff of the Italian Consulate, and unintentionally—and against their own best interests—they forced the Italians into the strange position of serving as some sort of defense counsel for Jews. In fact, as the Italian diplomats had to handle the affairs of the Italian Jews, and as the files wandered from room to room in the various branches of the German Military Government offices, the Italians found themselves on constant guard, forced to intervene to prevent the "temporary" appointment of French commissioners or to make sure that any such appointments be retroactively rescinded. The Italians were forced to ensure that Jewish property was not confiscated or that it be restored to them (for otherwise, how could they appoint their own commissioners in the future?). And finally they found themselves responsible for collecting the mass of documents demanded by the Germans and then submitting them on behalf of the Jews to the economic department of the Military Government. This cooperation, which initially took place out of necessity and for different purposes, placed them in one line with the Jews, as though the two parties were on the same side of the table. In the course of time, this led to a certain degree of closeness and even the creation of more or less normal human relations—within the bounds of the distorted norms of those days.

The consul general in Paris, Gustavo Orlandini, who reported regularly on the measures taken by the occupation authorities against the Jews, also pointed out the damage to Italian interests liable to arise from these measures and the untiring efforts made by the consulate in order to protect them. On 18 February 1941, Orlandini raised a question of principle: whether he should continue to restrict himself to the demand that Aryan Italian commissioners be appointed, or whether "it was preferable to ask the local German authorities that the measures [against Jews] not be implemented against Italian citizens."[13] In this proposal one may possibly identify an attempt on the part of the consulate staff not only to be relieved from part of the bureaucratic burden but also to ease the situation of their Jewish citizens. If that is the case, then the reply from the Foreign Ministry was totally unencouraging. Although the head of the Department for Italians Abroad did in fact warmly praise the action of the consulate, he reconfirmed the previous instructions: there would be only one demand— that the commissioners appointed to oversee Italian Jewish property should themselves be Italian Aryan citizens.[14]

Following the same line, the Italian Foreign Ministry again denied another request made by Consul Orlandini on 28 February 1941. He proposed that the consulate ask the German authorities to set special working procedures for the Italian commissioners (apparently more convenient than those of the French commissioners).[15] From Rome he was unequivocally informed that there was no reason for asking the Germans to treat the property of Italian Jews differently from the property of all other Jews and that the Italian commissioners would have "to adapt themselves to the general instructions issued by the military governor."[16] This reply in fact arrived after a considerable delay, and meanwhile, on their own initiative, the consulate staff had negotiated with the German authorities and agreed on more conducive working conditions.[17] Even so, the bureaucratic burden imposed on them was too heavy to bear. Just on one day alone, 10 May 1941, the consulate had submitted to the economic section of the Military Government the files of thirty Jews, Italian citizens according to their own claim and as certified by the consulate, on whose property the consulate wished to appoint their own commissioners, for whom the consulate also had to submit full documentation concerning their identity, their professional skills, and political loyalty.

Whether because of this intolerable burden or because the situation of the Jews in France had steadily deteriorated, toward the end of May, the consulate once again raised their proposal to exclude Italian citizens from the general application of the measures already taken or due to be published against the Jews in France. This time the reason for renewing the initiative came from outside France and from an entirely unexpected source. At the beginning of March 1941, Jews of Italian nationality residing in Vienna had applied to the Italian consul in that city, complaining that the authorities had exchanged the food ration cards that had been in their possession for others that were marked with the letter *J*. These papers, so the consul explained to the Italian Ambassador in Berlin, would restrict their bearers to buying necessities "only during a few hours in the afternoon and so they would suffer serious harm." On complaining to the local authorities, the consul received the reply that this had been done in accordance with the state law of 6 December 1940 that equated the status of "all members of the Jewish race," foreigners as well as Germans. Strict instructions had been received to exempt from the law only Jews bearing U.S., Russian, and Turkish citizenship. The consul regarded this as discrimination against Italian citizens and informed the Italian ambassador in Berlin of this, with the request that he be sent instructions on how to behave in the situation.[18]

Serving as ambassador of Italy in Berlin in those days was Dino Alfieri, one of the veterans of the Nationalist movement that preceded the establishment of the Fascist party, a man who came to the diplomatic service after having held senior political positions. (Among others, he served as minister of propaganda in Mussolini's government from 1936 to 1939, and in this capacity he had to explain the internal logic and the political necessity of the legislation "for the protection of the race").[19] In his report to Rome, Alfieri expressed his belief that the case of the Viennese Jews, which had been brought to his attention, was only one expression of a more extensive problem affecting the standing and rights of all Jews holding Italian citizenship and living in Germany. He therefore proposed to deal with the subject as a whole and even suggested two guidelines for determining the policy of the ministry on the subject: first, that under no circumstances were discriminatory laws to apply to Italian citizens living abroad, who were not defined as Jews in accordance with the Italian race laws; and second, that the Italian racial legislation be considered a domestic matter, just as the German racial legislation was a German domestic matter, and therefore did not apply outside the borders of the state. As for the specific case under discussion, Alfieri proposed that the Foreign Ministry instruct the consulate in Vienna to act in accordance with the precedent set in Prague and ask the German authorities, "without raising the question of principle," that the indicated measures not be applied to Italian citizens.[20]

As was customary, Ambassador Alfieri's proposals were sent to the Political Department of the Foreign Ministry, not to the Department for Italians Abroad (to which only the delegations of the Armistice Commission in France were subject). A short time later, Count Leonardo Vitetti replied that the Foreign Ministry shared the ambassador's opinion, demanding of the Germans that measures against the Jews of Germany be not applied against Italian citizens—all this "without raising the question of principle."[21] This reply, the first statement delivered by the political department of the ministry, was transmitted to the embassy in Berlin and from there to the consulates under its jurisdiction throughout the Greater Reich, in Prague, Vienna, Danzig, Luxembourg, Metz, and Mulhouse, among others.[22] Copies of the correspondence between Vienna, Berlin, and Rome were also transmitted to the Italian Consulate in Paris, after the latter had approached the ministry on its own initiative, wanting to know about the fate of Jewish Italian citizens living in Germany.

Relying on this precedent set for the Jews of the Reich, the consulate in Paris asked, apparently at the end of May 1941, its superiors in Rome for permission to approach the German authorities in France and demand that the measures against the Jews "which are about to be published" not apply to the holders of Italian citizenship.[23] It is not difficult to guess what Consul Orlandini referred to in his words. On 28 May 1941, a few days after he had sent his letter, the "Fourth Order" of the German Military Government in France was published, with the intent of widening the operation of confiscating Jewish property.[24] This time the targets of the legislator were the small businesses over which the authorities had until then not succeeded in appointing commissioners. The owners of these businesses were now also forbidden to realize their liquid assets and other means of payment at their disposal if these exceeded a certain sum, unless they had obtained a special permit from the responsible office. It was clear that these measures, of which Orlandini had probably heard from his German colleagues a few days before their publication, were liable to cause severe harm to the Jews of Italian nationality, many of whom were making their living from small businesses in trade and handicrafts. It was also clear that following the Fourth Order the consulate staff would have to take upon themselves an additional burden of administrative work, no less weighty than the one that had come earlier: they would now have to serve as "trustees" for the frozen assets of their Jewish nationals and have to prevent the impounding of these accounts by other bodies, on behalf either of the German Army or the Vichy authorities. (And for each case, of course, the Italians would have to collect thick files of documents and certificates to prove their demands.) For those reasons, and perhaps also out of genuine concern for the victims themselves, Orlandini raised the aforementioned proposal for an overall exemption from the instructions of the order, which would benefit the Italian Jews.

From the documentation that has survived in Rome and Paris, there is no way of knowing whether a direct answer was ever given to this enquiry, but in fact a solution of compromise was found on the local level. In negotiations conducted in Paris between Advocate Indelli, the legal adviser of the consulate and Dr. Blanke, the person in charge of Jewish affairs in the economic department of the German Military Government, it was agreed that the private assets of Italian Jews would be unfrozen (and would remain—so it should seemingly be understood—at the disposal of their owners), whereas sums of money that would be received from the sale of Jewish businesses would be delivered to the consulate. The Italians on their part undertook to ensure that in no case would Jewish money, no matter where it originated, be transferred from the Occupied Zone into the domain of the Vichy government.[25]

The question of the transfer of Jewish property from zone to zone was raised from time to time in discussions held between the Italian representatives and the German military authorities. Everyone understood that, despite all the prohibitions of the German administration, the Jews who had crossed the "line of demarcation" and sought asylum in the region under Vichy control were trying to transfer at least a part of the property they had left behind. The officials in the economic department of the German Military Government suspected that the "preferential status" enjoyed by Jews with Italian citizenship was likely to assist them in performing such an illegal operation and even in smuggling out capital for other Jews. German willingness to meet the requests of the consulate concerning the frozen assets of their Jewish citizens was therefore made conditional on an arrangement on this subject to which the Italians agreed.

At that very same time, although there was no connection between the events, the question of the transfer of Jewish property was also raised on the other side of the demarcation line, by the Italian Consulate in Nice (that was still operating as the Delegation for Civilian Affairs of the Armistice Commission). This time, apart from the usual economic arguments, the Italians raised political considerations that had not been heard in France yet and that are worth examining.

The affair began at the initiative of an Italian citizen called Reginella Goetz, a Jewess previously residing in Paris who had fled to Nice during the fighting and left behind the bulk of her property. Her request was that the Italian delegation should assist her in restoring possession of her property or gaining its cash equivalent. From the beginning of the summer of 1941, the delegation in Nice was headed by Count Quinto Mazzolini, who one year before had been serving as consul general in Jerusalem (and was not known for his sympathy to the Zionist cause), a man whose loyalty to the fascist regime was certainly not under any shadow of doubt.[26] On 12 June 1941, Mazzolini wrote directly to the minister's office at the Foreign Ministry, enclosing the detailed request from Mrs. Goetz; he expressed the opinion that there was room to accede to her request, not only out of concern for Italian interests, "which must be protected irrespective of the race of the Italian citizen concerned," but also for political reasons. Mazzolini explained that the population in the Alpes-Maritimes district was composed of various ethnic groups, hostile to one another. "Sympathetic interest" on the part of the Italian authorities in the affairs of the Jews—not necessarily Italian citizens—could not be without advantage to "our standing in the area, at present and in the future."[27]

It is almost certain that when Mazzolini raised this argument, which was novel in principle, he saw before his eyes the reality with which he had become acquainted during his years of service as consul in various Mediterranean countries. In the course of this, he came to know the distinguished part played by the Jewish communities in local society and the benefit they brought, at least until the publication of the racial laws, to the cultural and economic presence of the Italians in the area.[28] However, at that time, the middle of 1941, Rome was not yet ready for considerations such as these. On 28 June the Department for Italians Abroad replied to the consulate in Paris, with a copy of the letter sent to the delegation in Nice, that the affairs of Mrs. Goetz were to be handled in accordance with the long-standing general instructions, according to which "the racial legislation of the French Government applies also to Jews with Italian citizenship living in France." Although the Italian government was in the habit of protecting the interests of its citizens abroad, "irrespective of race and religion," as stated in that letter, they did so always within the framework of the law of the country where they were residing; namely, in the case of Mrs. Goetz, within the framework of the German and French legislation against the Jews. Moreover, the letter concludes, "it must not be forgotten that the well-known laws for the protection of the race are also in force in Italy and that, for the sake of good public order, these have been put into effect also against foreign Jews."[29] Was it at all conceivable that the Foreign Ministry oppose the application of laws such as these to Italian citizens residing abroad?

While the Italian representatives in Paris were still negotiating with their allies in the German Military Government and with French officials over the crumbs of Jewish property in France—or over matters of procedure connected with the future of this property—far-reaching changes were taking place in the arena of French internal politics and in the European war theater. In Vichy, on 13 December 1940, Pierre Laval, veteran parliamentarian and one of the architects of the policy of cooperation with Germany, who since 12 July had served as deputy prime minister and was the decision maker in Marshal Pétain's government, was dismissed. Appointed in his place was Admiral Darlan, an experienced technocrat with no clear political identity, who took on not only the positions of deputy prime minister and commander-in-chief of the navy but also the portfolios of the interior, foreign affairs, and propaganda ministers—in other words, all the posts that are important in a totalitarian state. During the last months of 1940 and during the course of 1941, both Laval and Darlan attempted to improve the troubled relations between their own government and that of Italy, in the hope that cooperation between the two countries would one day create a kind of counterweight to the mighty power of Nazi Germany. But these attempts were to no avail: Mussolini eyed the steps of rapprochement taken in those days between the Vichy regime and the German leadership with suspicion. He feared that if an understanding were to be achieved between the two governments, it would weaken his own international status and would in the long run come at the expense of Italy's territorial demands. He therefore rejected any idea of reaching an agreement with French statesmen before meeting them as victor at peace treaty talks.[30]

In truth, the last attempt made to reach agreement between the Germans and the Vichy regime in those days also failed: the Paris agreements, initiated 28 May 1941 and intended to create a broad foundation of collaboration between the two countries, even going so far as direct intervention by France in the war alongside the Axis powers, were after all not approved either in Berlin or in Vichy.[31] During the spring and the start of the summer of 1941, the German leaders, both political and military, were deeply immersed in the last preparations of Operation Barbarossa and in the execution of first stages of the operation; they did not have the time—and most probably not even the inclination—to compromise on agreements with defeated France. Politicians in the Vichy regime were deluding themselves when they believed that they would succeed in negotiating with the Germans as equals: under the conditions that had been created, the Nazi leadership was not interested in partners but in submissive and despised collaborators.

The opening of the eastern front at dawn on 22 June 1941 was an event of decisive importance in the course of World War II, and not only from the military aspect. It cast its threatening shadow over the future of all the nations of Europe, their liberty, their civilization, and, for some of them, even their physical survival. In the wake of this, and to a large extent as a result of it, the German leadership set new, extremely far-reaching objectives for their policy toward European Jewry, among these the Jews of Western Europe. In Western Europe, German policy till then had been to strive to isolate the Jews and to force them out of society and the economy by confiscating their possessions. When conditions eventually became ripe, apparently after the end of the war, the Germans intended to remove them completely from the region, by means of expulsion or forced emigration. The German order of 27 September 1940, whereby Jews who had fled to southern France were forbidden to return to their homes in the German Occupied Zone, the expulsion of the Jews of Alsace in July 1940 into the zone under the Vichy regime, and later the expulsion of Jews from the cities of Bordeaux, Baden, and Saarpfalz, are a few of the more prominent examples of this policy. On the other hand, at the beginning of the summer of 1941, with the start of the invasion of the Soviet Union, the picture already changed, and preparations were made toward implementation of the "Final Solution of the Jewish Problem" in Western European countries, too.

On 1 July 1941, SS-Obersturmführer Theodor Dannecker, the adviser for Jewish affairs in France of the Reich Security Main Office (Reichssicherheitshauptamt—RSHA), sent his superiors in Berlin a long and detailed memorandum in which he discussed the "way of handling the Jewish problem in France" in its various stages and within the framework of Germany's general policy toward the Jews. He mentioned—for the first time in connection with the operation in France—the Final Solution of the Jewish Problem, as well as the fact long known to him, that "the head of the Security Police and the SD had received from the Führer the task of preparing the Solution of the Jewish Question in Europe." Dannecker therefore believed that the preliminary preparations required for the execution of this task should also be made in Vichy France, not only in the Occupied Zone, for "if not today then in the near future we shall be faced with the inevitable necessity of also finding a solution for the Jewish problem in unoccupied France."[32] In fact, at the time these words were written, preparations had already begun, at least in the Occupied Zone, simultaneously in three principal spheres: the prohibition of emigration for Jews, the arrest of foreign Jews, and their imprisonment in detention camps (that later on became the points of departure for the deportations "to the East") and the establishment of a central organization for all the Jews of France.[33]

The prohibition of emigration, which applied to all Jews, foreign as well as French, reflects perhaps more than anything else the change taking place in those days in German policy—or more precisely in the objectives of that policy. In the past, the German leadership had regarded emigration as one of their principal objectives in their struggle against the Jews, in Germany proper and in all the countries under her control. On 16 July 1941, SS-Sturmbannführer Dr. Helmut Knochen, the commander of the Security Police and the SD in France, informed his subordinates in Bordeaux that the emigration of a small group of Jews there was not to be permitted. (As indicated, the Jews of Bordeaux had already been expelled into the region of the Vichy government during the first months of the occupation.) This order was sent because "the Reich Security Main Office on principle had once again decided on the prohibition of emigration of the Jews from the areas of occupied Western Europe and, insofar as this was possible, also of those in the Unoccupied Zone of France."[34] From then on this decision became the rule, which could only be broken in a few very special cases on which, in the opinion of the government authorities in Germany, the vital interests of the Reich were dependent.

At the same time, the mass arrests began. Initially, 3,733 foreign Jews were arrested on 14 May 1941; these were men of working age who had been called to the offices of the French police in Paris, supposedly "for the purpose of examination of status," and on the spot, with no further explanation, they were sent to two camps in the Loiret district, Pithiviers and Beaune-la-Roland.[35] Three months later, the first manhunts took place in the streets of Paris. On 22–23 August French policemen raided first the 11th district of the city and later also others, going from street to street and from house to house; they arrested 4,232 Jews, mostly foreigners, and transferred them to a new place of detention constructed near Paris—one that for tens of thousands of Jews would later become their last station on French soil—the Drancy camp.[36]

The order given to the Paris police on the eve of the operation was "to arrest every Jewish male between the ages of 18 and 50, except those of American nationality"—this until completion of a quota of approximately 6,000.[37] Those who had planned the operation were thus aware of the possibility that in the course of the manhunt nationals of friendly or neutral countries would also be arrested, but for their own reasons they had decided not to take this into consideration and exempted only U.S. citizens.[38] From this it follows that Italian citizens, not only their property, were also liable to be affected.

Already on 22 August, while the operation in the streets of Paris was still in full swing, Consul Orlandini urgently informed the German Embassy in Paris of the arrest of a number of Italian nationals in the course of the manhunt conducted in the 11th district. In polite but forceful language the consul raised the problem, enclosed a list of the names of Italian Jews who had been arrested—many of them born in Turkey, Greece, or Bulgaria— and asked to be informed when they would be released and whether instructions had been issued that in the future Italian nationals were to be exempt from this kind of arrest, should there be any.[39] Thus began a new chapter, which for four months engaged the Italian and German delegations in France, who negotiated stubbornly over the release or retention of a handful of Jews imprisoned in the Drancy camp whose numbers, even according to the Italians, did not exceed thirteen. The Germans tried to gain time and for weeks did not reply to the communications of the consulate. They transferred the handling of the matter from office to office, from the embassy to the Military Government and within the Military Government itself, from one department to another and back again. The Italians—may it be said to the credit of Consul Orlandini and his deputy Giovanni Luciolli[40]—did not let the matter drop and emphatically stood by their demands that their citizens be released at once. They maintained contact with the prisoners' families at all times, supplied them with the necessary certificates, and eventually obtained what they demanded. On 9 December 1941, the German Military Government announced that it had decided to release eleven of the thirteen Jews under consideration,[41] and on 20 January 1942, they had indeed been released.[42]

The bundle of letters sent by the arrested men to the consulate requesting intervention on their behalf (some of which have been preserved among its documents), are human testimony, both sad and precious, reflecting the feelings and thoughts still current among the Jews. These were in the first place feelings of surprise, dismay, and inability to grasp the meaning of the events in which they had become involved, as though as the result of some mysterious mistake over which there was no control and the origins of which they were unable to fathom. The common argument (in fact the only legitimate one, but under those circumstances the most irrelevant) was: I have done nothing bad, I committed no offense, I am innocent, my conscience is completely clean. Only hidden between the lines could there be seen the terrible doubt that many probably harbored in their hearts concerning their future. "If I turn to you today," wrote Nissim Calef, one of the arrested, to Consul Orlandini on 9 October 1941, "it is to beg of you to finally let me know . . . something precise about the fate that awaits me. I do not of course expect from you to spare my feelings—let that be clear. I would like to know the truth and I rely on you to tell me that." [43] The consulate's reply has not been preserved. The staff was not in the habit of writing directly to the prisoners but rather maintained contact with their families, if those had turned to them. This particular inquirer was in any case released three months later, and the episode of his suffering came to an end, at least for the time being.

At this stage, for a better understanding of the motives for the consulate's actions, the main question still remains: What did the consulate staff at that time really know of their allies' plans concerning the Jews, and what did they imagine would be the fate of the thousands of Jews who had been arrested in Paris and the surrounding country, and of the tens of thousands who were then already detained in the camps within the territory of the Vichy government? The impression obtained from the sources is that in the course of the autumn months of 1941 there was a change, perhaps even a substantial change, both in the quality of the information reaching them and in the understanding of its significance (and hence also in their readiness to contend with the Germans).

At the beginning of September, the consulate was still regarding the problem from the same vantage point as in the past. Although they were being called upon to act for the release of their imprisoned citizens, the main concern of the consulate staff as before was to prevent matters concerning Italian Jews, or their property, from passing into the hands of Vichy government officials. They therefore repeatedly demanded that the administration of the confiscated businesses of the Jews and their frozen assets should remain in their hands, as had been agreed on several times in the past, although it was still not put into practice, at least not on a regular basis.[44] They also insisted that their citizens be allowed to deposit their wireless set in the consulate (on 13 August the Jews in the Occupied Zone were forbidden to keep a radio receiver in their possession), and not in the offices of the French police.[45]

In the middle of October, on the other hand, a new note may already be recognized in the consulate reports, and another aspect of the problem was expressed. The racial policy was no longer regarded only in the local context, concerning the status and the property of the Jews in France, but was beginning to reveal itself in a broader pan-European dimension, with its horrifying implications, although these were still somewhat nebulous and unclear. It appears that in the course of discussions in Paris between the Italian and German delegations concerning Italian Jews, something of the Germans' intentions toward the "Solution of the Jewish Problem" was revealed, either intentionally or out of carelessness. Vice-Consul Luciolli reported on 16 October 1941 to his superiors in Rome, "in the course of my talks with them, I was able to understand that on the side of the Germans new and more severe arrangements for the Jewish problem as a whole were in the stage of development"; in France, new pressure was to be exerted on the Vichy government to make them adopt a more severe stand in the region under their control; and "on the question of the arrests and internment in camps, the interpretation given them by the Germans of being a prelude to a European solution of the Jewish problem and other similar phrases have allowed us clearly to understand that in the near future more severe measures will be put into effect, among them the indiscriminate internment of all Jews must be considered possible." On the basis of this analysis—that was the first clear evidence of the quality of the information in the hands of the consulate at that time—the vice-consul reached the conclusion that there was room to doubt whether in the future the consulate would be able to protect its citizens, let alone their property. He therefore proposed the possibility of their early repatriation to Italy and, insofar as was possible, with the bulk of their possessions.[46] The same proposal, with similar reasoning was repeated two months later by Consul Orlandini in one of his reports to Rome.[47]

From the middle of 1942, Italian diplomats and military officials serving in the Italian zones of occupation in Croatia, Greece, and southern France raised proposals from time to time for the transfer to Italy of Jews whose lives were endangered in their places of residence. For the most part, these proposals were met with opposition by the Ministry for the Interior, which for obvious reasons was not interested in permitting the entry into Italy of thousands of refugees, some of whom were undesirable elements from a political point of view and most of whom would become a burden on the public coffers. However, even the position taken by the Foreign Ministry on the subject—at least until the end of 1942—was not unequivocal.

It appears that at the time when the consulate in Paris was presenting its proposal to discuss the repatriation of Jews with Italian citizenship, repatriation was already taking place in practice. In the second half of 1941 and at the beginning of 1942, with the situation of the Jews in France growing steadily worse, Jews despaired of the hope that their Italian citizenship would protect them from further decrees (just as at the same time doubts arose in the minds of the consulate staff that they would be able to continue to protect them). They therefore applied to the consulate in Paris, asked for, and received the necessary travel certificates, and, as stated in the documents, set out to be "repatriated." However, when they arrived at the border post between the two countries, in the Italian township of Bardonecchia, they met with disappointment: they were stopped by the border police and were not allowed to continue their journey unless they had first obtained, from the office of the *prefetto* (the Italian district governor) of the town in which they intended to settle, permission to make their homes there. This permission was, for the most part, not granted, or it arrived a long time later and after numerous interventions. The *prefetto* of Turin, who was also responsible for the township of Bardonecchia and its surroundings, complained on this unsatisfactory situation in a report he sent to his superiors in the Ministry of the Interior in Rome on 23 March 1942. He indicated that "for some time" there had been a considerable increase in the stream of Italian citizens "of the Jewish race" returning from France and being delayed in Bardonecchia, "sometimes for months," while waiting for permission to settle in the place of their choice. The *prefetto* believed that this situation was in itself undesirable from a police aspect but, more so, it was worrying because "according to their own declarations the Royal Consulate in Paris was encouraging them to repatriate, and that is seemingly in contradiction to the instructions whose purpose is to encourage the departure of Jews from the Kingdom, even if they are Italians." [48]

This statement, in which a note of criticism of the actions of the consulate in Paris could be clearly distinguished, was brought to the attention of the Foreign Ministry, which on 24 May 1942 transmitted it to the embassy and consulate in Paris, the latter being requested to reply and clarify their position. Ambassador Gino Buti, who had been appointed to serve in Paris a few months previously, with the reopening of the embassy at the beginning of January, replied briefly that he had noted that the return to Italy of "Italian citizens of the Jewish race" was not to be encouraged. He also added that it was not inconceivable that in the future the Germans would decide on the expulsion of these Jews to Italy, "in place of deportation to the regions of Galicia and the Ukraine," and then there would in any case be no avoiding their return, whatever the general policy on the matter might be.[49] Consul Orlandini discussed the arguments raised against the actions of the consulate and rejected them vigorously—perhaps with an element of feigned innocence. According to him the consulate had never encouraged repatriation of Italian citizens. It issued travel documents to Jews only when they applied on their own initiative and declared that they did not intend to continue living in France. This was a routine administrative operation, which to the best of the Consul's knowledge was not in contradiction to any other instructions whatsoever. In connection with the bureaucratic difficulties that had arisen at the border post, Orlandini added that there might be room for approaching the Ministry of the Interior with the request that they grant blanket approval for the return to Italy of Jews who wished to do so and inform of that the *prefetti* concerned, thereby terminating the embarrassing episode.[50]

It is difficult to decide whether Orlandini truly did not know the stand taken at the Ministry of the Interior on this subject, or whether he pretended he did not know in order to justify his actions (and maybe tried in this way to probe the real stand of his superiors in Rome). Either way, the Marquis d'Ajeta, the head of the foreign minister's cabinet, replied to him two weeks later, leaving no room for doubt: Italian general policy was that "the return of Jews was not to be encouraged," and the explicit instruction to Italian consulates everywhere was that renewal of passports of Jews living outside the borders of the state, or the granting of "repatriation visas," in every case, needed a prior approval from the Ministry of the Interior.[51] The episode thus seemed to be at an end. In practice, Jews continued to infiltrate to the south, into the Vichy territory, and a few of them even tried to continue across the border into Italy, making use of certificates they had received from the Italian Consulate in Paris or some other town in France.

At the end of 1941 and the beginning of 1942, after the manhunts of May and August 1941, life in the Occupied Zone of France, at least outwardly, reverted to its previous course of social and economic discriminations, and the consulate was forced to intervene time and again to protect the interests of its citizens. On 14 December 1941, the Military Government imposed on the Jews a one-time fine of 1 billion francs, as an act of supposed retaliation for the attacks made on German soldiers.[52] Making his habitual detailed report on this to the Foreign Ministry, Consul Orlandini expressed the hope that he would succeed in obtaining the consent of the German authorities to exempt Jews of Italian citizenship from paying the fine or alternately, that the amounts collected from them should be transferred to Italian charitable institutions in France.[53]

Discussions on the method of selecting the commissioners over the property of Italian Jews were becoming almost routine and continued during the first months of 1942. This time, the subject arose following the opposition by the Commissariat Général aux Questions Juives (General Commissariat for Jewish Affairs)[54] of the Vichy government to the granting of extraordinary powers to the Italians—opposition that, according to some indications, had been "invited" by the Economic Department of the German Military Government.[55] In the end the consulate officials overcame these obstacles, and on 27 June 1942, they met with a few of the most senior representatives of Italian financiers then in Paris, among them the directors of the three Italian banks in France, to settle the concluding stages in the operation of the "liquidation of the property of Italian Jews." At the same meeting, it was decided that the proceeds from the sale of Jewish businesses would be deposited in accounts with one of the Italian banks in France from which any withdrawal of money would only be possible with the approval of the consulate, even though these accounts were to be in the names of the commissioners. After conclusion of the sale procedure (and thereby after the consequent termination of the function of the commissioners), all the sums of money deposited in the banks would be paid to the Jewish owners, in monthly instalments, in such a way as to allow the latter to receive their money "as quickly as possible." It was also decided to allow the Jews, who so desired, to transfer their money to Italy without delay. Those who preferred to transfer their money to the zone controlled by the Vichy government would be permitted to do so, although with certain limitations and, where necessary, through third-party Aryan Italians, in order thereby to circumvent the German opposition.[56]

On 29 May 1942, the Eighth German Order was published, forcing the Jews from the age of 6 onward in the Occupied Zone to wear the badge (the "Jewish star" in the words of the order) on their clothes, starting 7 June.[57]

The Italian Embassy in Paris demanded of the German authorities that the decree not be imposed on their citizens, and their request was granted.[58] There was still room for concern, however, that the publication of this order would be the last stage before the Germans applied their concepts and methods, used on the Jews of Eastern Europe, to the Jews of Western Europe. The tragic events that would befall the Jews of France in the days that followed were to confirm this fear beyond anything that could previously have been imagined.

# The Massive Manhunts and the Deportation to the East

## (JULY–NOVEMBER 1942)

In the spring and the beginning of summer 1942, the Axis powers reached the peak of their success in the battlefield. On the eastern front, the German Army renewed its offensive with full strength, and its units reached the gates of Stalingrad and the foothills of the Caucasus mountains. In North Africa, the Axis forces defeated the British Army in Cyrenaica and penetrated deep into Egypt, reaching the approaches to El Alamein, not far removed from the Nile Valley and the Suez Canal. It seemed that nothing could stand before the might of the Axis powers—joined a few months earlier by Japan—and in particular the might of the German Army that already controlled most of the countries of Europe and North Africa, either directly or by means of satellite governments. In these countries, the Germans had subjected the defeated nations to a regime of unbridled terror; together with that, they also acted with fanaticism and determination in putting their policy of what they called the "Final Solution of the Jewish Problem" into effect, in more or less close collaboration with the local population.

In France, the Germans had demanded that Pierre Laval, the faithful proponent of their cause, be reinstated to the leadership of the Vichy Government, and on 16 April their demand was fulfilled. René Bousquet, one of his close associates, was appointed two days later as head of the French police (Secrétaire Général à la Police au Ministère de l'Intérieur),[1] and on 6 May, Xavier Valat, the commissioner general for Jewish affairs who had been considered too moderate in his relations with the Jews, was replaced by Louis Darquier de Pellepoix, a fanatical veteran antisemite and a faithful follower of the Germans.[2] Meanwhile, at the beginning of May, SS-Brigadeführer Carl Albrecht Oberg was appointed senior SS and police commander (Höherer SS und Polizeiführer) in France,[3] and all matters concerning the affairs of the Jews, or at least all important decisions concerning their fate, were now taken out of the hands of the army and entrusted to him and to the new adviser for Jewish affairs, SS-Obersturmführer Heinz Röthke.[4]

With the political groundwork prepared and the organizational framework complete, the Germans started determining the practical steps for extending the operation of liquidating the Jews in the countries of Western Europe. On 11 June, at a meeting that took place between officials of the Reich Security Main Office and the three advisers for Jewish affairs in France, Holland, and Belgium, the latter were ordered to act without delay for the transfer of Jews "from the conquered western states to the Auschwitz concentration camp." The quota determined for the two zones of France was 100,000 Jews.[5] Immediately afterward, the German security services in Paris began negotiating with the French on ways to collaborate in performing the task. Speaking in the name of Pétain and Laval, Bousquet at first requested that the arrests in the Occupied Zone be carried out by the German Army, not by the French police, and that in the Vichy Zone only foreign Jews should be arrested. "On the part of the French Government," Bousquet declared, "there is no objection to the arrests themselves, and only their performance in Paris by the French police was a matter for embarrassment" (*gênant* in the German source). But because of pressure from the Germans, the men from Vichy gradually withdrew most of their reservations. In the end they agreed that within the entire territory of France, in the Occupied and Unoccupied zones, "foreign" Jews would be arrested by French policemen in any numbers the German authorities might demand.[6] The big manhunt, or Operation Spring Wind as it was called at the time, was ready to go.

The Italians were no doubt aware of these dramatic developments to some degree or another;[7] their impressions were reinforced by the horrifying news reaching Rome in those days about the events in neighboring Yugoslavia.[8] This news forced the Foreign Ministry for the first time to adopt a clear overall stand concerning the steps the Germans were taking, or were about to take, against the Jewish population of the countries the Germans had conquered and concerning their applicability to Italian citizens. On this, the Marquis d'Ajeta informed the Italian Embassy in Paris on 25 June 1942 in these words:

> [F]or reasons connected with the defense of the positions attained by the Italian communities in the different countries of the Mediterranean Basin, particularly in Tunisia, Greece (Saloniki), in Morocco, and in Egypt, we cannot be disinterested in the fate of the Jews forming a part of these communities. We cannot on the other hand agree that measures be taken discriminating against Italian Jews residing in other foreign countries [in addition to those mentioned above], and in particular in the territory of Metropolitan France, in favor of Aryan Italian citizens; this is so, both because those Jews are in possession of Italian citizenship as well as Italian passports that guarantee them our protection, and also because a possible lack of interest on our part would place us in a delicate situation in the actions that we might intend to take in defense of the Jewish communities [in the countries listed above], particularly those of Tunisia and Saloniki. It is therefore opportune that this Royal Delegation should let the competent authority know that we would be grateful if these strict measures that have to be applied for reasons of policy of a general or policing nature were not applied en bloc to the Italian Jews in France. Should there be cases in which it might be considered necessary to apply such measures, it would be necessary that they be taken in agreement with our Royal Consulates.[9]

Even though this stand was still entirely based on economic and political considerations, there is already a considerable difference from that taken about two years earlier, according to which the royal government "would reveal no interest" in the measures that were going to be taken against their Jewish citizens in France, and particularly in the fate of those Jews who had settled in France after the publication in Italy of the racial laws.[10]

In early July, a few days after this new and clear position had been determined by the Italian Foreign Ministry, German diplomatic circles were also aroused, demanding that "a comprehensive and suitable solution" be provided for the question of the status of Italian Jews residing in France. It seems that both sides simultaneously recognized that, under the circumstances then prevailing and in anticipation of the operations that were about to take place, it was no longer possible to be satisfied with partial solutions similar to those that could be reached within the narrow framework of "working discussions" between officials of the Italian Consulate in Paris and the people from the Economic Department of the German Military Government. They therefore arrived at the conclusion that it was essential that differences of opinion be settled at the highest political or diplomatic level, in Rome and Berlin.

First to be heard were the words of Otto Abetz, the German ambassador in Paris, a man more than once considered as one of the supposedly most moderate and enlightened among the German diplomats.[11] On 2 July 1942, at the height of the preparations before the launch of "Operation Spring Wind," he approached his superiors in Berlin to express his satisfaction that, according to the information he had been given, the Hungarian government had given its consent to the inclusion of its citizens in France in the operations about to be undertaken against the Jews (information that later was found to be inaccurate); he also indicated the necessity to act urgently and energetically so that the other countries friendly to the Reich, "particularly Italy," would also take this course. The ambassador argued that every effort should be made to persuade the Italians that they would have to choose between giving their consent to the deportation of their Jewish citizens and repatriating them to their country. Indeed, the ambassador made it clear that, in any case, one could no longer tolerate the embarrassing situation in which Axis policy would be seen to be clearly disunited.[12] Two days later, in a conversation with the Italian General Fernando Gelich, then serving as general secretary of the Franco-Italian Armistice Commission,[13] Abetz stressed the importance of French anti-semitic legislation, "which is intended to remove the Jews once and for all from European living space," and asked that the Italian government renounce their opposition to applying this legislation to their citizens. Abetz added that the subject was of considerable importance in the eyes of the Reich, that "regards with great favor this legislation that could be of help to the Axis in that it would separate France from the Jewish world."[14] That same day, Abetz reported to Berlin on his conversation with the Italian general and also repeated his opinion that in anticipation of the execution of the deportations from France ("the steps of evacuation to the Auschwitz labor camp," as he was in the habit of saying) it was of special interest that the holders of Italian nationality be no longer exempt from measures to be taken toward foreign Jews in general.[15]

The proposals from Ambassador Abetz were passed to State Under-secretary Martin Luther, who, in his capacity as director of the German Department (Abteilung Deutschland) in the Foreign Ministry, was in charge of Jewish affairs and was also acting as liaison among the ministry, SS headquarters, and the Security Police.[16] In his usual manner, Luther summarized the subject in a long and detailed memorandum, which on 24 July, together with an expression of unreserved support for the ambassador's proposals, he presented to his superiors, Secretary of State Ernst von Weizsäcker[17] and Foreign Minister von Ribbentropp for their decision.[18]

Before the minister had time to make a decision on this matter—despite the small number of Jews concerned, it involved very delicate political and diplomatic sensitivies—the massive manhunt after foreign Jews had begun in the streets of Paris. At dawn on 16 July, with the assistance of hundreds of volunteers from the pro-Nazi Parti Populaire Français (PPF) and according to a card index prepared in the *préfecture* of Paris, thousands of French police raided the homes of Jews and arrested their occupants— men, women, old people, and children. First they were brought to the collecting point at the Vélodrome d'Hiver, the stadium for bicycle racing, then from there to the Drancy camp (from which, during only two weeks, between 17 and 29 July, five transports of Jews were sent to the "Auschwitz Labor Camp"). For two days the manhunt continued in the streets of the French capital, the city that not long before had been one of the centers of European civilization. At the end of the operation, it was found that, from the point of view of its planners, its results were fairly disappointing: from a quota of 22,000 Jews, whom they had planned to arrest in the first stage, 12,884 were arrested—5,802 women, 4,051 children, and 3,031 men. (Many of the foreign Jewish men had already been detained in earlier operations.) A few hundred more Jews were arrested in the same period in other cities in the Occupied Zone, and they too were transferred to the Drancy camp.

On that same 16 July, only a few hours after the start of the operation and while it was proceeding at full blast, Ambassador Gino Buti reported on it to Rome in an urgent telegram. In his words, the French police were carrying out mass arrests among the foreign Jews throughout the Occupied Zone, in collaboration with the German police and at the latter's initiative. The object of the operation, as he had been informed by German sources, was twofold: "to eliminate those elements on whom English and Communist propaganda makes the most impression, and at the same time to recruit working hands for industrial production and even more for agriculture in Poland, the Ukraine etc." The ambassador added that the arrests had left an impression of gloom, "but the population suffered them without opposition, as they usually have suffered all the other steps taken against the Jews."[19] In this report, as in others he sent during the period immediately following the completion of the operation, the ambassador was unable to report on the arrest of Jews with Italian nationality. In the course of time, such cases did in fact occur, and the Italian Consulate was asked to deal with them, but before the tiring procedure over the fate of these individuals could get under way, there arose the main dispute between Germans and Italians on the question of principle of relations as a whole to the Jews of Italian nationality residing in France.

On 31 July 1942, a meeting took place between Vice-Consul Cesare Pasquinelli[20] and SS-Obersturmführer Heinz Röthke, the adviser for Jewish affairs—two officials who had just recently taken up their new positions in Paris. Pasquinelli, who had initiated the conversation, wanted to come to a general agreement, in the spirit of the guidelines of 25 June that he had received from the Foreign Ministry, concerning the Italian Jews in France. Opinions later differed on the nature of the verbal agreement reached between the two (and whether any general agreement was reached at all), and two different, mutually contradictory versions have been preserved. Pasquinelli reported his impressions of the conversation to Orlandini, and these were it seems extremely optimistic. More experienced than his colleague in negotiations with the Germans, particularly on matters connected with Jews, Orlandini considered it necessary to ask the other side for written confirmation of what had been agreed in that conversation. On 4 August, he therefore wrote to Röthke (and this time in German, as he was in the habit of doing when he was especially interested that his words should be clearly understood or that they should be dealt with quickly) and informed him that he confirmed the matters that had been agreed between him and Pasquinelli, "namely that the measures against Jews not be executed against Italian Jews if prior consent of the Royal Italian Consulate was not obtained." The latter would be prepared to discuss the measures that German authorities considered appropriate and would as always do this in the spirit of comradely cooperation; in each case, however, the approval for the execution of these measures against Italian citizens would be dependent on whether they conformed with the Italian racial laws and with the general guidelines received from the consulate's superiors in Rome.[21]

We do not know to what degree of accuracy these words reflected the agreement reached between the two. Röthke, in any case, totally rejected them and even regarded them as an attempt to mislead him. He therefore refused to reply directly to the Italian consul, and instead, on 21 August, he conveyed Orlandini's letter to the German ambassador in Paris. In his own hand he wrote a number of comments in the margins of the paper to indicate his indignation: "This is completely incorrect! Absurd! Impertinence! This was not approved by me!" On the subject itself Röthke argued that he had never agreed to these things and that the opposite was true: at the meeting with the vice-consul, with no possibility of being misunderstood, he had made it clear that the Italian Jews would only be exempt from wearing the "Jewish star," but that all the other measures that had been taken or would be taken would, without exception, apply to them. Röthke wrote that "the letter from the Italian Consulate-General contains a conscious distortion of the actual conversation," and because the consulate had already adopted an expressly, incomprehensibly pro-Jewish stand in the past, he had come to the general decision that he would no longer be able to remain in direct communication with them; he therefore requested that the embassy should inform the Italian Consulate of his decision and would in future act as intermediary between them and himself whenever they should have need of him.[22]

It does not appear that the embassy fulfilled his request in full. They certainly did not inform the Italians of this "severance of relations," even though they apparently found a way of letting them know of the displeasure their stand had aroused.[23] The Italians on their part, in their internal correspondence, did not conceal their satisfaction with the solution that they supposedly found for the problem of their Jewish citizens. On 4 August, Ambassador Buti reported on this to the Political Department of the ministry, stressing the importance of the matter and the particular urgency attributed to the finding of a solution, for an "increased harshness in the anti-Jewish decrees in the nearest future may be considered a certainty."[24]

In truth, both sides had erred in their estimations: the Italians were deluding themselves when they believed that they had so easily solved the problems of their Jewish citizens in France. The Germans on their part were incapable of understanding that at that stage, after the significance of their policy toward the Jews, or a part of it, had become known, there was no longer any chance that they would be able to persuade their allies to follow their lead on this subject (and that as yet they did not have the power to impose their wishes and methods on the latter). The developments of the days to follow were destined to make both sides aware of their error.

Toward the end of August and the beginning of September 1942, the focus of activities for the arrest of Jews had moved to the Unoccupied Zone, that is, into the territory of the Vichy government. At the same time, however, the Germans were not neglecting their treatment of those Jews of the Occupied Zone whom they had in their own hands and who, because of their "privileged" citizenship, were enjoying a form of full or partial immunity to measures taken against foreign Jews in general. It might appear that the reference was to the citizens of many countries in Europe and America—friendly, allied, neutral, and hostile countries (excluding the defeated). According to the German point of view the problem in France in mid-1942 was in fact of consequence only in connection with Jews who were nationals of Hungary (some 1,500), Romania (some 3,800), Greece (some 1,500), Italy (some 1,500), and Bulgaria.

The Greek Jews were included in this category only because of uncertainty, lest they demand Italian protection, since their country was largely occupied by Italy, and there the Jews were not obliged to wear the badge. Unfortunately for them, this immunity did not last for long: when Greek Jews approached the Italian delegations in France and requested their protection, the embassy in Paris asked for a ruling from their superiors in Rome. The latter's reply was explicitly negative. On 15 September 1942 Ambassador Buti informed the Italian consulates in Paris, Bordeaux, Le Havre, Nancy, Nantes, Reims, and Vichy[25] of this, and the fate of some 1,500 Greek Jews was thereby sealed: at the beginning of November 1942, nearly all of them had been arrested and had joined the other Jews on their way from Drancy "eastward."[26]

A short time before, the fate of Romanian and Bulgarian Jews had also been decided: on 20 August 1942, Martin Luther announced to the German representatives in France, Belgium, and Holland that the Romanian government no longer had any objection to the deportation of their citizens residing in these countries.[27] At about the same time, the Germans also obtained a similar consent from the Bulgarian government.[28] Hence, apart from isolated Jews who were citizens of neutral countries such as Switzerland, Spain, and Portugal, in Autumn 1942 no Jews with "privileged" nationalities of European countries were left in France apart from the Hungarians and the Italians. As for the Hungarian government, according to its ambassador in Berlin, it was prepared to give its consent to the deportation of its citizens from France on the condition that the Italian government give similar consent concerning its citizens first.[29] This situation, too, reflected the narrow and crooked path of Italian-German relations; a path that, in regard to policy on the Jews, had become by that time a maze out of which it was very difficult to find a way.

Altogether, only some 3,000 Jews were involved (Italian as well as Hungarian citizens), but at that time the German security authorities in France were having difficulties in filling the deportee quotas that they themselves had set, and 3,000 Jews could fill three transports "to the East." Furthermore, the Germans apparently could not reconcile themselves, as a matter of principle, to the idea that in a region under their control Jews would enjoy privileged treatment thanks to their citizenship. This phenomenon not only conflicted with their outlook on life, but also they believed that in the eyes of the French people it was liable to be interpreted as a sign of weakness, perhaps even as proof, that in reality they did not regard the Jewish problem as "a question of race but rather of nationality."[30] One way or another, the Germans in Paris and Berlin did not allow the matter to drop. On 16 August 1942, Ernst Woermann, the director of the Political Department at the Foreign Ministry, announced his support for the recommendations of Ambassador Abetz proposed in the beginning of July concerning the steps that were to be taken against the Jews of France and their applicability also to Italian citizens. Five days later, in a long and detailed memorandum, Martin Luther once more described the political and diplomatic problems that had arisen in different countries following the execution of operations whose purpose was the Solution of the Jewish Problem within the sphere of influence of the Reich. In the section dealing with France, he once more advised implementing the recommendations of Ambassador Abetz and avoiding the continuation of the preferential treatment of the Italian Jews.[31]

Despite all this, Foreign Minister von Ribbentropp was in no hurry to decide the issue. Perhaps he felt no urge to assist his rivals within the Nazi leadership: Reichsführer–SS Heinrich Himmler and his people from the Reich Security Main Office, who were likely to be the principal beneficiaries from his intervention in this matter, should it be successful. Maybe he also feared that the Italians would reject his approach, just as unofficial feelers and approaches made through various diplomatic channels in connection with the Jews of Croatia and Greece had been rejected at about that time.[32] Somehow in the end the decision was made, and it was carried out in the second half of September: on the 17th of that month Luther gave instructions in the name of the foreign minister to the German Embassy in Rome to take action in the matter,[33] and on the 22nd Embassy Counselor Prince von Bismarck issued "a verbal note" (which, as usual, was delivered in writing) to the officials of the Political Department of the ministry.

The note indicated that "for political reasons" it had recently been decided to force the Jews in the countries of Western Europe, first and foremost in France, to wear the Jewish star. This step in itself was received favorably by most parts of the French population. On the other hand, the population expressed open dissatisfaction with the fact that a section of foreign Jews was exempt from this obligation. Even more so, this applied to the act of deportation ("removal of the Jews," in the refined language of the German diplomat), that had not yet been carried out for certain groups of foreign Jews, who for some reasons were considered "privileged." In consideration of this and to prevent the great damage these Jews were capable of causing, the German authorities decided that, from 1 January 1943, all Jews had to wear the badge, whatever their citizenship might be. They also decided that all the other obligations and restrictions that had been or were to be imposed on the Jews of France in general would also apply to Italian Jews. If the Italian government came to the decision that they could not allow their Jewish citizens to be included in these steps, "including their removal toward the East," they would do well to repatriate them from German-occupied areas in Western Europe by that date.[34]

This was the content of the "verbal note," delivered, in writing, to officials of the Foreign Ministry. What explanations Prince Bismarck added verbally in the course of that meeting, we do not know. It is, however, well known that one month earlier, when he had brought to the Foreign Ministry the request from his government that the Italian authorities extradite the Jewish refugees from Croatia who had found refuge in the areas occupied by them, he had seen fit to whisper in his hosts' ears that "mass transfer of the Jews of Croatia to the Eastern territories . . . in fact would mean their dispersal and elimination."[35] It can be assumed that this estimate did not change in the course of the month that had passed; one may be certain that the German prince and his Italian partners to the conversation correctly understood that the fate of the Jews "removed" from France to the eastern territories would be no different from the fate of the Jews "transferred" there from Croatia. It was therefore to be expected that the officials of the Foreign Ministry would recommend rejecting out of hand the German approach and that Minister Count Ciano would back them up. However, the stand that would be taken by Mussolini, who had the last word on all matters of importance (in his estimation)—among these everything with any bearing on Jewish affairs—was certainly not known in advance. One month earlier, he had offhandedly given his consent to the extradition of the Jews from Croatia and had not held back, even in view of the severe and explicit warning of the German diplomat (that had been brought to his knowledge and that he even had initialed). Even if this time the circumstances were a little different from those in the previous case—involved in this case were Italian citizens, concerning whom the Germans had proposed an alternative solution to deportation, namely, their repatriation to Italy—certainly nothing in his earlier reply augured well.

On 22 September 1942, the very same day on which von Bismarck had delivered his note, officials of the Italian Foreign Ministry prepared a short memorandum for Mussolini, in which they presented the problem in a general outline, with the implications, both political and of principle, involved; in conclusion they unequivocally recommended rejecting the German approach and both the solutions proposed therein. The memorandum, which was submitted unsigned, that is, with the consent and at the responsibility of the minister, repeated in its main arguments the stand of the ministry in the course of the preceding year. However, there was a new tone unusual for an official document, especially one intended for Mussolini's eyes. Particularly prominent is the allusion to the Germans' policy toward the Jews, along with the desire not to be identified with it, its tendencies, and "its tragic consequences." These are the words of the memorandum:

> In the enclosed note the German Embassy gives notice that their government intends no longer to grant the special treatment that at our request they had granted to Italian Jews in France, Belgium, and Holland. The intentions of the German government are that Italian Jews would also be identified by the Jewish Star and that starting January 1943 they would also be included with those to be deported to some region in Poland.
>
> The request of the German government creates a delicate problem regarding our position toward the Italian Jews resident abroad, in whom the Italian government has taken an interest not as such but as Italian citizens who often represent prominent Italian interests abroad.
>
> The deportation to Poland, which could have tragic consequences, is a step not in tune with Italian racial policy, which starts out from the concept of distinguishing and separating the Jews in order to preserve the racial characteristics of the nation, without however going so far as persecution. In addition, bearing in mind that there are notable groups of Italian Jews in foreign countries in which we have a special interest, in particular in the Mediterranean Basin, where they represent a lively and active force in our communities, we have in the past therefore pursued a policy of defence against measures that under the pretext of racial concepts are in reality de-

signed to compromise the moral, political, and economic standing of our community.[36]

In this context and in accordance with this stand we have recognized the incidentally extremely modest interests of the foreign Jews in Italy, in order not to leave room for complaint of conflict between our requests to the foreign governments and the situation of foreign Jews in Italy. This stand, that has allowed us to keep effective the groups of Italian Jews in Tunisia, Morocco, Algeria, Greece and the Levant, cannot be reconciled with the consent we are requested to grant for the deportation of the Italian Jews from France, Belgium, and Holland. We have always understood and applied the concept of "defense of the race" so as to harmonize with the other principle, equally fundamental, of protecting Italian citizens abroad, protection that we have had to promote because of conditions of a political, economic, and military character, particularly those confronting the Italian community in the Mediterranean.

Besides, the racial policy implemented by us with enlightened criteria and applied with equanimity and measure, differs profoundly from the concepts that have inspired the recent drastic provisions put into operation against the Jews in France and which have aroused lively reactions in all circles. Furthermore, it should be noted that the legitimacy of a provision, by which the occupying power deports en masse not only persons belonging to the occupied territory but also foreigners and even citizens of an allied state, was highly disputable from a juridical aspect. An Italian stand of consent to the deportation of Italian Jews from France would create a woeful impression in many circles and could create problems concerning Jewish Italians in different countries. For these reasons, it seems appropriate to make it clear to the German authorities that it is impossible to accede to their request, even more so since the treatment presently given to the Italian Jews in France has not resulted in any inconvenience that could justify such a grave worsening in their conditions.[37]

There certainly is room for differing with the writer concerning the "enlightened" nature and supposed "fairness" of the racial policies pursued in Italy since 1938. In truth, this policy, both from a political and an intellectual point of view, was a foolish and absurd act that, from the start of its implementation, had aroused the opposition of many Aryan citizens, even in the circles that at that time were supporters of the fascist regime. But the writers of the memorandum were correct in pointing out the essential difference that existed between the aimless purposes of the fascist "racial policy" and the world of dark and repulsive concepts from which the Nazi leadership drew their inspiration when formulating their policy concerning the "solution" of the Jewish problem. The problem in which the two sides had become entangled really did have its roots in this essential difference: from it arose most of the friction, the misunderstandings, acts of subversion, and sometimes opposing stances adopted that characterized the relations of the two allies whenever they came to deal with the question of the fate of the Jews in the countries they occupied, particularly during 1942–1943, the years of the most intensive implementation of the Final Solution. A further contribution to the rift between the positions of the two powers vis-à-vis the Jews (a factor that found expression in this memorandum, as in other earlier documents) lay in the attempt by the Italians to protect their economic and social positions in the Mediterranean countries and the Balkans, positions that were often held by Italian Jews.

For some reason, the original copy of the memorandum presented to Mussolini for perusal, and on which he might have written his comments and his final decision, as was his custom, has not yet been found. However, clearly written on the copy preserved in the archives was: "Visto dal Duce" (Has been seen by the Duce). This means that the Ministry recommendations had received his approval, at least in principle.

Mussolini thus did not accede to the German demands over the Jews in France, as he had done one month earlier concerning the Jewish refugees from Croatia.[38] It also appears that he did not approve the recommendations of the Foreign Ministry in full and that he adopted a position that was hesitant and lacked courage (and, in the opinion of several of his close collaborators, was unworthy). He combined his refusal to hand over the Jews of Italian nationality into the hands of the Germans with his consent to other steps, intended to appease his ally and "meet them half-way."

This may be seen from a telegram the Foreign Ministry sent to the Italian Embassy in Paris on 10 October 1942; it reported in detail both the approach by the Germans on 22 September and the reply by the Italians. According to the writer, the royal government had decided it could not agree that the measures taken against the Jews in the Western European countries occupied by the German Army, and "among these the removal to the East," also apply to their citizens. "They had no objection, however, that, subject to certain reservations, the steps intended to restrict their [social and economic] activities apply to them." More important, though, they would not object from now on to their Jewish citizens residing in France wearing the yellow star, like the other local Jews.[39]

In the Italian view, this last item most probably seemed in the nature of a far-reaching concession. Nevertheless, it did not in the least suffice to meet German expectations, as the latter had intended the imposition to wear the badge to serve as a starting point in equating the status of the Italian citizens to that of all the other Jews and to prepare the ground for "their removal to the East." On this, they insisted explicitly, both in the conversations they conducted with their Italian colleagues in Paris and in the note that von Bismarck had delivered on 22 September. The Italian reply therefore did not in any way satisfy them, and they interpreted it as a rejection pure and simple of their message and the two alternative solutions it contained. They revealed no interest in the proposed concession concerning the application to Italian citizens of the duty to wear the badge. What is more, if, as the Italians had proposed, this obligation were really to be imposed without entailing the implementation of the other decrees— and primarily divorced from the decree of deportation—it was liable to stress even further the privileged status enjoyed by a small group of Jews and indirectly, the inability of the Germans to impose their will on their ally. The German security authorities in France therefore decided to ignore the Italian proposal and at that point refrained from making changes in the arrangements agreed until then between the Italian consular officials in Paris and the personnel of the German Military Government. In Berlin, however, Martin Luther summed up the entire subject in a memorandum of 22 October 1942 that was intended for von Ribbentropp and in which he indicated the serious dangers a continuation of the present situation held in store for both Axis powers. He proposed that the whole question of the fate of the Italian Jews in Italy itself and in the countries within the sphere of influence of the Reich be considered at the highest political level; the chances that it would find a solution at the local level were in the writer's words very weak, and it could no longer be tolerated that "on such an important matter the Axis would in the eyes of the whole world adopt a disunited policy." [40]

Against this position, which completely discounted the practical importance of the concessions the Italians were prepared to make, there were those who regarded the moral implications of these concessions with great severity. Count Luca Pietromarchi, a senior official of the Italian Foreign Ministry, who on the strength of his position as director of the Department for Matters of Armistice and the Peace [41] did much to save Jewish refugees from Croatia, wrote in his diary on 10 December 1942: "The Duce has agreed that the Italian Jews in France should be forced to wear the 'Star of Solomon.' This is the civilization introduced by the New Order. Is it any wonder that no one believes in victory by the Axis? This is repugnant to everyone who preserves a feeling of human dignity. In this way the Axis alienates the best part of public opinion."[42] This is evidence that by that time disgust at the German policies toward the Jews had already affected the highest ranks of the Italian diplomats (and had spread among broad circles even in the army, particularly among soldiers serving abroad, in the Balkans or Eastern Europe, where they witnessed the results of that policy).

On 11 October 1942, only one day after the telegram from the Foreign Ministry had been dispatched to Paris, Heinrich Himmler arrived in Rome on a personal mission from the Führer for a series of meetings with the senior personalities of the fascist leadership. The Reichsführer of the SS came to the Italian capital directly from an extended visit to the eastern front, and according to Ciano he brought with him memories "which for him were a nightmare and he did not conceal this."[43] Nevertheless, in his talk with Mussolini, Himmler apparently succeeded in overcoming his own distress, because he described in detail the steps that the German Army was taking against the Jewish population in Eastern Europe. He mentioned the high "natural" mortality that affected those engaged in forced labor, in particular those paving roads, the mass executions of men, women, and children, also announcing that the intentions of the Reich government was "to remove the Jews from the whole of Germany, from the area of the General Government and all the occupied countries." According to Himmler, Mussolini's reaction was that in fact "this was the only possible solution."[44]

For the third time in forty-five days Mussolini was thus required to consider the fate of the Jews in the areas occupied by the Axis powers: on 21 August on the matter of the refugees in the area of Italian occupation in Croatia, on 22 September on the question of the status of the Italian citizens in the zone of German occupation in France, and on 11 October on the general topic of German policy toward the Jews in the areas occupied by them. Each time Mussolini's replies were different, but they were always general, evasive, and given to interpretation one way or another.

This only means that the man, whenever he was forced to adopt a stand concerning the fate of large numbers of Jews, found himself trapped between opposing trends and considerations, and he could not or would not decide which stand to take. On the one hand lay his personal inclinations and his political views, which had always been charged with a burden of suspicion, intolerance, and even hostility to the very particular existence of the Jews. On the other hand, the policy of the Final Solution of the Third Reich, with its horrifyingly murderous revelations, was not his own policy, did not suit his own view on life, and certainly was no part of the world of concepts and of values acceptable to the majority of the Italian people, including the majority of fascists. In the face of this dilemma and in face of the unceasing pressure from the Germans, Mussolini did not find the courage to make a clear-cut and unequivocal decision. He was prepared to appease his allies at the cost of concessions that were far-reaching even in the eyes of some of his assistants and in at least one case would have entailed the abandoning of thousands of Jews to their bitter fate. However, Mussolini refrained from imposing his decisions in this matter on his subordinates at the head of the army and the Foreign Ministry, as he most probably could have done if he had really wanted it. As a whole, in this as in many other matters, Mussolini thus demonstrated a lack of determination, a lack of courage, and a large measure of cynicism and opportunism, but also recoil from a policy of murder and bloodshed and a lack of desire to be an active partner in the performance of these deeds.[45]

The question of the status and the ultimate fate of the Italian Jews residing in France was therefore discussed during the months of September and October 1942 in the embassies and the foreign ministries of the Axis powers and in Rome even, at the desk of the "Prime Minister and Duce of Fascism." Meanwhile, a stubborn and long-lasting struggle was taking place in Paris at the modest local level of the officials of the Italian Consulate and of the German Embassy and security forces over the fate of individual Jews holding Italian citizenship or claiming the right to such citizenship. These Jews had been arrested in Paris or its vicinity during the summer of 1942, detained in the Drancy camp (or in one case in the Beaune-la-Roland camp), and awaited their transfer "eastwards." It will be remembered that in the first reports by Ambassador Buti on the great manhunts in the middle of July, nothing had been said of the arrest of Italian citizens,[46] and there is no information on whether in fact there were any such arrests at that time. From the beginning of August at the very latest, however, Italian Jews were from time to time being arrested for various reasons by the French police, on the pretext of not observing one of the special decrees applying to the Jews, or in a few cases for criminal offences, real or imaginary, concerning food rationing, the black market, and the like. For the most part, these Jews were brought before a French court, sentenced to a fine or a short term of prison, and after they had served their sentence or were in the course of serving it, they were transferred to the Drancy camp. A few of them were not even brought to court or were not even officially charged with a crime of any sort, and after being arrested they were taken directly to Drancy.

It was clear to the Italian Consulate that from the Drancy camp these Jews were going to be sent to Poland and that in this way the Germans were in practice going to circumvent the agreements concerning the applicability of the deportation decree on Jews with Italian citizenship. When the news of the first arrests became known, the Italians therefore went into action in order to close the breach. The first two approaches to the German authorities, reference to which has been preserved in writing, were of 4 August 1942.[47] In them, Consul Orlandini demanded the release of two Jews: one, Josef Catarivas, had been caught as he tried to cross the demarcation line between the two zones and was detained in the Beaune-la-Roland camp (the consul notes that this man's father had fought in Spain "against the Reds"); the other, Daniel Roditi, had been arrested on the charge of "being suspected of trading in jewellery," was not brought to trial, and was transferred to Drancy. A few days later, on 14 August, the consul wrote about Renata Gabbai Mizrachi, who had been arrested in the city of Tours for unknown reasons, and "according to rumor had already been sent to Poland"; on 22 August, concerning Moshe Yerushalmi, who had been detained in Drancy "apparently only for racial reasons," and on 25 August, concerning the affair of Giovanna Levy Piperno who had been arrested at the Paris railway station because she was not wearing her badge.[48] In addition, at the beginning of September the consulate demanded the release of Vittoria Levi,[49] of Maurice Sardos,[50] of Abramo Hassan, of Sara Levy,[51] of Samy Cohen,[52] and also Lucia Danon Cohen, an Italian citizen by origin, who had received French citizenship on her marriage and was detained in Drancy with her two small children. The consul notes that Mrs. Danon Cohen had a nephew who was a lieutenant in the Grenadier Corps, at that time serving on the eastern front.[53] Altogether, between 4 August and 11 September 1942, some twenty letters have been preserved regarding Jews with Italian citizenship or who claimed the right to this citizenship and were detained at the Drancy camp (or Beaune-la-Roland) whose release the consulate was demanding (or at least the postponement of their deportation to Poland until their citizenship could finally be determined).

These letters, signed by Consul Orlandini or his deputy, Pasquinelli, were all addressed to the headquarters of the Reich Security Police in Paris, without indicating the name of the recipient; they were therefore intended for the adviser for Jewish affairs, SS-Obersturmführer Heinz Röthke. They did in fact reach their destination, and many of them have even been preserved, with the comments written on them in the handwriting of Röthke or of one of his assistants.[54] It seems, however, that not one of them was favored with a reply. Röthke regarded the "incomprehensible" intervention of the Italian Consulate on behalf of their Jewish citizens with open displeasure and even a certain amount of anger, on the grounds of which he had, as previously mentioned, decided to break off all contact with them.[55] On 12 September, Orlandini made an additional attempt to talk to him. He sent him a detailed memorandum in which he expressed his protest that "despite the repeated approaches of the Consulate, no way had yet been found to clarify finally even just one case." He enclosed a list that included the names and other details of twelve Jews of Italian citizenship who were still detained in the Drancy camp. Orlandini asked to speed up the processing of their cases by the normal legal procedures: to bring to court anyone suspected of breaking the law and to release without delay anyone not found guilty and anyone who had completed their sentence.[56] Four days later, when he did not receive a reply, Orlandini sent Röthke—this time by his full name—a few dry lines, in which he complained that he had not been allowed to make contact with him by telephone and requested urgently to make an appointment to meet Vice-Consul Pasquinelli.[57] But all was to no avail.[58]

Meanwhile, days went by, and time was pressing. Trains of deportees were setting out ceaselessly, almost every other day.[59] There was considerable concern that, while waiting for replies that did not come, the Germans would from time to time deport some of the Jews of Italian citizenship who were detained in Drancy, so that by the time the dispute was settled not one would be on French soil any longer. In the second half of September, Consul Orlandini therefore decided that he would no longer play into Röthke's hands. Concurrently with his approaches to Röthke, which were becoming more and more infrequent, he would try his luck with his colleagues, the diplomats at the German Embassy in Paris. On 20 September, he contacted Dr. Ernst Achenbach, the counselor for political affairs at the embassy, who directed him to his assistant, Dr. Karl-Theodor Zeitschel, who was according to him in charge of "the affairs of foreign Jews" at the embassy. (He in fact served as liaison officer between the embassy and the security services in Paris.)[60]

On 22 September 1942, the first meeting between the two diplomats, Pasquinelli and Zeitschel, did in fact take place in the building of the German Embassy.[61] Pasquinelli had found out that one day later, on 23 September, a train of deportees was destined to leave Drancy "for Germany or Eastern Europe," with several of the Italian Jews in it. Hence, before raising the subject he asked that immediate instructions be given to delay the deportation of those individuals. According to Pasquinelli's impression, Zeitschel began his reply in "a slightly aggressive tone." He complained that "Italy was the only country that was adopting a benevolent attitude toward the Jews, at a time when all the countries of Europe were taking ever more severe antisemitic measures"; he mentioned the example of Bulgaria that, according to him, had in those days published the most severe orders on the matter. Pasquinelli hurried to reply that the Italian government had recorded real "achievements" to their credit in this field, as they had already enacted racial laws in 1938, that is, long before such countries as Hungary and Bulgaria had seen fit to do so. He thought that he had succeeded in persuading his host, and in fact the latter did change his tone of voice and promised that he would issue instructions as soon as possible to delay the deportation of Italian Jews who were detained at Drancy.

In the same friendly tone, appropriate to conversations between diplomats of two allied nations, Zeitschel revealed to Pasquinelli that in accordance with the express wishes of the Führer all Jews presently in France, including those of French citizenship, must be deported, "so that before the end of the following spring at the latest not a single Jew would be left in France."[62] In view of this announcement, which to say the least was unusual and which Zeitschel asked to be officially conveyed to the Italian Embassy in Paris, Pasquinelli saw a need to react only concerning the small number of Italian nationals—or possibly he saw no possibility to act differently. He requested that these be taken off the list of the deportation order "until the Italian government is able to issue a declaration on the possibility of their repatriation to Italy." This last sentence, which Pasquinelli said on his own initiative, and possibly out of a certain rashness, since it ran counter to the position clarified during those very days in the Foreign Ministry, enabled Zeitschel to determine that the time had come "that the Italian government make a conclusive decision concerning the fate of the Italian Jews in France and choose between their return to their own country and their deportation"; and in fact, he added that he had heard that a request in this light would be presented within the next few days (in fact that very same day) by the German ambassador in Rome to the Italian Foreign Ministry.

So the conversation came to an end. Pasquinelli got the impression that he had achieved most of what he had wanted, that is, delaying the deportation of the Italian Jews detained in Drancy until the dispute over their fate (and the fate of all the Italian Jews in France) was settled in discussions scheduled to open at a high diplomatic level in Rome and Berlin. In fact, Pasquinelli was deluding himself, or at least erred in his estimations: his host, Dr. Zeitschel, the polished and "decent" German diplomat, was in actual fact an old and fanatical Nazi, a Sturmbannführer in the SS, who was ready to conduct a conversation with him on the "Jewish matter" only to mislead him and to allow Röthke to do his contemptible job with greater efficiency, speed, and a minimum of interference from outside. And in fact, only three days later, on 25 September, Pasquinelli was forced once more to call on Zeitschel, as information had reached him from reliable sources that, during the last few days and in spite of the promises he had been given, three Italian Jews had been placed on the deportation trains that had left Drancy. He demanded of Zeitschel that suitable instruction be given immediately that such events should not happen again, and that the three Jews who had been deported be returned immediately to France. Although Zeitschel did at first point out the difficulties that, according to him, would be involved in returning them, in the end he acceded to the pleas of his guest and expressed his readiness to inquire into the matter and to attempt to ensure that the operation would in fact be performed.[63]

Despite these promises, Consul Orlandini this time decided to try and act also in other ways: in an urgent message he contacted the Italian Consulate in Metz and asked them to try to locate the three deportees and release them, since in accordance with his information they were due to pass through that city and would perhaps even stay there for some time in the course of their journey "to Eastern Europe."[64] A few days later, the Italian consul in Metz contacted his colleague in Breslau and asked to continue the search for the deportees from his own place of operation, as he had been informed by the Metz police that the trains were traveling toward that city.[65] However, as might have been expected, these efforts were fruitless, and all traces of the deportees were lost somewhere east of

Breslau (needless to say, no trace was found in the records of any inquiries or efforts made by Zeitschel).

At the time when the conversations between Pasquinelli and Zeitschel were being conducted in a more or less friendly spirit (but without any real results), the officials of the consulate apparently felt that time was pressing and that every day was liable to be fatal. In view of this, they decided to take an additional, completely unconventional step, and on the 17th, 19th, and 22d of September 1942 Orlandini directly approached the commander of the Drancy camp, handed him a list of names of the Italian Jews who were detained there, and demanded that he refrain from deporting them to the "Eastern territories" until he completed clarifying their position with the German authorities.[66] Although these three letters, and perhaps also others that had been written on the same subject and for some reason have not been preserved, were in fact intended for the French officer who was in charge of the camp and apparently also reached their destination, they eventually found their way to the desk of Röthke, who in his accustomed way wrote on them his angry comments. On 19 September, the consulate sent an additional letter directly to Luisa Levy Andjel, a Jewess detained at Drancy, to inform her that her application for the restoration of her Italian citizenship was being processed and that the camp commander was requested not to permit her deportation until the end of her case. Within a few days this letter also reached Röthke's desk. In the margin of the document, some unknown hand had written: "Deportiert 23.9.42" (Deported 23 September 1942).[67]

When all was lost, Orlandini decided to send a detailed memorandum to the Italian Embassy in Paris concerning the Italian Jews detained in concentration camps in the Occupied Zone, most of them at Drancy, with the unequivocal recommendation that the subject be passed to the Foreign Ministry for treatment. According to Orlandini, until that day, 9 October, fourteen Jews had been arrested; some of them who had committed no offense, some for light offenses, mostly against the special regulations imposed on Jews. The consulate demanded their release countless times but was never given a proper reply; at times the replies from the German authorities were evasive, others were negative without any explanation. Meanwhile, one of the Jews, Riccardo ben Nachmias, died of a disease he acquired in the concentration camp. The consul indicated that this Jew had been a soldier in the Italian Army during World War I, had won a decoration, later became one of the earliest members of the Fascist party, and even participated in the March on Rome.[68] The other detainees, a man and two women, were deported to Eastern Europe, and despite all the efforts of the consulate, no way was found of discovering their fate.[69] Orlandini indicated that, although the Germans had undertaken to postpone the deportation of all Italian Jews until the two governments had found a solution to this problem, they did not keep their word, and the deportation was carried out in spite of everything. The consul therefore recommended that the matter be once more thoroughly examined in the Foreign Ministry, from which clear instructions could be issued to everyone concerned on how to act.[70]

The truth is that, even according to the reports of the consulate, until that date only three Italian Jews had been deported, out of a community of some fifteen hundred souls (by estimate) and another two women, one of them with her two children, who had married non-Italians and in consequence had lost their original citizenship. Nevertheless, in view of the magnitude of the danger hanging over the heads of a whole community (which was no longer a mystery for the Italian diplomats), one may understand the reasons for the consul's concern and the cause for his eagerness that the problem find a comprehensive solution with no further delays. Completely by accident, the consulate was granted an immediate reply to its approach, since at the time the letter went out to Ambassador Buti, a dispatch reached Paris from the Foreign Ministry, which included the announcement by von Bismarck of 22 September and the ministry's reply of 10 October. On 3 November, the embassy sent a copy of the two documents to the consulates in Paris and Vichy, who thus received the most authoritative instructions on how to act on the matter, as the reply of the Foreign Ministry to the German Embassy had, as indicated, been given after consultation with Mussolini himself and in accordance with his instructions. This reply contained an out-of-hand rejection of the two alternatives that the Germans had proposed (repatriation to Italy or deportation to the East) and as counterweight consented that Jews with Italian citizenship endure most of the economic decrees and the obligation to wear the badge.[71]

It would seem that the negotiations had returned to the starting point, or to a point extremely close to it. In fact, the episode stood on the brink of termination. With the allied landing in North Africa in the beginning of November, a decisive turning point in the battle was reached in the Mediterranean. As the military position of the Italians began to deteriorate, their political status within the Axis camp began to weaken. The more the days passed and their defeat seemed imminent, the less chance the Italians had of withstanding German pressure concerning both the cases of individual Jews interned at Drancy and all their Jewish citizens within the Occupied Zone.

# 3

# The Last Days of Italy's Axis Partnership

## (NOVEMBER 1942–SEPTEMBER 1943)

On 11 November the last trainload of deportees for 1942 left Drancy. By the time the deportations were renewed on 9 February 1943, the political and military array had already undergone fundamental changes, both in France and in the Mediterranean battlefield. On the night of 8 November 1942 the Allies landed in North Africa, opening a new front that presented a direct threat to the Axis forces in Libya and, in the long run, to their entire defense system in southern Europe. In retaliation, on 11 November, the Axis armies invaded the region controlled by the Vichy government[1] and completed the conquest of all the territory of France (although in Vichy the government of Marshal Pétain remained in place—for all purposes a satellite government, lacking any real authority). From then on, the center of operations against the Jews moved from Paris and its environs to the southern regions. Here also the dispute between the allies was renewed with even greater vigor on the Jewish Problem, although this time within a different political configuration, as the Italians physically controlled the southeastern districts of France and could intervene and enforce their own policy vis-à-vis the fate of the entire Jewish population, regardless of their citizenship (and not only regarding a handful of Italian citizens).[2]

In the German Occupation Zone, in contrast, the situation did not change, even after the events that occurred in the beginning of November, and in Paris negotiations and exchanges of memoranda continued over the Jews still detained in Drancy. These contacts, however, were lacking that feeling of urgency and fear that was evident earlier, as in practice the pause in deportations continued and no one knew if and when they would be renewed. On 30 November 1942, Orlandini reported directly to Rome on the daily events. This time he spoke of twenty Italian Jews who had been arrested up to that day—one of whom had died after his arrest, three had been deported to the East, and three had been released.[3] The Political Department of the Foreign Ministry responded to this information without delay, and on 11 December 1942 a telegram signed by the foreign minister himself was dispatched to the embassies in Paris and in Berlin. In it were instructions to act immediately for the release of the detained Jews and to obtain guarantees from the German authorities that such cases would not happen again.[4]

But these steps no longer had a real sequel. At the beginning of 1943 the position of the Italian Army had become extremely bad. They had been swept from the Western Desert and had retreated from the approaches of El Alamein across the border into Tunisia. It was clear to everyone that the hour of decision was approaching and that without large-scale assistance from the Germans in equipment and fighting units, the country would be unable to survive for long in the war. It was also clear, however, that the more dependent the Italian government was on its allies, the less freedom it had in operations and political affairs (among these Jewish affairs). The Italians, however, did not change their attitude or agree to compromise or abandon the Jews who had found refuge in the territories they occupied, in Croatia, Greece, and southern France until their surrender to the Allies in September 1943.[5] But regarding the Italian Jews residing in the areas occupied by the Germans, the Italians could not withstand the ceaseless pressure from their Axis allies.

On 13 January 1943, von Ribbentrop instructed the German ambassador in Rome to approach his colleague Foreign Minister Ciano and to inform him of the resolute decision of his government to solve once and for all the question of "the treatment of Italian Jews in the occupied western regions," either repatriating them to Italy or including them in the solution of the problem of all Jews who were residents of the Reich or of one of the countries under the rule of the Reich. "The Italian official position toward the question of the treatment of the Jews differed to a considerable extent from the German position," as von Ribbentrop explained in a dogmatic and somewhat threatening tone,

> While we have recognized Jewry as a disease, which threatens to decompose the body of a nation and which is seeking to prevent the reconstruction of Europe, the Italian Government believe they are able to treat the Jews individually, in that they prefer isolated Jews or groups of Jews above others. . . . It is inconceivable that we should reconcile ourselves to the Italian viewpoint within our own country and the areas under our control. . . . Jewry in

its entirety is the worst enemy to ourselves and our struggle, that is, both for Germany and for Italy. We can therefore never agree to exceptional treatment. In our view Jews of Italian nationality would also be considered Jews, who because of this are subject to our legislation for Jews.[6]

Von Mackensen, the German ambassador in Rome reported three days later that he had verbally delivered the contents of the transmission to Ciano, who had replied in general terms that the matter was complex and that it was desirable that the ambassador should provide these demands in writing so that it should be possible to consider them on their merits. Von Mackensen refrained from doing this, as in his words he had not received permission to do so.[7]

Despite their evasive answer, the Italian Foreign Ministry staff reached the conclusion that this time they would not be able to withstand the German demand. They had no choice but to agree to repatriating their citizens or let them be included in deportation from which there was no return. On 27 January, von Bismarck was already able to report to his superiors in Berlin that Ciano's cabinet head, the Marquis d'Ajeta, informed him of the decision by the Italian government to repatriate all their Jewish citizens from France, Belgium, and Holland.[8] On 3 February 1943, Foreign Minister Ciano in fact notified the embassies of Italy in Berlin and in Paris as well as the diplomatic delegations in the Hague, Oslo, and Brussels that "for political reasons" and "by prior agreement with the Reich government" it had been decided that all Jews of Italian citizenship and residing in the countries of Western Europe occupied by the Germans would be repatriated to Italy by 31 March 1943. Anyone preferring to remain in their place of residence after this date would no longer be able to enjoy Italian consular protection.[9]

In fact, some time before this, Italian Jews had again asked to be given the opportunity "to repatriate," and naturally, as the situation became more serious, the number of applicants increased constantly. Consul Orlandini reported this in a telegram of 14 November 1942, addressed directly to the Ministry of the Interior in which he stressed the serious danger awaiting these Jews, who any day were liable to be arrested without warning and deported to regions in the East.[10] This time the Ministry of the Interior replied without delay and promised that all requests in this matter made by citizens "of the Jewish race" living in France "would be answered speedily."[11] It was therefore clear that, despite the opposition to this solution that in the past had been expressed by both the Interior and the

Foreign Ministry (each for their own reasons), both ministries were now inclined to accept the fact that this was the most convenient and perhaps the only way to solve the problem.

At the beginning of February 1943, when the decision had finally been made, the Foreign Ministry instructed their representatives to make the administrative and economic arrangements required to facilitate the transfer of the repatriates and to allow them to bring the remains of their money.[12] Because of a lack of time and the scarcity of means at their disposal, the Italians did not succeed in completing the operation by the end of March. They repeatedly asked their allies for an extension of a few weeks, and this was granted.[13] In fact, the operation continued slowly until the beginning of September 1943, and in its course most of the Italian Jews residing in the Occupied Zone (as well as those in Belgium, who were included in the 3 February decision to repatriate)[14] were moved either to Italy proper or, if they preferred, to the parts of southern France occupied by the Italian Army. Meanwhile, most of those Jews still detained in Drancy were released and included in the repatriation.[15]

Thus ended this three-year episode, from June 1940 until August 1943, of Italian intervention on behalf of their Jewish citizens residing in the German Occupation Zone of France. During this time, Italian policy was guided by a few considerations, some based on principle, others dependent on changing political circumstances. At the beginning, the main goal of Italian officials in Rome and in France was simply to prevent the expropriated property of Italian Jewish citizens from falling into French hands. With time, the Italians reached the conclusion that, in order to preserve their international political position in the long run, it was important to uphold the rights of all their citizens abroad, and among them of their Jewish citizens residing in the countries conquered by Germany. Indeed, the fact that they were allies with such a superpower as Nazi Germany, which until the end of 1942 ruled most of Europe, obligated them, or so they perceived, to strictly maintain their image as a superpower in line with the Germans. The Italians also believed that to relinquish the rights of their Jewish citizens in one country—even if the interests represented by these Jews were relatively small—would sooner or later lead them to relinquish the rights of Italian Jews in other countries, where their political and economic interests would be much greater, as in Tunisia and Greece. The two choices proposed by Germans to solve the problem—the repatriation of Italian Jewish citizens or the removal of consular protection—both completely contradicted Italian policy. Thus as long as they believed their opposition would be successful, Italian diplomats fiercely opposed those two choices. In the beginning of 1943, when their military situation worsened and their political position was shaky, the Italians chose what they saw as the lesser of two evils, repatriation.

Beside those economic and political considerations, most of the Italian diplomats and military personnel in France and Rome arrived at the conclusion that there was a fundamental difference between the 1938 racial policy of fascist Italy and the actions against the Jews carried out by the German security forces throughout Europe, especially since the opening of the front against the Soviet Union. As they understood it, these were two different conceptions that could not be reconciled. In any event, the brutal behavior demonstrated by the Germans and their French collaborators during the manhunts and deportations of 1942 from both parts of France and the terrifying information arriving from "the East" about the fate of those deported (information that was confirmed on different occasions, although in general and ambiguous terms, by officials of the diplomatic delegation and German security services in Paris) influenced the Italian authorities to view their stand on the rights of their Jewish citizens not only as part of their duty to serve their country's interests but also as a moral duty in itself, outweighing all other considerations.

In the beginning of August 1943 (about two weeks after Mussolini was ousted), the German Foreign Ministry informed the Italian Embassy in Berlin, that from 10 September onward, "the status of all foreign Jews, in every country under control of the Reich would be equated to that of the German Jews."[16] In effect, the political and military circumstances that were suddenly created two days before the deadline made this ultimative announcement outdated and without purpose. On 8 September 1943, the headquarters of the Allied forces in North Africa unexpectedly announced Italy's surrender. In response, within days, the German Army took over most of the territory of Italy and of all the countries that until then had been under Italian rule. The fate of the Italian and foreign Jews, in Italy proper as well as outside, was from now on equated without any reservation to that of the rest of their people in all European countries occupied by the Germans.

# Part 2

## Southern France

# The Unoccupied Zone

## (JUNE 1940–NOVEMBER 1942)

On 3 October 1940, less than three months after the establishment of the new French state (état français) under the leadership of Marshal Pétain and the beginning of the "National Revolution," the Vichy government published the first basic law concerning the status of Jews (Statut des Juifs).[1] On its own initiative and free will, it thereby joined the camp of countries that made racialist antisemitism and discrimination against Jews part of their official and declared policy. The law, which had been formulated and submitted for the approval of the government by the minister of justice, Raphaël Alibert, was basically a colorless, abbreviated, and poor version of the race laws that had already been in force for some time in Germany and Italy. It contained ten clauses dealing with two principal topics: a definition of the term *Jew*—who was a Jew for the purpose of applying the law—and details of the restrictions that would be imposed on anyone included in this definition. Anyone who was the descendant of at least three grandparents "of the Jewish race" would be considered a Jew. The legislator thereby adopted the well-known definition of the German law but was more severe, adding that anyone with only two grandparents "of that race" would also be considered a Jew, if his or her spouse were a Jew. He thereby adopted the mingling of the racial and religio-national terms so characteristic of the Italian racial legislation.[2] Anyone considered a Jew according to these definitions was disqualified from holding positions of public office (with the exception of a few of them, in the very lowest grades, that were open to Jews "possessing special privileges" because of special services they had rendered to France). All Jews without exception were also forbidden any form of activity connected with the press or the radio, the theater and the cinema; in addition, the principle of numerus clausus was established in the free professions.

Published one day after the Statut des Juifs, which applied to all the Jews of France, whatever their nationality, was the law "concerning the foreign nationals belonging to the Jewish race," whom it would now be possible to arrest and imprison in "special camps," at the discretion of the regional prefect of their place of residence.[3] This law—one of the most extremely arbitrary, even in the France of those days—later on would provide the French police with the legal foundation for arresting tens of thousands of Jews and confining them in concentration camps within the borders of the Unoccupied Zone (and their subsequent surrender into the hands of the Germans, who deported them to the East). The second basic law on the status of the Jews was published on 2 June 1941, this time on the initiative of Xavier Vallat, the Commissaire Général aux Questions Juives,[4] an antisemitic lawyer and veteran member of the National Assembly. It was followed by a series of laws and regulations designed to restrict the employment of Jews in various branches of the economy—in industry, commerce, and the trades—and dispossess them of their property. The most important among them were the laws of 22 July 1941, intended to "eliminate all Jewish influence in the national economy," and that of 17 November 1941, extending the whole complex of restrictions imposed 2 June 1941 by the second Statut des Juifs.[5] Also published on 2 June 1941 was the law imposing on the Jews the duty to report within one month to the *préfecture* in their place of residence.[6] Jews who did not obey this order were liable to fines and imprisonment and, even if they were French, became liable to confinement in the "special camps" by administrative order alone.

By intensive legislative work that took a little over one year, the Vichy government thus successfully enacted far-reaching antisemitic racial legislation that in many aspects equaled in severity and arbitrariness what was customary in most of the fascist countries, Germany's allies or satellites. And this in France, the country that had been the cradle of human rights and the promoter of the emancipation of the Jews from the shackles of civil discrimination.

During all this time, from the end of June 1940 to the beginning of November 1942, the Italians took no formal stand on anything concerning the Jews in the zone under the Vichy regime, except for those few among them who held Italian citizenship.[7] Nevertheless, even during this period, short items of information concerning Jews came up from time to time in the routine reports sent by Italian representatives in France to the For-

eign Ministry in Rome or to the Armistice Commission headquarters in
Turin. These were for the most part factual reports concerning the laws
against the Jews enacted by the Vichy government or the measures that
government was taking in expropriating their property and interning foreign Jews in concentration camps in the southern regions of the country.[8]
The general tone in these reports is one of disinterest. Most of the writers
apparently regarded the Vichy legislation against the Jews as a matter of
routine, a natural phenomenon in the countries of the Axis camp that did
not require any special attention. Only a few of the writers found it necessary to add their own words of interpretation and evaluation. These did
so in most cases to commend the Vichy government on the measures they
had taken and to express their satisfaction with the fact that it also at last
had decided to take a joint stand with the Axis powers on such a sensitive
and important matter as the "race policy."

Excelling in this respect was Silvio Camerani, the consul general in
Nice, who on 29 July 1940 sent his superiors in Rome a lengthy and detailed memorandum, wholly devoted to describing the subversive activities
of the Jews in Cannes and Nice and the dangers inherent in this. The
writer starts with the hackneyed pun widely popular in those days, according to which, in view of the extent of the "Jewish invasion" into southern
France, it would be appropriate to change the name of the city of Cannes to
Kahan.[9] He recalls that included among the prominent representatives of
local Jewry, "who were hoping once again for victory of the British Army,"
there were also a few of the Italian citizens, among these the banker Angelo
Donati,[10] the brothers Viterbo, and Senator L. Louis Dreyfuss, "a war-
monger and Italophobe" (who, although not an Italian citizen, had married the Baroness Levy from Florence). The author of the memorandum
concludes with the warning that, if the Vichy government did not take the
most vigorous steps against Jews, "this would be further proof that the
new Government does not dare destroy all the focal points of political con-
tamination" that had spread among the French people, "of [which] that in
Cannes is perhaps not the least dangerous."[11]

A few months later, a member of the Armistice Commission in Nice followed his example: in the regular biweekly report he sent to his superiors,
this man pointed out the potential dangers of the "fifth column" from the
democratic countries that was operating in the region and that, according
to him, was based on some 2,000 members of the Evangelical Church and
on a similar number of foreign Jews. Logic would advise, the writer claims,

"that these people should be returned to their own countries or interned." What is more, the Jews were making use of "the skill they had acquired during the hundreds of years which they had spent in interpreting the Kabalah" to mislead people and spread the rumor that the Italian government had already renounced its historic claims to Nice and Corsica. As for the Italian Jews living in the region—whom the learned writer apparently did not consider to be authorities in the lore of mysticism—these had in the past pretended that they had remained loyal to their country even after the publication of the "race laws," but "they had for a moment thrown away the mask from their faces and revealed their Anglophile and anti-Fascist passions."[12] One more example: at the beginning of January 1942, in a general review of the situation in southern France written by a journalist close to Foreign Ministry circles who has remained unidentified, the Jewish colony in Nice is described in the following terms: "The Jews, chosen from the worst rejects of the society in central and eastern Europe, wander through the streets sometimes dressed according to the Mosaic Code, notoriously make their living from the most dubious business, contributing to starving the population."[13]

These voices and others like them did not in fact reflect, as a whole, the opinions of the Italian officials who in those days were serving in southern France. However, the very use of arguments of this kind by part of an elite in Italian society is an indication of the trends of thought during that period. (And, beyond that, they are an indication of the intellectual confusion and the deep moral and cultural distortions that twenty years of rule by the fascist regime had induced among the Italian people.)

The tragic turning point in the situation of the Jews of France during the second half of 1942, the massive manhunts both in the Occupied Zone and within the borders of Vichy France and the mass deportations that followed, roused the Italians into taking a closer interest in the subject, in most cases with a more sympathetic approach to the victims themselves. Two factors were at the root of this awakening: the shocked reaction to the inhumanity revealed in the operations against the Jews—in the course of which thousands of human beings were arrested under unbearably harsh conditions, families were separated, and children torn from the arms of their parents—and the fear that this operation would arouse widespread opposition among the French people, first and foremost in the French Catholic Church, in a way that would in the long run become a lethal weapon in the hands of enemy propagandists.

Ambassador Buti in an urgent dispatch of 16 July 1942 to the Foreign Ministry reported the start of the great manhunt in Paris on that same day.[14] A few days later, the ambassador again reported the beginning of arrests of foreign Jews in the Unoccupied Zone, where "up to now the number of foreign Jews arrested . . . has reached 10,000."[15] This cable was sent on 24 July 1942, and on that day the manhunts of the Jews in the Unoccupied Zone had not yet begun. However, for quite a long time there had been in this zone extensive arrests among the foreign Jews, who were being confined in internment camps in southern France on the initiative of the Vichy government.[16] Negotiations were also taking place in those days between the German security officials and representatives of the Vichy police concerning the "evacuation" of the Jews from the Unoccupied Zone; the French were requested to deliver a first quota of 10,000 Jews by 1 August 1942.[17] The ambassador probably had received some information about these negotiations, and in his report he referred jointly to the operations that had already begun in northern France and to those in preparation in the southern districts.

At the end of August, after the manhunts had also begun in the Unoccupied Zone, there were growing numbers of reports from Italian diplomats and military officials; this time, the events were presented in a new light and from different points of view. From Lyon, Nice, Chambery, and Marseilles reports were coming in from the Italian representatives there, on the arrest of thousands of foreigns or stateless Jews—men, women, and children—whose destiny was to be deported to "the East," a fate similar to that of their coreligionists previously arrested in the Occupied Zone. The evaluation of the writers was that the operation was being carried out under heavy German pressure and that it was liable to arouse extensive opposition among local circles, because these would accuse the Vichy regime "of accepting the German dictate in complete submission." Hence, the operation would eventually "serve the Anglo-Saxon propaganda in its efforts to arouse public opinion in France against the Vichy government."[18]

At the beginning of September 1942, the subject was also raised to an unprecedented extent on the pages of the *Bollettino Quindicinale* of the Italian Armistice Commission with France. This was a highly secret fortnightly publication, distributed in stenciled form among some of the security organs; it reviewed the principal events that had taken place in the preceding fortnight, both within metropolitan France and in the colonies, and also expressed the political evaluations of the commission staff officers and their conclusions on these events.

The first conclusion that arose from the description of the operation carried out against the Jews in southern France concerned the political damage that this operation had already caused and would still be likely to create.

> During the last days of the preceding fortnight [the second half of August] aversion to the policy of collaboration and to Germany has also been nurtured, in the Unoccupied Zone, by the measures taken against the Jews, which the dissident movement[19] has been quick to represent as being exclusively due to the complete and supine subservience of the Laval Government to German policy. The fact that these steps were taken, suddenly and following a long period of tolerance, concurrently with the vaunted progress made in the process of Franco-German rapprochement following Dieppe,[20] has played into the hands of the dissident movement in spreading alarm . . . over the consequences of a closer collaboration [with Germany].

The author of the item also touches on the horrifying display of inhumanity revealed in the course of the operation: "The harshness with which the arrests were carried out, which appeared so brutal, is able even to justify the suspicion that this way was deliberately adopted by the executors [namely, the French police], untrustworthy instruments of the Government they are supposed to serve, in order to place the whole operation in the most unfavorable light."

In other words, in the eyes of the writer, the acts performed so clearly contradicted any reasonable and acceptable human behavior that he could only explain them by going beyond their overt meaning. Finally, a stop-press footnote, added at the bottom of the page after the bulletin had already been printed, indicated that information had been received saying that Mgr. Saliège, the archbishop of Toulouse, had written a pastoral letter "On the humane person," in which he fiercely censured the measures taken against the Jews and the manner in which these had been put into operation. The archbishop also ordered all priests serving within his diocese to read the letter to the whole community from the pulpit of their churches on the following Sunday.[21]

The stand taken by the French Catholic clergy on the antisemitic policy pursued by the Vichy government and the possibility that they would openly and vigorously voice their opposition to the arrest of thousands of Jews and their deportation from the country, represented a cause for deep concern to the Italian representatives in France. Evidence of this may be found in the reports from the Italian Embassy in Paris during September and October 1942,[22] as well as in the evaluations reported in the *Armistice Commission Bulletin* for those months.[23] Prominent in all these was the fear that the French Catholic Church would openly adopt an unambiguous stand against the persecution of the Jews and would thereby become a hostile element in the political struggle raging in France and a focus of broadly popular resistance to the Axis powers. This worry did in fact have some foundation, at first sight at least, for at the end of August and the beginning of September, several of the senior clergy in southern France—headed by Mgr. Saliège, the archbishop of Toulouse; Mgr. Théas, the bishop of Montauban; Cardinal Gerlier, the archbishop of Lyon; and Mgr. Delay, the bishop of Marseilles—had raised their voices in a valiant and honorable protest in condemnation of the measures taken against the Jews: they had denounced them as inhuman acts, in total antithesis to Christian morality.[24]

A short time later, however, the Italians realized to their considerable satisfaction that they had erred in their evaluation and that their fears were groundless. The French public as a whole remained indifferent to the arrest and deportation of the "foreign" Jews. If there were some who were repelled by the demonstration of inhumanity that accompanied these measures or by the self-debasement before the dictates of the Germans that arose from them, there were also those who regarded the operation with more than a trace of satisfaction. As for the French Catholic clergy, for the most part they very quickly abandoned their opposition to what was being done to the Jews, under the influence of both the pressures by the Vichy authorities and the attacks on them from various platforms, mainly on the pages of the collaborating press in the two zones. Furthermore, on this subject they found themselves standing alone in the field (insofar as they had in fact entered it), with no support whatsoever, either diplomatic or theological, on the part of the Holy See. At the end of September 1942, the Italian officials of the Armistice Commission could already state that at a theological convention that took place at Lerins, the bishops of southeastern France had expressed their unconditional support for Marshal Pétain and their full appreciation "for his actions in favor of the religious, moral, and material revival of the new France." In the opinions of the Italian officers, this declaration constituted a kind of counterpoise to the harsh expressions included in the letters of Archbishop Saliège and

Cardinal Gerlier.[25] In the mid-October issue of the *Armistice Commission Bulletin*, these same officers indicated with satisfaction that "following the message of loyalty to Pétain by the bishops of the southeastern provinces, the pro-Jewish manifestations from part of the Catholic clergy . . . have been moderated during the past fortnight by some declarations of other Prelates."[26] At the end of October 1942, they could already report, with evident relief, that after the visit to Vichy on 27–30 October of Cardinals Suhard and Gerlier, who were officiating in Paris and Lyon, respectively, "The situation has been fully cleared up . . . the relations between Church and State remained founded on 'mutual trust'."[27]

By then, it had become clear to the Italians that two additional elements, who they feared were likely to express their protests against the deportation of the Jews—the Vatican and the U.S. government—were also not hurrying to do so (or confined themselves to vague words of protest, which everyone understood would have no real influence). Both the Vatican and the U.S. government had after all recognized the Vichy government from its very first days and were maintaining regular and orderly diplomatic relations with it. The brutal arrests of tens of thousands of Jews were therefore performed before the eyes of their representatives and with their full knowledge. There was room for fear (from the Italian point of view) that at some stage they would intervene in the events, expressing their revulsion and demanding an immediate halt of the operations, either for general humane moral reasons or for considerations of political expedience. The reality would prove that these fears were totaly unfounded.

On 3 September 1942, Ambassador Buti reported from Paris information according to which Mgr. Valerio Valeri, the apostolic nuncio in Vichy, in conversations with Vichy government officials had expressed "marked disappointment" at the arrest and deportation of foreign Jews residing in the two zones of France.[28] Only five days later however, the ambassador corrected his report. He announced that he had checked the subject, both at the German Embassy in Paris and among Vichy government circles, and it became clear to him that "the Apostolic Nunciate had taken no formal steps with the French government in matter of the recent intensification of the measures against the Jews, restraining itself to intervene . . . in favor of three or four individual cases."[29] There had in fact been rumors that on various occasions the nuncio had expressed his personal dissatisfaction with what was happening, and of course these rumors also reached the ears of the Italian diplomats in Paris.[30] However, in clarification talks conducted by Count Vittorio Zoppi, the Italian consul general in Vichy, with Charles Rochat, the secretary general of the French Foreign Ministry, the latter explained that, after Laval at the end of August had expressed his dissatisfaction with these rumors to the deputy nuncio (the nuncio was at that time in Rome), they had heard no more about it.[31] And in fact, from mid-September 1942, the subject of the Vatican's stand in this matter is only discussed in the Italian documentation at long intervals and in an offhand manner, without being treated as being of any real importance.

Concurrently, fears of intervention by the American government had arisen and were likewise dismissed. The first report on this subject reached Rome at the beginning of September 1942 from the Italian Embassy in Lisbon. According to this, "the Under-Secretary of State Sumner Welles . . . had presented the most severe protest to French high authorities concerning the mass-deportations of Jews."[32] A few days later, the *Armistice Commission Bulletin* wrote that H. Pinkney Tuck, the American *chargé d'affaires* in Vichy, had protested on these deportations in the course of his conversation with Laval.[33] In the same issue was also mentioned a report from Lisbon concerning the protest supposedly presented by Sumner Welles, but this time it said that the news had not been confirmed, and its veracity seemed doubtful. Also mentioned briefly in the same issue was the statement that American Secretary of State Cordell Hull had issued to the press, in which he described the deportation of the Jews of France as "disgraceful to the highest degree."[34] Concerning this statement, which was in fact the most important official American protest, and perhaps the only one on this subject, additional reports were received in Rome, both from the consulate in Vichy and from the embassy in Madrid. It became more and more clear that there would be no follow-up to these words and they would have no real influence on future political developments. Therefore, there was no reason for concern from this side either.

Toward the end of October 1942, Count Zoppi met Rochat in Vichy for a long conversation, in the course of which were discussed various aspects of the measures taken by the Vichy government against the Jews, among these political reactions that these steps had aroused. Rochat sounded relaxed and sure of himself. "The acute phase of agitation" that had arisen in the wake of the protests by some members of the French clergy had died down. "Most of the Jews concerned have already left the Unoccupied Zone toward Germany," the French official claimed, and no protest would be able to change what had been done. To Zoppi's question on the fate of the families of those "leaving for Germany," Rochat replied with supreme cynicism that "they were free to take their wives and children with them or leave them in France. Nearly all of them had preferred to take their families with them." When Zoppi persisted, asking how many Jewish children had remained abandoned in the Unoccupied Zone and what their fate would be, Rochat replied that there were no more than a few hundred and the Americans had in fact expressed their readiness "to receive them," but the French government had yet to decide on the matter.[35]

Thus came to an end this sad episode. No public or international element, religious or political, demonstrated any readiness to intervene in order to try to halt the dreadful debacle, in the course of which the fate of over 40,000 Jews was sealed in full view of the whole world.[36] The fears of the Italians that such intervention would take place, and their estimation that it would be likely to cause real political harm to the Axis powers—did not materialize. (It seems however that these fears confirm once again that the stand that various governments in the free world adopted, or avoided adopting, was a weighty factor in all the deliberations of the Axis powers, and to some degree was liable to affect the process of decision making in the matter of the fate of the Jews in France.) As for the Italians, they recognized with an evident feeling of relief that their fears had been unfounded. They continued to observe the events from the sidelines, possibly with a certain measure of discomfort and lack of consent but also without taking any form of action, apart from the intervention on behalf of their Jewish citizens.[37] However, there is no doubt that the moral they learnt in those days was not forgotten, and it became the starting point for their actions in the future.

# The Italian Occupation Zone: The First Days

## (NOVEMBER—DECEMBER 1942)

In the early hours of the morning of 8 November 1942 the armies of the United States and Great Britain landed on the shores of Morocco and Algiers and in the vicinity of the port of Dakar, quickly gaining control over extensive stretches of terrain extending from the Atlantic coast into the center of the territory of Tunisia. The fears expressed by the Italians two years earlier at the signing of the armistice agreements with France, that the French Empire across the sea would represent the weak link in the defensive array of the Axis and that the men of Vichy entrusted with its security would not fulfill their task and would change sides at the first opportunity, joining the enemies of the Axis powers, their own allies of yesterday[1]—these fears were realized in full. Within a few days, in a wide-ranging military move that surprised the Axis military commands, the Allies had succeeded in completely altering the balance of power in the Mediterranean. They opened a new front at the rear of the Axis armies fighting in the Western Desert and thereby brought nearer to a conclusion the blood-drenched military operations that had been conducted in this theater for over two years. They gained control of most of the territory of the African continent and created for themselves a giant base that allowed them to bring some of the mighty American military and logistic potential close to the battle zone, which was due to be opened on the soil of Europe. Above all, for the first time since the surrender of France, they succeeded in posing a direct threat from close quarters to the inner heart of the "Fortress of Europe," first and foremost to the territory of Italy and the Unoccupied Zone of France.

In view of this new strategic reality, and to counteract the serious dangers it posed, on 9 November the Germans parachuted army units into Tunisia. Two days later, at dawn, they invaded with large forces the districts of southern France that until then had been under the control of the Vichy government. At the same time, and by prior coordination between the two allies at the highest political level, the Italian Army also invaded southern France and took control of most of the districts east of the Rhône River and the island of Corsica.[2]

According to the agreement reached between the operations branches of the two armies on the eve of the invasion, the line of demarcation between the German and the Italian zones should have run along the course of the Rhône River on French soil, starting from the point where it left Swiss territory and continuing to its outfall into the Mediterranean. This agreement, however, was not in fact implemented, because of the opposition from the German High Command in France, who were not prepared to relinquish control of port, cities, and road junctions of such great strategic importance as Lyon, Avignon, Aix-en-Provence, Marseilles, and Toulon. Therefore, after the invasion moves were over, additional negotiations began between the two allies, after which, on 4 December 1942, the precise "tactical border" between the areas of occupation of their armies was determined.[3] This border, or demarcation line, began east of the town of Bandol on the shore of the Mediterranean, about half-way between Toulon and Marseilles; then it joined the Rhône River north of the city of Avignon (that is, Marseilles, Aix-en-Provence, and Avignon remained under German occupation); left the Rhône north of Vienne, continued as far as Nantua (so that Lyon was also left within the German area); and from there joined the Swiss border near the town of St. Julien.[4] The Germans thus got everything they wanted. The only city of military importance that had been included in the Italian zone of occupation was Toulon. But on 27 November 1942 it was already occupied by the German Army in the course of the latter's unsuccessful attempt to seize the French fleet, and from then on, in spite of all the agreements, the Germans occupied this city and the important naval base in its vicinity. After all this, seven whole French departments remained under the occupation of the Italian Army: Alpes-Maritimes, Basses-Alpes, Hautes-Alpes, Var, Savoie, Haute-Savoie, and Drôme; two departments almost completely: Isère, Vaucluse; and a small part of one department: Ain. Altogether, ten departments.[5] This complex situation, and the roundabout way in which it had been created, are apparently the reason why most research dealing with the subject presents contradictory data, mostly inaccurate, concerning the number of departments included in the Italian Occupation Zone.

The Italian zone of occupation, 1942–1943.
Based on a map appearing in Daniel Carpi, *The Italian Authorities and the Jews of France and Tunisia during the Second World War* (in Hebrew), © Zalman Shazar Center for Jewish History, Jerusalem.

The invasion of Vichy territory by the Italians at the beginning of November 1942 was carried out by the Fourth Army, then stationed in southern France until Italy's capitulation on 8 September 1943. During all this period, this army was under the command of General Mario Vercellino, one of the veteran commanders in the Italian Army, who had already served in senior posts during World War I. As a member of the old military school, Vercellino, as far as is known, was not among the closest to the fascist leadership. Ciano, who was not in the habit of flattering the intellectual capabilities and personal merits of the Italian Army commanders, describes him in his diary as a "worthy and honest man, of patriotic integrity."[6] Ciano also mentions the details of a conversation he had with Generals Vercellino and Vittorio Ambrosio on 20 January 1943, in the course of which the two generals expressed their opinion "that Germany will lose the war, and there is nothing left for us but destruction, death, and disorder" and asked him "how far we intend to go."[7] Six months later, General Ambrosio—who meanwhile had been appointed chief of the General Staff (Comando Supremo) of the Italian Army—was the man in charge of executing the order to arrest Mussolini. This is probably an indication of the general trend of thought of the two generals, at the time of their conversation with Ciano. Serving in France alongside General Vercellino were a number of commanders, who, owing to their positions, were directly involved in the implementation of the policy toward the Jews. Among these were the operations officer of the army, General Trabucchi, and his assistant, Lieutenant Colonel Duran.[8] Furthermore, from the middle of January 1943, General Carlo Avarna di Gualtieri was appointed as commander of the Italian military mission to Vichy.[9] In this capacity, General Avarna represented the Italian General Staff before the French authorities and, among his other duties, dealt with questions connected with the fate of the Jews in the Italian zone of occupation.

According to the official policies of the two Axis powers, the invasion of southern France was intended to be simply a measure to defend the country from any eventual landing of the Allies. Despite the "presence" of the German and Italian armies on its soil, therefore, there was no formal change in the legal status of the Vichy government, and nothing had supposedly changed in the scope of its sovereign powers. In fact, the two Axis powers contradicted their own policy and, in theory as well as in practice, assumed for themselves the widest possible powers, including over spheres that previously had been exclusively the Vichy government's.

On 17 December 1942, only a little more than a month after the invasion, the German Army Command in France announced that it was assuming for itself the full powers of an occupation army throughout the whole area in which it was stationed. One month later, on 15 January 1943, the Italians followed the example of their allies.[10] Thereby, the Axis powers in effect removed the foundation on which the armistice agreements of 1940 was based and put into question the very existence of an "independent" French government. At the same time, however, both the Germans and the Italians declared that these steps would do nothing to alter the legal and political status of the Vichy government in any way. In other words, the Axis governments wanted to seize both ends of the stick: rule the land with the full authority of an army of occupation, and continue to enjoy the services of a submissive and collaborating government (among these, the fulfillment under the armistice agreements of such obligations as meeting the costs of the occupation, the provision of raw materials, and the supply of hundreds of thousands of laborers for work in Germany). In fact, the two Axis powers largely succeeded in putting their policies into practice and extracted from them the greatest possible benefit. In consequence, however, they did create a mass of duplications in the implementation of the functions of the various organs, civil and military, Germans, Italians, and French, that were active. Because France and the Axis powers had never taken the time for an accurate delineation of the division of authority among themselves—and had possibly even deliberately avoided doing so—this sphere always remained unregulated and became a cause of misunderstandings and confrontations, considerably clouding relations between them.

This legal and political tangle was particularly acute in the Italian Occupation Zone, because there each of the two parties involved had a special interest in defending and even expanding its authority, including in expressly civilian fields: the Italians, because of their well-known territorial demands (to strengthen these they wanted to demonstrate that their presence in the region had a political significance going far beyond what derived from the performance of temporary military functions); the French for the same reason, but in the opposite direction (because of their endeavors to oppose these demands and to demonstrate that, despite the temporary presence of a foreign army on their soil, they were the only legitimate and sovereign rulers).

From the first days of the occupation, the question of the attitude adopted by the two sides on the fate of the Jews in the region was also interwoven into the framework of this political dispute. The men of Vichy more than once displayed their availability, or even their willingness, in taking part in operations against the Jews in the Italian zone of occupation, not only because of their hostile attitude toward them or because of their submissiveness to the German demands but also to demonstrate that they still had full authority in this region over domestic matters, including those connected with police activities. In contrast, the Italians wanted to prevent the execution of the measures enacted by the Vichy government against the Jews, not only for humanitarian reasons but also as a kind of test of their status in the region and, to some degree, as a form of demonstration of the permanence of their rule, at least in a few departments that were under their control.

For about ten months, from mid-November 1942 until mid-September 1943, this was the general political framework that to a large degree determined the nature of operations carried out in the Italian Occupation Zone. In complete contrast to the situation in those days in most of the European countries occupied by the Axis armies, in southern France, the national rivalry and political hostility between the two nations benefited the Jews, at least to a certain degree and for a limited time.

The first problem of any importance in domestic security that the Italians were asked to handle from the beginning of their rule in southern France did not at first sight seem to have a direct and specific bearing on the Jews. Large numbers of refugees, among them political refugees from Germany and Italy and tens of thousands of Jews from various European countries, had been living in the previously Unoccupied Zone for quite a long time. When the Axis armies took over control of the region, these refugees found themselves once again under the rule of regimes that had induced them to leave their homes and the countries of their birth. There was therefore considerable fear that under the newly created political conditions the lives of many among them would be in jeopardy. The German security forces, in fact, acted without delay in all the departments included in their zone of occupation and arrested their own countrymen and political long-standing enemies. The inclusion among these of the Jewish refugees, both the former citizens of the Reich and those coming from the occupied countries, together with the members of their families, was evident.

In that same period, the Italians were also faced with the problem of how to act toward their citizens, who in the past had been among the opponents of the fascist regime and whom the invasion had caught in one of the two zones of occupation.[11] They also had to decide what should be done with all the foreign refugees who had found asylum in the region now under their occupation; these, considering the small area of the Italian Zone, were in fact quite numerous. For various reasons, the Italian authorities were not inclined to hurry their decision on these questions, particularly as in many cases the solution would have to be found in cooperation with the German security forces, and in France during those days such cooperation was in most cases quite weak. It appears, however, that in this subject the Germans were not slow in displaying initiative.

Toward the end of November 1942, only about a fortnight after the invasion, SS-Sturmbannführer Rolf Mühler, commander of the German security services in Lyon,[12] contacted the delegation of the Italian Armistice Commission in the city and informed the latter that he had received instructions from his superiors to arrest anyone of German origin who had found shelter in the region (i.e., the Rhône department) and all the foreigners suspected of representing a danger to the security of the occupation army. In this connection, Mühler asked what were the plans of the Italians concerning their own citizens, "political refugees and Italian communists," residing in the department of which he was in charge. He also expressed the opinion that it was appropriate that, in the course of the operation he would carry out, all these should be arrested by his forces and delivered to the Italian authorities. The Italian delegate, whose name for some reason is not mentioned in the document, told his caller in a noncommittal manner that he could be certain of obtaining "the effective cooperation" of his ally. At the same time, he reported the conversation to his superiors, asked them to instruct him on how to act, and advised that a senior police officer be sent to him, authorized to come to an agreement with the Germans on "a joint line of action."[13]

In response to this call, and perhaps also out of recognition that in police matters the situation in southern France required handling at senior levels, it was decided in Rome to send a senior police official to Lyon, Ispettore Rosario Barranco. Inspector Barranco was instructed "to establish opportune contacts with the competent German authorities on the delicate question of handling the local undesirable Italian elements" (namely, those living in Lyon and the Rhône department). In a cable dated 14 December 1942, Ciano informed the Italian representatives in Paris, Lyon, and Marseilles concerning the decision reached.[14] Ciano added that in the future consideration would be given to the possibility of sending a police officer with the rank of Ispettore Generale, who would be authorized to coordinate with the Germans the measures to be taken toward "these elements" in all the departments occupied by them. Until then the ministry requested that no "definitive measures" be taken toward any Italian citizens, "even if they are not Aryans." From the outset, the Foreign Ministry interpreted the German approach concerning "political refugees and Italian communists" as including also the Jews (and in fact this was most probably the intention of the SS officer).

At that same time, the general outlines of the policy to be adopted toward the groups of "refugees" and "foreigners" living in the Italian Occupation Zone in southern France were also decided in Rome—by consent of the Ministry of the Interior, the Foreign Ministry, and the General Staff. An official notification on this was submitted by the Italian General Staff to the Supreme Command of the Wehrmacht on 4 December 1942, and this is its content: "1. In the Italian Occupied Zone of France orders have been issued to arrest anyone originating in countries in a state of war with the Axis; 2. In this Zone the Italians would intern all the Jews and their families."[15]

This short announcement, formulated in the somewhat terse and concise style customary in military circles, was later interpreted by the Germans as a clear evidence of the Italian General Staff's resolution to adopt a joint stand with them in all that concerned the implementation of the measures against the "undesirable elements" living in the Italian Occupation Zone, among these, Jewish refugees. German diplomats and security officers repeatedly insisted from now on on this interpretation in their approaches to their Italian colleagues, during which they often expressed their dissatisfaction with the noncompliance of the Italian military officials in France with what they consider as unambiguous instructions of the Italian General Staff.

In fact, there were no grounds for this interpretation and for these claims, as from the outset the intention of the Italian officials, and consequently the meaning of the instructions issued by the General Staff, were completely different. This may be most clearly understood from the detailed explanations of the decisions taken that Lanza d'Ajeta, Ciano's *chef de cabinet*, sent to the Italian Embassy in Berlin on 19 December 1942, to be brought to the attention of the competent German authorities. In the words of d'Ajeta, the Italian Foreign Ministry had learned that the Germans had recently sent special police units to the zone occupied by them to "purge the territory from German refugees, most of them Jews, and in general from subversive and other dangerous elements." The Italian Foreign Ministry therefore found it necessary to send "high-ranking Police functionaries" (in fact one officer) to this region to collaborate with these units and "to avoid possible mistakes in the choice of the elements to be removed" (that is, as implied further on, to prevent the arrest of the holders of Italian citizenship). It was also decided that, at a later date, "a special unit of the Italian police" would be established to operate in the Italian Occupation Zone within the framework of the Fourth Army. Its task would be to arrest without delay the citizens of enemy countries representing a danger to security, "to proceed with the internment of the Jews,"[16] and to take the necessary measures against all foreign citizens suspected of subversive activities. For the moment, d'Ajeta concluded, arrangements must be made with the central German authorities for them to instruct their subordinates in France "not to take definitive measures toward Italian citizens, even if they are non-Aryans, unless these were previously agreed with our police or consular authorities."[17]

This was the position adopted in those days by the Italian officials, and these were the guidelines for action set out by them—and officially brought to the attention of the German Foreign Ministry—in regard to both the "undesirable" Italian citizens (and among these the "non-Aryans") resident in the German Occupation Zone and the foreign citizens residing in the zone occupied by the Italians themselves. In the following months, these lines of action did in fact serve as a basis for the policies of the Italian authorities in southern France and for the measures they took there concerning the Jews (even though some of these decisions were not fully put into operation, or were carried out after delay or with some changes, as we will see).

While discussions on the fate of the foreign refugees who had found shelter in the two zones of occupation in southern France were in progress between Rome and Berlin in a practical and even somewhat relaxed atmosphere, dissent rose between the Vichy government and the Italian authorities concerning the fate of the foreign Jews residing in the Italian Occupation Zone.

At the beginning of December 1942, only a short time after the invasion of the Axis armies, the Vichy government decided on a series of new measures against the Jews, in addition to those it had taken up to that time. The first and most severe of all was taken on 6 December, when instructions were given to the department prefects on the Mediterranean coast to remove all the foreign Jews who had entered France after 1 January 1938 from a 30-kilometer–wide strip of territory along the coast. The people evacuated were to be transferred to two departments in the interior, Ardèche and Drôme. Ardèche was included in the German Occupation Zone, and Drôme bordered on this region. There was therefore considerable fear that sooner or later most of these Jews, or perhaps even all of them, would be surrendered to the Germans and would eventually be deported "to the East."[18] On 20 December 1942, this fear became even greater, among the Jews and the Italians alike, when the Alpes-Maritimes prefect, Marcel Ribière, published an order decreeing that all foreign Jews residing in the department who had entered France after 1 January 1938 were to be prepared for evacuation "to the interior of the territory" within seventy-two hours.[19]

As soon as this became known, Alberto Calisse, the Italian consul general in Nice, approached Prefect Ribière and demanded that he refrain at once from including Italian Jews in the evacuation order. Four days later, on 24 December, Calisse reported to his superiors in Rome on what was happening. He drew their attention to the fact that, according to the orders of the Vichy government, "foreign Jews in the Alpes-Maritimes Department would be sent to enforced residence in a department under German occupation" (a claim that as indicated was only partly correct), expressed his concern over the fate "of a number of Italian citizens among them," and asked that instructions be sent to him as soon as possible "indicating a line of conduct in connection with the latter's protection."[20] At the same time, other warning voices reached Rome, originating from the Fourth Army headquarters that indicated that "the initiative of the Vichy government . . . inside the territory occupied by the Italian army and under its control is heavily wounding to our prestige and the ruling authority of our occupation forces."[21] Inspector Barranco, who meanwhile had been placed in charge of police operation in the whole Italian Occupation Zone, also reported, both to the Fourth Army headquarters and to his superiors in Rome, on what was about to take place, pointing out that the French initiative was liable to harm "all the foreign Jews in the Alpes-Maritimes department, without distinction of nationality, age, or sex" or, in other words, that thousands of people who had done nothing to endanger the security of the Italians in the area would be harmed.[22]

In response to these communications the Marquis d'Ajeta on 29 December 1942 announced to the Fourth Army Command that "it cannot be tolerated that in zones occupied by Italian troops the French authorities would force foreign Jews, including Italian citizens, to move to localities occupied by the German troops. . . . The measures concerning foreign and Italian Jews should be taken only by our organs, which have long since received clear instructions [on how to act in the matter]."[23]

One day later, on 30 December 1942, General Trabucchi, the operations officer of the Fourth Army, informed the corps commanders of the Fourth Army that "the Supreme Command had ordered to forbid the prefects to carry out the internments of people of the Jewish race" and that the prefects of the departments in the Italian zone were to be informed of this decision without delay, stressing that "the Italian government will not permit people likely to have been involved in activities against the Italians or against the Axis to be taken away" from their surveillance. At the end of the communication, Trabucchi ordered all units of the land and sea forces belonging to the Fourth Army "to intervene in order to avoid any eventual attempt by the French authorities to put into execution the orders of the Vichy government."[24]

A notification repeating Trabucchi's words almost verbatim was delivered that day to the French Colonel Bonnet, who was serving as liaison officer with the Armistice Commission delegation in Nice,[25] and through him it was delivered that same day to the Vichy government. It appears that these authorities correctly understood that this time the stand adopted by the Italians left no room for bargaining: on 31 December they therefore ordered Ribière "to postpone for the time being the implementation of this measure"—that is, the order of evacuation of foreign Jews from the department.[26] "And in fact this is what happened," Calisse reported on 6 January 1943 to the Foreign Ministry, "even if only after some opposition, arising from the desire to reconfirm, in this case too, the rights of French sovereignty" in the area.[27]

Concurrent with the order concerning the evacuation of foreign Jews "to the interior of the territory," the Vichy government instructed the department prefects, in two circulars dated 6 and 8 December 1942, on the conscription of the foreign Jews into special labor battalions. According to the text of the order, the duty to enlist applied to all foreign Jewish men, between the ages of 18 and 55, "lacking consular protection . . . or . . . originating from neutral, allied, or enemy countries of the Axis."[28] That meant all Jews, excepting those of French nationality. A few days later, on 11 December 1942, the Vichy government once more dealt with the Jewish issue and published a law that provided that "every person of the Jewish race" (that is, including French citizens) had to report to the police station in his area of residence, in order to have the word *Juif* (Jew) stamped on his or her identity card.[29]

This time Ribière acted with caution and ordered that the Jews conscripted for labor would be attached to a battalion of foreign workers located near Entrevaux in the Basses-Alpes Department, so it would be impossible to argue that these "would be taken away" from the surveillance of the Italian security forces, as the Basses-Alpes Department was wholly within the Italian Occupation Zone.

It seems that these two measures caused a certain amount of uneasiness among the Italian representatives in southern France. On the one hand, the measures did not in principle deviate from the framework of the race laws implemented since the end of 1938 in Italy itself and, needless to say, in all the European countries in the German sphere of influence. Yet, on the other hand, in the political conditions in France of those days, they represented a clear and possibly demonstrative challenge to the authority and the standing of the Italian occupation authorities. What is more, this time the decrees also applied to Jews of Italian citizenship, and these hurried to apply to the Italian consulates in their places of residence and demanded that they intervene on their behalf. For these reasons, the steps planned by the Vichy government quickly became the subject of a lively exchange of letters among the Italian representatives in France themselves and the subject of approaches by these to their superiors in Rome and Turin (seat of the Armistice Commission headquarters). The main purpose of the writers was to clarify what was being done in the various places and to ask for instructions on how to act.[30]

Finally, on 2 January 1943, unequivocal instructions were issued by Ciano to the liaison officer of the Foreign Ministry at the Fourth Army command in this form:

> For additional clarification of what we have communicated in the quoted cable [of 29 December 1942]: This Ministry maintains that the adoption of precautionary measures regarding these Jews, without exception [i.e., all foreign Jews], must remain the exclusive responsibility of the Italian authorities. You are therefore requested to draw the attention of this Command to the necessity and the urgency of informing the French civilian

authorities that the orders concerning these Jews must be suspended. The measures of internment of them and others [similar measures] belong solely to our authorities, who will act as they see fit and based on the instructions they have been given.[31]

A few days later, Consul Calisse contacted Prefect Ribière: first he asked the latter verbally to postpone the date of conscription of the foreign Jews for labor; after that he demanded, once again verbally, not to apply meanwhile the obligation of stamping the identity documents to Jews holding Italian citizenship; finally, on 14 January, he informed him in writing that he was to refrain completely from implementing the latest instructions from his government concerning the Jews, except those of French nationality, "since all measures concerning the problem of the Jews in this zone must be put into effect exclusively by Italian organs."[32]

Ribière, stirred and shocked, apparently felt that this time the Italians had gone too far. He contacted Laval by phone on the spot and reported the astounding changes that had taken place in the Italian position: first, they had objected to the transfer of the foreign Jews to the Ardèche and Drôme departments, arguing that they could not agree that elements suspected of subversive activities should be taken out of their surveillance. After that they objected to the conscription of these Jews for labor, despite the fact that from the outset they were to have been sent to a battalion stationed inside the zone entirely occupied by the Italian Army. Finally they objected to stamping their documents, claiming that taking steps in matters concerning the Jews was the sole responsibility of their forces. According to Ribière, all these were no more than idle claims. The reason for the Italian stand was, in his belief, political both in its motives and its final aim—the strengthening of their standing and their hold in the region. Support of his opinion, Ribière added, may be found in the information that had reached him from reliable sources, according to which all the steps by Italian representatives in France on this subject were taken on the personal instructions of Count Ciano.

Laval heard Ribière's complaints, asked that they be submitted to him in writing and with all the details, and advised his caller to meet the local Italian representatives and propose to them a new idea for solving the problem, namely, that the Italians evacuate to their own country all the foreign Jews to which the Vichy instructions applied.[33] However, the information given him by Ribière had so much disturbed him that he did not refrain from immediately phoning the Italian Embassy in Paris. In this conversation, Laval repeated the gist of Ribière's arguments and expressed his astonishment at the stand taken by the Italians, as it found expression in the notification delivered by Consul Calisse. He also pointed out that any relief given to foreign Jews only would be discrimination against the holders of French citizenship and concluded "that he would see rather with favor the transfer to Italy of the Italian Jews and perhaps of the foreigners too." It is not known for certain to whom Laval spoke at the embassy, whether it was the ambassador himself or Count Zoppi, and what his replies were. In any case, that same day Zoppi reported the contents of the conversation to the Italian Consulate General in Vichy and instructed them to inform the French authorities that "for reasons of military security the Italian authorities had decided to take upon themselves the exclusive competence on the precautionary measures to be taken toward the Jews, according to criteria that they consider to be the most suitable."[34]

Thus, in the course of one day, 14 January 1943, the fate of some thousands of Jewish refugees occupied the attention of officials and politicians, Italians and Frenchmen, in Nice and in Rome, in Paris and in Vichy, and even led to the personal intervention of Foreign Minister Ciano and Prime Minister Laval. It is almost certain that among the many civilian topics discussed in those days between the representatives of the two countries, only few, if any, were granted such energetic treatment at such a high level, all this despite the fact that, from the point of view of each one of the two countries, it was after all only a question of a marginal group of people, who for the most part were still strangers to the surrounding society, without connections or means, so it would have been unreasonable to assume that they could represent a security risk of any kind. It was therefore clear—as both sides openly admitted in their internal correspondence—that the struggle taking place between them was of a political nature and that it was essentially intended to achieve political objectives that had nothing to do with the fates of the Jewish refugees who were the subject of the dispute. This struggle was therefore destined to go on as long as the two sides saw a chance of success (and as long as they had the means to continue it). In this complex situation, the Jews in the Italian zone found quite good conditions to organize themselves to prevent the implementation of the Vichy's measures against them and to assist the numerous refugees who fled to the region and create for them the minimal conditions for a decent life.

The arrival of the Italian soldiers in the departments east of the Rhône was generally received with satisfaction and with a feeling of relief among the Jews in southern France. At the beginning of the period of occupation there were however some fears in the hearts of many concerning the stand the Italian Army would adopt on the Jewish question in general and on the fate of the foreign Jews in particular.[35] After all this concerned the army of a fascist country that for years had implemented an intensive anti-semitic racist policy and that had gone to war as the ally of Nazi Germany. However, there could be no doubt that, for the Jews, Italian rule would in every case be by far preferable to the other alternative—the only one and the worst of all—namely, that they fall once again into the hands of the German Army and security forces.[36]

In the second half of December, these evaluations were already confirmed, even more positively than had at first been expected, when it became known that, following intervention by the Italian Army, the Vichy government had been forced to retreat from its intentions to impose new decrees on the Jewish refugees.[37]

As the *Armistice Commission Bulletin* of the beginning of January reported, in Jewish circles in Nice and surroundings "there are widespread feelings of gratitude toward Italy (which also found expression in a religious ceremony in the synagogue), following the intervention of our military authorities aimed at preventing the evacuation of Jews resident of the zone occupied by us, to other zones, where they would for the most find their way to concentration camps."[38] Two weeks later the same source indicated once again that "The Jews resident in the Alpes-Maritimes Department have expressed their gratitude for the attitude taken toward them by the Italian authorities, in objecting to their internment and to stamping their food ration cards to indicate their race; the French Jews of Grenoble have approached our Delegate on the spot and asked that they be given the same treatment."[39]

Rumors concerning the fair position adopted by the Italian Army quickly spread among the Jews in southern France, including those living outside the borders of the Italian zone, and soon individuals and even organized groups were beginning to stream toward it from all directions. Toward the end of 1942 the leadership of the Mouvement de Jeunesse Sioniste (Movement of Zionist Youth)[40] moved from Montpellier to Grenoble; they were joined some time later by groups of the movement from Toulouse, Montauban, Lyon, and Périgueux. Also transferred to Grenoble was the Documentation Center, which had been founded within the framework of the Mouvement de Jeunesse and had been operating for two years at Moissac. Meanwhile, two of the principal activities carried out within this movement were transferred to Nice: the laboratory for forging documents and the rescue network (which called itself "physical education").[41] At the same time, Jews who were veteran inhabitants of the Italian zone established new institutions, intended to assist in the absorption of the new wave of refugees, or expanded the activities of institutions that already existed and were devoted to the same cause. In the course of 1943, three children's homes were opened in the Italian Occupation Zone—at La Grave, Sappey, and Saint-Etienne-de-Crossey—in addition to the centers for assistance to refugees that were operating in Nice and in a few provincial towns. A broad range of activities in the fields of welfare, education (including vocational training), and culture was going on there under the protection of the Italian authorities.[42]

However, the most important Jewish center within the Italian Occupation Zone at that time was in Nice, where the largest concentration of Jewish refugees was also found.[43] In order to alleviate the situation of these Jews, especially during the initial period of their stay in the city, a small committee of volunteers was established apparently during 1942, called Comité d'Aide aux Réfugiés (Refugees' Aid Committee). Its seat was in the Ashkenazi synagogue in boulevard Dubouchage, hence the name applied to it in the course of time, Comité Dubouchage (Dubouchage Committee).[44] The principal activities of the committee at that time were the collection of contributions from the few Jews of means who remained in the city, the distribution of small sums of money among the most needy, and sending parcels and providing other assistance to Jews imprisoned in Nice prison and Vichy's concentration camps, especially at Gurs and Les Milles.

With the beginning of the Italian occupation, the activities of the committee expanded considerably, for the stream of applicants asking for support grew at the same time as the number of its active members increased. At the head of the committee stood at that time a Jew of Russian origin, an old man of majestic appearance called Jacob Doubinsky. He was assisted by a few colleagues, the most active of whom were Ignace Fink and Michel Topiol.[45] But the principal change, both in the character of the committee's activities and in the scope of its functions began a few weeks later, when a Jewish banker of Italian origin, Angelo Donati, became a partner in the leadership, if only behind the scenes.[46] Donati, a man of great initiative and remarkable political intuition, had good connections with the Italian authorities in France (and to some degree also with a few figures in the central administration in Rome). Thanks to him, the committee quickly became the center of activities for the Jewish refugees in the region; and in many respects, in fact if not officially, it even served as a kind of representative body for the Jewish refugees—that is, for most of the Jews in the city—in their relations with the local military authorities.[47]

From the end of 1942 or the beginning of 1943, the Jewish refugees arriving in Nice could in fact receive not only initial material assistance at the committee offices but also a special kind of temporary "identity card." This document, which certified the identity of its bearer and his intended place of residence, was issued by the committee and signed by one of its members. It bore a stamp with an inscription in Hebrew and French that read in Hebrew: "Synagogue for the Jewish Community of the Ashkenazi Rite in Nice," and in French: Association Culturelle Israélite du Rite Ashkenasi à Nice (Israelite Cultural Association of the Ashkenazi Rite in Nice); at its center the stamp showed a drawing of the star of David, and inside it a drawing of the sabbatical candelabrum.[48] Details of the registration of the refugees were regularly dispatched by the committee to the Italian police office in the city that confirmed the validity of the certificates issued by the committee by adding another stamp, without any delay or additional examination, all based on the registration previously made by the committee at its offices.[49]

In this way people who, until then, had been without any legal standing, overnight became legal residents, protected from arbitrary orders of arrest or deportation on the part of the French police. In addition, the holders of these certificates could join the groups of refugees to be settled in the interior of the territory, in departments occupied by the Italian Army (an operation discussed in greater detail in Chapter 4). It has been estimated that, during the ten months of Italian rule in Nice, over 4,000 Jewish refugees benefited from the services of the Dubouchage Committee. During this period, they enjoyed acceptable living conditions, and, above all, there was some alleviation of the dreadful feeling that had been their first lot for years of their lives hanging in the balance every day and every hour. On the other side, the Italians too benefited from the arrangement, for they were saved the trouble and the large financial costs involved in dealing with thousands of refugees, their registration, and the organization of their transportation to the new places of residence that had been allocated to them. What is more, all the work was done under the close and constant supervision of the Italian police, who did not overlook any detail liable to be connected with political or security matters. In the creation of this atmosphere of trust and cooperation, from which both sides benefited to the full—each for the advancement of its own objectives—the part played by Donati was almost certainly very great.

Angelo Mordechai Donati was born in Italy in the city of Modena on 3 February 1885 to an old and well-to-do Italian Jewish family.[50] He completed his studies of law in that city and started work, conducting a banking business in Milan and Turin. On the outbreak of World War I he was conscripted into the Italian Army, served in various combat posts in the infantry and the air force, and in 1917 was appointed liaison officer to the French Army Staff. From then he linked his fortune with France. After the war he settled in Paris and engaged in the management of banks and financial concerns. He was successful in his business and also won the recognition of society for his successes: he was elected president of the Chambre de Commerce Italo-Française (Franco-Italian Chamber of Commerce) in Paris and was awarded high decorations by the governments of France and Italy. At the same time, Donati took a part in Jewish and Zionist activities: he stood beside Chaim Weizmann at his appearance as head of the Comité de Délégations Juives auprès de la Conférence de Paix (Committee of Jewish Delegations to the Peace Conference) at the Versailles Peace Conference, was active in the Keren Hayessod (the "Foundation Fund" of the World Zionist Organization) from its beginning, and in 1931 he assisted Zeev Jabotinsky during the negotiations with the Italian authorities on the opening of a naval school for members of the young Zionist movement Betar in the harbor town of Civitavecchia near Rome.[51] In July 1940, after the military defeat of France, he fled from Paris to Nice, where he settled down and continued to engage in banking (particularly in the management of the Banco Italo-Francese di Credito) until the Italian capitulation, on 8 September 1943.[52]

On his arrival in Nice, Donati met again one of his old-time acquaintances, Count Quinto Mazzolini, who from July 1940 was serving as consul general in the city. Mazzolini, who in his time was among the senior Italian diplomats most closely identified with the fascist regime, had previously served as consul general in Jerusalem, where he adopted a completely unfriendly attitude toward Zionism in general and the Jewish resettlement of the country in particular. Nevertheless, there reigned between the two relations of friendship, originating in the time of their military service during

World War I. When they met again in Nice, even in the unusual circumstances of those days, Mazzolini did not hesitate to stand by his friend. In a letter to the deputy inspector general of the Italian police in Rome, he emphasized that he "had known and highly esteemed him for 25 years," and he successfully asked that Donati be granted far-reaching relief in the sphere of police supervision. Among other things, he was able to obtain for him a special permission to travel to Italy and return to Nice without all the bureaucratic practices required in those days from anyone wishing to cross frontiers, especially so for a Jew. Furthermore, toward the conclusion of his task in Nice, in June 1942, Mazzolini commended his friend Donati to his successor in the post, Consul Alberto Calisse. In fact, Calisse also trusted him, and he also recommended that the police command in Rome continue to grant him the same reliefs he had enjoyed in the past; more than that, he extended him his assistance in the activities on behalf of the Jewish refugees who had begun to concentrate in the city at an ever-increasing rate since the beginning of Italian rule there.[53]

In evidence he gave in 1944 when already free on Swiss soil, Donati described some of his activities in southern France during the ten months of Italian rule. According to him, his activities began in December 1942, when he first heard of the decree for evacuation "to the interior territories" of the Jewish refugees in southern France enacted by the Vichy authorities. He then approached his "personal friend" Consul Calisse and asked him to intervene with his superiors in Rome in order to save those Jews. He even pointed out that he advised Calisse on the form of approach to the Foreign Ministry, suggesting that he stress that "Italy would bear moral responsibility for this measure" taken by the men of Vichy in the Italian zone. Consequently, when he heard that an unequivocal order had been sent from Rome to prevent the execution of the decree, Donati believed that it was his intervention that provided the grounds for the adoption of this decision. After the war, on looking back over the events of those days, he reached the further conclusion that his intervention was to some degree "the genesis of the Italian action" on behalf of the Jewish refugees in the zone occupied by them in southern France.[54]

This assumption, explicitly arising from what Donati had written in 1944,[55] has since then become generally and undisputedly accepted. Most scholars have used it to register one more credit point to all the achievements of Donati for his praiseworthy activities in those days.[56] Some scholars have gone even further in their interpretations and found therein a solution for the supposed puzzle of why the fascist government treated these refugees so mercifully after having introduced the infamous "race policy" against the Jews in their own country.[57] In fact, all these suppositions are without substance.[58]

We may accept Donati's words concerning his initiative and his emotional approach to Consul Calisse unquestioningly. There is also no doubt that Calisse treated him with respect and listened to him sympathetically. However, it is clear that an approach of this kind by one individual—however respected he may have been—was and could only have been of very marginal weight in the decision-making process of the Italian Foreign Ministry. This assumption, quite reasonable in itself, is unambiguously confirmed by the documentation of those days. In the dispatch of 24 December 1942 from Consul Calisse to Rome, in which he reports about the new measure of the Vichy government,[59] he does not mention Donati's call even by one single word and does not use or even hint at the moral and general arguments Donati had raised before him. Even assuming that Donati's intercession with the consul had preceded the writing of the latter's letter to Rome—and there is no evidence on this—Calisse meticulously avoided any mention of it in his approach to Rome. The same applies to the other dispatches that Calisse had addressed to Rome on this subject in the months that followed. In all these, the consul took care of Italian interests, including the welfare of Italian citizens, and expressed his deep concern that the new measures planned by the Vichy government should also harm Jews holding Italian citizenship. It may be assumed that the Italian officials in Rome correctly understood what was his position concerning these measures and the whole problem of the Jewish refugees in southern France. Most of them probably even agreed with him, especially in view of the frightening informations that reached them in that period about the fate of the Jews deported "to the East" from the European occupied countries.[60] Nevertheless, even within this framework, Donati's intervention could not have represented a factor of prime importance in the decision-making process in the Italian Foreign Ministry.

On the other hand, Donati's activities in Nice during the subsequent months were a factor that greatly helped the implementation of the favorable Italian policy toward the Jewish refugees there. Furthermore, the rumors circulating among the Jews concerning Donati's connections with the Italian consul and with the Italian authorities in general, were of great importance in the struggle in which the Jewish community was engaged on the internal front. These rumors, which in some cases had become legends, were able to hearten the Jews, enhancing their staying power and their readiness to act in unison within an organized framework. They were also capable of sustaining within their hearts the hope, no matter how feeble it might be, that one day their lot would improve.

On 6 January 1943, at the height of the activities to prevent the evacuation of foreign Jews from the coastal strip "to the interior," in a memorandum he submitted to Consul Calisse, Police Inspector Barranco presented the main points of his own program for solving the problem of these Jews.[61] The timing in introducing the subject, as well as the contents of the memorandum itself, clearly show that the intention of the police officer had been to propose a plan that would be not only an answer to the security needs of the Italian forces but also a kind of alternative to the measures taken by the Vichy government in those days.

Barranco opens by recalling that he had recently been appointed "to direct the police services in the French territory occupied by Italian troops"[62] and that the main task imposed on him had been "to purge this zone of the suspect elements and of the foreigners belonging to nations with whom we are in a state of war." For the performance of this task it had been decided, in coordination with the army authorities, to set up a concentration camp near Sospello, a township near the Italian border, some twenty kilometers north of Menton, which would serve for the confinement of the "most dangerous elements." For the "other elements" the possibility would be examined of imposing "enforced residence" in small settlements in the Alpes-Maritimes and the Basses-Alpes departments.[63] As for the foreign Jews residing in the Alpes-Maritimes—altogether 3,500 persons, according to the detailed list in his possession—the Vichy government had recently published a series of orders, whose object was the evacuation of all of them "without distinction of nationality [that is citizenship], age, or sex." It was, however, well known that the competent Italian authorities had given instructions to prevent the implementation of these measures. He had therefore decided to present his plan, according to which "the old, the crippled, single women, and children would be allowed to remain in their habitual residence," while the remaining Jews would be transferred to a place of settlement in the "departments of our occupation." These localities "would preferably be chosen from among those possessing a well-developed network of hotels, so it would be possible to provide conveniently[64] lodging and eating for such a crowd of people transferred in the mentioned places; I would recommend to allocate [those people] in such a way as to keep families together. The hotels in these townships have in any case been standing empty since the beginning of the war; accordingly, if the program is approved, it will be possible to start its implementation without delay or postponement. I believe that this proposal conforms to the criteria of justice and humaneness, and it should therefore be favorably received."

It is not known when approval from high echelons was granted for implementing this plan (which for the most part is confused with the initiative of Lospinoso). In any case, a short while after it had been put into writing, preparations were begun for its implementation, and it was even decided that it would be put into operation in the second half of February.[65] It appears that the plan was favorably received among the Jewish refugees concerned and that their organizations expressed their readiness to cooperate with the authorities and even "to attend to the livelihood of their needy coreligionists" in their new places of residence.[66]

Inspector Barranco's program, which at the time involved a small number of Jews, served a few months later as a model for the broader operation carried out by the Italian police headed by Inspector General Guido Lospinoso. Therein lies its direct importance for what happened to the Jews of southern France. It did, moreover, acquire additional importance within the general political framework. The very adoption of this decision concerning the internment of the Jewish refugees in southern France—on the initiative of the Italian Army and under its supervision—served as a central argument in the hands of the Italian Foreign Ministry officials, in the course of the negotiations forced upon them by their allies in 1943. In the face of the recurring arguments raised by the German diplomats concerning the security dangers to the Axis powers created by the very presence of the Jews in the region, it was easy for the Italians to reply that the subject was well-known to them and that it had already been dealt with in a thorough manner. In proof, it had long since been decided to concentrate these Jews in several localities, under the supervision of the Italian Army and police forces, and the implementation of this decision had already begun, so that there were no grounds for any fear that they could cause any harm whatsoever to the security of the Axis powers.

It may be readily assumed that the Italians were also aware of the fact that their solution of the problem did not conform to the Germans' methods and that in the long run the latter would not under any circumstances accept it. However, this way, the Italians succeeded both in gaining time and in creating for themselves a more convenient bargaining position, one that served them well in the months that followed during the negotiations conducted between them and their allies.

# The Struggle over the Fate of the Jewish Refugees in the Italian Occupation Zone

## (JANUARY—FEBRUARY 1943)

During the first months of the occupation of southern France, the struggles waged over the fate of the Jewish refugees in the Italian zone were mainly between two contenders: the Italian military and diplomatic echelons on the one side and the Vichy government on the other. Both of them, however, must have been aware of the fact that there was an additional actor in the region, one also interested in what was being done in this matter and that would certainly not refrain from intervening when and if this should be considered necessary—namely, the Germans. Furthermore, the French authorities had several good reasons for encouraging such intervention, because they would find themselves linked with a powerful ally who would without a doubt support their demands for imposing new decrees on the foreign Jews, even against the wishes of the Italian authorities. In this way the Vichy government was due to enjoy a stronger position in the region, and indirectly this would strengthen its chance to oppose the territorial aspirations of the Italians. This was after all a national matter of first importance in the eyes of the French government and in the eyes of most French people—this and not the questions involving the standing or even the fate of several thousands of Jewish refugees in a few southern departments of the country.

Indeed, on 8 January 1943, in the course of a routine working discussion that took place between SS-Brigadeführer Oberg, the commander of the police and the SS in France, and René Bousquet, the secretary-general for the police in the Vichy Ministry of the Interior, the latter raised the subject. He complained that in view of the stand recently taken by the Italian Armistice Commission in Nice, the French authorities had been unable to implement the measures planned against the Jews in the south of the country, including the expulsion of all Jews from the departments on the Mediterranean coast and the internment of the foreigners among them in concentration camps. In the margin of the record of the conversation, Oberg indicated that Bousquet had already complained several times, that the members of Italian Armistice Commission tended to protect their Jewish citizens against the measures of the Vichy government, and that, following them, the governments of Spain and Romania also demanded that their citizens be exempt from these measures.[1]

A few days later, the French officials once more raised the question with the German authorities, this time in view of the extreme position lately taken by the Italian authorities, a position that in their estimation would lead to a complete breakdown in the policy toward all Jews throughout France. Jean Leguay,[2] Bousquet's representative in the Occupied Zone, approached Knochen, commander of the SD and the Security Police in France, and in the name of Prime Minister Laval informed him of a message recently received in Vichy from the Italians, announcing their firm opposition to "the taking of any measures against Jews of foreign nationality." Leguay claimed that this meant that from now on the Italians intended to protect not just their own citizens but all Jews in their zone of occupation, except those of French nationality. Laval had asked him "to notify officially that under these circumstances his government was naturally in very great difficulties before the French people, and requested appropriate support from the German authorities."[3]

Knochen, who for more than a year had been watching with suppressed anger the protection that the Italian Consulate in Paris was extending to its Jewish citizens,[4] hurried to report this development to the Reich Security Main Office in Berlin, together with an unequivocal recommendation that the subject be brought to Himmler's attention as soon as possible. Knochen stressed that the protection the Italians were extending to their Jewish citizens, even though their number was very small,

> had already caused considerable difficulties, since it is incomprehensible that our Axis partner has not yet adopted our point of view on the Jewish question. . . . If the Italians are now going to intervene on behalf of all the

foreign Jews, they will make the implementation of a Jewish policy in our sense impossible. That is, in the coming months we will not be able to count on having Jews of French citizenship delivered to us and on being able to deport them.[5]

Ten days after this approach, which was made at the level of the police and security services, a similar message was passed through regular diplomatic channels, from the German Embassy in Paris to the Foreign Ministry. On 23 January 1943, the first counsellor at the embassy, Rudolf Schleier, reported to his superiors in Berlin on "the present situation of the Jewish question in the newly occupied region, particularly concerning the seizure and evacuation of stateless and foreign Jews." He dealt extensively with the various stages of the negotiations that had been conducted up to that time between the Italian and the French authorities, stressing that the German Embassy in Paris and the SD Command in France shared the opinion, that a thorough settlement of the "Jewish problem" in the newly occupied region would only find a solution if "it becomes possible to bring the Italians into line on our measures towards the Jews." Schleier also indicated that, although the Italian General Staff had communicated on 4 December 1942 that all Jews and their families would be interned in special camps, up to this time the actions of the Italians did not conform to their declared intention.[6]

The news concerning events in the Italian Occupation Zone in France drew considerable attention in Berlin, both in Foreign Ministry circles and in the security services. What is more, rumors concerning the dispute that had arisen between the Axis partners on their policy toward the Jews in general, and on the Jews of France in particular, had leaked out beyond the borders of the Reich and had even reached journalists in the free world. These of course hastened to publish them to bring damage to the enemy.[7] It could therefore have been expected that the Germans would no longer restrain themselves in face of the Italian stand and that they would react quickly. The reaction in fact came—and in the long run it was insistent and powerful enough to constitute an indication of the special and completely irrational importance that the Germans ascribed to the solution of the problem.

First, on 29 January 1943, Himmler raised the subject in a cable to von Ribbentrop (a cable apparently written after he received the memorandum from Knochen of 13 January). In the opening of his communication Himmler stated simply and decisively that "it is important . . . that Jews of foreign nationality residing in the Italian Occupied Zone of France, whether of Italian or other citizenship, be eliminated. Jews are the origin of the resistance activities and of communist propaganda in the region and represent a serious danger to the Italian forces."

Furthermore, "many people in France and in Europe" are refraining from acting energetically against the Jews in their country, arguing that "even our Axis partner is not prepared to follow our lead on the Jewish question." Himmler therefore demanded that the Foreign Ministry do everything in its power to bring about a change in Italian policy.[8] Two days later, still independently of Himmler's approach, two cables went out from Berlin signed by Martin Luther, the official who in his capacity of head of the Abteilung Deutschland (German Department) was responsible for Jewish affairs at the Foreign Ministry. One cable was sent to the German Embassy in Rome, which was asked to approach the Italian government and demand that they order their forces in southern France to assist the French authorities in the implementation of their policy against the foreign Jews. Another cable was sent to the German Embassy in Paris, which was asked to draw the attention of the Italian authorities there to the fact that the German government expected greater cooperation on their part in enforcing the measures against the Jews in southern France.[9]

Following these instructions, Prinz von Bismarck, the first counsellor at the German Embassy in Rome, approached Count Vidau, the newly appointed director of the Political Department (Affari Generali) at the Italian Foreign Ministry, and on 3 February he presented him a short memorandum on the position of his government and its desiderata in everything concerning "the policy toward the Jews in the newly occupied territories." Although still quite politely, the German document openly criticized the measures taken by the headquarters of the Italian Army in southern France in general and the instructions issued on 30 December 1942 to the *préfets* of the southern departments in particular. The German government had long since reached the conclusion that for security reasons all the Jews together with their families had to be "evacuated" from the region, and in the completion of this task they expected more cooperation on the part of the Italian Army and security services, especially as the German measures conformed with the declared policy of the Italian General Staff, as expressed in its communication of 4 December 1942 to the German Supreme Command.[10]

At the meeting following the consignment of the document, a conversation developed between Bismarck and his Italian colleagues, in the course of which the "Jewish matter" was also extensively discussed. According to Bismarck, who reported to his superiors in Berlin on this conversation, the Italian diplomats replied to his arguments that the operation of concentrating the Jews in southern France had been going on for some time on the initiative of the Italian Army there and was proceeding in an orderly way and without any delays. As for the general question that had been raised concerning the measures to be taken toward the Jews in the Italian Occupation Zone, they believed that the topic was mainly political in nature and that therefore it would be appropriate to discuss it between the two governments and not just at the level of army commands. Concerning the specific questions contained in the German document, the Italian diplomats announced that the Foreign Ministry would do the best it could to answer them as soon as possible.[11]

The days of the end of January and beginning of February 1943 were days of untiring, almost incredible activity on the part of German and Italian diplomats and military officials on the question of coordinating policy toward the Jews between the two Axis powers.

The first subject raised in this context was the fate of Jews with Italian citizenship residing in the Reich and the countries it occupied. This topic had been extensively discussed for almost two years between the two Axis partners, and the Germans were now determined to bring it to a conclusion. On 13 January 1943, Foreign Minister von Ribbentrop instructed the German ambassador in Rome to approach his colleagues at the Italian Foreign Ministry and in effect to deliver them an ultimatum: they should either order the immediate return to Italy of their Jewish citizens or agree to their deportation "to the East." At this stage, in view of their precarious military situation and their absolute dependence on German military and economic aid, the Italians could no longer resist their ally's pressure. On 27 January, d'Ajeta informed Bismarck of his country's readiness to repatriate the Italian Jews "from the Western European countries," and on 3 February an explicit order on this, signed by the foreign minister himself, went out from Rome to the diplomatic representatives in these countries.[12]

That same day, 3 February 1943, a memorandum reached Rome from Dino Alfieri, the Italian ambassador in Berlin, concerning the measures taken during the last years in the "Great German Reich" and the countries it occupied in order "to solve the Jewish problem."[13] This memorandum is an astounding document, unique in the Italian documentation of those days because of the detailed description it contained of the atrocities committed against the Jewish population (that were still being perpetrated). No doubt this document was capable of shocking its readers. There is in fact clear evidence that it had a real influence on Foreign Ministry personnel and on their decision-making process on the subject. First, Alfieri explained that he had found it necessary just then to compose a kind of summary of the measures taken against the Jews in Germany since the rise to power of the Nazi party, because "these days the Jewish problem in Germany seems to have arrived at a 'solution'." [14] The number of Jews "evacuated" from the area of the "Great Reich" had in his estimation already reached some 500,000.

> About the fate that was reserved for these, as the fate toward which went, and still are going, the Polish, Russian, Dutch, and also French Jews, there cannot be many doubts. . . . The German authorities did not conceal and are not concealing the aim they have set themselves . . . they confirm their willingness to exterminate the Jewish race completely, and they qualify this total extermination as a humanitarian action, because it would be able to restore the European peoples to health.

Confirmed reports had reached the Italian Embassy, according to which the ghettoes of Poland had recently been emptied of their inhabitants. In Warsaw alone, where some 600,000 Jews had been confined in the ghetto (in an area that could have accommodated some 100,000 inhabitants), today there remained only some 53,000. The rest had died of starvation and disease or had been executed. On the executions themselves, horrifying reports were reaching the embassy from various German sources, even from the SS sources. There were reports of documentary films shown to German officers that showed mass executions of Russian Jews, some of whom were thrown into the flames of fire while still alive. Pictures were also shown of long lines of women and children, standing naked on the edge of pits waiting to be executed by shooting. Recently, an SS officer had even informed one of the embassy employees that he himself had smashed the skulls of Jewish babies against a wall "in order to set an example to his men, tired and shocked after an execution particularly horrifying." In conclusion, Alfieri recalls that the German authorities had always striven to implement their measures against all Jews, including those of foreign nationality. He therefore welcomed the order issued by the Foreign Ministry, which had reached him that day, concerning the repatriation to Italy of Jews holding Italian citizenship.

That same day, 3 February 1943 (or perhaps one day later), Prinz von

Bismarck as indicated took the diplomatic step designed to persuade their allies to alter their stand and cooperate with the Vichy government and the German security forces in solving the problem of all Jews in the Italian-occupied zone in southern France, whatever their citizenship might be.

Concurrently, the various branches of the German security forces in Paris were active in the same matter. As was usual for him, SS-Standarten-führer Knochen overreached himself in this matter and in the course of three days sent four memoranda that once more described in full detail the incomprehensible and potentially dangerous attitude taken by the Italian authorities in France. On 2 February, Knochen wrote to Müller,[15] on 3 February, to the head of the Supreme Command-West of the German Army,[16] that same day once more to Müller,[17] and on 4 February to Department IVB4 of the Reich Security Main Office.[18] Two of his colleagues followed his example: on 2 February, the diplomat Rudolf Schleier wrote to the head of the Supreme Command-West,[19] and on 4 February, SS-Sturmbannführer Hagen, Oberg's assistant, once again dealt with the subject in an "internal note."[20] All were on the same subject, the implementation of the measures taken by the Vichy government against the Jewish refugees in the Italian Occupation Zone in southern France.

It seems as though in those hours so fateful for the future of their country and people, the German diplomats and security forces commanders in France had nothing more important to deal with than the fate of a few thousand Jewish refugees, without means and helpless, for whose extradition and extermination they labored tirelessly, as though possessed by a real devil. The Italian diplomat Luca Pietromarchi described the events in those days well, writing in his diary, sadly or perhaps wonderingly: "Despite all the disasters befalling them, the Germans are ceaselessly insisting that we should surrender to them all the Jews in the areas under our occupation. They confirm that by the end of 1943 not a single Jew should remain alive in Europe. It is clear that they want to implicate us in the brutality of their policy."[21]

During the first half of February 1943, there were dramatic developments on the interior political stage in Italy that today may easily be recognized as an omen heralding the approaching end of the fascist regime. In a desperate attempt to bolster up his standing in public opinion, which was progressively eroding following the worsening military situation on all fronts, Mussolini decided on a number of sweeping changes of the guard in the army command and in the ranks of his government. Among others dismissed from their posts were the chief of the General Staff, General Ugo Cavallero (on 1 February), who had been regarded as responsible for the defeat of the Italian Army in North Africa, and Foreign Minister Ciano (on 6 February), who was suspected of not believing in victory for the Axis and of no longer wholeheartedly supporting the continued association with Nazi Germany. Ciano was sent to a kind of gilded exile, being appointed Italian ambassador to the Holy See.[22] Appointed in his place to head the Foreign Ministry was one of the senior ambassadors, Giuseppe Bastianini,[23] although only with the title of deputy minister, for Mussolini once again took this portfolio for himself.

Bastianini was an experienced diplomat and a fascist of the first hour. He was apparently considered the most suitable person to stand by the Duce in those difficult times, to assist him in managing the Foreign Ministry, and, primarily, in faithfully implementing his policies. On the face of it, the rare combination of this man's political connections and his high professional competence seemed to justify this choice. In truth, despite his stormy past in the ranks of the fascist movement, Bastianini was a level-headed diplomat of independent mind: during the 1930s, while serving as deputy foreign minister he had opposed the closer ties with Nazi Germany and in 1939–1940, while serving as ambassador in London, he had consistently acted to avoid a final breach between his country and Great Britain. Despite his sincere and true loyalty to Mussolini, from the outset, Bastianini did not support the pro-German reorientation that was taking shape in his country's policy, and in 1943, with the decline of this policy, he was certainly not prepared to lead the foreign ministry to embrace the dictates from Berlin.

Furthermore, Bastianini's stand concerning the fate of the Jews certainly did not conform with that of the Germans. In the spring of 1941, after the invasion of Yugoslavia by the Axis armies and the dismemberment of that country, Bastianini had been appointed governor of Dalmatia. In that capacity, he had seen the terrible tragedy that befell the Jews of Croatia at close quarters. He had also become acquainted with the problem of thousands of Jewish refugees seeking refuge in the Italian-occupied zone (or in the areas annexed to Italy), their surrender persistently demanded by the German diplomats and the Croat Ustasa authorities. At that time, Bastianini was directly involved in the extensive activities performed to prevent the extradition of these refugees; and by his acts, he demonstrated his determination to protect them, whether for political reasons or because of his personal adherence to general moral values.[24] General Vittorio Ambrosio, who was appointed on 1 February as chief of the General Staff, had also direct knowledge of the problem of the Jewish refugees in Croatia, as he had served as the first commander of the Italian Army there. The events of the following six months would prove that the new appointments at the Foreign Ministry and the General Staff did not endanger the situation of the Jews and their expectations to continue enjoying the protection of the Italian authorities in the Italian-occupied territories in general and in southern France in particular.

Significant changes were also made at the beginning of February 1943 among the personnel of the German Foreign Ministry (without of course any connection with the events in Rome). Dismissed from their posts, within the framework of these changes, were two officials who had been directly entrusted with Jewish affairs at the Foreign Ministry: Martin Luther, until then head of the Deutschland Department, and Franz Rademacher, until then director of the Third Office (Referat DIII) in the same department. Luther was arrested and imprisoned under preferential conditions at the Sachsenhausen concentration camp, and Rademacher was first placed under house arrest and later conscripted into the Navy. Appointed in their places to these two posts, so crucial for the Jews in countries that were satellites or allies of Germany, were two professional diplomats, Horst Wagner and Eberhard von Thadden.[25] Judging by the actions of these two individuals over the following two years, their readiness to contribute to the implementation of the policy of "the Final Solution" throughout all of Europe, was in no way inferior to that of their predecessors.

The fact that at the beginning of February the leaders of the Axis powers, both in Rome and in Berlin, were busy with the changes and internal power struggles did not prevent the official of the German administration entrusted with the execution of the "solution" of the Jewish problem from continuing their labors in the countries of occupied Europe in general and in the "newly occupied areas" of France in particular. On 9 February 1943, after a pause lasting three whole months, the departure of the deportation trains from Drancy to the death camps of Auschwitz, Sobibor, and Majdanek was renewed.[26] From then until 25 March, within only forty-five days, 8,000 Jews were deported from France, among them many who had recently been arrested in the southern departments, including the victims of the manhunts carried out in Marseilles on 22–25 January 1943.

These deportations of the beginning of 1943 were carried out under more difficult initial conditions than in the past. Ever since the landing in North Africa and the enlistment of the French Army and administration there into the Allied camp, a change had begun to take place in the stand adopted by French public opinion toward the regime of Marshal Pétain in general and the policy of collaboration with Germany in particular. Victory of the Axis did not appear as certain as it had before, and the followers of Nazi Germany among the men of Vichy no longer enjoyed the same broad popular support to which they had been accustomed since their rise to power in the summer of 1940. In consequence, some of these politicians had reached the conclusion that from now on they would do well to act more cautiously, particularly concerning the acceptance of dictates from the Germans, else their image and standing would suffer even greater harm in the eyes of their fellow countrymen.

In this context, a change also began to be felt in the degree of readiness among the Vichy government to collaborate with the Germans in implementing the decrees against the Jews. There was above all increasing opposition to the involvement of the French police in the arrest of Jews of French nationality (unlike the other Jews, stateless or of foreign nationality, who remained as before the prey of the French police). The Vichy government also insisted on their opposition to applying the obligation to wear the badge on Jews within their borders, that is, the residents of the former Unoccupied Zone. In vain did Adolf Eichmann visit Paris at the beginning of February 1943 in an attempt to persuade the Vichy government to change its position. They refused to do so, among other things relying on the argument that the Italians, the closest allies of Nazi Germany, were habitually protecting their Jewish citizens. Furthermore, they refrained from taking measures against any Jews in their zone of occupation, regardless of nationality, and they even prevented the implementation of the steps that the Vichy government wanted to take against foreign Jews.[27] Why, therefore, should the Germans complain about the Vichy government?

This confrontation with the Vichy regime over the arrest of Jews with French nationality, as well as the urgent need to supply the quotas of Jews for deportation regularly and without delay (as indicated, the deportations had been renewed at full blast from the beginning of February), forced the German security officials to act with additional determination in the manhunts after foreign Jews throughout the whole of France, including the Italian Occupation Zone. There was thus an escalation in the struggle that had been raging for some time between the two Axis partners on the "Jewish subject."

In the course of the conversation already mentioned, which von Bismarck had held on 3 February 1943 with some employees of the Italian Foreign Ministry, he had been promised that a reply would be given as soon as possible to all those objections and complaints that he had presented in the name of his government. In fact, despite the upheavals affecting the Foreign Ministry staff in those days, this time they kept their word. On 10 February, Count Vidau informed von Bismarck without any reticence that the Italians saw no possibility of entrusting the fate of the Jews residing in their zone of occupation into the hands of the French authorities "since that would mean, in a subsequent stage, their surrender into the hands of the German police for deportation to Poland." Furthermore, Vidau added, the principle has long since been established that in the Italian Occupation Zone all Jews, no matter what their nationality, would be under the exclusive authority of the Italian authorities there, and the Italians did not intend to change this policy.[28]

A few days later, perhaps to soften somewhat the impression of these harsh words, the Italian Fourth Army Command stationed in France informed the German Supreme Command in the West again that the operation of concentrating the "dangerous Jewish elements" had already begun and that within the coming few days a start would be made on "the concentration of all the remaining Jews in the places selected for this purpose."[29] The Germans did in fact take note of the "conciliatory" information from their ally and even expressed satisfaction, although quite reservedly.[30] However, they had no intention of being content with the measures that the Italians had decided to take, and they were certainly not ready for their sake to renounce the implementation of their policy in the Italian Occupation Zone.

On 11 February, one day after the presentation of the replies from the Italian Foreign Ministry to von Bismarck, the German Embassy in Paris informed Knochen that explicit instructions had been received from the Foreign Ministry in Berlin, that execution of the measures planned against the Jews of France was to be continued also in the newly occupied areas. If in the course of implementing these measures the French authorities encountered difficulties on the part of the Italian Army Command, they would have to report them precisely and in full detail to the German security officials to enable the latter to inform the Italian government of events in the field.[31] It appears that the opportunity to test the real intentions of Italian policy was not long in coming.

On 20, 21, and 22 February 1943, the Vichy police began widespread manhunts after foreign Jews who were residents of the former Unoccupied Zone. This time, the operation was performed following heavy pressure from the German security authorities, who demanded the delivery into their hands of an ever-growing number of Jews in order to fill the quotas of deportees to the East. In the course of these manhunts, extensive arrests were also made in the former Unoccupied Zone, including three departments in the Italian Occupation Zone, Savoie, Haute-Savoie, and Drôme. According to the Italians, the representative of the Commissariat Général aux Questions Juives stationed in Annecy, a Mr. Bérard, was to ensure that only "elements suspected for political reasons" would be arrested, and that in any case "no one . . . would be transferred across the demarcation line of the zone under Italian control."[32] But this was said quite insincerely, for the purpose of misleading the Italians and to prevent them from interfering. According to Mr. Marchais, the French police officer in Lyon who had ordered the arrests in the Italian Zone, he had been informed in advance that the operation was intended to arrest 200 to 300 Jews to be interned in France and further deported "to Germany to a camp," together with all the Jews arrested in other departments.[33] In evident contradiction to the prior undertaking given by the representative of the Commissariat Général, Jews were in fact arrested indiscriminately; they were concentrated in two places close to the German Occupation Zone, at Bassens and Annecy, and while the manhunt was still going on, the first group of them was sent to the Gurs camp at the foot of the Pyrénées, well inside the German Occupation Zone. Under those circumstances, no one could sustain any doubt about the purpose of the operation and what fate these Jews could expect. It was similarly clear that the operation was in obvious conflict with Italian policy and that the Italians could not accept or ignore it without bringing about the most serious damage to their image and standing in the whole region.

On the second day of the operation, units of the Fourth Army were therefore already in action to prevent its implementation. On 21 February the commander of the Pusteria Division, operating in the northern part of the Italian Occupation Zone, ordered the department prefects of Valence, Chambéry, and Annecy to halt the arrests immediately. These tried to evade fulfilling the order, claiming they were obliged to carry out the instructions of their government. A day later, in reply to this, the commander of the Fourth Army, General Vercellino, asked the General Staff for permission to order these department prefects once again to release the Jews immediately, with the explicit warning that if they did not do so they themselves would be placed under arrest.[34] In Grenoble and Annecy, the commanders of the military units stationed there demanded of the French authorities the immediate release of all those who had been arrested. When these were slow in carrying out the order, the Italian commanders sealed off the local police stations, first, to prevent deportation of the prisoners being held inside them and in the second stage, to obtain their release. In the Drôme department, the Italians warned the local French authorities that they were determined to use force to prevent the removal of the Jews from the region.[35] The *Armistice Commission Bulletin* of the end of February opened the chapter dealing with events in the Savoie Department by stating that "the salient local event in the second half of the month has been the operation by the [French] police against Jews." The same source concludes his review by describing the positive results of the Italian reaction in these words: "The immediate intervention of our authorities . . . has been effective in halting the departures and placing at liberty a part of those arrested. . . . Quite naturally the intervention has aroused gratitude in Jewish circles and also appreciation among Catholics."[36]

The attempts to extend the manhunts after foreign Jews also to the area of the Italian Occupation Zone thus did not produce the results the Germans had expected. Furthermore, they revealed to the world that the two Axis powers were not pursuing a united policy concerning the "solution" to the Jewish problem. Hence, other governments might arrive at the conclusion that the policy of Germany in the matter was not necessarily the only policy that any country sheltering under the wings of the Axis had to adopt and meticulously apply. Helmut Knochen, in a dispatch addressed on 22 February to the Reich Security Main Office, described the situation that had been created and the dangers inherent therein from the German viewpoint; these are some of his conclusions:

> If the highest Italian military authorities continue to protect the Jews from arrest by the French police, the result will be that not only the French authorities but also French public opinion as a whole will be immediately provoked into most severe criticism of the relations between Germans and Italians. In addition, ever growing opposition may in future be anticipated

on the part of the French government to our demands connected with the final solution of the Jewish problem. Consequently I therefore ask if you would intervene, in order that the civil and military authorities receive instructions from the Italian government in the quickest possible way, that they are not to make difficulties for the final solution of the Jewish problem in the zone in France occupied by Italy. It must be emphasized from the very beginning that, if a way cannot be found of imposing this demand, the final solution of the Jewish problem in France as a whole will be placed in jeopardy.[37]

The subject of the fate of Jews in the Italian Occupation Zone had therefore reached the verge of a crisis. Furthermore, it threatened to lead to a complete collapse of the Reich policy in the region. The German security authorities therefore came to the conclusion that it was essential to have the problem discussed by the two powers at the highest political levels and that a solution had to be found as soon as possible once and for all. The opportunity for this was in fact not long in coming.

On 20 February 1943, the day the manhunts began in southern France—but, of course, independently of them—the German ambassador in Rome informed his colleagues in the Italian Foreign Ministry that Foreign Minister von Ribbentrop intended to visit Rome within the next few days and meet with Mussolini "in order to discuss with him a number of topics of great importance." He also intended to deliver a personal message from the Führer to the Duce. The minister did not find it necessary to explain the nature of so many important topics, whether in his approach to the Foreign Ministry in Rome or in a conversation he had with Ambassador Alfieri in Berlin.[38] Today, it is known that the main object of the visit was to foster closer military and diplomatic cooperation between the two countries in general, and between their diplomatic representatives and military commands in the occupied and satellite countries in particular. This collaboration had considerably deteriorated in recent months, particularly after the serious defeats at Stalingrad and El Alamein. In the opinion of the German leadership, it was of great importance to restore it to its previous level in order to ensure a united effort for the common victory. In addition, von Ribbentrop planned to ascertain the real meaning of the change that had taken place some two weeks earlier at the head of the Italian Army and in the government, including the leadership of the Foreign Ministry itself. He found it difficult to believe that these were matters of mere routine, as the official spokesmen of the Italian government were trying to represent them.

Within the framework of the broad topics related to strengthening the collaboration between the two partners, von Ribbentrop was also instructed to raise in his talks with Mussolini the question of the solution of "the Jewish problem in Italy and the territories occupied by the Italians."[39] It appears that, despite the somewhat surprising mantle of secrecy in which the Germans enfolded the purpose of von Ribbentrop's visit, this last detail, "following a fortunate indiscretion," reached the ears of the director general of the Political Department in the Foreign Ministry. In view of this, Count Vidau urgently ordered his staff to collect the large quantity of factual material that had recently reached the ministry, concerning the atrocities performed on the deported Jews. He also ordered to prepare a detailed memorandum on the subject to be presented to Mussolini, if this should be required, in order to persuade him "not to submit to German demands."[40] Italian sources do not of course reveal the identity of the individual responsible for that "fortunate indiscretion," whose source must have been in the German Embassy in Rome. There are, however, few doubts that it was Prinz von Bismarck himself.

In contrast to this swift operation made in the Italian Foreign Ministry, the preparations among the German officials were by far less efficient. In view of the planned consultation on "the Jewish problem in Italy and the territories occupied by the Italians," von Ribbentrop had asked his assistants to prepare a detailed memorandum. This memorandum would include both the general desires of the German government on the subject and specific examples of measures taken by the Italian authorities that had not been agreed on in advance with their allies or were even in contradiction to the policy they were pursuing. For this purpose, the Foreign Ministry officials—this time without the two outstanding experts on "Jewish affairs," Luther and Rademacher—approached their colleagues at the Reich Security Main Office and asked for the material they had required.[41] For some reason, the instructions to prepare the memorandum were only issued on 23 February, and the officials at the Foreign Ministry were asked to complete their work within twenty-four hours, as the minister's train was due to arrive in Rome late in the evening of the following day. Because the time at their disposal was so short, the ministry officials were unable to produce a detailed paper as requested, and in fact they only succeeded in composing a document that contained just two recommendations. The one, about the Jews of Italy, said it was desirable for the Italian government to take the same measures in their country as those implemented in the Reich. The other, concerning the Jews outside Italy, stated that the Italian government be requested to stop their army from acting to foil the measures the Germans were taking against the Jews in the countries occupied by the Italians, "particularly in Greece and France." In an additional document, apparently attached at the last minute to the first one before it was sent off, some information was given on what had happened a few days earlier in Grenoble and in Lyon in the course of the manhunts carried out by the French police.[42]

These memos apparently did not satisfy the minister, for, on the morning of 25 February, when he was already in Rome, he demanded once again to be given the detailed requests of the SS command concerning "the Jewish problem in Italy and the areas occupied by the Italians."[43] This time the Reich Security Main Office complied with his demand and that same day sent him a detailed and documented memorandum that included a description of a number of incidents where the Italians had foiled the policy of their ally on the subject.[44] As will be seen, however, it was already too late, and von Ribbentrop did not have the chance to make use of the document in the course of his talks in Rome.

The German foreign minister's visit lasted four days, in the course of which he met Mussolini three times, on 25, 26, and 28 February. Also present during the first and third meetings were Deputy Minister Bastianini and the two Ambassadors, Alfieri and von Mackensen. Participating at the second meeting were two generals, one from each side: Warlimont and Ambrosio. On 28 February, there was also a tête-à-tête meeting held between the two leaders. Quite detailed information has been preserved on all these meetings, except the tête-à-tête, thanks particularly to the summaries that officials from the German Foreign Ministry recorded, probably from the participants themselves.[45]

On von Ribbentrop's initiative, the question of policies to be pursued against the Jews was raised at the first meeting between the two leaders.[46] In accordance with the German summary, the Reich foreign minister had seen fit first to present to the Duce the background of the problem and its development in general lines. According to him, "Germany took up a radical position on the question of the treatment of the Jews," and this attitude "had gained even greater clarity" as a result of the development of the war in Russia. "All Jews have been transported from Germany and from the territories occupied by her to reserves in the East." The Reich foreign minister knew that these measures were described as cruel, particularly by the enemies of the Reich. But they were necessary in order to be able to carry the war through to a successful conclusion; and, considering the enormous importance ascribed to them, they should be regarded as "relatively mild." The damage the Jews were causing by spreading Anglo-American propaganda was enormous. It was essential "to apply special measures against them, not only for general ideological considerations but also for purely practical ones." After this introduction, the minister went on to deal with the actual subject. France had also taken measures against the Jews, "that were extremely useful," but they were only temporary, "because here too the final solution would be in the deportation of the Jews to the East." He himself as Reich foreign minister knew that circles in the Italian Army did not always understand the Jewish problem in all its significance (just as occasionally happens among German military people too). This is the only explanation for the order issued by the Italian General Staff, cancelling the measures that had been taken by the French authorities, on German initiative, against the Jews in the Italian Occupation Zone.

At this point, Mussolini intervened in the course of the conversation and contested the accuracy of the information on which his visitor had relied. He said this was nothing but a rumor spread by the French in order to cause dissension between Germany and Italy. The fact was that, on the initiative of the Italian Army, the Jews had long since been concentrated in various camps. Nevertheless, he admitted that von Ribbentrop "was right with regard to the remark that the military people had not got the right conceptions concerning the Jewish problem." And, as though reverting for a moment to the anarchic anti-bourgeois roots of his youth, he ascribed this "among other things, to their dissimilar mental preparation."

At that time, as mentioned, von Ribbentrop had not yet received the detailed material on events in the field, and therefore could not produce for his host clear and substantiated examples of acts by the Italian Army on behalf of the Jews in the territories it occupied. He was therefore forced to return the conversation to the somewhat hackneyed lines of a description in general terms of the great dangers inherent in "the Jewish problem." The Jews are Germany's and Italy's greatest enemies, they will always hate both national-socialist Germany and fascist Italy fanatically. If 100,000 Jews were allowed to remain in Germany or Italy or one of the countries occupied by them, it would be as though 100,000 enemy secret service agents had been admitted into one's country, allowed to operate there and even given the camouflage of German citizenship.

Here Mussolini once again interrupted the conversation and began to recall the measures that fascist Italy had already taken against Jews, as though attempting to prove the remarkable weight of his government's contribution to the struggle against Jews. It had concentrated them in special camps (he was apparently referring to the Jews of southern France). It did not treat them too gently, and this is also proved by the fact that Libyan Jews, after their liberation by the British, had declared that "the behavior of the Italians toward them had been worse than that of the Germans to the Jews in Germany."

It is doubtful whether von Ribbentrop was convinced by these shallow and flaccid boasts and even more doubtful whether he regarded himself as qualified to issue judgment in the name of his colleagues standing at the head of the security organs of the Reich on the orthodoxy of this anti-semitic policy. In any case, he merely added a short comment concerning the wealth of the Jews of Trieste, which according to his information still amounted to 4.5 billion lire. These Jews still continued to have an influence on 200 companies and consequently, in a disguised manner, they were able to act and exert an influence on the country's economy (as had happened in the past in Germany). They were therefore liable to be more dangerous than British agents.

Thus ended the discussion on the Jewish topic, in the course of the first conversation that took place between the two leaders (and in all their talks, for, according to the summaries drawn up by the Germans, this subject was not brought up again between them).[47] Following inadequate preparation and the small amount of material at his disposal, von Ribbentrop had been forced to present his government's demands for greater cooperation on the part of the Italians in implementation of the policy toward the Jews only in general terms, in an unconvincing manner, and above all completely ineffectively. His inability to highlight the differences displayed in the policies of the two allies on the basis of detailed examples and to display in full the scene arising from them found prominent expression in the concluding portion of the minister's presentation. In this piece he produced "facts" and accusations concerning the Jews of Trieste that, by their nature, would have formed part of the subjects raised in the course of the fascist race campaign of 1938–1939. These subjects, however, had no bearing on the reality of the beginning of 1943, completely overshadowed by the execution of the last stages of the Final Solution throughout most countries all over Europe. Fortunately for some tens of thousands of Jews in Italy itself and the countries it occupied, this time the legendary German efficiency had not been in evidence.

Italian sources—all of them of a literary nature—confirm this picture in general terms and provide some additional details, some of them quite interesting. Ambassador Ortona, one of the figures close to Deputy Minister Bastianini, mentions in his diary that he had read the personal message from the Führer to the Duce and that it contained "precise and insisting hints of the danger inherent in Judaism." Ortona himself was not present at the talks between the two leaders, and he did not have a lot to say about them. He participated, however, in the discussions of the joint team that composed the closing announcement. In the course of these, the German representatives so persistently urged their Italian colleagues to include a clause concerning the Jewish problem that Ortona asked himself, perhaps with some degree of hyperbole: "Had this not been the 'marotte' [the fad] for their coming to Rome?" [48]

Count Pietromarchi, in his capacity as head of the Department for Armistice and Peace at the Foreign Ministry (a department responsible mainly for events in Croatia and Greece) dealt with the subject in two entries in his diary.[49] On 1 March 1943, in summarizing the contents of the talks with the German foreign minister, he wrote:

> Von Ribbentrop briefly brought up the question of the Jews, with the object of obtaining our consent to new measures against the Italian Jews abroad.[50] On this subject had been prepared a courageous and skilful memorandum for the Duce, in which were repeated our instructions on the subject. The purpose of these instructions were to exclude any foreign intervention concerning our citizens and to prevent that a race policy that differed from ours would be conducted against them. The Duce, who found the memorandum very satisfying, interrupted Ribbentrop's words stating that in Italy the Jewish question had long since found a solution.
>
> "Nevertheless," Ribbentrop remarked, "in Trieste there are interests to the value of 4 billion lire in Jewish hands."
>
> "Really," the Duce replied, "I will order this to be investigated." And thus the discussion ended.

On 11 March, in mentioning the information reaching the Foreign Ministry on the liquidation of the Jews in the countries occupied by the Germans, Pietromarchi wrote:

> Information is arriving from London that the slaughter of the Jews in Poland was continuing. Eden confirmed in the Commons that Poles and

Yugoslavs were also being massacred in addition to the Jews. Our Embassy in Berlin reported macabre details of mass executions of Jews concentrated at the places of massacre from all the occupied territories.[51] The only ones to be saved are the Jews who put themselves under our safeguard. Our military authorities, it may be admitted to their credit, maintained a firm opposition to the brutal measures of the Germans. In France they demanded the local authorities to cancel all the instructions against the Jews, such as the duty to wear "the star of Solomon,"[52] conscription for forced labor and the like. This is perhaps the only action earning us respect among the French. The same happens in Croatia and in Greece. The Germans manifest strong disappointment. Ribbentrop did not restrain to express it in a note of 26 February, in which are enumerated all the attitudes taken by our authorities in occupied countries on behalf of the Jews. He added that such behavior on our part encourages other governments to behave in the same way. I told my colleagues to preserve this document jealously, since it is an irrefutable evidence of our ways of acting: a valuable evidence in front of history that will redeem us for too many cowardices.

Ironically, this very document that Pietromarchi had ordered "to preserve jealously" was not saved in the archives of the Italian Foreign Ministry (or at least it has not so far been found). Nevertheless, its contents are known today thanks to the Germans, since the "note" that von Ribbentrop delivered to the Italians on 26 February at the end of his talks in Rome was certainly based on the memorandum from the Reich Security Main Office of 25 February (if it is not a literal copy of it), and this memorandum has been preserved among the German documentation.[53]

Von Ribbentrop's talks in Rome thus ended fruitlessly, as far as coordination between the two countries' policies toward the Jews was concerned. Despite their serious military and economic weakness and their ever-growing dependence on German assistance, the Italians still found ways to maneuver between needs, pressures, interests, moral bonds, and time-guided constraints. Nevertheless, there could be no doubts that the affair was not yet over and that it would not easily find a solution, because the difference of views between the two sides was so great that it was doubtful whether any form of compromise could be reached.

At the beginning of March 1943 two requests concerning the fate of the Jews in the Italian Occupation Zone in southern France lay before the Italian policymakers in Rome—two requests that were totally different and conflicted with each other. The one, from General Vercellino, originally addressed to the General Staff, contained the proposal to demand once again that the French department prefects immediately release the Jews arrested in the Italian Occupation Zone, with the explicit warning that if they did not do so, they themselves would be arrested.[54] The other, from Foreign Minister von Ribbentrop, containing the demand that unequivocal orders be issued to the military commands in southern France to desist at once from their deliberate actions aimed at canceling the measures taken by the Vichy government against the Jews and to the best of their ability to provide assistance to the French authorities and German security forces in performing their tasks.[55] It was evident, however, that the adoption of a clear-cut stand could not be evaded.

This time the first to take a stand were the military authorities. On 1 March 1943, General Ambrosio, chief of the General Staff, sent a cable to the Fourth Army Command with short and clear instruction on how to act, saying:

> With reference to your cable 2501 dated 22 February.[56] This is to inform you that measures concerning arrest and internment of Jews, residents in the territory of France occupied by our armed forces, whatever their nationality, are the sole responsibility of our military authorities. I also inform you that we have instructed COLFRAN[57] to demand the Vichy government to cancel arrests and internments of Jews put into effect so far, and to order the Prefects to refrain from taking measures such as these taken at present. I wish for the moment to delay the arrest of the Prefects.[58]

That same day, 1 March, the chief of the General Staff sent to General Avarna, head of the COLFRAN in Vichy, detailed instructions concerning the demands he had to present to the French government.[59] The following day, General Avarna presented his well-known letter to Admiral Platon,[60] in which in general terms he repeated the contents of the instructions he had received from Rome. This is the text of Avarna's letter to Platon:

> Vichy, 2 March 1943
>
> Dear Admiral,
>
> In the name of the Italian Supreme Command I have the honor to inform you of the following:
>
> On the instructions of the French government the Prefects of Valence, Chambéry, and Annecy have recently carried out arrests of numerous Jews holding foreign nationality. Eight of them, who had been arrested in Annecy, have been transferred to the Pyrénées.[61] When the Italian military authorities intervened in the matter, the Prefects replied that they were obliged to carry out the orders from Vichy.
>
> In view of these facts, the Italian Supreme Command wishes to make

clear that the question of these arrests does not differ in character from that which arose during last December, following anti-Jewish instructions of the Prefect of Alpes-Maritimes. Furthermore, the Italian Supreme Command cannot consent that the Prefects take measures involving arrest, internment, and the like of Jews resident in the region of France occupied by the Italian armed forces, irrespective of whether they are Jews holding Italian, French, or foreign citizenship. These measures lie within the exclusive competence of the Italian occupation authorities. For this reason the Italian Supreme Command demands that the French government:

a) cancel the arrests and internments carried out so far;

b) order the Department Prefects in all the territories under the control of the Italian armed forces to refrain from taking these measures in the indicated region, whether they involve arrests or internments of Jews of Italian, French, or foreign nationality.

signed: Carlo Avarna di Gualtieri, Brigadier General[62]

Platon apparently rejected the Italian move on the spot, or at least announced that he had "certain objections" to it; and Avarna reported on this in a dispatch to the General Staff on 3 March, in which he also requested that additional instructions be sent to him on how to act in the matter.[63] Concurrently, Laval, acting through René Bousquet, the secretary general for police of Vichy, contacted the German Embassy in Paris and stated that he was "greatly astonished" at the Italian move. According to Bousquet, the French prime minister did not query the rights of the Italians to intervene on behalf of their citizens, but he is in no way prepared to accept their demands to release French or foreign Jews from arrest. This step contravenes both the laws of France and the policy of Germany toward the Jews in France. Counsellor Schleier of the German Embassy in Paris, who reported the conversation to his superiors on 4 March, enclosed a copy of the letter from General Avarna to Admiral Platon. He also saw fit to add that the fact that the Italians had raised these demands in writing— according to him, for the first time—had created a bad impression in the French government, concerning the degree of coordination in the policies of the two Axis powers. What is more, everyone understood that the Italian step this time did not originate at the local level but had come from high up. The German Embassy raised the assumption that the step taken by the Italian authorities was related to their intention to transfer all the Jews resident in their zone of occupation to the interior of the country; except that, according to reports from the German Consulate in Marseilles, this operation was still only in its initial stages.[64]

It was clear that this report, and especially the contents of the Avarna letter, would not fail to elicit a firm German reaction. Nevertheless, at this stage, the Italians were not prepared to let the subject drop. On 5 March, immediately after the "objections" raised by Platon had become known, the Italian Foreign Ministry contacted the General Staff and asked that urgent orders be given to the Fourth Army Command to intervene without delay with the French prefects, so that the measures concerning the Jews decided by the Vichy government would not be put into operation:

> The purpose, the message said, is to prevent the mentioned measures from being implemented in the field, while the step by General Avarna is still under discussion, thereby frustrating our intentions. . . . In this regard it should be stressed that our intervention is not a mere request or a matter of negotiation, but an express notification to the French government, according to which all that concerned the policy toward the Jews in French territory under Italian occupation should be of our exclusive competence. Our line of conduct in this matter is based both on the instructions given at the time by the Duce and on the well-known political guidelines concerning Jews resident in territories over which our authority is exercised.[65]

The officials at the Foreign Ministry thus wanted to invoke high places; or, more accurately, the highest place that could be imagined.[66] Nevertheless, they apparently felt that time was short and that their intervention would be too late if it were discussed after the Jews arrested had already been transferred to the German Occupation Zone. Two days later, they therefore contacted again the General Staff and repeated their request that urgent instructions be sent to the Fourth Army Command to take forceful action for an immediate halt of the operations and the release of the Jews already arrested, without waiting for the outcome of the talks that General Avarna had begun to conduct in Vichy.[67] The following day, 8 March, two urgent messages did in fact go out from General Ambrosio, the chief of the General Staff, containing detailed instructions on the subject of "The arrest of the Jews"—one to the commander of the Fourth Army, and one to COLFRAN, the liaison unit of the General Staff with the Vichy authorities.

The one message, addressed to General Vercellino, mainly repeats the instructions of 5 March from the Foreign Ministry.[68] The other, addressed to General Avarna, is a little more detailed. It is phrased in quasi-legal language and divided into clauses but does not differ substantially from the preceding one. The only new clause added said that Jews who had committed criminal offenses could be judged by French civil courts but could not be sentenced to deportation (*deportazione esclusa*).[69] "The removal of the Jews," the document explicitly stated, "is to be regarded as inconceivable, since as a result of their removal from the territory of our occupation they would be deported."[70]

While the matter was under discussion at the military level, the officials of the Foreign Ministry still had before them the note from Foreign Minister von Ribbentrop—delivered, as mentioned, on 26 February[71]—that also required an answer. This time the Italian diplomats apparently saw no cause for urgency in the matter, or perhaps they preferred to wait with their reply until after instructions had been issued from the General Staff to the Fourth Army in France. Either way, the Italian note was composed on 9 March and was delivered to Prinz von Bismarck a day or two later. The note included three clauses. The first discussed the question of Italian Jews in the German Occupation Zone of France. This problem, according to the writer, had been solved long before that, and these Jews were in the process of repatriation to Italy. The second clause, the most important of the three, discussed "the security measures to be taken toward Frenchmen, dangerous foreigners, or members of the Jewish race in the French territories occupied by the Italian forces." The authors of the note state somewhat categorically that "although the military authorities and the Italian police appreciate the offer of collaboration, they would take the necessary measures alone, and therefore the intervention of the German police in these zones will be superfluous." The third clause discussed "the eventuality that foreign or French Jews would cross, or try to cross, from the zone of German occupation to that of the Italian occupation." According to the writer, clear instructions had already been issued on 29 December 1942 to the military authorities, according to which they had to prevent the entry of "these undesirable elements," and these orders are still in force and are reconfirmed.[72]

The Italians thus seemed to have brought back the matter to the starting point. In fact, the affair had already been provided such an impulse that the clock could no longer be turned back, certainly not by the rather meaningless arguments and excuses that the Italian diplomats had used until then.

On 9 March—the day on which the Italian Foreign Ministry note was written, but before it had arrived at the German Embassy in Rome—von Ribbentrop ordered von Mackensen to go to Mussolini and personally deliver a message from him. The long and detailed message opened with a factual review of incidents in which the Italian Army in France had foiled the measures taken by the Vichy authorities "against the Jews and other enemies of the Axis." The author of the review, relying among others on the complaints from Laval and Bousquet,[73] cited word for word the text of the letters from General Avarna to the Vichy authorities and from Colonel Romolo Zorio to the prefect of Basses-Alpes and mentioned other letters from Italian commanders on the same subject. After this factual review, von Ribbentrop discusses the subject itself, raising evaluations and proposals over the situation created and the steps to be taken to correct it. He stated that agreement had been reached between him and the Duce during his visit to Rome, according to which the two powers would act on the question of the Jews in full coordination and cooperation. At the time, Mussolini had claimed that he could not believe information that Italian commanders in France had acted against German policy and frustrated the measures taken by Vichy against the Jews. He even expressed the conjecture that the source of this information lay in French intrigues, aimed at sowing discord and embarrassment between the two allies. Von Ribbentrop now claimed that the letters from Italian commanders quoted above are "the clear evidence that the Italian military authorities, and even the Supreme Command itself, were apparently conducting in France a policy diametrically opposed to the concepts and intentions of the Duce." He therefore asked that Mussolini urgently and forcefully intervene to put an end to this intolerable situation. In practice, von Ribbentrop stated, the Italians are to choose between three alternatives: that (1) the matter be deferred to the exclusive competence of the French police; (2) the matter be submitted to the care of the Italian civilian police, who would act on this subject totally independently of the army authorities (according to von Ribbentrop, SS-Reichsführer Himmler favored this solution); (3) the matter be submitted to the SS-Reichsführer, who would act in cooperation with the French police, without leaving the Italians any say in the matter. Von Ribbentrop indicates that the Führer himself is aware of this approach and had even called him for a special interview in order to hear details on it.[74]

It appears that in presenting the choice of these three courses of action, particularly in raising the second choice (and also giving it first priority), the Germans displayed a very low measure of understanding about the structure of the Italian establishment of those days. The decision to take the subject out of the army's field of operation and to submit it to the authority of the police, could have been, and usually was, of decisive significance in Nazi Germany. It was meaningless in fascist Italy, where there was no real difference between the police and the army from the point of view of their subordination to government's bodies (the Ministry of the Interior for the first and the Ministry of War for the other, both of which at that time headed by one man—Mussolini).[75] The German leaders thus projected the situation they knew in their own country to that in Italy, which they supposedly knew in every detail. (As is well known, both von Ribbentrop and Göhring considered themselves outstanding experts on Italian affairs). But in this case at least, their expertise failed to pass the test.

This time, however, it was clear that in Berlin the subject was considered of great importance, and they expected it would be given first priority. Nevertheless, Mussolini was in no hurry to receive the ambassador in audience. Those days were among the most difficult experienced by the Italian Army since the outbreak of war. At the end of January the troops of the British Eighth Army had completed the conquest of Libya, had crossed the border into Tunisia, and were getting into position for the final attack on the Axis forces there. At the hour when the Italian Empire on African soil was collapsing and the danger that military action would overflow onto the soil of the home country had become imminent, the aging, ill, and tired leader seemingly was not able to devote his mind to the matter of the fate of the some Jewish refugees in southern France. Mussolini only replied on 9 March to the long personal letter the Führer had sent him a fortnight earlier through von Ribbentrop. In his letter, the Duce dealt with ways for closer cooperation between the armies of the two powers in the Balkans and the need to take a line of defense on the eastern front in order to reach a separate agreement with the Soviet Union. He also stressed once again "the unshakable intention to march with Germany to the end of the road."[76] On these matters he talked extensively, apparently that same day, with Fieldmarshal Göhring, who was staying in Rome for a few days on a visit.[77] However, both in his letter to the Führer and his conversation with Göhring, Mussolini refrained from raising "the Jewish topic."

Mussolini found time only on 17 March to receive Ambassador von Mackensen bearing the personal message from the German foreign minister. But before this meeting took place, on 11 or 12 March, von Ribbentrop had received the memorandum dated 9 March from the Italian Foreign Ministry.[78] As expected, the minister found it necessary to react to it immediately, and on 13 March he sent his ambassador in Rome a new version of the second part of the dispatch, emphasizing that the ambassador was to read these things to Mussolini in person. Although the new version expanded on the arguments that were in the previous letter, it contained no substantial innovations. Von Ribbentrop stressed that from the Italian document it may be understood that the Foreign Ministry had known of the letter from General Avarna of 2 March, as well as the measures taken by the Italian authorities in southern France at the end of December 1942. In view of this, he was more certain than ever that the Duce should be asked "to intervene immediately and personally by issuing draconic orders, in order to bring this intolerable situation to an end." As for the three options he had raised in his previous letter, von Ribbentrop repeated them with the addition of a few explanatory comments that did not alter the substance of the matter. The second option was still preferred, both in his own view and in that of SS-Reichsführer Himmler. Furthermore, on the first option he found it necessary to remark that, in his opinion and under the present circumstances, it was almost certain that it could not be accepted by the Italians, because its implementation would involve overt disregard of the actions by the Italian command—and that in full view of the French authorities.[79] This evaluation was perhaps the most reasonable and logical in the entire document; nevertheless, as we will see, it came close to being refuted.

Ambassador von Mackensen was received in audience by Mussolini, as mentioned, in the evening of 17 March 1943.[80] A detailed report of the course of the meeting has been preserved, prepared that same evening by the German Ambassador and sent to Berlin the following morning. According to him, Mussolini had read the first factual part of the document and heard him read the text of the second part most attentively, nodding his head from time to time as a sign of agreement with its contents. After that, he declaimed his reply at length. "The imperative necessity for [taking] radical measures against the Jews . . . still remaining in the Italian zone of occupation could not be presented more clearly and irrefutably." If the Italian generals opposed the implementation of these measures, they did this because "they had not grasped the full significance of all the measures." Furthermore, he believed that "the behavior of these generals was the result not only of the indicated lack of understanding concerning the significance of the action being taken, but also the consequences of a misguided humanitarian sentimentality, which is inappropriate to our harsh times." On the subject itself, the ambassador could inform the Reich Foreign Minister that "he would that same day issue suitable instructions to the Chief of the General Staff General Ambrosio, so that from now on the French police would have a completely free hand [*völlig freie Hand*] in this operation." When the ambassador remarked that an order of this nature was liable to encounter opposition among the Italian generals, who might possibly regard it as detractive to their standing, the Duce replied by raising his hand as he was saying, according to the ambassador's interpretation, "Only one man gives orders here, and that is I." "Hence I have the clear impression," von Mackensen concludes, "that the Duce has decided in favor of a solution that matches option no. 1 in our proposal."[81]

What had inspired the Duce to reach this astounding decision that was illogical even in the eyes of its German sponsors? Seemingly only one factor. The man had not fully understood the matter, took no interest in what was under discussion, and had not given a thought to the results of the decision he had taken. At a time when the Italian Empire was collapsing before his eyes, when hundreds of thousands of young Italians were disappearing in the wilds of Russia or were being taken prisoner in the deserts of Africa, with the enemy pressing on the very gates of the homeland, in this fateful hour when his whole personal, political, and ideological world was facing ruin, what interest did this tired old man have in the mess of conflicting authority between Italian generals whom he had never liked and the Vichy authorities that he despised over the fate of a few thousand Jews who at best had always been repulsive to him? He therefore tried to get rid of the troublesome ambassador, who was taking up his time in the late hours of the evening in reading a long document and—what is more—in German, a language he had difficulty in understanding, and chose the first option that occurred to him, or the only one that was not flattering to the men of the Italian Army or to German security forces. He certainly could not have imagined that he would thereby arouse into counteraction the heads of the Foreign Ministry, the Italian Army staff and the police command, as well as a factor from outside the Italian establishment, the Segreteria di Stato of the Vatican.

An accurate reconstruction of the meetings and events that took place 18 and 19 March for the purpose of changing the Duce's decision, is not possible in all its details. It is based largely on literary sources—the books of memoirs by Senise[82] and Bastianini, Lospinoso's evidence, and the diaries of Ortona and Pietromarchi—whose authors did not always record the dates of events to which they were witnesses, and if they did so, they were not always careful to be precise (or did not remember the exact date). Anyway, the overall picture is definitely clear.

In the early morning of 18 March, Bastianini heard about Mussolini's decision from Ambassador von Mackensen, who called him over by telephone—according to him on the Duce's advice—and asked him to inform the Italian Army Command in France of the decision that had been taken. As might have been expected this approach, which deviated from all the rules of diplomatic etiquette and protocol, met with an unsympathetic reaction on the part of the deputy minister, who replied immediately that he was not in the habit of receiving instructions from his superiors through a third party. On the matter itself, Bastianini added, he did not believe the Italians could agree to "the transfer of people" who had asked for asylum in territories occupied by them into the hands of other authorities.

Shortly afterward, at 11:30, Bastianini went in to see Mussolini for the regular daily consultation between the minister and his deputy. Bastianini immediately raised the subject and in emotional words persuaded Mussolini to retract his decision. Delivery of the Jews in the Italian zone of southern France into the hands of the Germans, he said, was equivalent to a death sentence for 20,000 souls—men, women and children—who had not been accused of any crime. Their surrender would heavily damage Italian prestige in France and in other countries occupied by Italy. If the German authorities believed that all these Jews, including the infants among them, were spies, they would have to provide prima facie evidences of their accusations, and the accused would be legally brought to trial before Italian courts. Similarly, it was in no way acceptable that the subject be handed over to the Vichy authorities; the matter of the Jewish refugees being after all of a political nature, which had to remain within the authority of the occupation authorities. To Mussolini's question, how he could change his mind after he had given his agreement to the German ambassador, Bastianini suggested that a decision in principle be taken, under which the Jewish refugees really would be transferred "to the interior," but only to one of the departments in the Italian zone of occupation and that the whole operation would be carried out by the Italian police and under its exclusive supervision.[83]

Perhaps a short time earlier Bastianini had heard from the German ambassador of this option that from the outset had been preferred by both Himmler and von Ribbentrop, and he reached the conclusion that this option was also preferable for the Italians. Perhaps he had raised his suggestion under the influence of the reports he had received from Nice from Consul Calisse and Police Inspector Barranco, details of whose recommendations were clearly seen reflected in his words. In either case, Mussolini accepted the advice of his deputy—according to Bastianini "with evident relief"—and asked him to inform the German ambassador of the change that had taken place. On the spot, Mussolini called Chief of the General Staff General Ambrosio[84] and Chief of Police Carmine Senise in to see him and in Bastianini's presence gave them the necessary instructions for putting the decision into operation. Ambrosio was ordered to inform the Fourth Army Command that "the Italian military authorities would no longer deal with the Jewish question, but the Italian police would from now on be competent for all that concerned the Jews residing in our zone."[85] With Senise it was agreed that a police officer of the rank of inspector general would be sent to France, to be responsible for the implementation of the plan and for the "Jewish topic" in general there.[86]

In the evening of that day so crammed with activity on this subject, Ortona, with his characteristic restraint and brevity, wrote in his diary: "Today was discussed with the Duce the question of the Jews in French territory occupied by our forces. The German view was not accepted. Without a doubt this will be a subject to be extensively discussed with the Germans. Information was received that a meeting would be held in a week between the Duce and the Führer."[87]

"The German view was not accepted," Ortona concluded, meaning that the terrible danger hanging over the heads of over 25,000 people was averted at that point.

While the Italian organs of government occupied themselves on this subject, a discrete approach was made by an actor who until then had not been known to have intervened concerning the Jews in the Italian Occupation Zone in southern France, the Segreteria di Stato of the Vatican. It appears that the Vatican had very efficient sources of information in the Italian capital, for already on 18 March information had arrived there on the decision taken the previous evening in the course of the tête-à-tête conversation in the Duce's room between Mussolini and the German ambassador. (The source of the leak is not of course known, but again it could only have come from the German Embassy in Rome.) That same day, Monsignor Montini, the deputy secretary at the Segreteria di Stato, instructed the Vatican nuncio in Italy, Monsignor Borgongini Duca, to approach Ortona "that same evening" in order to arrange a meeting the following day between himself, the nuncio, and Deputy Minister Bastianini, "to ask him to intervene in the question of the Jews in France."[88] The meeting did in fact take place on 19 March as requested, except that at that hour there was no longer any need for lobbying by the nuncio, as Bastianini could already inform his visitor that the problem had been solved, at least for the foreseeable future. The nuncio could therefore merely express "his great satisfaction" and report to his superiors concerning the reassuring words he had heard from the deputy minister.

Both Bastianini and Pietromarchi, who were devout Catholics, described with some emotion the words of blessing and esteem that the nuncio pronounced on hearing the reassuring information. According to Pietromarchi, although he had not been present on the occasion, the monsignor had said: "In that case I would like to announce that the Holy Father blesses the Italian government";[89] whereas, according to Bastianini, the monsignor "asked me to inform Mussolini that the Holy Father blesses him, for saving the lives of some thousands of human beings in this way." Bastianini, who as mentioned was very close and devoted to Mussolini, found it necessary to add in his memoirs, that he hurried to report these words to Mussolini and that the Duce was pleased with this and even raised a smile on his lips "after such an extended period in which only sadness had marked his face."[90]

Apparently, this was quite an unusual result of dealing with "the Jewish question," as a result of which a veteran atheist like Mussolini had won—without any merit on his part—the apostolic blessing! (And, who knows, perhaps he had smiled merely at the thought.) Anyway, on this occasion, as previously in the case of the Jews holding Italian citizenship in France, Holland, and Belgium,[91] the man again had displayed neither courage nor decisiveness. Nor did he display concern whatsoever "for the lives of some thousands of human beings," as the nuncio had said; rather the contrary. By the light of the mentioned facts, Mussolini was blessed thanks to others. But at least he proved once again that he was repelled by bloodshed[92] and was not prepared to impose on anyone under his command, diplomats or generals, the execution of actions that went completely against their conscience (and in their estimation also against the interests of their country).

As soon as they received the new orders from the Duce, at noon on 19 March, both General Ambrosio and Chief Police Senise began taking practical steps for their implementation. At the General Staff the task was given to General Castellano, the assistant to the chief of staff.[93] On his orders Colonel Cesare Cremese, head of the Office for General Affairs (Capo Ufficio Affari Generali), went the following day to the Fourth Army Command at Menton. He carried with him a short message from the foreign minister (i.e., Mussolini) to General Vercellino, as well as written and verbal explanations from the chief of the General Staff. The message from the foreign minister read: "On receipt of this note the problem of the Jews resident in the territories occupied by the Italian army in France will be handed over to the Italian civilian police. Until the Italian police start fulfilling their duties no changes are to be made in existing conditions."[94]

In a short letter to General Vercellino, Ambrosio explains that it was intended that the Italian police, not the army, deal with the concentration of Jews in special places of settlement. Verbally it was explained to the Fourth Army Command, as explicitly expressed by Colonel Cremese on 23 March, that the object of the Duce's orders concerning the Jews was twofold:

1. To save the Jews, whatever their nationality—Italian, French, or foreign—resident in the French territory occupied by our forces.
2. The military authority would no longer be concerned with the Jewish problem, which is transferred into the hands of the Italian police; nevertheless, the mentioned authority would assist that Police in the performance of their duty.[95]

It is not known who at the General Staff was responsible for inserting the key word *save* that indicates so clearly the intention of those who gave the order and that until then had not been used in the diplomatic or military documents of the period. These documents always speak in a generalized and discrete manner of the need for the "internment" of the Jews in the Italian zone and prevention of their "removal" to the German zone. This intention had also found no expression in the discussions taking place in those days with Mussolini, insofar as they are reflected in the literary or documentary sources that have been preserved. From the report delivered by Colonel Cremese we now learn that toward the end of March it had become understood at the General Staff that the purpose of the new instructions issued in connection with the Jews in southern France was simply to "save" their lives, whatever their citizenship might be. At that stage the General Staff also did not refrain from verbally announcing this clearly, even if for obvious reasons they still preferred to refrain from putting it down in writing. As for Colonel Cremese's report, this too was originally delivered only verbally, and it was later quoted in the internal memorandum of the General Staff, apparently without a thought by anyone that this detail must first be deleted.

Concurrently with these extensive activities carried out at the General Staff, preparations required for completing this task were also being made at police headquarters. On 19 March Chief of Police Senise had already submitted to Mussolini the names of four high police officials who, on the strength of their record and professional skills, seemed to him to be the most suitable to be placed in charge of the operation in southern France. Of the four candidates Mussolini selected Inspector General Guido Lospinoso.[96]

That same day, in the late hours of the evening, Senise called Lospinoso and ordered him to report immediately to the Duce, in order to receive from him instructions concerning an unusual mission that had been entrusted to him.[97] A short time later Lospinoso reported at the Palazzo Venezia, and around 11 P.M. he was received for an interview with the Duce. At the outset, Mussolini indicated that he remembered him from other services he had rendered in the past, among them the mission he had performed for him a year earlier in Germany. "This time," he added, "you must leave at once for Nice and deal with the internment in places at least one hundred kilometers from the coast, of many tens of thousands of Jews who have settled on the French Riviera, something that represents a danger from the military aspect." The Duce further added that by the end of the month he wanted to receive a report on the completion of the operation. "You have received my orders," he said, "Carry them out." With that the conversation ended, according to Lospinoso's own evidence. He gave the fascist raised arm salute and left the room. That same night, he called on Senise, reported to him on the details of the interview with Mussolini and a few hours later left for Nice to take up his new position.

After all the loose ends had been tied up with all the bodies involved—the army, the police, the Foreign Ministry, and the "foreign minister" himself—nothing remained but to inform the German ambassador of the decision that had been taken. After all, he was the man who, on a mission from his superior the minister, had raised all this commotion. Deputy Minister Bastianini called him to his office for a conversation, apparently on 20 March[98] and, to his visitor's great surprise, informed him that the Duce had finally decided to accept the second option. On the Ambassador's query as to what had caused the man to change his mind, as during their conversation he had given him to understand that he had in fact chosen the first one, Bastianini replied that his impression was in fact correct but that both General Ambrosio and he himself had afterward explained to the Duce that the French police could in no way be trusted. The latter had on more than one occasion acted in collusion with the Jews, either under the influence of Jewish money or of Jewish women, or because they implement "the measures backed by the Berlin-Rome Axis with mixed feelings." The Duce had therefore ordered that the whole matter be entrusted to the Italian police, on the orders of Inspector General Lospinoso, who would be solely responsible for the arrest and internment of the Jews resident in the region.[99]

Count Pietromarchi, who had expansively recorded the details of the conversation in his diary, obtained the impression that "the old fox understood the Latin language," that is, he understood the intentions of the words and "found the Deputy Minister's argument was quite correct."[100] In the report he sent to Berlin, von Mackensen gives no expression to this view, if in fact that had been his view. On the contrary, he repeatedly stresses that he had asked Bastianini to specify what measures the Italian authorities intended to take in order to ensure speedy and complete performance of the operation, and in order also to prevent actions by the army commanders that would foil the Duce's policy. According to him, he had even inquired, whether it was possible to regard the planned Italian operation concerning the internment of the Jews as a first step toward "their deportation," but to this Bastianini replied in diplomatic language that for the moment this measure was not included in the plans.

We do not know what really was in the man's heart, and there is no point in raising conjectures. Anyway, after all the changes and reversals through which the subject had gone, and after all the efforts they had invested in it, the Germans had no choice but to wait and see how things would develop: whether the Italians' decision would be put into effect soon and with determination, and to what extent it was likely to serve German policy in the matter. After all, Mussolini's choice had been among the proposals they themselves had raised, and it was even the one that in their (short-sighted) estimation was the best for their interests. Now that the Italians had complied with their requests, the Germans could only watch over their ally's action and hope that it would become within a short time a preparatory stage toward the implementation of the one "solution" that was acceptable to them.

# The Italian "Race Police" in Nice

## (MARCH–JULY 1943)

In the evening of 19 March, when Police Inspector General Guido Lospi-noso presented himself to the Duce at the Palazzo Venezia, the latter gave him—according to Lospinoso's testimony—only one order and even that only in very general terms: he had one month in which to transfer all the Jews living in the Italian Occupation Zone in southern France to new places of residence, at least 100 kilometers from the coast. He testified that he was told nothing, either on that occasion or at the meeting immediately afterward with his superior Chief of Police Senise, on the political and humanitarian objectives of the mission entrusted to him. Namely, what would be the fate of these Jews after their removal, and how he was to be-have toward the German security organs in France, who probably expected him—as the police functionary in charge of Jewish affairs in the region— to regard them as partners, even active partners in deciding this fate.

This presentation of the events could create the impression that every-thing done afterward—ensuring the safety of the Jews and preventing their surrender into the hands of the Germans—had been done on Lospinoso's initiative, according to his own judgment, and thanks to his steadfast re-sistance to the pressures applied to him;[1] and that is, in fact, the way the episode is described in most of the research on the subject that has been published so far. This picture, however, does not reflect what really happened.

Lospinoso set out on the morning of 20 March, but not alone as might be deduced from his testimony and not for Nice. He traveled with Colonel Cremese of the General Staff to the township of Menton where the Fourth Army Command was stationed. There, the two consulted the following day with General Trabucchi, the Fourth Army operations officer and his assis-tants, who until then had borne direct responsibility for all that concerned the Jews in the region. Colonel Cremese informed his hosts of the contents of the orders signed by Mussolini, which he carried with him and according to which the subject of the Jews in southern France was from that moment transferred to the sole competence and responsibility of the Italian police. He also transmitted the brief written instructions, which the chief of the General Staff had attached to the Duce's order, and the detailed verbal instructions according to which the purpose of the operation was "to save the Jews, whatever their nationality—Italian, French, or foreign—residing in the French territory occupied by our forces." Discussion took place after which, based on these three messages—that were in effect explicit orders from the two highest military authorities, the Duce and the chief of staff— the officers present expressed their opinions on how to implement them.

Lospinoso started by saying that he intended to transfer the Jews to places of residence in the Haute-Savoie Department. General Trabucchi argued against this, that one-time members of the French Army and young men evading *la relève* (conscription for labor) had recently found hiding places in this department, so that in the near future it may be expected to become the scene of military operations. It would be preferable to choose the Drôme Department, a quiet department at some distance from Fourth Army lines of communications. Trabucchi also announced his readiness to place Lieutenant Colonel Duran,[2] the officer who until then had been in charge of the subject of the Jews at the Fourth Army headquarters, at Inspector General Lospinoso's disposal as well as an officer from the Carabinieri (whose name he did not specify, in all probability Captain Salvi), one who knew well the departments in the Italian zone of occupation and could assist him in finding suitable places for housing the Jews. In summing up the discussion, Lospinoso said that as a first step he intended to conduct a census of the Jews who had "not yet been interned." These would be moved to places in the Drôme Department that would be proposed by the Fourth Army, although it was possible that at a later date he would decide to transfer them to other places of settlement "less remote." (That is, further from the demarcation line with the German Occupation Zone, on which the Drôme Department bordered. In fact, no Jews at all were transferred to the Drôme Department.) Lospinoso also expressed his full appreciation of the officers of the Fourth Army for their readiness to assist him and cooperate with him.[3]

The following morning Lospinoso traveled to Nice, and that same day, 22 March 1943, he started to work.[4] He requisitioned a villa at 42 Boulevard Cimiez, not far from the building that housed the Italian police commanded by Inspector Barranco. There he set up the headquarters of his office, the R. Ispettorato di Polizia Razziale (Royal Inspector's Office of Race Police). At the start of his work he had at his disposal his deputy, Vice Questore Tommaso Luceri and ten plainclothes policemen. When necessary, he could count on the help of units from the Carabinieri regiment attached to the Fourth Army Command.[5] With time, it was decided to enlarge the staff of the "Race Police," but it is not certain that this decision was ever carried out.

From the development of the events, and especially from the contents of the discussions held on 21 March at the Fourth Army headquarters, it may be clearly seen that Lospinoso knew the written and verbal instructions issued by the General Staff concerning the objective of the operation due to be executed in southern France. He knew these orders from the outset, first-hand, and in every detail. In fact, it could not have been otherwise, as he had been charged with heading the operation, and those who had appointed him to the task must have been interested that it would be carried out in the best way possible, according to their original objectives and intentions. The argument raised by Lospinoso, which he repeated over and over in his evidence that supposedly nothing had been explained to him and nothing was said to him on the true objectives of the operation (and, therefore, all he did in the field had been on his own initiative), this argument does not stand up to the examination of logic, and it does not agree with what may be learnt from the documentation of the period. (To the question that might be asked—even though it is not the concern of the subject under discussion here—What were Lospinoso's motives in representing things in this fashion?—the answer is that after the war he apparently had good reason to stress his part in the affair even beyond its real dimensions, as we will see in Chapter 8, n.58).

The decision of the Italian authorities to send a high-ranking police officer to southern France, one who would be responsible for "race policy" in their zone of occupation, was at first interpreted by many residents as a submission to German pressures and naturally gave rise to great anxiety in the hearts of Jews, both refugees and French citizens. There was great fear that the arrival of the officer foreboded a fundamental change in Italian policy toward Jews and that from then on they would be liable to become the victims of the persecution, arrest, and deportation "to the East," that had long been the lot of Jews in the other parts of France. In consequence, as soon as the news got out, Jewish representatives sought ways to make contact with the officer in order to discover what type of person he was and, insofar as this was possible, to find out what instructions he had brought with him and what they could expect of him. The way to approach him was quickly found out by the Jewish banker Angelo Donati, through a monk of the Capuchin Order, Father Marie-Benoît.[6]

Father Pierre Marie-Benoît, a man of noble mind and high moral character, one of the righteous gentiles who was awarded the Distinguished Order of the French Resistance Movement, was born in 1895 in a small town in the department of Maine-et-Loire. Between the two world wars he had lived in Rome, and from the 1930s he had served as professor of theology at the International College of the Capuchin Order of Rome. As a French citizen, he had to leave the country on Italy's entry into the war in June 1940. He returned to France and moved into the Capuchin monastery in Marseilles, where he lived for three years until he was allowed to return to Italy just before the fall of Mussolini. In Marseilles the father first became aware of the sufferings of the foreign Jews, for whom, in his own words, "France had ceased to be a safe place and a land of liberty." For them he organized an extensive and praiseworthy operation of assistance in a number of spheres, ranging from obtaining identity cards and food coupons under false names, concealing persecuted Jews with people he trusted, obtaining means of livelihood for the neediest, to finding ways of crossing the borders into Spain or Switzerland. For these tasks, the father often benefited from assistance of nuns from the Notre-Dame de Sion convent in Marseilles. He himself also maintained contact with French underground organizations, with "various Jewish committees in Marseilles" whose names he does not mention, and with Catholic and Protestant clergymen.[7]

The entry of the German Army into the territory under the Vichy regime in November 1942 raised new and almost insurmountable obstacles for this activity and greatly restricted the chances for Jews to escape across the border. The focus of all aid and rescue operations carried out by both Jews and Christians was then transferred to the Italian Occupation Zone, and Father Marie-Benoît was not slow in getting involved in the operations being conducted there. Every week on Sunday night the father made it his habit to travel from Marseilles to Nice accompanied by "his secretary," the Jew Joseph Bass. In this city he regularly stayed for three days, sometimes even four, and, in cooperation with the two Jewish organizations there, the Dubouchage Committee and the Union Général des Israélites de

France (UGIF, General Israelite Union of France), he engaged in various activities on behalf of the Jewish refugees. This activity brought him into contact with Donati, who at that time was one of the principal active members of the Dubouchage Committee, and this acquaintanceship quickly became true friendship. According to Father Marie-Benoît, it was Donati who voiced his desire that he should meet with Lospinoso and appeal to him as a Christian clergyman to one of his flock. He consented willingly and did this without delay. Father Marie-Benoît describes the conversation between himself and the chief of the Race Police in the following words:

> I visited him. He welcomed me and since I addressed him in Italian the conversation from the outset was conducted on a cordial and informal note. He asked me whether my Superiors knew of my approach to him. I replied that my Superiors in Rome were perfectly aware of my activities and they fully approved. Mister Lospinoso was a straightforward person, not particularly well versed in Jewish questions. He wanted to know for example whether the God of the Jews was the same as the Christian God, and why I as a Catholic occupied myself with them. I had no trouble in enlightening him and justifying my actions and he declared that he only wanted to show his good will toward the Jews.[8]

Lospinoso's promise that he would behave humanely toward the Jews (that is, that he would act to prevent their surrender into the hands of their persecutors) was certainly sincere. This was, after all, the reason he had been sent to Nice, this was the purpose of his mission, and this was probably also in tune with his personal inclinations. However, it is clear that by his remarks concerning the Jews and Judaism he quite simply misled his visitor. The naive Father Marie-Benoît could not imagine, either on that occasion or in the years to come when he gave his evidence, that the "straightforward person" before him, a veteran and experienced police officer, was pretending ignorance in the matter he was sent to deal with, all this to make the implementation of his own task easier. To Father Marie-Benoît's credit it may be said that even some of the German security officials, who in general were by no means naive people, would later also fall into the traps laid for them by Lospinoso. Despite a certain hesitation, they also were inclined to accept his version, that he knew nothing of the Jewish problem and that he should be given some reasonable amount of time in order to study the subject. For some reason, even after the end of the war Lospinoso preferred to refrain from "confessing" to the deception he had practiced on Father Marie-Benoît. In consequence, most of the scholars who dealt with the subject were deceived by his pretense from 1943,[9] which from the start had only been designed to deceive his colleagues from the German security services.

The true picture, however, arises out of Lospinoso's own testimony, and it differs totally from the image he was trying to create. In recalling the tasks he had fulfilled in the course of his career, Lospinoso indicated that before the war he had served for twelve years at the Italian Consulate in Nice, a place where he had gotten to know "all the people and everything." In Nice he had also gotten to know many Jews, especially those of Italian origin, and according to him some of them had become "his personal friends or friends of the family." Amongst these were the banker Angelo Donati (who, although his permanent home was in Paris, was in the habit of going to Nice from time to time for a holiday) and the industrialist and businessman Viterbo.[10] It may therefore be easy to assume that, with such friends and during such a long period of living there, Lospinoso would have had the time to become closely acquainted with Jews and Judaism. And even if he had not become "particularly well versed" in matters of religions, and in the mysteries of the Jewish religion amongst them, he had probably already discovered that both Christians and Jews believed they address their hearts to the same god. He certainly must also have learnt about the Jewish refugees from Central Europe, on whose problems both Donati and Viterbo had been working devotedly since the mid-1930s. Furthermore, there is no doubt that during the years he was attached to the Italian Consulate in Nice Lospinoso's functions were mainly in the intelligence field. After all, he was a senior police official, not a clerk of the consular section of the Foreign Ministry. His particular task in Nice was to gather information on the political tendencies amongst the Italian colony in the city in general, and on the activities of those elements in particular—such as antifascist exiles, left-wingers, liberals, Freemasons, Jews, Zionists—who because of their political inclinations or international connections, real or imaginary, were considered by the fascist police as potential enemies of the regime.[11] In this capacity, Lospinoso knew local conditions inside out, including the Jewish circles, French and foreigner, and it is almost certain that this experience stood in his favor when he was chosen by his superiors, and by Mussolini himself, to serve in the new and sensitive post. In fact, this consideration turned out to be justified during the months he acted as commander of the Race Police in southern France, because his knowledge of local conditions—in addition to his shrewdness and his sophisticated pretense of being a man who knew nothing—helped him considerably in overcoming the many difficulties with which he was faced in fulfilling his task.

According to his own plans and the program made at the Fourth Army headquarters, Lospinoso's first step in his new-old residence should have been to make a census of the Jewish refugees in the region. On taking up his post, however, he was informed by sources at the Armistice Commission in Nice, that the number of Jews in the city and its surroundings at that time had been estimated as approximately 22,000 souls.[12] It appears that Lospinoso relied on the accuracy of this evaluation, estimated the number of Jews in the remaining departments of the Italian occupied zone at a few thousand and arrived at a total estimate of at least 30,000 souls.[13] In view of this, he decided to postpone the census taking to a later date and thereby was able to act without delay on the most urgent and important subject of all that faced him at that time, choosing the departments and the places of settlement to which the Jewish refugees were to be taken.

As mentioned, Lospinoso had been inclined from the outset to choose mountain locations in the Haute-Savoie Department. These were places with well-developed tourist facilities, including large numbers of hotels that had stood deserted since the outbreak of war, where thousands of people could be accommodated without a great deal of preparatory work. Moreover, the Haute-Savoie Department was far removed from the communication lines of the Axis armies and bordered on the German-occupied zone only along a very small mountainous sector. The officers of the Fourth Army, however, advised him to choose the Drôme Department, and Lospinoso expressed readiness to consider their proposal. But as soon as he arrived in Nice on assuming his post he decided to reexamine his original plan.[14] He therefore went to the Haute-Savoie Department and, through a staff officer of the Fourth Army who accompanied him, he requisitioned a number of hotels in the townships of Saint Gervais and Megève, at the foot of Mont Blanc near the Italian border; these two townships later housed the largest concentrations of Jewish refugees. In the course of time and by the same method, additional centers were also set up in the townships of Saint Martin-de-Vésubie, Venanson, Castellane, Barcellonnette, and Vence, all towns far from the German-occupied zone and close to the Italian border.

On his arrival in Nice, Lospinoso conferred with the three prominent members of the Dubouchage Committee—Angelo Donati, Michel Topiol, and Ignace Fink—in order to plan with them the method of executing the whole operation.[15] The first and most serious problem of all these confronting them was to find the means of transportation for the thousands of people who had to be moved to their new places of residence. Although there was a railway line between Nice and the departments of Savoie and Haute-Savoie, it was practically impossible to make use of it, because it went through the city of Marseilles, which was controlled by the Germans, and no one was prepared to put their readiness to cooperate to the test. It was therefore necessary to use trucks; but at that time there were already so few vehicles available to the Italian Army—some already unusable because of the serious shortage of spare parts—and such a tiny supply of fuel that it was hard to imagine that the Fourth Army could allocate their own resources for the operation. Lospinoso therefore suggested that the Jews should provide the required trucks and fuel by their own means (that is, by turning to the black market), for they had to understand that their fate depended on this. His proposal was in fact accepted, and the Jews undertook to provide transportation (which they in fact did). It was also agreed by Lospinoso and those same Jews, either at that meeting or at one of the subsequent ones that took place from time to time, that the Dubouchage Committee would be responsible for preparing the lists of Jews who were to be transferred to the interior of the country. These were divided into groups of about 100 persons who left the city every few days, accompanied by a few soldiers from the Carabinieri or policemen from the Race Police.

At the beginning of the operation, some hesitation could be discerned among the candidates for transfer, and even a degree of anxiety of what awaited them. But when details became known of the conditions placed at their disposal—there were direct communications between the Jews who remained in Nice and those already transferred—many people asked to be included in the groups that were leaving. The members of the Dubouchage Committee therefore decided to give first priority to the neediest refugees. These would find quite comfortable accommodation in their new places of residence, either in hotels or in private homes requisitioned for them. Various Jewish organizations, in particular the "Joint" and "Ose," provided them with reasonable means of livelihood (according to the standards of those days),[16] as well as modest but quite effective services in the fields of education, culture, and health care.[17] A committee was established among the refugees in each locality, which was responsible for the internal living arrangements and maintained close contact both with the Italian authorities and the Dubouchage Committee. The Dubouchage Committee on their part took care of collecting the assistance funds from the Jewish organizations and transferred them to their destination.[18] At St. Gervais the support for refugees at the end of May amounted to 1,000 francs per person per month; of this, 800 francs were required to pay for the accommodation and two meals a day, with some 200 francs left for other expenses.

This is how a young Polish-born refugee girl, who arrived to St. Martin-de-Vésubie from Nice in September 1943, described the conditions of the Jews living there:

> St. Martin, a small settlement in the mountains some sixty kilometers from Nice, was before the war a holiday and convalescence resort. There the Italian occupation authorities have set up one of the places of *résidence forcée* [enforced residence] for the Jewish refugees, who reached France during the war from the countries occupied by the Germans. Here the refugees were accommodated in houses and villas. Twice daily they have to report to the police offices; they are also not allowed to go outside the village or to leave it. At this time some three hundred families of Jewish refugees are living here. They are well organized: a Jewish committee elected by the refugees is responsible to the Italian authorities. They have schools for their children and there is also a Zionist youth movement. Despite the state of emergency life goes on normally, and thanks to the young Zionists cultural life is very well developed. Of course the refugees do not have the right to take jobs. The rich ones live off the money they have succeeded in saving from the Germans and the poor receive assistance from the committee, which is supported by the "Joint." The refugees are allowed to receive visits from their friends and families. On the whole their situation is not bad. If things could only remain like this until the end of the war![19]

In spite of these favorable conditions, many of the Jews were conscious of the uncertainty of their situation and of the terrible dangers now lurking all around, awaiting them in a future that was still completely shrouded in fog. This is how one of the refugees at St. Gervais expressed these fears:

> We are like survivors on the high sea. The sea is still stormy. An iceberg has been signaled in the vicinity. The collision could occur at any moment, but it could also be avoided. Uncertainty and anxiety. If the collision does take place, it is liable to be terrible. There will be an "every man for himself!" or an organized rescue. That will depend on many factors. But the captain and the crew have only one objective: to maintain and ensure until the last moment a little order and happiness to the passengers.[20]

During the four months in which the operation continued, from the time Inspector General Lospinoso was appointed until the fall of the fascist regime (that is, from the end of March 1943 until the end of July of that year) some 4,500 Jewish refugees were transferred by the Italian police, with the help of the Dubouchage Committee and the financial assistance of Jewish organizations, from the coastal region to inland localities.[21] Really, in the course of his hasty night-time meeting with the Duce, Inspector General Lospinoso had actually been ordered to carry out the whole operation by the end of the month—that is, to transfer more than 25,000 Jews within ten days. But perhaps even Mussolini himself, when he gave this order in his usual imperial determination and theatrical tone, did not expect that the operation would be completed within such a short time. In any case there is no information that he ever took any interest in finding out how his order was executed. Lospinoso on his part regarded the number of refugees transferred as quite a success, under the given logistics difficulties, and he refrained from addressing superfluous questions to his superiors. As for the Jews, they certainly had good reasons for satisfaction, both from the operation itself and from the manner in which it had been put into effect.

It seems that there is no more genuine and natural expression for the feelings of the Jews toward the people who had performed the operation than two certificates of recognition that were composed in their honor. One, in Hebrew and Italian, was delivered to Consul Calisse on 10 May 1943, on the occasion of the termination of his duties in Nice. The other, completely in Hebrew, was delivered to Angelo Donati in July 1943. This is the translation of the original Hebrew text of the certificate presented to Calisse:

> An eternal keepsake and sign of gratitude / to the majestic glory and excellency the great minister Master / ALBERTO CALISSE / may his name shine like the sun, the Chief Consul for the Italian Kingdom in Nice / We express our deep thanks, in our names and the name of all our miserable and wandering brethren, who found refuge in his shadow to rescue them from the oppressor during the time of his officiating in Nice, and on the occasion of his leaving here wish to extend to him our blessing, the parting blessing in the words of David King of Israel: / May the Lord preserve you from all evil, guard your soul, the Lord will watch over your coming and going from now and forever.[22]

And this was the text of the certificate presented to Donati:

> We will welcome him with thanks, with singing we will applaud him / to the honored very exalted prince / Mordechai son of Rabbi Yehoshua Aaron Donati, may his light shine, / as a memento of thanks, may he accept from

us the feelings of our hearts, who as one man we praise his honor with
sounds of gladness and thanks, for if we had not had him when a man rose
against us, that one would have swallowed us live. May he be blessed for not
leaving us a prey to their fangs. May the Lord repay his actions and may
his reward be complete. And may he have long life to see the Lord's salvation and the salvation of Israel his people on the mountains of Zion and
Jerusalem. / St. Martin, in the month of Sivan 5703.[23]

Nevertheless, there still remained one side whose willingness to support
the operation was doubtful: the Germans. It is true that the solution the
Italians had provided, namely, the decision to entrust the problem entirely
to the police's hands, conformed at least in principle with one of the alternatives the Germans themselves had offered. But soon, even the Germans
had to recognize the fact—that should have been clear from the beginning—that the decision to remove the competence of the problem from the
Italian Army and to entrust the Italian police with this responsibility did
not change and could not change anything. The origin of the problem did
not lie in the different disposition of these two branches to fulfill the orders
given from above about the fate of the Jews in the Italian-occupied territories. The problem was that the solution the Italians intended regarding
the fate of these people was fundamentally different from the "solution"
their ally was striving to implement. The differences of opinion between
the two totalitarian states on this subject were not over the means but on
substance. And, as is well known, to find a compromise for substantial
differences of opinion is an almost impossible task.

On 18 March 1943, in summing up a day crowded with meetings and
decisions concerning the fate of the Jews in the Italian-occupied zone in
southern France, the Italian diplomat Ortona wrote in his diary that "without a doubt this is a topic that will still be extensively discussed with the
Germans."[24]

However, even Ortona probably did not imagine that only nine days
later the commander-in-chief of the Gestapo himself, Heinrich Müller,
would arrive in Rome on a personal mission from the SS-Reichsführer in
order to deal with the subject (which in the eyes of the German leadership
was, it seems, so essential to the war effort that the Axis powers would be
unable to be victorious without its receiving an immediate and fitting solution). On 27 March, Müller was received for an interview with Mussolini,
in the presence of Ambassador von Mackensen and Chief of Police Senise,
and there he raised before him the "Jewish problem in the newly occupied

French territories." As was his custom, Mussolini replied briefly and in a resolute manner: on his personal orders the Italian police had recently sent Inspector General Lospinoso to France, together with Deputy Inspector Luceri and some additional assistants, for the purpose of solving the problem "in the German sense" (*im deutschen Sinne*). This they were to carry out in close collaboration with the German police and, where necessary, also with the French police.[25] The subject was therefore closed and there was no need to discuss it again.

Müller received these words with satisfaction, and on his return to Berlin he hurried to inform SS-Standartenführer Knochen of the results of his mission, in a message dated 2 April. He also ordered him to contact Inspector General Lospinoso without delay to verify the nature of the orders he had been given.[26] (Müller was certainly far from doubting the veracity of the Duce's words, but from his experience he had learnt that not infrequently, on the road from Palazzo Venezia to the commands in the field, changes occurred in the spirit of the orders that had been issued. He therefore wished to ascertain that the order had really reached its destination without misleading alterations or interpretations). On receiving this message, the personnel of the Security Police in Paris went into action without delay to carry out the task they had been given. Seemingly, nothing could have been easier, since Lospinoso's unit was part of the Italian "establishment" in France, with which they were in constant, almost daily (even if not always particularly friendly), contact. In practice it would be found that this task was not at all simple and that the route to Lospinoso's headquarters was strewn with numerous traps and obstacles that even the renowned German security services, well-known for their efficiency and success, found difficult to overcome.

On 3 April 1943, Knochen contacted Lieutenant Francesco Malfatti, a young officer who a short time before had been placed in charge of military intelligence matters at the Italian Embassy in Paris, and asked him to clarify at the Fourth Army headquarters the details of Inspector General Lospinoso's planned journey in France.[27] Next morning, however, Knochen was already surprised to hear that no news had been received either at the embassy or at Fourth Army headquarters concerning that journey.[28]

Officers of the Fourth Army, if at that point they really had been asked —what is not at all certain—pretended they knew nothing—and that for good and well-understood reasons. As for the embassy in Paris, it is almost certain that until that day they really had received no official information whatsoever on Lospinoso's mission. To prove this, on 5 April, immediately after the conversation between Knochen and Malfatti, Ambassador Buti sent an urgent dispatch to the Foreign Ministry and reported, with a certain note of anxiety, that "This SS command has received information according to which Inspectors Lospinoso and Luceri, at present at Menton, had been ordered soon to go to Paris in order to make contact with these German authorities, concerning questions connected with the treatment of the Jews in the territories under Italian occupation." The same SS command had asked for additional clarification on the subject, and Buti asked for instructions on how he was to act.[29]

The "information" supposedly received at the SS command in Paris, according to which Lospinoso and Luceri were due to visit there soon in order to coordinate their action with their German colleagues, was of course the product of Knochen's imagination, or perhaps the interpretation he had given to Müller's cable of 2 April, reflecting what he would have liked it to read. On the other hand, it is not clear what was the origin of the belief that Lospinoso was still in Menton, a supposition that at that time was to circulate in different forms among the Italians and the Germans. In any case, only two days later, on 7 April, the deputy foreign minister's *chef de cabinet*, Francesco Babuscio-Rizzo, replied that the Ministry of the Interior (which was responsible for the police) totally denied that Inspectors Lospinoso and Luceri had been given the indicated instructions. Accordingly, Babuscio-Rizzo added, the Italian Embassy in Paris would also in future act in accordance with the instructions sent to them in the dispatch of previous 13 March (which as indicated had stated that it had been decided to reject the German offer of assistance in solving the Jewish problem and that in future the handling of the subject would also remain in the hands of the Italian Army and police authorities).[30]

That same 7 April Müller replied to Knochen and instructed him to inquire once more, before he would approach a second time the chief of the Italian police, whether Lospinoso really had not yet reached France; for, according to what Mussolini himself had told him only a few days earlier (that is, in the course of Müller's visit to Rome), Lospinoso should have been in France some time now.[31] It appears that this time Knochen did not need to make too many inquiries, for that same day, and independently of Müller's approach, SS-Sturmbannführer Herbert Martin Hagen, assistant for political affairs to General Oberg, met Lieutenent Malfatti, who informed him that after staying three days in Menton Lospinoso had returned to Rome. When he returned from there he would come to Paris and meet General Oberg. Meanwhile, Lospinoso would like to direct the following three questions to the Germans (according to Hagen's report):

1. Whether the steps to be taken against the Jews in the newly occupied region [namely, all the former Unoccupied Zone] were to be performed by the French?
2. Have we [that is, the Germans] demanded mass internment among the Jews of French nationality in the newly occupied region?
3. Have mass arrests already been carried out among French nationals by the German authorities?

Hagen adds that he had delivered the questions to Knochen, asking for his reply.[32] It is not clear who among the Italians had formulated these strange and pointless questions, which clearly would contribute anything to furthering Lospinoso's mission. We also do not know who decided to spread the news that Lospinoso had returned from Menton to Rome, whereas he had arrived in Nice a fortnight before. Perhaps the intention of this source had been merely to mislead the Germans and gain time to allow Lospinoso to take up his duties with a minimum of outside interference. Either way, Malfatti repeated the same questions a day later in a conversation with Röthke. According to the latter's report to Knochen on this meeting, Malfatti also remarked on that occasion that in his opinion these were not Lospinoso's questions but rather they had originated at the Fourth Army headquarters.[33]

As may have been expected, these strange developments were not to Knochen's liking, and in his usual way he did nothing to conceal this. On 7 April 1943 he contacted the Reich Security Main Office and demanded once again "that all means be used in order that the Italian military and civil authorities be induced to change their attitude concerning the Jewish question."[34] A day later, in a cable to Müller, he reported in detail the contents of the talks conducted with Malfatti during the preceding two days. He indicates that he had not replied to the questions presented by Malfatti in Lospinoso's name "out of considerations of principle," as he believed no negotiations on such an important subject should be conducted with a junior officer, a mere lieutenant, and what is more, while awaiting the arrival of Inspector General Lospinoso, who was due to negotiate with him directly and in person. As for Inspector Lospinoso, Knochen added in conclusion, it would be proper that he himself should ask the questions to which he wanted a reply and not use the services of a third party.[35] Müller again replied the next day, informing Knochen that he had contacted the chief of the Italian police through the attaché for police matters at the German Embassy in Rome and had asked him to instruct Lospinoso to come to Berlin to meet him or to contact Knochen directly in Paris, and that as soon as possible.[36]

This time Senise's reply is not known, nor whether he even had the time to reply, as on 14 April, he was suddenly dismissed from his post on personal instructions from the Duce, who expressed his wish "to have in such a position 'a true Fascist'."[37] Appointed in place of Senise was Renzo Chierici, a high-ranking officer in the Ministry of the Interior, who in the past has held senior posts within the Fascist party and on its behalf. In the long run, this appointment was not to Chierici's benefit: he only had three months and ten days to serve as chief of police. At the end of July 1943, after the fall of the fascist regime, he was dismissed from his post by the new government, who distrusted him because of his fascist past, and five months later he met his death under circumstances that have so far not been clarified while a prisoner in the hands of the fascists of the Salò Republic who accused him of not doing enough to defeat the deposition of their leader.[38] In any case, during the three months in which he served as chief of police, there is no evidence that Chierici tried in any way to worsen the policy pursued by his predecessor in relation to the Jews in the Italian-occupied countries, including the Jewish refugees in southern France.

Toward the end of April and the beginning of May 1943, hope weakened among the German security officials for a meeting with their colleague from the Italian Race Police, Inspector General Lospinoso, even though they had not completely abandoned their demand that he should come to Paris and negotiate with them on coordination of policy between the two allies toward the Jews in France (that is, according to their views, on implementing their policy also in the Italian-occupied zone).

Von Thadden, the man responsible for Jewish affairs in the Inland 2 Department of the Foreign Ministry, reported on 6 May to the Reich Security Main Office concerning a meeting of the German ambassador in Rome with Deputy Foreign Minister Bastianini. Following instructions he had received from Berlin, von Mackensen once again raised the question of the Jews in the Italian-occupied zone in southern France and reminded the deputy minister that, on the basis of information in his hands, the Italian Police in Nice had not yet received appropriate instructions on the subject. According to von Mackensen's report, Bastianini was extremely surprised to hear these remarks, and on the spot, in the ambassador's presence, called on the telephone Chief of Police Chierici in order to make clear what steps had already been taken "in our sense" (*um sich im Sinne unserer*, that is, in accordance to the Germans' views). To this Chierici replied that he had only begun to deal with the subject in those days and that on Lospinoso's request he had given orders to increase the number of policemen at his disposal for the implementation of his task. Following the deputy foreign minister's request, Chierici also promised that he would bring the urgency of the matter to Lospinoso's attention. Bastianini for his part found it necessary to remark that he had not been aware of these delays, and that these had probably occurred because of the replacement of the chief of police. However, when von Mackensen proposed that Inspector General Lospinoso meet an authorized representative of the German Security Police in France, Bastianini was not prepared to commit himself on this point and replied that he would consider the ambassador's proposal and when the time came would inform him on his own stand on the matter. "Should this proposal be acceptable to the Italians," von Thadden indicated in conclusion, "the [German] Embassy [in Rome] would propose that the meeting should take place on 18 May at the office of the commander of the Security Police and SD in Paris, 72 Avenue Foch."[39] Thus, this time, the Germans were careful to plan the meeting in all its details, except that only four days later they realized that all this planning had been premature.

On 10 May, von Thadden again reported to Eichmann that a reply had been received from the Italian Foreign Ministry concerning the proposed meeting with Lospinoso. The Italians claimed that the inspector general had only recently begun to put the planned measures into operation, after having received the supplementary manpower he had requested. It would therefore be best if for the moment he did not leave the place where the operation with which he had been charged was being put into effect and did not go to Paris or anywhere else. Furthermore, "Lospinoso had received his orders directly from the Duce. Hence discussions with other authorities concerning these measures, being direct orders of the Duce, could easily create a delicate situation. The Reich authorities were therefore asked to leave to the Italians the care of deciding further whether a conversation with the German representative was in fact necessary."

If this version, as it was reported by von Thadden, did in fact faithfully reflect the words used—and there is no reason to doubt this—the Italian reply this time was totally unequivocal and even assertive to an unusual degree. The German diplomat could therefore only make clear to Eichmann that, if it should nevertheless be decided at the Reich Security Main Office that the meeting was necessary, he, SS-Obersturmbannführer Adolf Eichmann, would have to visit Lospinoso in southern France, but, even then, not in order to discuss with him the orders he had received but "merely to obtain information" about them. In that case, the Foreign Ministry would be prepared to contact the German Embassy in Rome, so they should ask their Italian colleagues where Lospinoso was if until then the security police had not discovered the police official's whereabouts.[40]

It seems that for the first time the German Foreign Ministry officials had come to the conclusion that it would be impossible at that stage to obtain a clear-cut decision concerning the fate of the Jews in southern France according to their views. They also reached the conclusion that they would do well to reduce, if only to some extent, the pressure they were applying to their allies on this topic in general and on the task entrusted to Lospinoso in particular. After all, not one of them dared to demand, or even contemplate a demand, that negotiations, or even discussion, be conducted over instructions issued "directly by the Duce." Even though the Germans had so far not in any way abandoned their well-known demands, at that point they were left no choice but to wait and see what would develop: what Lospinoso would do with the instructions he had received and what good for their plans would come out of his activities in the foreseeable future.

The strange fact should be mentioned that some two months after the arrival of Lospinoso in Nice, and after he had started his operations as commander of the Race Police for the whole region, not only had the Reich security services in Germany and France not succeeded in bringing about a meeting between him and their own people, but they seemingly had also failed to discover whether he had even arrived in Nice or what was his address. That in any case is the picture that clearly emerges from the official German documentation. In fact, on 24 May 1943, Knochen still reported to Müller that Inspector General Lospinoso had so far given no sign of life and that nothing whatsoever had become known to the Security Police in France "of his possible presence in the Italian Occupation Zone."[41]

This situation of total lack of information changed a few days later, when Knochen finally uncovered the desired information on his Italian colleague, and even then, only after "intelligence work" was carried out not by his own people but by the French Police aux Questions Juives (Police for Jewish Affairs). On 12 May, Röthke contacted the commanders of the Gestapo units and the Security Police in Dijon, Lyon, and Marseilles: he informed them that from then on "the Jewish Problem" in the Italian Occupation Zone would be handled by the Italian police and not by the Italian Army, and he asked them to report to him without delay on the steps being taken by the Italian police in their department toward a solution of the problem.[42]

The first to reply was the commander of the Gestapo in Lyon, SS-Obersturmführer Klaus Barbie, who on 15 May briefly reported that information had been received from the representative of the Commissariat Général aux Questions Juives in Lyon, according to which the Italians had transferred 400 Jews, mostly foreigners, to the township of Megève.[43] Two weeks later, on 26 May, came the reply from SS-Obersturmführer August Moritz, the Gestapo commander in Marseilles. He reported that the Italians had set up a "Commissariat for Jewish problems in Nice, at the Villa Surany on [Boulevard] Cimiez, headed by the Italian General Lo Spinoso." He was assisted by two officers, Lieutenant Colonel Bodo and Captain Salvi, and "his most important partner in the work was supposed to be the half-Jew Donati." (Röthke rightly commented in his own handwriting in the document margin that Donati was "one hundred percent a Jew"). The Italians' intention was to evacuate within three months all the Jews from the coastal region, from a strip of land 50 kilometers wide. Those evacuated were being transferred to the interior in small groups, by trucks. Up to 25 May a total of some 2,400 Jews had been moved from Nice and its surroundings, mostly belonging to the poorest section, to the townships of St. Martin-de-Vésubie, Vence, Megève, and St. Gervais.[44]

Even though Moritz had refrained from mentioning it in his report, this detailed and fairly accurate description relied on a document written in those days, entitled "General Reflections on the Jewish Problem in Southern France." At the time this document, undated and without mention of its author, came to Röthke's attention, who wrote on the paper in his own handwriting: "To Standartenführer Dr. Knochen for information. This review comes from the ex-director of the anti-Jewish police. Röthke, 1 June."[45] Hence, the review had been written by Jacques Schweblin—who had been the commander of the infamous Police aux Questions Juives that had been disbanded a few weeks earlier, or by one of his assistants on his orders.[46] The review was written after 25 May, because it mentions the number of Jews moved inland "up to May 25," and had already reached the Gestapo staff in Marseilles on the 26th. On that day Moritz took the second part of the document, the part dealing with the situation of the Jews in the Italian Occupation Zone, simply copied it word for word, with a few deletions and the addition of a few inaccuracies of his own, and sent it to his commanding officer over his own signature, as though this had been the result of his own work in the field. Schweblin's review describing activities in the Italian zone thus reached the desks of Röthke and Knochen from two different sources almost at one and the same time, at the end of May or beginning of June. It was to the best of our knowledge the first detailed and authoritative source received by the Security Police command in Paris concerning Lospinoso's location and the nature of his activities.

In their internal correspondence the German officials did not raise the question of how it could happen that this information, on a matter so important in their eyes, only came into their hands some two months after Lospinoso's arrival in Nice. Apparently, this question is still unsolved and will probably remain an astonishing puzzle. They were, however, conscious of another question that considerably occupied them during those days, quite rightly from their point of view. In the margin of the report he had received from Moritz, Röthke comments among other things: "It is really strange that the Italian Embassy claims they know nothing of Lospinoso's activities." Really a surprising fact in his eyes, whose meaning today is not difficult to understand.

While the discussions between the two Axis powers were going on at an accelerated pace and at the highest political levels between Rome and Berlin, diplomatic contacts between Rome and Vichy had not ceased. These for the most part were conducted in a minor key, through local military channels, either through representatives of the Armistice Commission or by means of the military mission in Vichy headed by General Avarna di Gualtieri.[47]

On 2 March 1943, as mentioned, General Avarna had delivered an official note in the name of the Italian General Staff to Admiral Platon, one of Laval's close assistants. The note dealt with the measures taken a short time before by the Vichy authorities, and it stated categorically that the handling of the Jews' affairs in the Italian-occupied zone was, as in the past, "the exclusive competence of the Italian occupation authorities." Consequently, the Vichy government was asked to order the immediate release of the Jews arrested and to refrain in the future from taking any measures whatsoever against the Jews resident in that region, whether they were of Italian, French, or foreign citizenship.[48] It seems that on that occasion Platon had raised "certain objections" to the Italian demands.[49] Although these "objections" are not known in detail, from the Italians' reaction it is quite clear that they would have emptied the document of its principal contents. The Chief of the General Staff General Ambrosio reported on this development in a dispatch dated 8 March to the Fourth Army Command, in which he also gave the clearest orders on the subject: "In order to prevent the further execution of possible measures of arrests or deportation against Jewish elements, while the step taken by General Avarna is being implemented, this command is ordered to take action in the meantime with the department Prefects involved and the local French authorities, in order that these same measures should not (I repeat should not) be put into operation."[50]

In the field these orders were translated into direct and simple military language: a few days later one of the Italian commanders delivered a written order to the representative of the Commissariat Général aux Questions Juives in the Savoie and Haute-Savoie departments that read: "Any transfer of Jews from the Italian-occupied zone to this under German occupation is strictly forbidden. This prohibition remains fully valid even if the [local] *Préfecture* has received orders to the contrary from other authorities. Any planned measure that the local French authorities intend to take against the Jews in the region must be submitted for our approval. Giovanelli."[51]

A few days later, on 17 March, General Avarna informed Admiral Platon of the reply from the Italian General Staff to his objections. The General Staff insisted on their demands of 2 March, but it was ready to agree that Jews suspected of civil offenses be arrested by the French police and be tried before the civil courts, on condition that in each case the Italian authorities be provided with detailed information on the circumstances of the arrest and the evidence on which it was intended to base the accusation. In addition, in no case will these courts have the authority to pass sentences of deportation from the country.[52] The notification of 29 March from General Avarna to Vice-Admiral Bourrague, in charge of the Armistice Services of the Vichy government, in principle dealt with the same subject. This time Avarna based the demands of the Italian General Staff on "urgent and overbearing motives of security needs" facing the Fourth Army Command.[53] In his note of 27 April 1943 to General Bridoux, the Vichy Secretary of State for Defense Avarna once more repeated these demands and this reasoning.[54]

Despite these constantly repeated approaches, the French persisted in their refusal to accede to the Italian demands, at least for appearances' sake. The French argued that Italian demands concerning the transfer of the handling of the "Jewish subject" to the sole authority of the Italian occupation army were not only unacceptable for political reasons but also from a legal aspect, because it explicitly contravened clause 43 of the Hague Convention, under which the occupying power is not permitted to impose its own laws in the region occupied by its forces.[55] It is most probable that against this argument the Italians raised the "motives of security" mentioned, because under the same convention this was the sole legitimate reason for which it was permissible to base the transfer of civil juridical powers to the occupying authorities. (As for the attempt by French jurists to make use of a clause in the Hague Convention to allow in practice the deportation of a complete civilian population for the purpose of their destruction, this attempt raises profound speculations concerning the intellectual integrity of those jurists, even within the framework of the very distorted norms of those days).

Toward the end of March and the beginning of April, this shallow and pointless debate was dying down. Neither side had moved from their initially declared positions. In fact, the French did refrain from then on from carrying out operations against the Jews in the Italian-occupied zone. Perhaps they had despaired of the possibility of doing so, in the face of the opposition of the Italian Army units who controlled the area. Perhaps also the Vichy authorities did not altogether regret the existence of a precedent wherein a power allied to Nazi Germany was protecting the Jews within its borders; in those days, they themselves were beginning to take the same route, even if only toward those who were its own citizens and with clear hesitation and a lack of perseverance.

On 22 March 1943, Jean Leguay, Bousquet's representative in the Occupied Zone, informed Röthke that the matter of the deportation of the French Jews had been discussed at Vichy, up to the level of both the prime minister and the head of state. According to Leguay, "Marshal Pétain had expressed his lack of understanding toward the deportation of Jews with French nationality, while there were still so many other Jews in France."

Bousquet had therefore given instructions to the French police not to participate in "the evacuation of the French Jews." Leguay found it necessary to apologize to his German colleague for the "disagreeable task" he had to fulfill: he had been ordered to bring to the latter's attention his own government's decision, according to which the fate of the French Jews must remain the sole responsibility of the French government, which would deal alone with the solution of the problem.[56]

As might have been expected, these decisions aroused considerable indignation among the German security officials. Then and there, Röthke expressed his "astonishment" at the decision of the Vichy government to handle the solution of the problem of the French Jews itself, and this "at a time when the Führer's wishes concerning the final solution of the Jewish problem was well enough known."[57] General Oberg asked to inform Leguay of his deep concern at the fact that "the French government had still not abandoned its 'emotional' point of view, despite the latest declaration of the Führer concerning the Jewish problem."[58] Knochen summed up his own opinion in a short and somewhat laconic cable to the Reich Security Main Office for the attention of Eichmann, in which he announced that in the immediate future no transports of Jews would be leaving France, because "the measures against the Jews of French nationality could not be implemented for political reasons, due to the stand taken by the Marshal." (In fact the deportations were renewed only three months later.) The French government, Knochen added, "is constantly taking into account the attitude of the Italians, who declare that they were not treating the Jews like the Germans [were doing], and that on the contrary they were opposing the continued implementation of the anti-Jewish measures."[59]

Indeed, these words were more a matter of settling accounts with the Italians—and Knochen did have good reasons for a reckoning with them —than a very accurate quotation from the declarations by the French. There is also no doubt that additional important factors may be found to have influenced the stand taken by the Vichy government, such as the change taking place at that time in public opinion inside France on the whole policy of collaboration with the Germans and the feelings of protest spreading among the clergy against the continued deportation of Jews. Thus, it seems that the Italian example made it very difficult for the French authorities to agree to the execution of widespread manhunts against their Jewish citizens. Indirectly, this example was therefore, to some degree, a factor restraining the implementation of the German policy in France against the Jews, even outside the Italian Occupation Zone (particularly concerning Jews of French citizenship).

As for Inspector General Guido Lospinoso, if we were to judge by his own evidence, all this time he was sitting quietly in Nice, supervising the operation of transferring Jews "to the interior" in accordance with the orders he had received "directly from the Duce," without knowing anything whatsoever of all the commotion that had arisen around him and about him. He did not even imagine that the German security services were looking for him, and he heard nothing of the pressures the latter were exerting at various diplomatic levels in Paris, Berlin, and Rome to find someone who could order him to make contact with them. Only after the war, he related, did he discover from the book by Poliakoff (which came into his hands by chance, a present from his friend Angelo Donati) that SS-Obersturmbannführer Adolf Eichmann and some of his superiors and subordinates had been interested in meeting him to discuss the coordination of operations by the two police forces toward providing a permanent solution to "the Jewish problem" in the region. At that time the subject no longer had any relevance.[60]

This picture, arising in its general lines from Lospinoso's own evidence, is part of the image he was interested in creating for himself at the actual time of the events and also after the end of the war, but it is far from reflecting facts. On the contrary, even in the evidence that Lospinoso gave in 1962 (in reaction to press publications during the Eichmann trial, which were not to his liking), a detail is mentioned that clearly does not harmonize with the general picture he presented and that contributes to a correct understanding of the subject.

Lospinoso related that while he was in Nice, completely immersed in the implementation of his duties, a German officer from the unit of the Security Police in Marseilles dropped in at his office on a "courtesy visit." Lospinoso entertained him for lunch, as is fitting between colleagues, in the course of which a conversation developed between them over many and varied subjects, particularly on Lospinoso's souvenir from his mission in Berlin one year before. Incidentally, the German officer, whose name was not introduced in the evidence, asked what was being done to solve the problem of the Jewish refugees in the region and mentioned that his commanding officer had instructed him to invite Inspector General Lospinoso to visit him in Marseilles to decide on the measures they had to take jointly

for providing a permanent solution to the Jewish problem. As a junior officer, the visitor said, he did not know anything about the nature of these
measures. Before taking leave of his host he also asked that Lospinoso give
advance notice of the date of his visit so as to allow them "to repay the
courtesy" properly.

Lospinoso did take advantage of the invitation, and a few days later
went to Marseilles, but for some reason he refrained from giving advance
notice of his coming. For that reason, he was unable to meet the commander of the German unit, who was away, and only met his deputy. The
latter apparently did not know exactly what he had to tell his visitor and
what he had best conceal from him. He leafed through the papers, talking
in general terms of the plan for transferring Jews from the Italian-occupied
zone to Drancy and from there to Germany. Finally, and after a lot of stut-
tering, he spoke of the necessity for Lospinoso to go to Vichy as soon as
possible to meet "the Gestapo general, Eichmann, . . . who often comes
there from Berlin" and to agree with him and the French police officials on
the practical steps of the operation due to be put into action in connection
with the Jews. Lospinoso testified to having been completely surprised to
hear these things, but he controlled himself; he refrained from making any
meaningful reply and merely said that for the moment his hands were full
working to complete the task he had been given and that he would only be
able to find time for such a journey at some later date.[61]

It is however clear that some details in this testimony were incorporated
in it under the influence of information that Lospinoso received after the
war or that reached the headlines during the submission of the evidence
(as, for example, the insertion of Eichmann's name as one of the security
officials operating in France, and what is more in Vichy). Nevertheless,
there is no cause to doubt the information itself concerning the holding
of such meetings with German security officials in Nice and Marseilles.
Hence, even according to his evidence itself, Lospinoso knew of the Germans' efforts to meet him and, what is more, on the subjects they were
interested in discussing with him. As for the date of the meeting, which
is not included in the testimony, it cannot be determined with any certainty. It seems reasonable that it took place after Röthke and Knochen
had learned the details contained in the Schweblin document, perhaps only
a short time after receipt of that document (which, as mentioned, reached
Paris at the end of May).

Almost a month had passed since Moritz's report to Röthke was written, when around 20 June 1943, on his own initiative, Lospinoso visited Vichy. As was his habit, he refrained from announcing his coming to the officials of the German Security Police, except that this time he also refrained from meeting them and limited himself to a working conversation with René Bousquet, the French secretary general for the police. The Germans learned of the visit in Vichy by their Italian colleague from Bousquet, who hurried to report the contents of the conversation to Hagen, quoting sentences that were or were not said, which were likely really to jar on German ears ("The Germans are very harsh in the execution of the measures against the Jews . . . while Italy wanted to implement a humane solution to the Jewish problem"). As for the purpose of the meeting itself—during those days Lospinoso had planned the transfer of an additional 6,000 Jews "to the interior" and was interested in reaching agreement with Bousquet on the practical aspects of the operation, particularly on the question of selecting the places to which the Jews would be taken, whether to Megève or to other townships. Despite his general readiness to cooperate with the French police, Lospinoso found it necessary to emphasize that as in the past the entire operation would in the future also have to be performed by the Italian police alone. Bousquet for his part reminded Lospinoso that General Avarna had already been made aware of the strong opposition of the French authorities to the continued transfer of Jews to Megève, indicating that in his opinion it was preferable that the operation should be carried out by the French police.[62]

There was thus no common ground in the positions of the two sides over which it would be possible to conduct practical negotiations; hence, the meeting apparently ended without reaching any kind of understanding. It is difficult to draw clear conclusions based on second- and third-party reports, for Lospinoso himself makes no mention of this meeting in his evidence. What is clear is that the very holding of the meeting without the knowledge of the Germans, without their participation, and to some degree even behind their backs, was due to arouse a great deal of anger on their part. In his usual aggressive and angry tone Knochen hurried to report on what had occurred to his superiors in Berlin, Kaltenbrunner and Müller. He suggested that they "express to the Italian Government our surprise at seeing Inspector-General Lospinoso evading a visit to the Höheren SS und Polizeiführer und BdS [Supreme Chief of the SS and Commandant of the Police], yet at the same time establishing contact with the chief of the French police about the application of the anti-Jewish measures." Especially as, "in such a complex subject," it would be appropriate that the two Axis powers "should confront the French government with an absolutely identical conception." In Knochen's words, such behavior was "an extremely serious matter, and endanger[ed] the implementation of the new measures against the Jews."[63] That is, it was liable to thwart the planned operation of deporting tens of thousands of French Jews, whose French citizenship was about to be withdrawn under a special law, whose details were under discussion at that time between the Vichy government and the German authorities. (In fact it was never approved because of the opposition of the Vichy government.)[64]

After the officials of the German Security Police despaired of negotiating with Lospinoso directly, they approached Inspector Barranco, the officer in charge of the Italian police in southern France and asked to meet him in order to agree on the policy of the two police forces "concerning the Jewish problem in the Italian occupied zone." As may have been expected, however, Barranco refused to discuss the matter, claiming that the matter had recently been entrusted to Inspector General Lospinoso, the head of the Race Police in the region, and he advised his callers to contact him directly. SS-Sturmbannführer Mühler, one-time commander of the German Security Police in Marseilles, did in fact call Lospinoso's office on the phone and arranged to meet him—apparently in Nice, at Barranco's office—at the beginning of July.[65]

If the Germans thought that this time they would be able to discuss the matter directly with the man responsible for its conduct on behalf of the Italian government, they were again disappointed. Lospinoso did not arrive for the planned meeting and instead sent his deputy, Deputy Inspector Luceri. As soon as the meeting began, the latter announced that he was not authorized to make any decision concerning the Jews and that for that purpose it would be necessary to wait for the meeting with Lospinoso that would "take place shortly." On the activities of the Race Police, Luceri reported that until that day 22,000 Jews had registered,[66] and their transfer to townships in the interior of the country had begun not long before. The Jews "classified as dangerous, that is, those actively engaged in politics," were being transferred to a concentration camp under construction near the township of Sospello. In the conclusions to his report on the meeting, Mühler remarked that this way of conducting negotiations on the part of the Italians created the impression that they were doing everything they could to prevent the measures that they were taking against the Jews from being adopted to suit the method acceptable to the German side. He also pointed out that enemy propaganda in France frequently presented these differences in treating the Jewish problem as proof "of the supposed beginning, or even of an already very far advanced stage of disagreement within the Axis camp."[67]

These words, written on 10 July 1943, sound somewhat anachronistic today after all the proofs the Italians had presented, especially starting in November 1942, of their unwillingness to accept the German example in all that concerned the "solution" of the Jewish problem. What is more, these words were written the day the Allied armies were beginning their landings on the shores of Sicily, when it should have been clear to any clever observer that Italy was already involved in a dispute with "its partner in the Axis camp" over matters much more fateful for itself and the Axis as a whole than the policy toward the Jews. (In fact, Italy was already standing with one foot outside the Axis camp, and outside any belligerent camp, as it was no longer able to continue to participate in military operations.)

A few days later, on 21 July, one day after the first bombing raid on Rome by Allied aircraft, it was the turn of the delegate of the Commissariat Général aux Questions Juives to meet with Lospinoso.[68] It seems that this meeting—which apparently took place in Nice—was even more ineffective than the preceding ones. Lospinoso started by apologizing that he had never heard of the existence of such a Commissariat. For that reason, he argued, when he had gone to Vichy to discuss matters concerning the Jews in the Italian-occupied zone, he conferred with Bousquet and not with a representative of the Commissariat. The French official, whose name is not recorded, regarded "the intrusion" of his colleague and rival, the secretary general for the police, in a matter under the authority of his own office, with evident displeasure. He therefore tried to explain to his visitor the functions and fields of operation of the Commissariat, and he did that with such prolixity that Lospinoso apparently lost his patience. He interrupted the flow of words from the French official and asked him, with pretended ignorance that bordered on discourtesy, "whether the Minister [i.e., Darquier de Pellepoix] and he himself were Jews," since they were so immersed in Jewish affairs. One might seemingly have thought that this time the Italian police official had crossed the border of credibility; but the French representative, who apparently was a small bureaucrat, was not particular about this. On the contrary, he considered Lospinoso as a man "animated by a certain spirit of understanding," and he reacted forgivingly to his question as expressing his crass ignorance of anything that concerned the Jewish problem. At the end of the conversation the two agreed that Lospinoso would be given a list of foreign Jews, whom the French were interested in conscripting for forced labor.[69] It was also agreed that they would have an additional meeting in Vichy on 27 July 1943.

This meeting of course did not take place, and this time Lospinoso had indisputably good reasons for canceling the journey. In Rome, on the night of 24–25 July, the great majority of the members of the Fascist Grand Council voted for the deposition of Mussolini, thus terminating the twenty-year regime of the Fascist party in their country. This event was destined to have a decisive influence on military and diplomatic events inside Italy itself and in the countries it occupied, including on the fate of tens of thousands of Jews—refugees or residents—of these countries. In southern France then began the last chapter of Inspector General Lospinoso's mission, a chapter that would finally end forty-five days later, on 8 September 1943, with the sudden announcement of Italy's surrender to the Allies.

# The Forty-five Days of the Badoglio Government

## (25 JULY—8 SEPTEMBER 1943)

The first half of 1943 witnessed a great deterioration in the military and strategic situation of the Italians on the Mediterranean front. On 23 January the forces of the British Eighth Army entered the city of Tripoli, and at the beginning of February they crossed the border of Libya into Tunisia. For three months, fighting continued to rage on the soil of Tunisia between the Axis forces trying to defend their last position on African soil and the Allied forces applying pressure from Libya and Algeria. Finally, on 13 May, over 200,000 German and Italian troops surrendered, when they were trapped in the narrow region between the cities of Tunis and Bizerta. Some seven months earlier, the Italian Army was still standing victorious in the heart of Egypt and at the gates of the Nile Valley, overlooking the Suez Canal and the sea lanes to the Far East. Now, their last hold on African soil was lost, and the fascist leadership's glorious dream of resurrecting the mighty Roman Empire from its ruins had escaped from their grasp and vanished.[1] Moreover, following the loss of the military bases in North Africa and in view of the heavy losses suffered by the Italians in the course of the fighting—equipment abandoned, planes shot down, ships sunk—the control of the sea and air lanes in the whole Mediterranean Basin had slipped out of their hands; without it, there was no chance they would be able to protect their own country from invasion by the enemy armies. When, at dawn of 10 July, Allied troops in fact landed on Sicilian soil to set up a rapidly expanding bridgehead, most of the people came to the conclusion that the war was lost and that Italy would not be able to stay in it for long.

At the same time, and closely linked to these events, inside Italy itself the internal front was beginning to disintegrate. A mood of opposition and indignation was beginning to spread among the working and middle-class masses, who had to bear the major brunt of the everyday burden of the war effort in the front lines and the rear. It was directed against a leadership that, with astounding irresponsibility, had led them into a military adventure that had already become a grinding defeat and was threatening to bring down a terrible disaster onto the whole nation. Besides, from the outset many had doubted the logic and benefits of a war alongside such an unloved ally as Nazi Germany. These moods rose to the surface unexpectedly during the months of March and April 1943, when the first massive strikes of workers in heavy industry broke out in northern Italy, and within a short time involved over 100,000 people. It was clear that beyond the economic demands raised by the strikers (which in themselves had good grounds) were political aims connected with the very existence of the regime.[2] During the first months of the year, there were in fact growing underground activities among the left-wing parties and within circles of intellectuals and politicians from the parties disbanded after the rise of fascism, all trying to find a way to put an end to fascist rule, and with it, to Italy's unfortunate part in the war. Things went so far that of three divisions that the General Staff was forced to transfer from southern France to Italy in order to protect the soil of the homeland against the foreign invader approaching from the south, one division was stationed in the north of the country "in order to protect public order."[3]

The Jews in the Italian Zone in southern France regarded these events with mixed feelings. On the one hand, they were naturally pleased to see the defeats suffered by the Axis armies and the great change that had occurred in the course of the war (especially as in that period the fortunes of war were also reversed on the eastern front, with the great victories of the Red Army). On the other hand, they did not overlook the fact that the reversals suffered by the Italian Army would be liable sooner or later to force Italy to surrender to the Allies and withdraw from the war. There was therefore great fear that the day was coming when the Italians would withdraw from the region and that with them would disappear the one and only remaining force standing between them and their surrender into the hands of the German Army and security forces.

The astounding news of Mussolini's deposition by his own people, the members of the Fascist Grand Council, on the night of 24–25 July was received with outbursts of joy among the Jews and most of the French population in the Italian-occupied zone. They were also joined by many of the Italian troops stationed in the region, who followed either their own political views or because they deluded themselves that their part in the war would thereby come to an end. A young Jewish girl, who had found shelter in Nice with her family, reported that 26 July "was a night of delirium." People celebrated the event "as though it was the 14th of July. . . . The cafes remained open all night. It seemed the nightmare was nearing its end and the war would be over any moment—as though Europe was not still under German rule, as though there were no deportees and prisoners in Austria, Poland, and in Germany."[4]

The following day, however, after they sobered up from their intoxication of joy and their sweet delusions, the Jews inevitably began to think what might be expected to happen in their places and what they could expect for themselves in particular. The scene they now realized was in fact most ominous, especially as only a few days after news had come of the establishment of the new Italian government under Marshal Badoglio, the German Supreme Command-West began to move large army forces into the Italian zone, with the pretense that they were transit units making their way south to the battleground in Sicily. (In fact, part of these forces were moved to Italy, mostly to the central part of the country, where at the beginning of September they participated in taking over the country).

The *Armistice Commission Bulletin* from the end of July 1943 described the new problems arising in the department under Italian occupation in these words:

> The situation seems to be characterized by the repercussions of the presence of German army units in the region and the change of the regime in Italy. The first fact reinforces among the local population the belief that the Italian military units are preparing to leave the French territories occupied by them. There is even a rumor that the date of departure had been fixed for 5 August. The most tangible effects of these rumors are observed among the Jews resident in the region, foreign as well as French: these are crowding to the army Commands and Italian Consular Offices, asking that they be allowed to move to Italy together with our units.[5]

Two weeks later the same source again reported on the mood that had spread among the Jews, and this time the feeling was one of genuine despair: "Following persistent rumors current in the region, the fear has arisen that in the very near future control of the Nice department would pass from the Italian authorities to the Germans. This fear causes panic particularly among the Jews, both foreign and Italian: the latter were doing everything they could to obtain the documents needed for their repatriation, while the foreigners among them are making every effort to cross the border into Italy illegally." [6]

In fact at that time the refugee committee in St. Martin-de-Vésubie sent a group of young people, members of the Movement of Zionist Youth, to explore two mountain passes in the Alps near the township, in order to get to know the escape trails into Italy that they would use in time of need, if that should ever come. [7]

The Jews' desperate demand—that the Italian authorities not abandon them if it was decided to evacuate the region and would act to bring them to safety inside Italy—greatly concerned the Italian diplomats, both in France and in Rome during the forty-five days that passed between the fall of Mussolini and the surrender of Italy (that is between 25 July and 8 September 1943). First and foremost to participate in the operation on behalf of the Jews were the Italian Consul General in Nice, Augusto Spechel, the head of the Political Department at the Foreign Ministry, Count Luigi Vidau, and to some extent the new-old chief of police, Carmine Senise. (As mentioned, Senise had served in this position until April 1943 when he was dismissed by Mussolini, then reinstated to his post after the establishment of the Badoglio government.)

On 31 July Consul Spechel first addressed a short official letter to the Political Department of the Foreign Ministry and asked that in view of the present circumstances he should be permitted to grant Jews of Italian citizenship the necessary visas for returning to Italy, without waiting as usual for approval by the Ministry of the Interior. [8] At the same time he also sent a long and detailed personal letter to Count Vidau (who, it seems, was a personal friend) and raised the question of all the Jewish refugees in the region, stressing its extreme seriousness. Many Jews of various nationalities had approached him in the few preceding days, following the spreading rumors about the eventuality of the Italian Army's withdrawal, and had asked to be allowed to enter Italy. They also stated that, if these rumors were to prove true, they would "cross the Italian border by any possible means, for they are determined to risk a concentration camp in Italy rather than go once more through the painful events that had brought them there from various and far-off countries." The problem was therefore complex and serious, and "ought to be studied from nowadays on the whole and in its detail, since it is liable to appear suddenly and in all its serious implications." In the consul's estimation some 12,000 to 13,000 Jews were involved in the Alpes-Maritimes Department alone.[9] (But in a report he sent a week later he amended this estimate to at least 20,000.)

The officials at the Foreign Ministry did not think they were empowered to circumvent the authority of their colleagues at the Ministry of the Interior and the police (after all, only five days had passed since the fall of the regime, and this ministry still headed the hierarchy in the country's administration). On 2 August, they therefore contacted these colleagues, explained the problem raised by Consul Spechel, and suggested that the Italian representatives in France be empowered to issue the necessary visas for entry into Italy at their own discretion and without additional confirmation, to all those Jews whose Italian nationality was not in any doubt and against whom there were no complaints or suspicions of any kind.[10] Two days later, Chief of Police Senise did in fact reply that the Ministry of the Interior was prepared to approve the request by the consul general in Nice concerning the "repatriation" of Jews holding Italian citizenship and residing in the Italian-occupied zone, under the conditions specified in the letter from the Foreign Ministry.[11] After a further two days, on 6 August, Vidau so informed the Italian delegations in southern France, the Fourth Army Command, and the Italian Embassy in Paris.[12]

When the problem had been solved for the small group of Italian Jews, whose numbers did not exceed a few hundred, Spechel raised the problem of another small group, that of Jews of Italian origin who had renounced their citizenship and had chosen the French one. Spechel claimed that there were altogether about 100 of these Jews, many of them had moved to France following the "race laws" of 1938. Now they faced the tragic danger of being deported; they therefore asked to be allowed to return to Italy, in view of their exceptional case, even though they held no legal right to it. On 7 August, the Foreign Ministry again asked for the consent of the chief police officer at the Ministry of the Interior[13] who did not hesitate and a day later gave his approval.[14] That same day, August 7, Spechel again reported to Count Vidau on the Jewish refugees in the Alpes-Maritimes Department.[15] He cleared up that their number was at least 20,000, and not 12,000 to 13,000 as he had stated a week earlier. But in a meeting he held with their representatives, he was told that many of them did not want to move to Italy and that many of those who did want would come with financial means, so they would be able to provide for their support without living on public relief in the places where they would settle.

We do not know to what extent Consul Spechel himself believed the accuracy of these declarations. Either way, his message reached Rome at the right moment, as the cable of Spechel was received at the Foreign Ministry on 10 August, just the day before the heads of the ministry met "to examine the problems arising out of the decision by the General Staff to bring back to Italy the occupation forces from the metropolitan territory of France." Participating in the meeting was Augusto Rosso, the newly appointed Secretary-General of the Ministry, who also took the chair, as well as the heads of the principal departments: Amedeo Giannini (Department of Commercial Affairs—AC), Leonardo Vitetti (European and Mediterranean Affairs—AEM), Luca Pietromarchi (Cabinet, Armistice and Peace—GABAP), and Luigi Vidau (General Affairs—AG).

According to the very confidential summary prepared by the officials of the Department for European and Mediterranean Affairs, only two matters were discussed in the course of the meeting: (1) the economic problems liable to arise following the withdrawal (this subject was presented in detail by Giannini); and (2) the "very delicate situation in which many thousands of Jews, around 15,000, mostly foreign citizens . . . were liable to find themselves" (this subject was presented by Vidau). Count Vidau apparently assumed that all those present at the meeting agreed with him that "these Jews should not be abandoned to their fate"; he therefore did not say a great deal in support of this and proposed "to reach an agreement with the Ministry of the Interior, so that their officials would put a blind eye to the illegal entry of these Jews into the kingdom. These would later be considered political refugees and be sorted out in suitable ways through several provinces." Vidau believed that his proposal was likely to be accepted by the Ministry of the Interior. He found support to his belief in the fact that the ministry had already agreed to the return of Jews who had left the country after 1938 and accepted French citizenship, for these had for all purposes become foreign citizens. It seems that no one opposed Vidau's proposal, and it was submitted, together with the recommendations on economic matters, for the perusal and approval of the new foreign minister, Raffaele Guariglia.[16]

It thus seemed that the problem of the Jewish refugees in southern France was about to be solved, perhaps by the easiest and most convenient solution that might be imagined. In fact, under the conditions of those days, even if the silent approval of the Ministry of the Interior had been obtained—something that was very much in doubt—the proposed solution could not have been implemented. At the end of August 1943, Italy could no longer serve as a refuge for the tens of thousands of Jewish refugees, most of them stateless and without means, who were crowded into southern France, not only because of the practical difficulties involved in the secret transfer of these people through the Alpine passes but also and primarily because of the serious economic and social situation in which the country was. At a time when its major cities were being ceaselessly bombed from the air, when masses of their inhabitants had fled from them and sought refuge in the country, internal transport was almost totally paralyzed, and most of the population was suffering shortages of the most essential necessities. Under such conditions it was not possible to absorb tens of thousands of foreign refugees and provide for their needs. The fact that in those days a way had been found to absorb a few hundred Jews who once had Italian nationality, most of them genuinely with means, could not serve as a precedent for the rest. Furthermore, even only for political reasons, it was very doubtful whether the Italians could permit themselves either secretly or openly to bring these Jews into their own territory while evacuating their army from southern France. This operation would in any case come to the knowledge of the German security services, and it was liable to arouse their angry reactions at the highest political levels. After Mussolini's fall, relations between the two Axis partners had already become very strained, and the Italians certainly were not interested in making them any worse and even less in bringing them to a breaking point. This difficulty was clear to everyone, and Vidau himself hinted at it during the meeting held by the heads of the Foreign Ministry's departments.[17]

The logical conclusion from all of these factors was that everyone understood the dreadful danger to the lives of the Jewish refugees in southern France, but that the problem could be solved, if at all, only outside the borders of Italy. It could find a solution in the region that would remain under the control of the Italian Army in France, if there was such a region, in one of the neutral countries, namely, Switzerland, or in one of the countries that had already been liberated by the Allies, such as the North African countries. In fact, on the initiative of the Italian authorities as well as that of Jewish bodies, a number of attempts were made in those days in every one of these directions to provide a solution for the problem of the Jewish refugees in southern France.

On 15 August 1943, a meeting at the highest level was held in the city of Bologna between the commanders of the two Axis armies. In its course, it was decided that the Italian Fourth Army would be withdrawn from

France in the coming weeks, but, even after completing the evacuation (which should have been over by 9 September), an enclave of territory in southeastern France would remain under control of the Italian Army. This enclave was due to include the part of the Alpes-Maritimes Department between the line of the Var and Tinea rivers and the old international border between the two countries. This way, the Italians intended to retain control of a region vital to them for the defense of their country but also— and perhaps this was the most important—one that had always been at the very heart of their territorial demands toward France.[18] This decision, whose implementation would start ten days later, was able to provide a convenient, almost natural solution to the problem of the Jews who had found refuge in the Italian Occupation Zone. The great majority of these Jews was in any case already concentrated in the enclave that was due to remain under Italian control and that included the city of Nice. In this enclave, it was therefore easy to create the conditions for the continued existence of those Jewish communities already there and for the absorption of the quite small number of Jews who were due to move there from the departments the Italians would evacuate. Being an operation of limited extent, which would be carried out entirely within the Italian zone, it could all be completed without creating an excuse for new German protests and without the need to invest a great deal of material resources that in any case were no longer available.

On 28 August 1943, only three days after the evacuation of the Italian forces from southern France had begun, a new meeting took place in Rome, at the Ministry of Interior, this time at the highest interministerial level and with one single item on the agenda: the evacuation of the Jews from Provence. Participating in the meeting were Umberto Ricci, minister of the interior; Raffaele Guariglia, foreign minister; Carmine Senise, chief of police; Count Vidau, head of the Political Department of the Foreign Ministry; and a representative of the General Staff, a general whose name was not recorded. In the course of the meeting, the following five brief operational decisions were passed and were given on the spot to an officer who had come specially from the Fourth Army Command, for immediate implementation:

—The Fourth Army Command will make the arrangements for the establishment of one or more concentration camps for the Jews living in French territory that we have to hand over to the Germans.

—This camp must lie in the territory included between the old Italian-French border and our future demarcation line in France (Var-Tinea or Cap d'Antibes).

—The Jews would have to reach the concentration camp under their own means (the Fourth Army would eventually assist them), and would have to provide for their own subsistence at their own expense (assistance would be given in obtaining the supplies and their transportation to the camp).

—Supervision of the camp would be in the hands of the Italian police bodies that would remain in the French occupied territory.

—Crossing the border to Italy would be forbidden. The Foreign Ministry would consider further solution for the Jews, as the present situation changed.[19]

Information on how these decisions began to be implemented is very scarce. It seems that up to 8 September—that is, until the announcement of Italian surrender—only the first steps had been taken for the transfer of Jews to the enclave close to the Italian border and in the preparation of their accommodation. Thousands of Jews nevertheless began to flock to the enclave on their own initiative, either in the belief that the Italians would not give up this piece of land or because of rumors that had spread in the meantime concerning negotiations that Donati had begun to conduct in Rome for the transfer of the Jews to North Africa.[20] Many people thought that, in view of the execution of this rescue plan, it would be best to concentrate in the city of Nice and its surroundings in order to be ready to leave whenever required.

On 3 September Consul Spechel reported in a personal cable to Vidau that the Fourth Army Command had recently received instructions to assist in concentrating the Jews "in the territory that remains under our occupation," east of the Var-Tinea line. He also reported that Police Inspector General Lospinoso had been charged with carrying out the operation and that the necessary vehicles had even been placed at his disposal. It had been agreed with the latter that the Jews living in Nice, who represented the majority of the Jewish colony, would not for the moment be transferred, since there was no room for them in the small townships inside the enclave. However, "should a sudden need arise also to transfer the Jews of Nice," it would be possible to settle them in the township of Menton, which the Fourth Army Command had recently left after being transferred to the township of Sospello and where in consequence many hotels had been vacated. Spechel further added that Inspector Barranco, who was in charge of the police in the region, had submitted a detailed memorandum a few days earlier to Chief of Police Senise concerning the Jews. Barranco had recommended the transfer to Italy of those Jews who were citizens of countries not at war with the Axis, concentrating all other Jews in Menton. According to Spechel, Barranco was due to go to Rome that same day and intended to discuss his plan with Senise. Spechel himself regarded "the ever-growing and pressing intervention of the German troops and the Gestapo . . . in a zone occupied by our troops" with great concern and gave unreserved support to Barranco's recommendations. Inspector General Lospinoso and Captain of Carabinieri Salvi had also expressed their opinions in favor of these recommendations, and they too believed that the township of Menton was the most suitable place to settle the largest group of Jews (that is, those who were stateless or citizens of countries at war with the Axis).[21]

That same day, 3 September, Lieutenant Malfatti, who meanwhile had been appointed consul in Chambéry, also reported to the Foreign Ministry that the Jews at his place of service were contacting him in great anxiety, asking that they be given asylum in Italy. Malfatti had apparently not been informed of the changing versions of the decisions that had been taken, as he proposed allowing some of the Jews to enter Italy and others to cross the border into Switzerland.[22] Two days later, Vidau replied to Malfatti that these Jews would have to leave their homes and move to the area that was to remain under Italian control and that he would have to coordinate the operation with the consulate general in Nice.[23]

On 6 September Augusto Rosso, the secretary general of the Foreign Ministry, again informed the General Staff that the decisions of 28 August 1943 were to be implemented without delay and that the conscription of Jews for work in the framework of the Todt Organization (a German organization for large-scale construction works), as demanded by the Germans, was not to be tolerated.[24] At the same time Rosso informed the Italian Embassy in Paris that the local Italian Consulate was authorized to repatriate even those Jews who it may be assumed were able to prove they were Italian citizens. Those who claimed they were entitled to this citizenship may be transferred to the region that was to remain under control of the Italian Army until their rights were finally established.[25] We do not know when the cable from Rosso of 6 August reached the General Staff; but we do know that its contents were brought to the attention of the operations branch of the army on 8 September at 2:00 P.M. Exactly four and a half hours later General Eisenhower broadcast his dramatic announcement concerning the armistice agreement signed five days earlier by himself and a representative of the Italian government, with the agreement of the governments of Great Britain, the United States, and the Soviet Union. A short time after, Marshal Badoglio broadcast an announcement in which he instructed all units of the Italian Army to cease hostilities against the Anglo-American forces and to react to any attacks that might be made on them "from any direction."

This event in itself had not been unexpected, but its timing took unawares even the Italian government and brought all the planned operations to an end. The Italian Army disintegrated and gave up its arms; the decision to set up an enclave under Italian occupation on French soil never materialized, and the plan to provide a solution to the problem of Jewish refugees within its frame hence came to nothing. The terrible trap into which these Jews had entered now closed on them, and no one was able to provide any help whatsoever.

During the forty-five days of the Badoglio government, some leading Jewish figures also raised proposals to provide a solution for the increasingly worsening situation of the Jewish refugees in southern France, in one of the neutral countries or one of the countries already liberated. First, practical steps were taken to put some of these plans into operation.

The boldest and best-known of all these plans was that of the Jewish banker Angelo Donati, who suggested that tens of thousands Jews be moved from the Italian Occupation Zone to North Africa. During the few weeks that remained at his disposal, he even engaged in feverish activity to obtain the consent of the international bodies involved, and the instruments necessary for the implementation of such an extensive and complex operation. In fact Donati's initiative found expression in two different schemes that he proposed in two different times—before the fascist regime's fall and after it—and that were tailored to the special political conditions of each one of the two periods. Standing behind these two initiatives was once again Father Marie-Benoît, who was the key figure in many of the moves made.[26]

Donati apparently raised his first plan in the spring of 1943, after the surrender of the last of the Axis troops in Tunisia, when it had become increasingly clear that Italy would not remain in the war for long and would probably be unable to retain control over its zone of occupation in southern France. Donati then traveled several times to Rome, conferred with officials in the Foreign Ministry, principally with Count Vidau, presented before them the serious dangers awaiting the Jews in the case of a withdrawal by the Italian Army, and tried to obtain the consent of the Italian authorities for the transfer of these Jews into Italy. According to him, he found a sympathetic ear with his hosts, and he also heard that Deputy Minister Bastianini did not oppose the idea. However, he was also told that his plan was liable to meet strong opposition at the Ministry of the Interior, whose hands at that time were full with the evacuation of masses of inhabitants from the bombed cities, and it would probably not be anxious to undertake the additional work involved in caring for tens of thousands of foreign refugees.[27] Furthermore, the ministry had not until then been known to be particularly lenient to Jews. In a totalitarian country like the Italy of those days, it would not occur to anyone that it might be possible to overcome the opposition of this all-powerful ministry, which since 1926 had been headed by Mussolini himself, except by intervening at the highest level.

Donati did in fact think of such an intervention in June 1943, when he heard that Father Marie-Benoît had received permission to return to Rome after three years of "exile" in Marseilles to resume his senior position at the Capuchin Monastery in that city. Before the father left for Rome, Donati asked him to intervene with Pope Pius XII, in order to get him to support the idea of transferring Jewish refugees to Italy and to obtain his apostolic intervention to the Italian government or to its head on behalf of his plan.[28] In his customary manner Father Marie-Benoît undertook the mission without hesitation; but when he arrived in Rome he discovered that he would not find it easy to carry it out, because, he was told, "the Holy Father no longer received anyone for a private audience."[29]

After a number of attempts, Father Marie-Benoît was finally allowed to see the pope on 16 July 1943, but even then only to accompany his superior, Father Donato Wynant a Welle, and without having his name recorded in the visitors' book.[30] He handed Pius XII a long and detailed memorandum on the situation of the Jews in France, to which he had added four appendixes (the first two were lists of those deported from France whose relatives wanted to obtain news, the third contained "information about the camps in Upper Silesia," and the fourth described the conditions reigning in the camps in France and the merciless way in which deportations were carried out). In the last paragraph of the memorandum he dealt with the problem of the "foreign Jews" in the Italian Occupation Zone (whose numbers he estimated at 8,000 to 10,000) and the serious dangers threatening them in case the Italian Army was evacuated. He concluded this section somewhat hesitantly with a question—whether the Holy See could bring up before the Italian government the question of transferring these Jews to Italy. It is possible that Father Marie-Benoît was also given the opportunity to explain the subject with some more detail, but this is not in the evidence. In any case, two days later Monsignor Tardini, in charge of the *Congregazione per gli Affari Ecclesiastici Straordinari* (Assembly for Special Ecclesiastic Affairs) in the Secretariat of State of the Vatican, that is, the Vatican's foreign minister, wrote a brief note in the margin of Father Marie-Benoît's memorandum saying: "It will be possible to say a good word to Italy."[31] It is not known whether the apostolic nuncio in Rome did in fact have the opportunity to put in such "a good word" with the Italian policymakers. Anyway, a few days later the fascist regime collapsed, and the Jews were once again facing new and changing political realities and dangers.

As for Angelo Donati, even before this event, he apparently felt that the time was ripe for far-reaching changes, and on the eve of Mussolini's dismissal, somewhere around 20 July, he arrived once more in Rome in order to try and advance his plans for the evacuation of the Jews from southern France. The fall of the fascist regime and the establishment of a new government—which, although it was composed of gray technocrats, was on the whole in favor of peace and democracy—aroused his hopes that from now on it would be easier for him to achieve his purposes. He also understood that under the new conditions Italy would no longer be able to serve as a country of asylum for masses of refugees (and perhaps also would no longer be safe from the long arm of the German security forces and army). Donati therefore conceived a new plan—or another version of the first plan—under which the Jewish refugees would not be absorbed inside Italy but would only pass through this country and be at once sent on to North Africa to one of the countries of the French Maghreb that had already been liberated.

For the implementation of this plan Donati needed the agreement and the support of three bodies: the Italians, who more or less controlled the exit routes from France, the Allies, who controlled the Mediterranean sea lanes and the countries of North Africa, and the international Jewish organizations, who would have to finance the operation. Donati tried to enlist all these, with rare talent and in a mad race against time.

As usual, Donati conducted the negotiations with the Italians at the Foreign Ministry with Count Vidau (although at least once he met Mario

Badoglio, who in those days was acting as his father's *chef de cabinet*). This time, Donati's position was better than in the past, for he came not only as a petitioner but also as someone who appeared to have something to offer. After a short negotiation the Italians did in fact give their consent to the transit of tens of thousands of Jews (this time there was already talk of 30,000 people) from southern France to North Africa, through one of the ports in their country. They even agreed to place four passenger ships at the disposal of the operation, some of the biggest and most modern that at that time were still available to them,[32] at a cost of $5,500 a day for each one of the ships (not including fuel that the Allies were to supply or other current expenses such as food, marine insurance, and the like that the Jews were to cover). In return, Donati undertook to transmit a message to "the Anglo-Saxon Jewish organizations" and through them to their governments, saying that the new Italian government favored a liberal policy and that it was ready to assist as best it could to save the Jews from German persecution.[33]

The truth is that neither side arrived at this agreement with entirely clean hands. The Italians did not reveal to Donati their fear that the open transportation of tens of thousands of Jews through the Alpine passes to Italy was liable to meet with German opposition and that there were great doubts whether it could be put into operation. Donati on his part well knew that his message to the Jewish organizations, and through them to the governments of Great Britain and the United States—even if it reached its destination, which was not altogether certain—would only be of dubious importance. At all events, the two sides reached in a quite short time a positive and detailed agreement that could be regarded as a considerable achievement for Donati, especially as the Italian agreement was a prior condition to opening negotiations with the other parties.

As a matter of fact, while the talks with the Italians were still under way, Donati had already begun to seek ways for making contact with authorized representatives of the Allies, without whose involvement in the operation nothing could be done. It was well known that in the Italy of those days these representatives were to be found in only one place, in Vatican City, the seat of the British minister to the Holy See, Sir Francis Godolphin Osborn, and the chargé d'affaires of the United States, Harold H. Tittmann. It was, however, also generally known that the approach to them was absolutely forbidden to anyone who was not part of the establishment of the Holy See and was apparently only possible under conditions of absolute secrecy, out of sight of the Italian police, and only by agreement with the Vatican authorities (so that in practice this approach was almost impossible). Donati therefore asked again Father Marie-Benoît for help, and again Father Marie-Benoît consented. He contacted Mgr. Hérissé, one of his acquaintances who was serving in the Church of St. Peter and lived not far from the residences of the two diplomats. Thanks to the latter's assistance, Father Marie-Benoît succeeded several times in secretly introducing Donati into Vatican City, where he met members of the British and American missions, apparently also Osborn and Tittmann themselves, presented his plan before them, and asked that they should act to obtain the support of their governments. At least some of these meetings were also attended by Father Marie-Benoît.[34]

At the same time, Father Marie-Benoît prepared a memorandum—according to him on Donati's detailed instructions—specifying the subjects on which the Holy See would be asked to assist the operation in progress; and on one of the last days of July, he submitted the document to the Congregazione for Special Ecclesiastic Affairs of the Secretariat of State. In the opening remarks, Father Marie-Benoît recalled that on 16 July, when he was received in audience by the pope, he had indicated the terrible catastrophe that was liable to befall the Jewish refugees in southern France, should the Germans take over the Italian zone of occupation. Now, he wrote, "the threat that we had feared is about to materialize." In view of this, an Italian Jew, Angelo Donati, "A brave man with a good heart," had come to an agreement with the Italian government, under which these Jews (some 30,000 in number) would be transferred to North Africa, together with the Jews who had already found refuge in Italy—altogether some 50,000 souls. The British government had already given the plan its consent in principle and would shortly discuss it with the U.S. government. His request was twofold, and in his customary way he formulated it in the form of a question: could the Holy See instruct his representatives in London and Washington to express their support of the plan to the governments there? Would the Secretariat of State agree to receive Mr. Donati for an interview "so he could explain and deal with the matter more directly and more specifically?"[35]

The reply of the Secretariat of State has not been preserved in the Vatican documents published so far, nor is there any other information indicating active intervention in the matter by the Holy See. There is nevertheless no doubt that the Vatican authorities knew of the activities of Donati within the walls of their city and hence that they gave them their tacit approval. It is also inconceivable that Father Marie-Benoît would have been willing to act contrary to the position taken by his superiors or even without their knowledge, and it is almost certain that he himself had found ways to keep them constantly informed of what was happening.[36] As for the real reactions of the two diplomats, the Briton and the American, beyond the optimistic rumors that Donati and Father Marie-Benoît had spread, either innocently or for well-understood tactical reasons, it seems that their replies contained nothing but just a noncommittal promise that the matter would be brought to the knowledge of their governments, and this was in fact done.[37] Donati himself, in his short memorandum of 30 August to his friends of the Dubouchage Committee wrote explicitly: "At this stage we are awaiting replies to the dispatches sent by the diplomatic representatives mentioned above."[38] That is, until that date the two diplomatic delegations had not given any binding answers.

Despite this uncertainty, Donati returned to Nice during the month of August in order to give his colleagues full and precise information on what had been done and to plan with them the steps that would be necessary for implementation of the plan. Toward the end of August he returned once more to Rome, and from there, with the help of one of Father Marie-Benoît's acquaintances who happened to be going to Portugal, at the beginning of September he sent a detailed report of what was being done to the representative of the "Joint" in Lisbon.[39] In this dispatch, Donati repeated the motives for his initiative—the Jews of southern France living under the threat of destruction that, although dormant at the moment, could erupt at any moment—and pressed the people of the "Joint" to intercede urgently with the British and American governments to get their consent for the execution of his plan. He also brought up the idea of approaching Lord Reading and Dr. Chaim Weizmann to ask them to exert the full weight of their influence on these two governments, as—and this is the first time that a hint of doubt may be discerned in his words—"The British government had replied that they would take the project into serious consideration and would discuss it with Washington, but sees difficulties of a practical nature that are almost insurmountable."[40] As for the financing of the operation, which the "Joint" was asked to provide, Donati indicated that when he (Donati) was in Nice, Mr. Jefroykin [41] had informed him that in his opinion the "Joint" would raise no difficulties and would undertake this obligation. He, Donati, was apparently inclined to believe (perhaps to some degree naively) that this matter was agreed and would require no further attention.

At 9 A.M. on 8 September 1943 Donati was still conferring with Ivanoe Bonomi, the veteran Italian politician who since the fall of the fascist regime had served as representative and spokesman of the democratic parties in their contacts with Marshal Badoglio; according to rumors, Bonomi was due to be appointed within a few days as minister of the interior.[42] Donati told him of his plan and of the preparations made for its implementation and obtained the promise of Bonomi that immediately after his appointment as minister of the interior he would give orders to the police to raise no difficulties for the Jews who wanted to cross the border. That same morning, Donati took care to inform the British and American representatives in the Vatican of the results of this conversation. A short time later, he boarded a train to Nice, where he intended to speed up the preparations for the evacuation of the Jews from the place. In his words, he felt that the ground was burning under the feet of the Jews and that every day that went by without action was liable to be fatal. This time, however, he did not arrive at his destination. During the journey, at one of the stations on the way, and while still on Italian soil, he heard that at 6:30 P.M. an announcement had been broadcast over the radio concerning the signing of the armistice agreement between the Allies and the Italian government. It was clear that it was no longer possible to act through the Italian authorities and that all his work and endeavors during the past months had been in vain. Once again, many Jews would fall an easy prey to their persecutors. Donati did not return to the train that he had left and did not continue his journey to Nice. A few days later, he succeeded in crossing the border into Switzerland where he was granted asylum until the liberation of Paris.

It seems that there can be no better summary of this episode than that written by Sir Godolphin Osborn on 11 September to the British Foreign Office, saying: "this will get known and lead to protests here and in the U.S., that an opportunity, however fraught with difficulties, was offered to the British and American Governments of rescuing some thousands of refugees . . . and was allowed to go by default."[43]

Another plan discussed in those days in diplomatic and political circles —and also quickly shelved—had been raised on the initiative of Jews in Switzerland. On 5 August the Italian consul general in Geneva, Cortese, announced to the Foreign Ministry that "the Chief Rabbi of the city, Signor

Salomon Poliakof," had visited him and talked to him on the question of the fate of the Jews in southern France. The Rabbi had thanked him for everything the Italian government had done for these Jews until then and asked that "In the eventuality of evacuation of the Italian troops from the occupied zone, the Jews would be allowed to enter Italy with our troops or, if the Italian government preferred it, that they be allowed to escape to Switzerland."

The Rabbi even announced that "he was certain that in this eventuality the Swiss government would give the entry visas" and the local Jewish community members would also contribute their part to the success of the operation.[44] It is not known on what the rabbi had based his unreserved confidence in the generosity of the Swiss government, which, however, regarded the matter in a different light. On 12 August, the Italian minister in Berne, Massimo Magistrati, met the president of the Helvetian Federation, who was also serving as minister of justice and police, and asked him what would be his stand on the matter. The latter's words were totally unequivocal: the Helvetian government is prepared to consider "individual cases with possible benevolence . . . but it is to exclude that they would permit the mass entry of these Jews." On that occasion, the Swiss politician found it necessary to stress that in his country there was a great deal of grudge toward "the international Jewish circles that, instead of being grateful to Switzerland for what it had done until then, blame its present attitude."[45]

The two initiatives taken by Jews at almost the same time during the forty-five days of the Badoglio government therefore bore no fruit. This, despite the fact that, in complete contradiction to the words of the British diplomat, there were no such "almost insurmountable" difficulties that could not have been overcome. On the contrary, the four ships intended for the transport of the Jewish refugees from southern France to North Africa had a short time before carried thousands of Italian citizens who had been evacuated from Ethiopia with the consent of the British and under their protection. They had sailed by way of the Cape of Good Hope and the Straits of Gibraltar to the ports of Italy. This operation, covering such a long route, probably involved far more serious practical difficulties than those anticipated in the short trip between Italy and North Africa. Italian citizens had been evacuated from the British Isles themselves after the outbreak of war, carried on board a British ship to Portugal and from there on an Italian ship to Italy. These operations and others like them were carried out in the course of the war, even in the days when the Allies did not have total control of the sea lanes, as they did at the end of 1943, particularly in the Mediterranean. There was therefore no practical obstacle to the transfer of the Jewish refugees from southern France to North Africa, apart from the lack of a genuine willingness on the part of the countries concerned to cooperate and open their gates (more correctly the gates of one of the countries under their control) before the Jewish refugees, even for a short transitional period until the end of the war.

The upheavals that took place in the period between 25 July and 8 September 1943 had left their impressions not only on the internal preparations of the Jews and of the Italian authorities but also on the relations between the Germans, the Italians, and the men of Vichy, in the three capitals as well as in southern France.

The news of Mussolini's deposition by his own people descended on the Germans and their collaborators among the French as a complete surprise. Laval hurried to express his concern to General von Neubronn, the head of the German military mission in Vichy. He stressed the possible reactions that the events occurring in Italy were liable to arouse among the "French extremist movements," and he suggested that the German and French authorities consider together what steps were likely to be required by the new situation in the foreseeable future.[46] German sources close to the army command in France expressed themselves at first cautiously about "the new stage in the war" that Italy would face following the resignation of Mussolini.[47] In fact, a great flow of German forces into the Italian zone began, together with the dispatch of senior commanders both of the army and the security services, to prepare the ground for taking over the complete control of the region in the near future, either in coordination with their Italian allies (or ex-allies) or without them.[48]

In contrast, the reactions of the Italian command showed a great measure of improvisation and stress, revealing most of the signs of confusion and helplessness that characterized the actions of the Italian authorities in those days. On 10 August, clear orders were received by the Fourth Army Command from the Army General Staff to defend themselves against any hostile act on the part of the Germans, the following day, a circular that had been prepared some time before was distributed to the units of the Fourth Army, still stressing the need to preserve "comradely collaboration" with the German units.[49] Additional instructions in the vein of the previous ones were received by the Fourth Army Command on 3 September.[50] In those days, however, the evacuation of the Italian forces from most of the departments was already in full swing, and even the Fourth Army Command had already been withdrawn from the town of Menton. Everyone already understood that the chapter of Italian occupation of the region had come to an end.

Even in those fateful days for the relations of the two Axis partners, the "Jewish question" was not neglected in the contacts between them. On 18 August SS-Sturmbannführer Hagen wrote a short protocol of a conversation he had held with Lieutenant Malfatti concerning "the treatment by the Italian government of the Jewish problem." According to him, the Italian junior officer had assured that "in all that concerned the Jewish question, the stand of the present Italian government did not deviate from what had been laid down in the Italian laws on the Jews."[51]

That same day, 18 August, also started the last act in the long extended saga of negotiations between Lospinoso and the German Security services. It appears that in the second half of July, before the fascist regime in Italy had been brought down, there had been negotiations between the two allies—possibly in the two capitals or in Paris—over the German demands for the delivery into their hands of Jews originally from Germany and Austria, whose numbers were estimated at many thousands, who had found refuge in the Italian Occupation Zone. The Germans demanded their delivery in return for the release of a few dozen Italian Jews whom they had arrested on various pretexts in their occupation zone, mostly in Paris (and most of whom had already been released). Details of the negotiations are not known. Actually, this was quite a strange matter, a kind of exchange of prisoners between allies, with the Germans seemingly concerned for their "citizens"—that is, people whose German or Austrian citizenship they had long since withdrawn. In any case, Chierici, in those days the chief of the Italian police, apparently instructed Inspector General Lospinoso to surrender these Jews into the hands of the Germans.

In evidence given on two occasions after the war, Lospinoso recalled receiving this order but claimed he had simply refrained from obeying it. According to him, he had adopted a policy of wait-and-see and allowed time to pass until the events of July–August had done their work and the matter was no longer of practical interest.[52] In fact, Lospinoso did deal with the matter. He, or someone acting in his name, also promised the commander of the German special security unit in Toulon that he would surrender the Jews, and at some stage he even supplied the SD Command in Marseilles with a list of the names of the Jews, or of some of the Jews, who belonged to the mentioned category. However, Lospinoso did not in fact surrender one single Jew, and after 25 July, when both the government and the chief of police in Rome had been replaced, he gave the matter no further thought. But not for long. During the second half of August, apparently around the 20th of the month, Lospinoso was planning to go to Rome for a few days. Being an old and experienced police officer, he rightly understood how dangerous a list of names in the hands of the police could become one day for people mentioned on it. He therefore asked to meet SS-Sturmbannführer Mühler, the commander of the SD special unit in Marseilles to try and get these lists back. On 18 August, the meeting did in fact take place.

According to Mühler's report to Knochen, Lospinoso came to the meeting only to announce that "in view of the changes of governments in Rome," he regarded as invalid the obligations he had undertaken in the course of his conversations with the chief of the German security services in Toulon concerning the surrender of Jews of German nationality. He also said that he was about to meet his superiors in Rome and intended to talk with them about the whole matter; on his return to Nice he would report the results of these meetings.[53] Knochen reacted to this on 26 August in his usual angry tone. He expressed his "astonishment" that Mühler had permitted himself to discuss a matter concerning Jews "with the official Italian representative without first getting in touch with us," and demanded an immediate detailed report on the topics raised in that conversation, particularly "the arguments that L. used."[54]

Reprimanded and confused, Mühler tried to justify himself, and, as frequently happened in such cases, he only made his situation worse. In his words this was not a discussion of an official nature, as Lospinoso had only been interested in a number of general matters. Moreover, Mühler added, "The principal reason for Lospinoso's visit was possibly something else." A short time earlier Lospinoso had supplied the German security services in Marseilles with "several lists of Jews living in the Côte d'Azur," without requiring that they be returned to him. It seems that he had now received new orders from his superiors, for he asked for the return of these lists. However, "he made a vague promise" that on his return from Rome he would bring them back again.[55] On the spot, Knochen wrote on the form of the cable from Mühler: "Were they at least photographed?" and asked one of his subordinates to put this question to Mühler.[56] No, Mühler replied, this had not been done. At first this had not been necessary, since nothing was said about the need to return the lists, while now Lospinoso "promised to place the lists at our disposal after he came back from Rome."[57]

Thus, in one stroke, in the course of one supposedly informal conversation, Lospinoso—the talented and cunning Neapolitan policeman—had wiped out the one and only achievement that the experienced German security services had obtained in months of long and weary negotiations. If this had arisen from Lospinoso's own evidence only, and had not been written black on white in the official German documents of that period, there would probably have been room to doubt the credibility of the information on such a surprising course of events.

The last dispatch that Mühler sent in this period to the command of the security services in Paris was dated 2 September. By that time, Lospinoso had returned to Nice, but, as could be expected, he did not find the time to contact the unit of the SD in Marseilles to report on the results of his talks in Rome and certainly did not return the list of Jews. A few days later, the announcement of Italy's surrender was published. The last units of the Italian Fourth Army still stationed in southern France disintegrated overnight or retreated across the border. According to Lospinoso's testimony, he succeeded only with great difficulty in escaping from there and returning to his country. Once there he hid for a few months in the Liguria district in northern Italy, fearing revenge from the German security services. In fact, in the second half of May 1944, shortly after his return to Rome, he claims the SS were looking for him both at the police headquarters in Rome and in his private home, and he was forced to ask a friend to hide him in his house. He only returned to serve in the police after the liberation in June 1944 (this too on his own evidence, but this statement is by no means certain).[58]

During the last days of August, a new and short-lived affair sprang up in southern France, connected at least outwardly with the conscription of Jews for labor within the framework of the German Todt Organization. This time the initiative came from the Vichy authorities. In February 1943, under heavy pressure from the Germans, these had introduced the Service du Travail Obligatoire (Compulsory Labor Service), and within its framework had conscripted hundreds of thousands of French youths, both for fortification works in France and for civilian work in Germany. In this framework, the Vichy authorities had decided to conscript also the Jews residing in the Italian Occupation Zone, the foreign Jews 18 to 50 years old, and Jews with French citizenship 20 to 30 years old. The Italian military authorities first heard about this in the middle of August from the prefect of Lyon. As in similar cases in the past, there were serious fears that once they were conscripted, these Jews would not end in labor battalions of the Todt Organization in France but rather deported "to the East." In view of this, and based on the orders from the General Staff stating that the transfer of Jews to the German Occupation Zone was to be prevented, the Fourth Army Command informed the French authorities of their objections to the conscription of the Jews.[59]

When the matter became known, Laval contacted Cristoforo Fracassi, at that time head of the Italian delegation in Vichy, and asked him to intervene with the Foreign Ministry to cancel the order from the military authorites. Laval claimed that if these Jews were to be exempt from conscription for labor, this would mean a discrimination in their favor compared with the rest of the French population and would seriously demoralize those who were ready obediently to fulfill the orders of the government. What is more, Laval added, "The Jews concerned are not due to be sent to Germany, but for work in France within the framework of the Todt Organization," and the duty of conscription did not apply to Italian citizens.[60]

The subject was discussed at the beginning of September in a fairly lively exchange of letters between the Foreign Ministry, the General Staff, the Army Operation Branch, the general consulate in Nice, and the Fourth Army Command.[61] Finally, the secretary-general of the Foreign Ministry, Augusto Rosso, in a dispatch of 6 September to the General Staff, again confirmed that in view of the decisions taken on 28 August, concerning the concentration of the Jews in southern France in an enclave that was due to remain under control of the Italian Army, implementation of the order concerning the conscription of Jews for the Todt Organization was not to be permitted. Rosso also added that "in view of the delicacy of the subject, the opportunity to act discretely is obvious, keeping as a last argument that these Jews are required for work in the zone occupied by our forces."[62] As already mentioned, these instructions from the secretary general of the Foreign Ministry were sent at noon, 8 September 1943, from the General Staff to the Operations Branch of the Fourth Army. The events that took place in the hours and days that followed made a dead letter of these instructions. In any case, until that day the conscription of Jews for forced labor throughout the departments occupied by the Italian Army was prevented, and so was their surrender into the hands of the Germans.

Although the news of Italy's surrender and its withdrawal from the war were announced on 8 September, the feeling that far-reaching changes were about to take place in the Mediterranean theater of hostilities had been in the air for some time—at least since the deposition of Mussolini. Since that event the Italian Army had also begun to withdraw their forces from the region, and it was easy to imagine the day when this operation would be completed. In evil anticipation, both the Germans and the Vichy government began to make advance preparations in readiness for the day when the Jews of the region would be stripped of their patrons' protection. For ten months, both had been suppressing their anger, observing this protection that they had been unable to destroy. Now their day of reckoning was approaching.

On 3 September, the head of the Department for Research and Control of the Commissariat Général aux Questions Juives in Vichy wrote to the Commissariat's representatives in Nice concerning the rumors he had heard that the Jews were plotting to continue to enjoy the protection of the Italian authorities. These rumors are completely false, the writer claims: "The happy days [for the Jews] are numbered: that I can solemnly assure you, and I call you to concentrate your efforts and those of your colleagues on preparing the lists and checking the index cards that you will need incessantly." [63]

The following day Röthke composed a kind of general operations order, whose object was the "preparations for the implementation of the measures against the Jews in the Italian Occupation Zone." This order, classified as "confidential," was based on the assumption that southern France's departments would cease to be under Italian occupation and that as soon as the change took place, they were to be purged of all Jews and their families, without consideration for their citizenship (with the exception of Turkish citizens). The arrested Jews were to be concentrated at temporary assembly points in Lyon and Marseilles that were to be prepared under the supervision of SS-Hauptsturmführer Alois Brunner. They would then be brought in groups "of 1,000 to 2,000 heads" to the camp in Drancy, from where "they will be immediately evacuated to the East." At the end of the document, Röthke concluded: "The complete evacuation of the Jews in the former Italian occupation zone is not only necessary in the interests of the final solution of the Jewish problem in France, but is also an urgent security need for the German troops." [64]

Only a few days passed, and these instructions actually became the operational orders for the German security personnel descending on the Jews of Nice. The period of Italian occupation in southern France had come to an end. The last chapter in the persecution of the Jews in the region, the hardest and most dreadful of all, had begun.

During the night of 8–9 September, a few hours after General Eisenhower's broadcast announcing the Armistice agreement, German Army forces in a lightning operation took over all the points of strategic importance throughout the former Italian zone of occupation. Units of the Fourth Army who still remained in the area—over 100,000 troops, including some 60,000 from elite fighting units—disintegrated within a few hours, lacking the ability or the desire to resist the German assault. Some of the Italian troops succeeded in escaping and crossed the old international border between France and Italy, but most of them were disarmed and taken prisoner by their allies of yesterday. Only one day later, on 10 September 1943, a special commando of the German security forces arrived in Nice under the command of SS-Hauptsturmführer Alois Brunner, who had been given the task of purging the region of Jews.

The great manhunt for the Jews of Nice began that same day at 3:30 P.M., when the German Army troops and security men were joined by French volunteers from the fascist movement Parti Populaire Français (French Popular Party). Jews were seized in their homes and hotels, in hiding places with Aryan friends, and on the roads, in their desperate flight from the city—the same city that until then had been a safe shelter and overnight had become a deathtrap. At the same time, German security officials visited the department prefect, Jean Chaigneau, and the Italian consul-general, Augusto Spechel, and demanded that they hand over the lists of Jews they had in their possession. In this, however, they were unsuccessful: Chaigneau had made certain of burning the lists in good time, and Spechel claimed he had long since transferred all the documentary material of the consulate to Rome (which in fact had been done).[65] However, it may be assumed that from the start the consulate only kept lists of Jews with Italian citizenship—who in any case had for the most part already left the city—and that the lists of all other Jews should have been at the headquarters of the Race Police. But when the Germans reached its offices, they discovered that this time they had arrived too late. The staff had already left the place, and their commander, Inspector General Lospinoso, before leaving had taken care—according to Donati, who probably relied on Lospinoso's own evidence—to burn all the lists and records that had been in his possession.[66]

Whether for this reason or because of the fact that this time many of the local inhabitants were extending considerable help to the persecuted Jews, the results of the cruel manhunt conducted by Brunner and his men were quite disappointing from their point of view. During the three months from Brunner's arrival in Nice on 10 September, until his return to Paris on December 14, out of a total of some 30,000 Jews who earlier had been in the whole previously Italian zone, he only succeeded in sending 1,819 Jews to the Drancy Camp, 1,100 of which came from Nice itself.[67] Additional Jews were arrested later, during the months that passed until the liberation, either on French soil or in Italy itself, which several groups of Jews had succeeded in reaching in the first days of the occupation. It is impossible to determine with any certainty what in the end was the percentage of survivors from among those Jews who until 8 September 1943 had taken refuge in the Italian zone, especially as some of them had scattered to various departments after the arrival of the Germans, where their fate became linked with that of the local Jews. But, if it had been correctly estimated that this percentage was somewhat higher than the overall percentage of survivors among the Jews in all of France, then the Italian civil and military authorities, in France and in Rome, had a part in this, and in some respects a very considerable part.

However, after the entry of the Germans into the city, the situation of the Jews in Nice was changed out of all recognition. This was observed with obvious satisfaction and malicious gloating by an official of the Commissariat Général aux Questions Juives, who in describing events in the city in those days writes, among other things: "Since the entry of the German troops, the city of Nice has lost its appearance of a ghetto. The Jews no longer walk in its streets; the synagogues are closed and the Promenade des Anglais offers the Aryan stroller many empty benches that until now had been occupied by Jews."[68]

As for the local Jewish leadership, on 9 September, when the first German troops were already marching through the streets of Nice, the last meeting of the Dubouchage Committee was held under the chairmanship of Joseph Fischer (Ariel).[69] The feeling was that all the points of support around them, on which the Dubouchage Committee had relied in its activities so far, had vanished. Donati at that time was in Italy, looking for a way to secretly cross the border into Switzerland. Father Marie-Benoît was in Rome, where during the nine months until the liberation he acted with great courage and devotion on behalf of the Jewish refugees who were reaching the city, including refugees from southern France.[70] The Italian authorities in Nice, who in the past had given reliable support to the activities of the committee, had mostly disappeared from the scene, and the few who had remained were powerless to help. The ship in which the Jews were embarked had not perhaps struck an iceberg, as the refugee in St. Gervais had feared a few months earlier,[71] but with its sails torn it was sailing on a stormy sea, mighty waves rising up all round it and no safe shore of any kind to be seen on the horizon.

The central topic discussed at that last meeting of the Dubouchage Committee was what would become of the thousands of Jewish refugees living in the localities at the interior, who they all thought were in the greatest danger. Special anxiety was aroused by the situation of the Jews in the townships of Megève and St. Gervais, two places west of the line of the Var and Tinea rivers, which held the two largest concentrations of Jews. It appears that the members of the Dubouchage Committee still considered that the Italian Army would hold this line and that the threatening evil would halt there, so by a majority decision they decided to bring these Jews into Nice (that is, east of the Var River) as soon as possible. In fact, the following morning the Jews from these two townships left in one long convoy of trucks going to Nice. Unfortunately, when they reached the bridge over the Var River they ran into a roadblock held by the German Army and security forces and many of the Jews—mostly those from Megève—fell into the hands of their persecutors.[72]

Another group of refugees who were living in the township of St. Martin-de-Vésubie wanted to make use of the geographic proximity of the place where they were living to the Alpine passes. In the night of 8–9 September, the first groups of these Jews crossed the border into Italy, using mountain paths that young Jews had explored earlier in readiness for any possible emergency that might arise.[73] In the days that followed, all the rest of the Jews from that place, over 1,000, went the same way, in the hope that in the future they would still continue to enjoy the protection of the Italians. This time, their hopes were dashed: Italy had already been occupied by the Germans, and quickly their units also reached the remote villages at the foot of the Alps on the Italian side of the border. In these villages, some 350 Jewish refugees were arrested by the Germans. They were initially concentrated in the village of Borgo San Dalmazzo, afterward returned to the Drancy camp in France, and from there they were deported "to the East."[74]

At the end of this meeting, the Dubouchage Committee's activities were in fact over. Most of the active members dispersed, left Nice, or found shelter in some hiding place in the city. The main activities within the Jewish community from then on were conducted by active members of the Jewish underground.[75] Thereby, a new chapter opened in the history of the Jews in southern France, a chapter burdened by great suffering and also great devotion, that was only due to end nine months later with the liberation of the region by the Allies.

The end of Italian rule in southern France also brought to an end their involvement in determining the fate of some 30,000 Jews who had found refuge in this area. From the outset, the Italians had had a special interest in this involvement, regarding it as a way to demonstrate that the significance of their presence there extended beyond the narrow interests of security and embraced local civilian matters of far greater importance. The Italians also believed that submission to German dictates (particularly on a matter that everyone understood to be one of Nazi ideology and not essential for security) would defile their honor in the eyes of allies as well as of the conquered nations, would undermine their position within the Axis itself, and would in the long run jeopardize their chances of taking their place at the peace table as one of the great victorious nations.

From the start of their rule in the region, the Italians had therefore decided that handling the affairs of the Jews living in their zone of occupation, of any nationality whatsoever, would remain the sole prerogative of their army there. The army headquarters would act only out of considerations of its security requirements and in accordance with the general instructions it would receive from Rome. The Italians did not budge from this stand during the whole period of their rule in the region, despite their growing dependence on German military and economic assistance and in the face of the heavy pressures brought to bear by their allies in France, in Berlin, and in Rome (and despite the fact that during the same period they had been forced to submit to German demands concerning Italian Jews who lived in the Occupied Zone in northern France and had agreed to their repatriation to Italy).

Concurrently, many of the people implementing the Italian policy in France and in Rome, diplomats and army personnel alike, considered it inconceivable that they should become direct or indirect partners to the brutal deportations perpetrated in France from the middle of 1942 against thousands of people only because they were "members of the Jewish race." This policy in itself, no less than its outrageous final purpose, in no way conformed to the Italian character and trends; it certainly did not meet the basic foundations of human morals accepted by most of those responsible for Italian policy, and their total rejection of it was therefore only natural.

The stand taken by the Italian authorities on the Jews who had taken refuge in the region under their occupation until 8 September 1943 prevented the latter's arrest by the French police and their surrender into the hands of the Germans. Indirectly, to some degree or other it also affected the attitude of the Vichy government and strengthened their stand in the face of German demands, at least on what concerned Jews with French nationality. There is also room to believe that the conditions created in the region during the days of Italian rule were of assistance to the Jews even after this came to an end: they helped at least some of them to go into hiding among the French population until the liberation, and to save their lives.

# Part 3

Tunisia

(JUNE 1940–MAY 1943)

# 9

# General Background

The 16th of June 1940, on the eve of his departure for the meeting with Hitler in Munich, at which they were to discuss the terms of the armistice to be imposed on France, Mussolini promised himself and his colleagues "that he would return with something, at least with Tunisia."[1] Indeed, at the conference in Munich, after initially raising a series of extreme demands— the handing over of the French naval and air fleets and the annexation of vast areas of metropolitan and colonial France—he finally agreed that only two demands be granted in advance, pending a final arrangement: the annexation of Nice and of Tunisia to Italy. Nice, birthplace of Garibaldi, was viewed as the cradle of the Italian Risorgimento movement. Tunisia, which had harbored a large and flourishing Italian community for hundreds of years, had, since the end of the previous century, become a symbol of Italy's unfulfilled colonial demands.[2] As a "partner" in the splendid victory over France, Mussolini could not have raised more modest demands than these.

Nevertheless, despite his intentions and promises, Mussolini returned from Munich empty-handed.[3] Tunisia was not given to Italy, either as a colony or even as an administered territory for the duration of the war. Instead, the parties agreed that the Commissione Italiana di Armistizio con la Francia (CIAF)[4] would provide a framework for discussing the overall Italian interests in the French colonies, and that fixed delegations of the commission would be installed in North Africa, Corsica, Syria, and French Somali for the purpose of supervising in loco the implementation of the terms of armistice in those places.[5] In all the Maghreb countries, the Italians were, at first, active on their own, as that area had not been covered by the armistice agreement with Germany. However, in February 1941, following the British attempt to take over Dakar, the Germans sent a military delegation to Morocco, which assumed sole de facto authority for local implementation of the Armistice.[6] In Algeria and Tunisia, on the other hand,

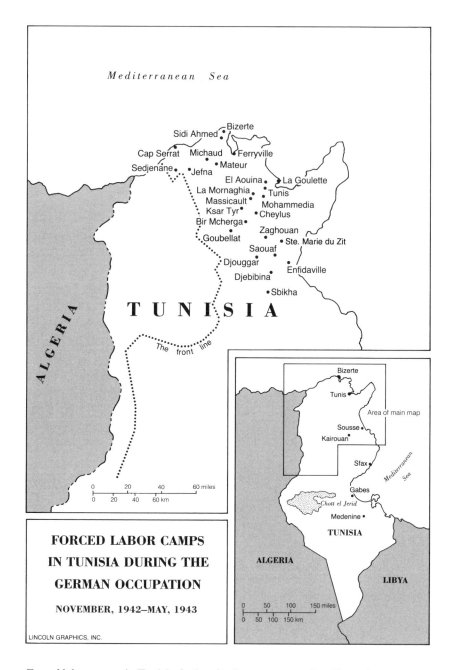

FORCED LABOR CAMPS
IN TUNISIA DURING THE
GERMAN OCCUPATION

NOVEMBER, 1942–MAY, 1943

LINCOLN GRAPHICS, INC.

Forced labor camps in Tunisia during the German occupation, November
1942–May 1943.
Based on a photo made available by Beth Hatefutsoth, the Nahum Goldmann
Museum of the Jewish Diaspora—Photo Archive, Tel Aviv.

the Germans contented themselves with dispatching liaison officers, who acted in more or less close coordination with the Italians.

In October 1940, in order to reinforce its presence in the area, the Vichy government appointed General Weygand as the délégué général du Gouvernement en Afrique Française.[7] Weygand, who had been chief of staff of the French Armed Forces in the last days of the campaign for his country, held the position of delegate general for only thirteen months. In November 1941, he was transferred from that post at the demand of the Italians,[8] who did not approve of his energetic activity in North Africa; on his return to France, the post was abolished completely. During his term in office, according to his own testimony, he took action to reduce the strength of the Italian delegation in North Africa from 570 to 400 persons.[9] Admittedly, the accuracy of these figures is not certain;[10] there can, however, be no doubt that the Italians were especially interested in making their delegations in North Africa much larger than would have been required to implement the supervisory role originally intended for them. It should be remembered that when Italy entered the war in June 1940, its diplomatic and consular representations in France and the French colonies were closed down, and the handling of its affairs turned over to neutral countries, as customary in such situations. In Tunisia—where the Italians had had a consul general in Tunis and vice-consul in Sousse, Bizerte, and Sfax—the many and varied Italian interests were handled by the Swiss Consulate.[11] The services rendered by that consulate, however, were quite limited and did not exceed the day-to-day handling of consular affairs in the narrowest sense of the word.

As stated, from a legal standpoint the signing of the armistice agreement did not put an end to the state of war prevailing between the two nations; nor, at least in theory, did it enable the Italians to reopen their diplomatic and consular offices.[12] This would have placed the Italians in a strange (and, from their point of view, somewhat embarrassing) position: following the "victory over France," Italy's status, presence, and freedom of action in Tunisia would have been more restricted than they had been before it entered the war. The solution found involved the delegation in North Africa of the Italian Armistice Commission. In the guis of commission's members in charge of the Department of Civil Affairs, the Italian consular staff were returned to their former places of office in September 1940. The four consular offices that had formerly existed in Tunisia—Tunis, Sousse, Bizerte, and Sfax—were reopened; former Consul General Giacomo Silimbani, an experienced diplomat who had served in Tunis since 1937, returned to that city, accompanied by a staff of advisors and functionaries. Nevertheless, the Swiss Consulate in Tunisia officially continued to represent Italy's affairs vis-à-vis the French government, and diplomatic connections between the Italians and the *résident général*, Admiral Jean-Pierre Estéva, were maintained through its intervention.[13] This legal status did not change in November 1942 with the landing of Axis forces in Tunisia, although, in practice, the six months of occupation were marked by frequent direct contacts between the French and Italian authorities (and despite the fact that, during the same period, the Swiss Consulate in Tunisia also represented the interests of Great Britain and of the United States). Only on 12 April 1943 did the Italian diplomatic representation in Vichy notify the French authorities that the Italian government had decided to restore its diplomatic offices in Tunisia to the status of consulates.[14] Yet this move—made principally to give the Italian representative a status equal to that of his colleague and competitor, the German diplomat Rudolf Rahn—did not have the power to alter the Italians' position or to promote their local interests to any great degree. By that time, the Allied offensive was already in full swing: the city of Tunis was liberated on 7 May, and the last Axis soldiers surrendered on 11, 12, and 13 May.

The population of Tunisia, according to the census taken by the French in 1936, numbered a total of 2,608,313, including 2,335,623 Muslims, 59,485 Jews, and 213,205 "Europeans." The "European" residents, according to that census, consisted of 108,068 French, 94,289 Italians, 7,270 Maltese, and 3,578 "others." These data were of great political importance at the time, as they indicated that, for the first time in the history of the protectorate, the local French colony had achieved a significant numerical advantage over its Italian competitor (in the 1931 census, the figures had been nearly identical: 91,178 Italians and 91,427 French). This census, its methods and findings, were subjected to a thorough examination in Rome, in an attempt to undermine its reliability, but with no real results.[15] Eventually, even Foreign Ministry functionaries accepted these figures, on which they based a great many evaluations and working papers concerning Tunisia's future, both before the outbreak of the war and after the signing of the armistice agreement. At most, they attempted to blunt their sting with occasional generalizations and vague formulations, such as "the population of Tunisia consists of 2,340,000 Muslims, 200,000 Europeans, and 60,000 Jews."[16]

In any event, the Italian authorities were aware of the fact that the total number of their colonists, as recorded in the French census, also included Jews of Italian extraction and citizenship, whose number, according to various estimates, was between 5,000 and 5,500.[17] It was therefore obvious that, if only from the statistical standpoint—even before taking into consideration the relevant economic and social factors—maintaining contact with this Jewish community was vital to Italian interests, as, without these Jews, the delicate numerical balance between the Italians and the French, which had already tipped to Italy's disadvantage, would have been utterly destroyed. By contrast, the Muslim population held only marginal interest for the designers of Italian foreign policy. According to the archaic colonialist viewpoints then still prevailing among Italian politicians and diplomats, that population was principally an object for negotiations between the Great Powers, rather than an independent subject of cultural or nationalist ambitions. Only a few Foreign Ministry functionaries immediately involved in this area were aware of the changes that had occurred in Muslim society during the 1920s and 1930s and were prepared to take those changes into account. Yet, even those experts limited their proposals to supporting movements hostile to the French colonial administration, in order to use them to promote Italy's plans for its own colonialism.[18] No wonder, then, that their attempts at practical implementation of this senseless policy, such as the negotiations with Bourguiba in Rome in early 1943,[19] encountered only failure and disappointment.

# 10

# In the Shadow of Vichy Government Policy

## (JUNE 1940–NOVEMBER 1942)

In July 1940, at the inauguration ceremony for the new *résident général* of Tunisia, the outgoing governor, Mr. Peyrouton, congratulated his newly appointed colleague, Admiral Estéva. According to his aide, Peyrouton's remarks included the following: "We are happy to hand Tunisia over to you. We hope you will manage to keep it for at least a month. In any case, it is not we who will be responsible for having lost it."[1] This wish may have been affected by the bitterness of the hour—one of defeat and humiliation for France. Yet, at the same time, Peyrouton's words reflected the opinion held in those days by victors and vanquished alike: that Tunisia would be one of the first fruits of victory to fall into the hands of the Italians, irrespective of the terms of the armistice agreements. This feeling overshadowed the relations between France and Italy to no small degree—especially right after the signing of those agreements, the last half of 1940 and the beginning of 1941—and sowed frustration and disappointment on both sides. The French viewed with a heavy heart the possibility of Tunisia's future and possibly imminent transfer to Italian administration, despite Italy's minimal (and, some said, dishonorable) role in the victory over France. The Italians, on the other hand, were disappointed at the fact that this transfer had been put off yet again, even though supposedly for only a short time; among themselves, they did not hide their fear that this deferment might injure their status in the eyes of the victors, not to mention those of the vanquished.

These feelings of frustration manifested themselves between the lines of the reports, memoranda, and messages composed by the various branches of the Italian administration active in the field, the consulate general in Tunis, the military delegations affiliated with the Armistice Commission, and the Military Intelligence Service (SIM), and transmitted to the For-

eign Ministry or the General Staff. These working papers also shed light
on the nature of the first encounter between the officers and senior officials
in charge of these organizations and the local Jewish community. This encounter, itself problematic for objective reasons, was at times accompanied
by manifestations of hostility and rather ugly overtones of antisemitism.

The reports composed in the first months following the signing of the
armistice agreement discuss in detail the main question that occupied the
Italians in those days: to what extent the various population groups in
Tunisia accepted the fact that, by contrast to popular expectations, their
country had not been transferred to Italian rule or even to Italian administration; and what these groups now expected Tunisia's political future to
hold. The reporting officials appeared to believe that a change had taken
place in the standpoint of the local population, both European and Muslim, over the past several months. At first, the majority had been prepared
to accept the idea of Italian military administration, believing such a move
to be inevitable following the defeat of France. However, when these fore-
casts had failed to be realized, new winds had begun to blow in Tunisia.
Some had gone so far as to spread the rumor that Tunisia would never be
transferred to Italian rule and that the preservation of the status quo was
an obvious sign of Italian weakness. General Roberto Lerici, head of the
subcommission "for the control of the Libyan-Tunisian border" (and, as
from May 1941, head of the ground forces subcommission in North Africa),
stated in August 1940 that the factors that had been and still were contributing to the dissemination of such rumors were (1) the independent status
enjoyed by portions of the Muslim population, especially along the Libyan
border, due to the laxity of the former French regime; (2) the subversive
activity of Libyan refugees hostile to the Italian regime in their country,
who had taken shelter in Tunisia; "(3) the deceitful propaganda of the
Jews, who, as in the past, maintain an economic and financial monopoly
over the country, and constantly keep up an extremely hostile attitude
toward Italy; (4) the incessant English propaganda, disseminated and held
to be true by the Jews."[2]

A report in the same spirit was dispatched several days later by the
Italian Military Intelligence Service to the Foreign Ministry; the service's
sources in North Africa were concerned by the rumors spreading among
the Tunisian population, according to which their country would remain
under French rule in the future. These rumors had first been reflected in
an "Order of the Day" issued on the date of the armistice agreement by

General August Noguès, former commander of the French forces in North Africa and now résident général of Morocco, who expressed his certainty "that the territorial integrity of North Africa would be preserved in the future as well." The author of the report went on to state that "the Jews, who have always been extremely hostile toward us, were first to express their immediate support of that opinion; they abandoned the restrained position that they had formerly held and began openly conducting intensive anti-Italian and pro-British activities, and did not hesitate to raise funds on behalf of England."[3]

This viewpoint was echoed on 31 December 1940 by Admiral Farina, head of the subcommission for the Navy (and subsequently head of the General Delegation for North Africa), who, in a report to his commanding officers in Turin, ascribed the unsympathetic attitude of the Tunisian press toward Italy to "elementi demo-giudaici" (democratic-Jewish elements).[4]

These and similar voices did not necessarily reflect the opinions held in this matter by all of the senior officials in the Italian administrative system. At the same time, ignoring them, or even underestimating their importance, would be an error on our part. These were not the unsupported voices of a few individuals but part of the complex reality of Italy in those days. They represented official government policy and were the "legitimate" (and, in several respects, the true) voice of the fascist regime. In Tunisia, France, and of course Italy, such voices were heard from more than one quarter, from the outbreak of the war until late 1941 or even early 1942. Only later, with the internal weakening of the fascist regime on one hand and the horrifying results of racist antisemitism on the other did they gradually die down, becoming at last the matter of a small and marginal faction.

The return of the Italian consular offices to Tunisia in the autumn of 1940, in the guise of the Armistice Commission, altered the rather amateurish political methods that had prevailed until then and improved the level and style of reporting, as well as the scope of problems reviewed. As stated, the consul-general in Tunisia, Silimbani, who had been the senior official present up to the landing of the Axis forces, was a professional diplomat of the old school. He observed the colonial problems from a distance, with neither inspiration nor imagination, but without losing his sense of proportion or falling prey to illusions, as many of his colleagues did during and following the great Axis victories.[5] His long and detailed reports, which he dispatched to Rome on a near-monthly basis, were concise and restrained in nature and gained the attention of his superiors in the Foreign Ministry.[6] His evaluations, mostly based on realistic data, were more or less fair—even when they concerned the enemy or the Jews. The grossness and profanity so typical of those trained in the fascist school were utterly foreign to him, nor was he known to make use of antisemitic metaphors or stereotypes.

At the same time, these differences of style did not reflect significant differences of opinion. Silimbani's conclusion regarding the position displayed by the Jews of Tunisia on their country's future were utterly negative from the Italian standpoint and not widely divergent from those previously or simultaneously expressed by the other Italian representatives in the area. All of the latter correctly estimated that the great majority of the Jews, both those holding French citizenship and the Tunisian subjects of the bey (or *tuansa*, as they were called), wholeheartedly supported the Allies and hoped for continued French administration in Tunisia. Some ascribed this attitude to the Jews' corrupt characteristics and "natural" tendency toward subversion; others were more aware of the objective reasons, centered on the political reality of the period, in which Jews everywhere supported whomever happened to be fighting against the Axis powers. Yet, reasons aside, the same conclusion was shared by all.

Accordingly, only one small group of Jews could possibly be of any advantage in the promotion of Italian affairs: those holding Italian citizenship. In the past, those Jews had demonstrated unblemished loyalty to their native country; some of them even supported the Italian Fascist party, thus constituting a sort of counterweight in opposition to their coreligionists active in leftist movements or local antifascist circles.[7] Admittedly, the race campaign and the policy of social discrimination enacted by the fascist government in Italy since 1938 had caused them bitter disappointment and cooled their patriotic fervor; at the same time, only a few of them had exchanged their Italian citizenship for French nationality. Accordingly, Consul Silimbani thought it appropriate to attempt to renew contact with the Italian Jewish community in Tunisia. He considered those Jews to be of considerable influence in the local social and economic systems, above and beyond their proportion among the population. Many of them practiced free profession—especially medicine, pharmacy, and law; the consulate estimated their property to be worth about a billion francs, or more than 50 percent of the total property held by the Italian colony in Tunisia.[8] Their support was likely to be of real advantage to Italian interests, especially as, from a numerical standpoint, those Jews constituted the focus of equilibrium between the two large European colonies.

On the basis of these reports, received by the Foreign Ministry from various sources during the first year of the war, the Italian authorities crystallized their position toward the various groups of Tunisian Jews. This position was formulated in the autumn of 1941 in a secret document dozens of pages long, that discussed Tunisia's economic social problems in general and Italy's plans for its political future. The section dealing with the Jews and the effect of the Vichy government's first race laws on their status contain the following statement:[9]

> Among the Jews of Tunisia, as we know, one must distinguish between those originating in that country (who are subjects of the Bey) and those who came from Livorno and settled in the area during the eighteenth century, who are Italian citizens. The former . . . whether by design or from natural inclination, support any form of subversiveness. They are often among the standard-bearers of Communist ideology; they were formerly among the supporters of the "Popular Front"; they have always sympathized with the democratic Great Powers and have taken a hostile stand, including noisy demonstrations, against all legitimate Italian claims. Many of them have requested and obtained French citizenship. By contrast, the Italian Jews, some six thousand in number, are on a higher cultural level, and a greater percentage of them are active in the free professions. Before measures concerning race were enacted in Italy, many of them, the most conspicuous in the lifestyle of the colony, were among those favoring the penetration of Italian influence. In the wake of the said measures, many have joined the other camp (and some have even requested French citizenship), some have maintained a restrained attitude, and only a very few have accepted the new situation in a disciplined and good-hearted manner.[10]

The attitude of the Italian Foreign Ministry was clear: the vast majority of Tunisia's population were considered incorrigibly hostile to the Axis powers. As for the small group of Jews of Italian origin, the Italian authorities did not entirely reject the possibility of regaining their support and expected that they would soon, and perhaps even imminently, find out whether there was any basis for that hope. While waiting for this situation to change one way or another, both sides—for the Italian Jews, too, were eager to ascertain the fascist authorities' position toward them—were faced with the new reality formed with the promulgation of the Vichy race laws and their application to the Jews of North Africa.

The laws against the Jews passed by the Vichy government[11] did not apply automatically to those territories "beyond the sea" that were legally subject to Vichy but in which the local regime had its own legislative branch. Nevertheless, the Vichy authorities took pains to stress their favoring of the adoption of a policy of discrimination and economic dispossession toward the Jews in those lands as well,[12] and primarily in the three Maghreb countries, Morocco, Algeria,[13] and Tunisia, whose Jewish population was large[14] and influential in the local free professions and commercial and economic systems. On 30 November 1940, Tunisia passed its first Statut des Juifs[15] (in the wake of the Alibert Statute); on 26 June 1941, its second Statut des Juifs (following that of Vallat); and, on 12 March 1942, two laws concerning the expropriation of Jews and the expansion of limitations on their professions (following the Vichy laws of 22 July and 17 November 1941). These laws were joined, in the autumn of 1941, by several orders regarding the implementation of the numerus clausus in the free professions; in the spring and early summer of 1942, new orders were published regarding the implementation of economic decrees.[16] These legal measures fitted into a rather wide and generalized array of antisemitic legislation that, had the authorities had time to implement its provisions in practice (which they did not), would have rocked the very foundations of Jewish existence.

The laws promulgated in Tunisia against the Jews corresponded, step by step, to those passed in France by the Vichy government. They differed, however, from the Vichy laws in several respects, some of them fundamental, that their legislators felt must be adapted to the special conditions of local society. Thus, for example, the Tunisian statute of November 1940 included two different definitions of the term *Jew*: one, based on the principle of religion and applying to the subjects of the bey, stated that *"tout Israélite Tunisien"*—that is, any native Tunisian of the Jewish faith—was to be considered a Jew; the other, based on the principle of race and nationality and applying to non-Tunisians (that is, mainly to citizens of European countries), specified the same rules given by the French statute. Anyone defined as a Jew by either of these criteria was subject to the prohibitions and limitations listed in the Alibert Statute. At the same time, the Tunisian legislators included a few mitigating details, permitting Jews to hold public office in the framework of Jewish institutions or as their representatives, to teach in Jewish schools, and to practice the free professions among the Jewish public, even in excess of the percentage stipulated by the numerus clausus. Jews were also permitted to publish a French-language newspaper, *Le Petit Matin*, intended as the organ "of the Tunisian Jews or of those Tunisians holding French citizenship." The scope of exemptions— deeds entitling Jews to exemptions from an admittedly minor portion of the limitations—was extended to include actions on behalf of Tunisia or by Tunisian citizens. The second Tunisian Statut des Juifs, promulgated on 26 June 1941, did not change either of the two definitions of the term *Jew* as stipulated in the earlier statute; it did, however, add that anyone descended from two Jewish grandparents and practicing the Jewish religion was also a Jew, and that all of those Jews had to undergo a special census.

Harshest of all, from the standpoint of their economic significance, were the two laws passed on 12 March 1942. The first, based on the amendment of 17 November 1941 to the Vallat law and applying to the Jews of Tunisia, listed in great detail the positions, professions, and functions that Jews were henceforth forbidden to exercise. In fact, according to that law, the only professions freely permitted to Jews were that of craftsmanship and retail commerce.[17] The second, intended by definition to ensure the "elimination of all Jewish influence on the national economy," dealt with the seizing of property owned or managed by Jews—both movable and fixed property (except for the dwelling occupied by the owner of the property), including industrial plants and commercial establishments "if the owners or the managers, any or all, were Jews." This property, stated the law, was to be managed by "provisional administrators," who would be entitled to run it as they saw fit, without having to report to the former owners.

These laws, although exceptionally severe and punctilious, nonetheless lacked (perhaps not by chance) that portion without which they had no practical value: paragraphs governing the implementation of the principles defined, such as the method by which the provisional administrators were to be selected, or the date on which they were to begin to act. These instructions, as the law put it, would be given separately for each specific category, by special orders issued by the *résident général*. Indeed, a few such orders were published between April and June 1942; however, even after their publication, the date of their implementation was deferred. Thus, up to the time of the Allied forces landing in North Africa and the takeover of Tunisia by Axis troops, no Jewish property (with the exception of newspapers and cinemas) was actually seized. By contrast, as early as the beginning of 1941, the Jews were dismissed from their posts in education, journalism, and civil service; their practice of the free professions, especially law, was strictly limited, particularly after the spring of 1942.

It may thus be seen that, up to the landing of the German and Italian forces (that left the Jewish community facing problems far above and beyond the framework of the antisemitic legislature), the Jews of Tunisia enjoyed a more privileged status than their coreligionists in the area under Vichy administration, in both France and North Africa. This was due to the position taken by elements of power within, or influence on, the Tunisian administration, who—for whatever reason—did not wholeheartedly accept the persecution of the Jews. The *résident général*, Admiral Estéva, and several of his senior assistants did not approve of the institution of a racist antisemitic constitution in Tunisia, whether their opposition resulted from moral reasons or from a belief that it would not serve their country's interests in the protectorate.[18] The "danger," in the eyes of French nationalists in Tunisia, involved the existence of a large and lively Italian community backed by a nation with expansionist interests in the area, not those of the Jewish community, which was generally sympathetic to France (as correctly believed by Italian Foreign Ministry sources) and could be considered as a potential ally in the competition between the two European colonies or in any struggle against the Axis nations. Admittedly, the French in Tunisia had a few longtime antisemites of their own—members of rightist movements, who favored the imposition of such laws on the Jews; and there were also recent converts to antisemitism, who sought a convenient opportunity to build their own economic careers by dispossessing the Jews and expropriating their property. These, however, failed to achieve a significant effect on the life-style of the protectorate; even after the takeover of the Axis forces, their influence remained rather limited.

The attitude of the two beys who successively occupied the throne during the war years was also relatively easygoing toward the Jews. Old, moderate Ahmed Pacha, whose rule was governed and guided by the French from 1929 until his death on 19 June 1942, granted two Jews, Dr. Nataf, a physician, and Paul Ghez, an attorney,[19] a full "exemption" from the limitations of the law.[20] His successor, Mohammed Almounsaf, attempted during his brief rule to reduce his dependence on the French, while forming links with the more moderate Arab nationalists, as well as with representatives of other sections of the local populace, including Jews. Italian intelligence sources, who followed the new bey's initiatives closely and with great interest, favored his steps of independence vis-à-vis the French authorities, stressed the rumors concerning his sympathy toward fascist Italy,[21] and emphasized (with some suspicion) his attitude toward the Jews. "Although aware of the natives' profound dislike toward the Jews," stated the *Armistice Commission Bulletin*,[22] "the Bey tends to bring them closer to him, perhaps because of the assistance in intellectual forces, organization, and money that he hopes to obtain from them, in order to implement his plans for independence." On the Muslim festival of Id al-Sajir, the bey hosted the heads of the Jewish colony, demonstrated his sympathy toward them, and awarded high honors to several of them; in a meeting with all the caidi of Tunisia, which had taken place a short time previously, he had "announced that he firmly intend[ed] to reinforce his sovereignty, asked those present to support him, and called on them to cooperate with the Jewish element." Nor did he refrain from speaking out in condemnation of the Vichy government legislation against Jews; in an audience that he granted to the head of the Tunisian branch of the Légion Française des Combattants,[23] a Petainist organization with conspicuous antisemitic tendencies, the bey treated him with obvious coldness and mockingly (according to the same Italian sources) pointed out "the anti-Christian nature of France's policy against the Jews."[24]

As for the Italians, their attitude toward the Vichy government's antisemitic legislation and its application to the Jews of Tunisia was not unambiguous. In principle, they could not but support it, as they themselves had passed similar laws in their own country several years before. In practice, however, they could not agree to its imposition on Jews holding Italian citizenship; their strenuous demand to exempt thousands of Jews from its provision not only improved the lot of those Jews but eventually weakened the entire system (and, in several instances, indirectly brought about the deferment of implementation of decrees affecting the public as a whole). This inconsistent position exhibited by the Italians in France and in Tunisia had a great deal in common with that held by them toward Jews in other countries under their occupation; yet, it had its own special and unique aspects as well.

The anti-Jewish legislation published in Tunisia between 1940 and 1942 had several aspects. Its main intention, naturally, was to damage the local Jewish populace and was part of the Vichy government's overall antisemitic policy. At the same time, it also served a specific French-Tunisian interest, as many of those laws eventually would have turned out to cause especially severe damage to Jews holding Italian citizenship. The proportion of the latter among property holders and practitioners of free professions was high, relative to their proportion among the general Jewish public, and very few of them, if any, were potentially eligible for the "exemption" granted by the law in return for special services rendered—generally military—on behalf of France or Tunisia. It was rather obvious that the protectorate authorities would appoint their favorites, holders of French citizenship, to the posts that the Jews were forced to vacate, in jurisprudence, medicine, and large-scale commerce; and that, in that way, the Italian colony would lose some of its most important positions. Moreover, the instructions concerning the confiscation of Jewish property and the appointment of "administrators" to run it were liable to become deadly weapons in the hands of the French. In an entirely legal manner and without the slightest difficulty, the French would be able to gain half the property of the Italian colony—property belonging to Jews of Italian extraction that would soon be taken from its owners and handed over to administrators, whom the authorities could appoint as they saw fit (probably not from among their Italian adversaries and competitors).

The problem facing the Italians in Tunisia, following the publication of the anti-Jewish laws, was thus different—and much more broad-based and complicated—from those they had encountered in other places. This was not merely a matter of protecting the rights of Italian citizens who happened to be non-Aryan, or of maintaining economic positions or a cultural "presence"—as had been more or less the case in other countries that had enacted anti-Jewish regulations. Here, they opposed measures that, in addition to the mentioned damage, were liable to strike a severe blow at the entire Italian colony (whose great majority was Aryan) and perhaps even to give the French a permanent and final advantage in the long-standing competition between the two communities. Ironically, the Italians were liable to suffer such a crushing defeat precisely because of the same sort of anti-Jewish legislation they had enacted in their own country several years before. To make matters worse, this situation had arisen in the wake of the "brilliant victory" over France that the Italians had expected and planned to be a starting point for satisfying their colonialist claims in general and obtaining control of Tunisia in particular. The Italians' objection to imposing the French antisemitic legislation on their Jewish citizens in Tunisia, then, resulted from the need to protect their vital interests; and even if this objection was apparently not in line with Italy's nature as a fascist power, a supporter of racist antisemitic policy and an ally of Nazi Germany, the Italians were still unable to refrain from exercising it consistently and forcefully.

Another question was Italy's attitude toward those Tunisian Jews who were not Italian citizens. In the areas under Italian occupation in Europe—Greece, Croatia, and the South of France—the Italians defended the lives of Jews in danger whenever possible, even those of foreign Jews (especially the latter, who were in greater peril). In Tunisia, on the other hand, they showed no interest whatsoever in the fate of non-Italian Jews.[25] Was this another expression of the shameful racist policy practiced by the Italians toward native Africans, especially toward black Ethiopians? We have no evidence of this. After all, Tunisia was not an occupied area from the beginning; and even after the landing of Italian forces on Tunisian soil, in November 1942, the influence of those forces on the management of Tunisian internal affairs, which, formally speaking, remained in the hands of the bey and the French *résident général*—was quite limited. There was, then, no legal basis for any attempt at Italian intervention on behalf of the Tunisian Jewish community; nor could such intervention have succeeded in practice—and, in fact, we have no evidence that Italy even desired to intervene in this matter.

The first action taken by Italy for the protection of its Jewish citizens was implemented immediately following the promulgation on 30 November 1940 of the first statute (the Alibert Statute) in its Tunisian version. The consulate-general in Tunis, still known at that time as the Sezione Civile della Delegazione Italiana di Armistizio, reported in detail to the Italian Foreign Ministry on the content of the new law and advised that action be taken to remove the Italian citizens in Tunisia from its jurisdiction, "for political reasons." In the opinion of the consulate general, the law contradicted the first two paragraphs of the 1896 consular agreements that had given Italian citizens residing in Tunisia the right to practice the free professions and to deal in business without limitation; there was thus a valid basis for the demand that this law not be enforced with respect to Italian citizens.[26]

The legal department of the Foreign Ministry gave this suggestion its protracted consideration; its response, on 13 March 1941, reflected the fear that the proposed argument had no real legal foundation. The said sections of the 1896 agreements had basically been intended to ensure that Italian citizens would suffer no discrimination relative to their French counterparts. The *Statut des Juifs* did not undermine the principle of equality between Italians and French, as it explicitly stated that the limitations would apply to all Jews, irrespective of citizenship. At the same time, the Foreign Ministry's legal experts found other points in the Alibert Statute that, in their opinion, were not in line with the 1896 agreements, such as the distinction between Tunisian Jews and non-Tunisian Jews, or the discrimination in favor of Jews who had given their services on behalf of France or of Tunisia. They suggested the use of these points in the appeal soon to be made to the Swiss authorities—that, as stated, formally represented the Italian interests in Tunisia.

Indeed, on 17 March 1941, the head of the Direzione Generale Affari Generali in the Foreign Ministry, Count Vitetti,[27] contacted the Italian Legation in Bern, briefly summarized part of the argument raised by the Foreign Ministry's legal experts, and requested that the message be conveyed to officials in the Swiss Foreign Ministry, so that the latter could pass it on to their consulate in Tunis, which would give the French officials of the protectorate the (amended) proposal originally submitted by the Italian Consulate in the same city. This route was indubitably long; nonetheless, as the *résident général* had not yet published any instructions for the implementation of the principles set forth in the statute, there was no reason to rush matters. On 15 April 1941, the Swiss consul in Tunisia, A. Petitmermet, submitted the Italian reservations to the French authorities; the French response was submitted by Admiral Estéva on 10 May. As expected, the admiral politely and somewhat hypocritically rejected the Italian claims, indicating that the law reflected the principle of absolute equality in its treatment of all Jews—Tunisian, French, or Italian—and promising that that principle would be observed in the future. Estéva's response traveled through channels no less slowly, by a long and circuitous route, and was finally transmitted from Berne to Rome on 5 June, and from there to the Italian Consulate in Tunisia on 7 June 1941.[28]

While the diplomatic messages were leisurely progressing between various cities and continents, far-ranging military developments were taking place throughout the area. After the gloomy winter, in which Italy suffered severe defeats in the Western Desert and along the Albanian-Greek front, the spring brought a counteroffensive by Axis forces in North Africa, bringing them back to the Egyptian border, as well as the invasion of Yugoslavia and Greece, following which all of the Balkan countries came within the sphere of influence of or were directly occupied by the Axis powers. From that point on, Nazi Germany had at its disposal military bases overlooking the Mediterranean coast, from which its vast armies could threaten nearby British positions in the area. These developments in general, and the Axis victories in North Africa in particular, generated various echoes and responses among the nations and camps facing one another in Tunisia. "The fact that there is no longer any chance of British armed forces camping on the Tunisian border," noted Consul Silimbani in one of his long and detailed reports, "caused bitter disappointment to the French and to all those who hastened to gamble on a British victory, and primarily to the Jews and the Maltese. Those who once arrogantly and noisily demonstrated their joy at every instance of our lack of success, now skulk about in silence."

Nevertheless, continued Silimbani, the Vichy propaganda against Britain and the Gaullists "is entirely ineffective among the French population and its Jewish supporters, as all of these consider British victory to be their only possibility of salvation." On the other hand, he noted, those French who lent their support to Pétain did so primarily in hope that a policy of cooperation with Germany would eventually constitute a barrier against Italy, the object of their greatest hatred. As for the Arab population, it was greatly encouraged by the Axis victories and clearly indicated that it was no longer prepared to accept continued French sovereignty in its country. On 12 May, a small demonstration of Arab nationalists—the first since 8 April 1938—took place in Tunis, calling for Habib Bourguiba's release from prison in the South of France. The demonstrators also expressed their denunciation of Britain and support of the Arab revolt in Iraq, emphasizing the assistance offered by Axis forces to the rebels. In the same breath, Silimbani noted that incidents "apparently also involving casualties" had taken place between Arabs and Jews in the city of Gabes.[29]

Those incidents, which took place on 19 and 20 May 1941 and in the course of which seven Jews were brutally murdered, were again reported by Silimbani on 23 and 27 May 1941.[30] He initially announced that the Arabs, embittered by the fact that the Jews had hoarded large quantities of food and were now in a position to evade the rationing orders, had risen against them, raiding their houses and stores. The local police had not succeeded in keeping order and had therefore had to bring in reinforcements from outside. It was now feared that Arab riots would spread to other cities, including Tunis.

In his second report, longer and more detailed than the first, the reported course of events was entirely different. According to that account, the incidents had begun on the night of 19 May, when an Arab had harassed a Jewish woman on the street and had been severely beaten up by four young Jewish men who happened to be on the scene. The Arab had complained to the cadi, who had sent him away in disgust, remarking: "This is the first time in my long career that I have had the opportunity of hearing that Jews beat up an Arab." This comment spurred the Arabs into action. On the morning of 20 May, Arab street gangs launched merciless attacks on every Jew they happened to encounter. By evening, seven Jews were lying lifeless ("beheaded," as described by Silimbani) in the streets, and the wounded were many. Only then did the French authorities manage to restore order, with the aid of military reinforcements called in to the city. Many of the Jews of Gabes fled to Sfax and did not intend to return to their homes until calm had been restored. In Sfax, stated Silimbani, some 150 Jews had assembled in the synagogue, to pray "that Italy would soon enter Tunisia, so that (the Jews) would, at least, be efficiently protected." This last piece of information had been given to Silimbani at second hand, and he himself expressed his doubts as to its veracity. Nevertheless, it was clear that the Axis victories had instilled in the Arab population the desire to revolt against the French colonial authorities and had deepened that population's traditional hostility toward Jews. It was widely feared that the violence in Gabes would sooner or later expand to the other cities of the protectorate.[31]

The second wave of antisemitic legislation in France, following the establishment of the Commissariat Général aux Questions Juives and the publication of Vallat's *Statut des Juifs* on 2 June 1941, aroused profound concern among the Jews of Tunisia who feared for their future. Although the laws previously passed in the protectorate had admittedly affected individual Jews, they had not undermined the status of the entire community. By contrast, the new constitution of the Vichy regime, were it to be applied in Tunisia in letter and spirit, was liable to cause extremely severe damage: "The Jews of Tunisia stood, and still stand, at the head of the free professions, of trade, and of industrial activity," noted Consul Silimbani in his report of 20 June 1941.[32] "If the French race laws are executed in Tunisia with the same consistency practiced in France, we will witness a total social and economic revolution in this country." Admittedly, the Jews hoped that the Tunisian legislators would once again modify and attenuate some of the sections of the original statute, as they had in the past. At the same time, the next steps to be taken by the Tunisian authorities were anxiously awaited; the Jews of Italian citizenship still trusted in the protection of the consulate and hoped that it would manage to protect them on the basis of the 1896 agreements.

The second Tunisian statute, published on 26 June 1941, was in fact incapable of significantly changing the existing state of affairs, as the only new section included therein provided for the holding of a census. Any practical action was deferred pending new legislation—which, by no means coincidentally, was held up for some time. This delay did not go unnoticed by the Vichy officials in charge of Jewish affairs.

On 20 August 1941, the *commissaire général* himself, Xavier Vallat, arrived in Tunis, in the framework of a visit to the three Maghreb countries. He met with the *résident général*, Admiral Estéva, and with his assistants in charge of the legal department.[33] According to the Italian vice-consul, Cesare Regard, he expressed interest "in the specific problems related to the local implementation of the race laws."[34] The details of these talks have not come down to us; apparently, however, they uncovered real differences of opinion between the parties. These differences are echoed in a statement made by Admiral Estéva on 18 September, on his return from a visit to Vichy, where he met with Pétain and with the ministers in charge of political and economic affairs. Admiral Estéva's statement was as follows:[35]

> The legal status of the Jews in Tunisia will be somewhat different from that of the other countries in Africa, as I must take into account the past of these Jews in Tunisia, who served France loyally, and many of whom have long since received French citizenship. I will implement the general measures with consistency, of course, but also with the requisite degree of moderation. Discussions are now going on toward the preparation of a *modus vivendi*, which will regulate the freedom of action to be granted to the various groups of Jews.[36]

These discussions do not appear to have taken too much time. As early as 9 October 1941, an order was issued stating that the quota of Jews among Tunisia's lawyers must not exceed 2 percent; a similar order, limiting the quota of Tunisia's Jewish doctors to 5 percent, was issued on 16 October.

These orders gave the diplomatic system a rude awakening. On 23 October 1941, in a message to the Italian Legation in Bern, Count Vitetti transmitted the Italian Foreign Ministry's response to Admiral Estéva's letter of 10 May (which, as stated above, had been sent in response to the Italian communication of 17 March). He rejected Estéva's claims and again stressed the discrimination liable to be suffered by Italian citizens as a result of the special conditions required by law for the "exemption." At the same time, added Vitetti, "the practical implementation of the measures will determine whether the persons of Italian citizenship will, in practice, enjoy the same rights held by the French and the Tunisians." [37] In other words, Italy was prepared to make concessions on the legal level (and aware that, in any event, its own legal position was weak) to safeguard its citizens' interests in practice.

Similar discussions, concerning a smaller Jewish community (and one far less important from the standpoint of Italian interests), were held at the same time regarding the rights of Jews holding Italian citizenship in Morocco (most of them residents of Casablanca). The second Moroccan *Statut des Juifs* appeared on 5 August 1941, following the Vallat Statute; it, too, stated inter alia that the Jews would have to undergo a census. The Italian consul in Rabat, Zappoli, who had been reporting to the Foreign Ministry on the details of the antisemitic legislation promulgated in his country of residence, raised a specific question on 20 September 1941: whether or not he should insist that those Jews holding Italian citizenship be exempt from that census. He added that he had been informed that the U.S. consul had instructed American citizens and British subjects not to report for census and that the Spanish and Portuguese consuls had decided to take the same position and were now waiting for their governments' approval. The response of the Italian Foreign Ministry was cabled on 11 October. Foreign Minister Ciano himself stated that the Italian citizens could not evade the requirement for census and that the same decision had recently been reached concerning the Italian Jews in France. At the same time, stated Ciano, the ministry intended to take firm and urgent action to ensure that the new laws would not injure the property rights of Moroccan Jews holding Italian citizenship. In fact, a detailed and well-reasoned claim to this effect was submitted on 28 November 1941 to the French authorities in Morocco, via the Italian Embassy in Lisbon and the Portuguese Foreign Ministry (which then represented Italian interests in Morocco.) [38]

In early October 1941, Tunisia was advised that the Italian authorities in Libya intended to deport all citizens of France and of the French protectorate states from that colony. According to Italian sources in Libya, this category included 2,315 persons—715 Muslims and 1,600 "of the Jewish race," most of them originally from the three Maghreb countries.[39] The French authorities did not conceal their displeasure at this prospect and demanded that the deportees be given the possibility of liquidating their assets and of transferring the funds thus obtained to their new place of residence. They also asked to be provided with lists giving the names and particulars of all candidates for deportation before their actual departure for Tunisia, the country that was to constitute their first stop on the road to exile. We do not know when the actual deportation began; it was apparently not until the early summer of 1942, as it was still going on in July and August of that year.[40] The Jewish community of Tunisia welcomed the refugees with open arms and extended all possible material aid to them.

In the late autumn of 1941 and early winter of 1942, the tide of war turned twice on the Western Desert front. A British offensive, starting on 3 December 1941 and ending on 11 January 1942 (known as Operation Three Cunninghams, after the three generals commanding it), proved successful, bringing the British forces back into Libya—more precisely, up to the border of Cyrenaica and Tripolitania. Rommel then succeeded in a lightning operation, between 21 January and 4 February 1942, in restoring the majority of Libyan territory (up to Ein al-Ghazala, a small point east of Tobruk) to Axis control. Meanwhile, in France, preparations were being made for the deportation of Jews "to the East." Initially, only aliens were scheduled for deportation; the first group of non-French Jews, more than 1,000, set out on 27 March. The scope of those included in the deportation process gradually widened and finally included all Jews residing in the Occupied Zone as well as in the area governed by Vichy. In the first days of May, Xavier Vallat, the *commissaire général* in charge of Jewish affairs, was ousted and replaced by Darquier de Pellepoix, head of the Rassemblement Anti-Juif (Anti-Jewish League) in France and trusted by the Nazis. Ended were the days of the New Order technocrats, rightist reactionaries who had believed in their own ability to negotiate with the German political leadership as equals. The time was now ripe for the collaborators, henchmen of various German police officers and security services.

In Tunisia, fortunately for the Jews, matters proceeded at a slower pace, in a more leisurely—or, let us say, more Mediterranean—fashion. The two laws concerning the limitation of Jewish economic activity and the transfer of Jewish property to the hands of "provisional commissioners" were published in Tunisia on 12 March 1942. As had been feared, these two laws at first seemed capable of inflicting serious damage to both the Jewish community and the Italian interests in that country. This fact was emphasized by Consul Silimbani in his report of 26 March 1942, in which he set forth an extensive analysis of the main items included in those laws, indicated the damage liable to be done to Italian interests, and raised several points that, in his opinion, contradicted the explicit obligations undertaken by France in the framework of the January 1884 and September 1896 agreements. Those agreements had stated that the Italian citizens of Tunisia (and this, interpreted Silimbani, referred to "any and all Italians, including those of the Jewish race") would enjoy total equality of rights and would be entitled to practice all professions and to hold all kinds of property without limitation. In his summary of the situation, Silimbani went on to state that

> The implementation of the provisions set forth in those laws will comprise an important stage in a gradual French plan, by means of which the power in charge of the Protectorate intends to take over the sources of wealth and the control of the country's economy, in order to deepen its roots there and to confront all those having ambitions toward (the Protectorate) with a *fait accompli*. The problems raised by the two laws of 12 March, as far as the Italians are concerned, are therefore more than the mere question of protecting the interests and rights of certain groups of citizens, which, in fact, are defined in a special legal framework even within Italy; this is a serious Mediterranean problem, of national political importance, whose solution may tip the balance to one side or the other in the sixty-year struggle between Italy and France for influence in the area.[41]

Silimbani considered the problem so important, and the need for its solution so urgent, that the very next day, 27 March, he transmitted to the Foreign Ministry the complete version—already translated into French— of the legal reservations that he proposed to submit, via the Swiss diplomatic delegations, to the protectorate authorities. Moreover, he announced that he had already contacted the Swiss consul in Tunis and that he had agreed that, on receipt of approval from his superiors in Bern, the latter would submit the detailed version given him by Silimbani. The Italian Foreign Ministry was apparently not impressed by Silimbani's fears and warnings and preferred to abide by more routine bureaucratic and diplomatic procedure. On 15 April, the head of the Italian foreign minister's cabinet, Marquis d'Ajeta, contacted the Italian Legation in Bern, conveyed Silimbani's reservations (in an abridged version, retranslated into Italian) to the legation staff, and asked that they be transmitted to the French authorities in Tunisia via the political department of the federal government.[42] The French response has not come down to us; however, we do know from one of Silimbani's cables to the Foreign Office that Admiral Estéva informed the Swiss consul that he would reply to the Italian missive on his return from Vichy, where he imminently intended to meet with the new Laval government for initial consultation.[43]

Meanwhile, in Tunisia, publication of orders regulating the implementation of the laws of 12 March 1942 had begun. An order regarding the legal profession was published on 30 March;[44] two laws concerning the confiscation of property, on 30 April;[45] and three orders imposing limitations on various branches of the economy—insurance, banking, the stock exchange, and so on—on 12 and 18 May.[46] Silimbani's response to the limitations placed on the legal profession is interesting in itself, especially in light of the details it includes regarding the Jews' activity in this profession. According to Silimbani, there were only two approved registers of lawyers practicing in Tunisia: one maintained by the court in Tunis, and the other in Sousse. Of the 316 lawyers registered in Tunis, 211 of them were "of the Jewish race." A total of 13 lawyers from that register held Italian citizenship, "only five of them Aryans." Of the remaining eight, two held "exemptions" as defined by the Italian race laws.[47] In Sousse, 28 lawyers were registered, 13 of them Jews. Only one lawyer in that city held Italian citizenship, was "of the Jewish race." Based on these data, Silimbani expressed the opinion that the order regarding the legal profession had no real adverse effect on important Italian interests; thus, in this case, Italy could content itself with demanding that the two Jews who had been granted "exemptions" by Italian law would be permitted to continue practicing their profession in the future. Moreover, added Silimbani, aside from those two, "the other Italian lawyers of the Jewish race have no political merit, and some of them are even among our declared enemies."[48]

Completely different, in the eyes of the Italian authorities in Rome and their representatives in Tunisia, were the other orders that, in their opinion, could cause their non-Aryan citizens to be dismissed from their posts and dispossessed of their property in favor of French citizens. This time, the Italians concluded that the routine handling hitherto given this matter via the Swiss consular delegations (and, concerning the Moroccan Jews, via the Portuguese delegation) was no longer sufficient. They decided that direct diplomatic contacts would be made with the Vichy authorities to inform them of the severity of the problem and to demand that the measures planned against the Jews not be put into practice, or at least that their implementation be deferred to a later date (in fact, until the final determination of Tunisia's political future). Detailed and explicit instructions to this effect, signed by Foreign Minister Ciano himself, were issued on 28 May 1942 to the Italian Embassy in Paris, delegating that institution to work with the French authorities through its representative in Vichy, Count Vittorio Zoppi.[49] Ciano's appeal centered on the question of the Jews in Tunisia (more precisely, the question of the Italian Jews in Tunisia) and was therefore extensively based on Silimbani's reports, especially that of 26 March, as well as on his legal and political arguments. However, at the end of the cable, Ciano noted that the claims also applied to the Jews in Morocco (where, as he knew, a Jewish lawyer holding Italian citizenship, Moreno by name, had already been dismissed from his post) and in "Free France," in those districts of the south of France under Vichy administration. Ciano concluded: "It is evident from this, that the attention of the French Government must be directed to this subject in energetic terms, which will leave no doubt of our firm intention to protect Italian interests in Tunisia and to prevent damage to our status in the guise of implementing measures of a racial nature."[50]

It may thus be seen that Italy decided to handle the matter as vigorously and aggressively as possible. At the same time, the Italians also arranged a way of retreat from their initial, far broader demands, should the Vichy government find these absolutely unacceptable. Indeed, in that same cable of 28 May, Ciano notified the embassy in Paris that, at a later stage, the Foreign Ministry would be prepared to discuss a solution based on the appointment of "provisional commissioners" from among "Italian Aryan" citizens for the property of those Jews holding Italian citizenship; these, however, would in any event have to be appointed on the recommendation and in accordance with the sole consideration of the Italian Consulate.

On 4 June 1942, the Italian ambassador in Paris, Gino Buti, confirmed the receipt of the new instructions;[51] on 13 June, he reported on the first meeting between Zoppi and Lagarde, the official in charge of political matters in the Vichy Foreign Office. Lagarde was already aware of the problem and its ramifications; these, as he stated, had already been discussed several days previously with Admiral Estéva during the latter's visit to Vichy. Estéva claimed that, if the Italian demands were met, there would be no alternative but to repeal the laws of 12 March altogether, as it would be impossible to restrict the execution of these laws to the Tunisian and French Jews alone, thus discriminating in favor of the Italian Jews. "The repeal of these laws in Tunisia," added Lagarde, "would mean, from the standpoint of the French Government, a renunciation of the anti-Jewish policy that it has recently launched and is now implementing. What is more, France would be liable to arouse the remonstrances of the Germans, who reproach France for not conducting that policy with the necessary vigor." When Zoppi insisted, emphasizing his demand for not implementing the expropriation law, Lagarde replied that he would convey this demand to Laval.

At this stage, Zoppi refrained from raising the second proposal, to which Italy was prepared to agree as a last resort, that is, that the commissioners of the seized property be appointed from among their Aryan citizens.[52] An arrangement of this type, however, had already been discussed by Zoppi and Lagarde regarding the Jews holding Italian citizenship in the zone of the Vichy government; moreover, a similar arrangement was more or less in force in the area occupied by the Germans.[53] It could, then, be expected that such a proposal would, sooner or later, also be brought up for discussion concerning the Jews in Tunisia. In fact, in the course of the second meeting between the diplomats, this proposal was made by Lagarde, who defined it as a good formula that would not prevent the French from applying the laws to Jews of Italian citizenship, while allowing Italy to safeguard its own interests. Zoppi did not reject the proposal out of hand (knowing that, under certain circumstances, it was likely to be accepted by the Foreign Office) but stressed that it could only be discussed if it were totally clear that the commissioners of Jewish property would be selected by the Italian Consulate alone. Italy was not prepared to consider the partial proposal alluded to by Lagarde at one of their previous meetings, during discussions on the Jews of the Unoccupied France, for the appointment of Italian "observers" alongside French commissioners.

Thus ended the second meeting between the diplomats, with the understanding that negotiations would continue after matters had been discussed with the two foreign ministers and their comments obtained. This, in any event, was Zoppi's understanding of the situation, as reported on 10 July 1942 by Ambassador Buti to Ciano.[54] The French, however, apparently understood things differently; to everyone's surprise, some three weeks later, Lagarde notified Zoppi that his government had "acceded to the Italian request" and had instructed the *résident général* in Tunis to ensure that the commissioners appointed for the property seized from Jews holding Italian citizenship be Aryan Italian citizens. Moreover, the *résident général* had already been instructed to confer with the Swiss consul in Tunis in order to select the said administrators "out of a common intent."[55] There could be no possible doubt: this was a French attempt to deceive the Italians and to confront them with a fait accompli. Not only was this not an "Italian request," but also the Vichy government had decided to "accede to" it by giving it an interpretation that stripped it of all positive significance and that ran absolutely counter to Italy's declared intentions. It was both natural and predictable that Italy would respond forcefully.

While negotiations plodded along between Rome, Vichy, and Paris, there suddenly appeared a new factor, not known to have intervened up to that point in the matter of Tunisia's Jews, Germany. Italy should have understood from the very beginning that, once the handling of that matter had been removed from the quiet peripheral channels of the consulates in Tunis and the political department of the federal government in Bern and turned into direct diplomatic pressure on the Vichy government, it could no longer remain a secret or even an internal matter between the two nations, and surely it could not fail to arouse German interest. Furthermore, the Vichy government had several good reasons to bring about such intervention, by which it apparently expected to win Germany's complete support. Vichy may even have hoped, with German assistance, to bring about a minor Italian diplomatic defeat that would put Italy in its place and teach it to stay out of Vichy's internal affairs—including those having to do with North Africa. The Italian government may not have foreseen this development; alternatively, it may have felt that the matter was sufficiently important to risk disputing it, if necessary, even with its own allies. In any event, the intervention came about only a few days after the first meeting between Zoppi and Lagarde.

The Italians raised a great number of complaints about the French treatment of Italian non-Jewish citizens, both in the occupied zone and in the area under Vichy control, in France and North Africa.[56] Protracted negotiations in this matter had been going on at various diplomatic levels ever since the signing of the armistice; the chairman of the Armistice Commission, General Vacca Maggiolini, reported on this in talks with Mussolini on 31 March and 27 June 1942. During the month of June, the heads of the two armistice commissions (Italian and German) met in Friedrichshafen; their discussions also covered these complaints. At that time, it was decided that the Italian secretary general of the Armistice Commission, General Fernando Gelich, would go to Paris to meet with the local German authorities and coordinate the details of the joint policy, which would be presented as an ultimatum to the Vichy authorities (with regard to the protection of Italian and German citizens, with no bearing whatsoever on Jews).

On 3 and 4 July, Gelich held long meetings with Ambassador Abetz, with Colonel Böhme of the German Armistice Commission, and with Baron

Dr. von Welck, the German Foreign Office representative on that commission. For a number of reasons, the opening positions of the two sides were divergent, and, in certain sections, even contradictory. Ambassador Abetz finally settled the issue: on the second day of deliberations, he surprised his colleagues by announcing that he accepted the Italian position without reservation and even pointed out several pressure tactics that could possibly be of use against the Vichy government, should the latter not cooperate in implementing the policy agreed on by the two Axis powers. Gelich's report included the following passage:

> Following the conclusion of the discussions, Ambassador Abetz hinted to me that he would like to take the opportunity to talk with me about another matter. His reference was to the recently published French anti-Semitic legislation, which included a series of economic and financial measures intended to expel the Jews from the European *Lebensraum* once and for all. For these reasons, the Reich Government is quite sympathetic toward this legislation, which is also likely to be of assistance to the Axis, by separating France from the Jewish world. It would therefore be wise for the Italian Government to give up its objections to the complete implementation of this policy with regard to Italian citizens of the Jewish race residing in French North Africa, particularly in Tunisia.

The hint dropped by Ambassador Abetz was none too heavily veiled; nor was his point in mentioning Tunisia as part of "French North Africa." Gelich had no choice but to reply that the matter was outside Armistice Commission authority and that all he knew was that the Italian government was firm in its intention to safeguard the property of Italians residing in Tunisia, *"which must become Italian"*[57] and to prevent that property from being turned over to the French by virtue of the race laws. Abetz commented that this aim could be achieved by entrusting the management of that property to "Aryan Italian citizens" without impeding the implementation of this legislation in its entirety. This ended the discussion between Abetz and Gelich.[58]

On the same day, 4 July, a meeting took place between Ambassadors Abetz and Buti. Abetz did not refer to the laws against the Jews of Tunisia but simply announced that he would "defer the discussion of this matter to another time." Nonetheless, on the same day, he submitted a report on his meetings to the Foreign Ministry.[59] The gist of that report was quoted in a memorandum dated 24 July 1942 and signed by Unterstaatssekretär Martin Luther, who emphasized Abetz's sarcastic remark: "It will not be in the interest of Italian colonial policy that, in Tunis and Algeria, the French appear as persecutors of the Jews and the Italians as their protectors."[60]

Meanwhile, in Tunisia itself, no real changes had taken place. Admiral Estéva had indeed returned from his visit to Vichy in the beginning of June. However, a month later, he had still not fulfilled his promise; nor had he responded to the reservations originally raised by Silimbani on 26 March (and apparently conveyed to him in late April via the Swiss Consulate) concerning the two laws of 12 March 1942. Additional orders limiting the professional and economic activity of Jews were indeed published on 30 May, 2 June, and 19 June; their actual implementation, however, was deferred to a later date—a month, or several months, away. Regarding the Jewish doctors, on the other hand, no additional legislation was published (the initial order of 16 October 1941 was already out of line with the provisions of the new law), and the Italians insisted that no new rulings be passed on this matter until a satisfactory solution could be found to the entire problem of Italian citizens' rights.[61] This objection may have been the factor impeding the publication of additional orders concerning the group of Jewish doctors as a whole; no further measures, in fact, were taken against that group throughout the remainder of the Vichy government's control over Tunisia.

The spring of 1942 was a time of great success for the Italians, a time of hope and illusion unparalleled since their country had entered the war. The Axis forces reconquered all of Cyrenaica, entered Egypt, and were threatening the Nile Valley. On 2 July 1942, they reached El Alamein, from which point a victory campaign was to set out toward the Suez Canal. In those fateful days, when the future of the entire Middle East hung in the balance and the Italian dream of hegemony over the area was about to come true, the tension around the measures taken by the Vichy government in Tunisia lessened somewhat, and the handling of Jewish issues in that country was put aside, or at least put off. Eventually, though, the diplomatic system was roused from its slumber by the military standstill in the heart of the desert on one hand, and, on the other, the receipt of information from Paris on 31 July concerning the unilateral instructions transmitted by the Vichy government to the authorities in Tunisia.

On 9 August 1942, two cables signed by Ciano were sent from Rome to the Italian Embassy in Paris. One, concerning the "Italian Jews in France, Tunisia, and Morocco," was sent in response to cables dispatched by the embassy on 13 June and 10 July and was apparently written before Ciano learned of the French decision to place the Jews' property in the hands of Italian Aryan commissioners. The other, more forcefully phrased, was sent in response to the cable of 31 July and concerned the French decision—utterly rejecting it.[62]

In his first cable, Ciano first mentioned the possibility of German intervention. In his opinion, the French had no basis for their claim that refusal to apply the race laws to Jews holding Italian citizenship might well arouse German protest.[63] The German authorities themselves, stated Ciano, put this principle into practice in Nazi-occupied countries: in the North of France, the Italian Jews were exempt from wearing the badge (the yellow star); and in Salonika, when the Jews in general were ordered "to report to the Greek authorities" for induction into forced labor,[64] the Italian Jews were released from that duty. Admittedly, in the north of France, the Italian diplomatic delegation had given its agreement to the confiscation of property belonging to Italian Jews, provided that the management of that property be turned over to Aryan Italian citizens; the situation there, however, was not the same as in Tunisia. The Italians in Tunisia had unique political and historical interests; moreover, the special rights granted to the Italian colony in that country were safeguarded by various international agreements. There was, therefore, no room for compromise regarding the Italian demand that no limitations whatsoever be imposed on the Italian Jews, nor was it possible at that time to accept Lagarde's demand for the appointment of Italian commissioners. Furthermore, added Ciano in an "eyes-only" remark, "it will be very difficult for us to find immediately in Tunisia Aryan Italian citizens with the qualifications required to manage the commercial and industrial enterprises to be expropriated, at the present level of profitability and success."

It may thus be seen that the Italian Foreign Ministry had noticeably hardened its position and had withdrawn even from its limited readiness (as expressed in its cable of 28 May 1942) to accept the solution of Aryan Italian commissioners as a last resort under predetermined conditions. Among the contributing factors to this withdrawal were the many and detailed reports dispatched by Consul Silimbani, who forcefully objected to that compromise, both because he considered it impractical and because he feared it to be no more than a distraction on the part of the French authorities, whose real intention was to damage the Italian colony in the course of time. One can easily imagine the extent of Italy's disappointment on discovering, on 9 August, that the Vichy authorities had confronted—or, at least, attempted to confront—the Italians with a fait accompli by instructing their representative in Tunisia to implement the proposed compromise, and to do so in accordance with Vichy's own interpretation, which had never been so much as discussed. Ciano responded to this discovery by asking Ambassador Buti to inform the Vichy authorities that the Italian Foreign Ministry utterly rejected the French announcement and demanded that no measures whatsoever be taken concerning the Italian Jews in Tunisia and their property until negotiations had been resumed and a mutually agreeable solution found. Several days later, on 17 August, the head of Ciano's cabinet, d'Ajeta, returned to this matter. In a long, detailed cable to Ambassador Buti, he extensively discussed the political and legal arguments justifying the Foreign Office position, stressing "the necessity of using every argument in order to defend the Italian nature of Tunisia, one of whose strongholds is at present the situation of the Jews."[65]

It may thus be seen that both Ciano and d'Ajeta, in cables to Ambassador Buti in Paris, rejected out of hand any possibility of German intervention. These, however, were outwardly aimed arguments, raised for the sake of negotiations with the French. Among themselves, the Italian Foreign Ministry staff may well have appreciated the significance of such intervention, should it occur. Ambassador Abetz's words to General Gelich—if they were indeed brought to the attention of the Foreign Ministry—could not have left the intentions of Italy's allies in doubt. This being the case, the Italians decided that it would be preferable to take the initiative and contact the German Foreign Ministry to request its intervention—naturally, in the direction favorable to Italy. In fact, a detailed memorandum in this regard was dispatched to the Italian ambassador in Berlin, Dino Alfieri, on 28 August 1942 and submitted by Alfieri to the German Staatssekretär Ernst von Weizsäcker on 2 September.[66]

The memorandum concerned the implementation of the French race laws in North Africa in general and in Tunisia in particular. It indicated the damage that those laws could do to Italian interests in those countries and noted the special problem of some 5,000 "members of the Jewish race" of Italian extraction then resident in Tunisia, stating that, should those Jews be dispossessed of their property, the delicate balance formed in the course of many years between the two European colonies could be grievously affected, to the sole advantage of the French. The document went on to state that the Italian government had contacted the Vichy authorities in this regard, claiming that the scheduled measures were in contravention of international law and of agreements signed between the two countries and demanding that those measures not be applied to Italian citizens. The Vichy authorities, however, had replied that they would have to implement them promptly, "due to pressure by the German government," which was demanding that the race laws be enforced in North Africa without delay. Accordingly, concluded the memorandum, in view of the Italian government's interest in the success of these negotiations, the German government was hereby requested to instruct its representatives not to view the implementation of the race laws in North Africa as urgent, and, if possible, to take action with a view to delaying their execution in Tunisia.

The documentation that has come down to us gives no indication of the feelings aroused in the German diplomats by what must have seemed to them a highly unusual request for action. In any event, that very day, von Weizsäcker forwarded the memorandum to Martin Luther for handling. Luther found it proper to contact Ambassador Abetz in Paris, both to obtain his opinion (knowing that Abetz had already conferred with Gelich and Buti) and to find out whether German elements had indeed been putting pressure on the Vichy government regarding the Jewish Italian citizens in Tunisia. The latter possibility struck Luther as puzzling, because, as he noted, Tunisia "is not French territory."[67]

In his cable of 12 September 1942, Abetz did not directly respond to the latter question. He did state that he had discussed the issue with Laval and with the secretary general of the Vichy police, René Bousquet. Both Laval and Bousquet had claimed that, following the French authorities' order for "Aryanization" of Jewish property in Tunisia, "Italian Jews had offered themselves as buyers." In other words, according to Abetz's version, they had offered to exploit their preferred status (which they did not yet enjoy in fact, but only hoped to obtain) for the purpose of fictitious purchases, in order to defeat the purpose of the law. Abetz took a severe view of these phenomena and expressed the opinion that they were liable to interfere with "both Italy's image and the implementation of National-Socialist race policy." He therefore asked the Foreign Office to enjoin the Italian government to desist from its objections to the "Aryanization" of Jewish property in Tunisia and to prevent its Jewish citizens from offering to buy the property of (non-Italian) Jews. At the same time, suggested Abetz, Germany should demand that the Vichy government prohibit its (non-Jewish) citizens from purchasing the property of Italian Jews. In this way, the policy of "Aryanization" in Tunisia would cause no damage to Italy's economic interests in that country.[68]

Abetz, who has several times been mentioned as one of the more moderate and enlightened German diplomats, thus took a rigid and totally uncompromising stand on this issue. Admittedly, his attitude may have been affected to one degree or another by the events of the period, during which persecution of Jews had reached its height—both in the Occupied Zone, starting on 16 July, and in Vichy France, starting on 27 August. At this time, with the French police carrying out extensive and cruel man-hunts against the Jews, arresting them by the thousands, and turning them over to the Germans for deportation "to the East," it was apparently not convenient for the "enlightened" German ambassador—nor for his collaborators, Laval and Bousquet—to lend a hand to the preferential treatment of Jews holding Italian citizenship, even in such an out-of-the-way, politically isolated place as Tunisia. Yet in Berlin, far from both the events themselves and the uproar occasioned by them, the Foreign Ministry staff were prepared to consider more broad-based political considerations, and it was these that led them to reject Ambassador Abetz's proposals.

On 16 September 1942, Luther (on von Weizsäcker's instructions)[69] replied to Abetz that, taking into account the Italian political claims on Tunisia, the Foreign Office had decided not to intervene in the policy of the French authorities in Tunisia regarding Jews. The problem, in Luther's opinion, would be best solved in the framework of the overall measures to be taken by Italy in the future against Jews residing in Italian territories. Until that time, the matter would best be left to direct negotiation between France and Italy.[70] Thus ended the Germans' (minimal) role in the deliberations on the fate of Tunisia's Jews, prior to the landing of Axis forces in that country; nor did any additional discussions on this matter (or, at least, any of which we are aware) take place with the Vichy government until then.[71]

In theory, then, the Italians' activity in this regard achieved nothing, as they received no explicit positive response to their claims throughout those two years. In practice, however, Italy achieved much more than it had requested, and perhaps even more than it had planned, as many sections of the antisemitic race laws were not implemented against the entire Jewish population, and not only Italian citizens profited from this. Admittedly, the Italian position was not the only reason for this; it was nonetheless a factor of considerable importance.

# 11

## Under the Heel of the Axis Army

### (9 NOVEMBER 1942–13 MAY 1943)

On 25 September 1942, Ambassador Abetz notified his superiors in Berlin that he had received reliable information from sources with access to Vatican circles that the United States and Britain were planning a large-scale landing of forces in Dakar and North Africa. This operation, to be implemented some time between mid-October and mid-November, would be the first stage in preparation for an additional landing in Sicily, Sardinia, and the South of France.[1] Admittedly, this was not the only warning signal concerning Anglo-American strategic plans to reach Berlin in the autumn of 1942; yet, it was certainly one of the most detailed and most reliable. Nevertheless, it did not convince the German political leadership that the Axis powers were indeed facing severe danger, in the form of a military move liable to alter the very nature of the balance of forces in the Mediterranean. In mid-October, Hitler rejected a proposal raised by the Supreme German Command to allow the Vichy government to reinforce its troop strength in North Africa beyond the quantities dictated by the armistice agreement. His argument—correct in itself—was that such a measure would arouse objections on Italy's part.

The landings of British forces in Madagascar[2] and of American forces in Liberia again raised the suspicions of the Vichy government and the Axis general staffs regarding the future destiny of the French Empire states in Africa. Accordingly, in the last half of October and the beginning of November, a number of emissaries of the highest military and political ranks were dispatched to the Maghreb countries, in order to ascertain the readiness of the French troops posted there and, if necessary, to make suggestions for the improvement of their deployment and preparedness. In the second half of October, General Gelich toured Tunisia. However, even this seasoned and experienced military man noticed nothing more serious than "complications likely to arise in the near future, in view of the logistic preparations that the Anglo-Americans are making in Equatorial Africa"; accordingly, he proposed "to keep a close watch and increase supervision, so that we can by no means be surprised."[3] Between 21 and 29 October 1942, Admiral Darlan, commander of the French armed forces and heir-apparent to Marshal Pétain, visited Dakar, Morocco, and Algeria. The purpose of these visits was to determine the effectiveness of the French defense array in those countries, the morale of French military and administrative personnel posted there, and their readiness to fight, if necessary, against their former allies. In the course of his visit, Darlan made several speeches to the French troops, calling on them "to respond to Anglo-American aggression, should it come, as they had in 1940" (the reference being to the British naval attack on Dakar, on 23 September 1940). Following his return to Vichy on 30 October, the admiral submitted a detailed report to his government; according to Armistice Commission sources, he indicated the "firm determination" of the French army and settlers in the Maghreb countries to defend themselves against "any aggressor."[4]

During Darlan's tour of Morocco, on 23 October, the British launched their large-scale offensive on El Alamein. After long months of slumber, the Western Desert front sprang into action, at a strength and on a scale unparalleled since the beginning of the war. This dramatic occurrence did not prevent the chairmen of the two armistice commissions with France, General Vogl and General Vacca Maggiolini, from leaving the next day on a two-week tour of Morocco, Algeria, and Tunisia. On 24 October, Vogl and Darlan met in Rabat for a long talk; the two agreed that no extraordinary political or military developments could be foreseen in the area. Vogl and Vacca Maggiolini continued their tour as planned, even after the German and Italian naval staffs received initial detailed information at the beginning of November on unprecedented concentrations of warships and cargo ships in the port of Gibraltar. There could be no doubt that this concentration represented the final stage of preparations for a vast landing operation. The target of that operation, however, remained unknown.[5]

Finally, on the night of 7–8 November 1942, while General Vacca Maggiolini was still in Tunis (in fact, during the gala reception held to celebrate the end of his visit), the landing of Allied forces began at Dakar, in Morocco, and in Algeria. A bit more than 24 hours later, on the morning of 9 November, the first German troops landed at the El-Awina airfield near Tunis. Additional forces, both German and Italian, arrived soon afterward

by air and sea; within a few days, the Axis forces held most of the popu-
lated areas of Tunisia, including all its major cities, without encountering
any real resistance by French forces.[6]

The landing of Axis forces in Tunisia, according to the declared policy
of the Italian and German governments, was not intended to take over
the country from the French but to defend it against the continued "aggression" of the Allied powers. Accordingly, it was decided at the outset of the campaign that no real changes would be made in the political status of the country or the authority of its institutions, French and
Muslim alike. In theory, then, the bey and his government and the *résident général* and his administration remained in power. In practice, however, the commanders of the German armed forces—General Nehring (up
to 8 December 1942) and General von Arnim; the representative of the
German Foreign Office, Rudolf Rahn[7]; and the Sicherheitsdienst leaders,
SS-Obersturmbannführer Walther Rauff and his aides[8]—were those who
made the real decisions on every military and civilian matter of importance.[9]

This control, which the Germans assumed over most of the political
positions and economic resources in Tunisia, became a source of concern
and complaint in Italian diplomatic and military circles, in Tunisia itself
and in Rome, not only because the Italian forces were full partners in the
military campaign for the defense of the country[10] but also because of
the special political status they wanted to claim in the area, especially in
Tunisia, after the end of the war. They were, therefore, quite sensitive to
any step that might overshadow them—or, worse, might present them as
a second-rate military and political power. However, their repeated attempts to change the situation and to assume control of local affairs proved
unsuccessful and received only declaratory responses.

A month after the start of the campaign, on 11 December 1942, the head
of Ciano's cabinet notified the German Embassy in Rome, on behalf of
Mussolini himself, that the Italian government forcefully objected to any
step that might be interpreted as a promise or an agreement to grant
Tunisia independence in the future. Three days later, von Ribbentrop replied that his government realized "that any decision of a political nature
relative to Tunisia must take into consideration the unquestionably preferred status of the Italians in the area" and that suitable instructions had
been given to the representative of the Foreign Office in Tunisia, Rudolf
Rahn, "to maintain close contact with the relevant Italian authorities,

and to limit his personal initiatives, if any, to the Algerian and Moroccan arenas."[11] The phrasing of the instructions given to Rahn has not come down to us. However, in practice, no significant change occurred in the behavior of the German authorities or in their domineering and contemptuous attitude; nor did they exhibit any tendency to discuss local policy problems with their Italian allies or to involve them in the decision-making process.[12]

As the differences between the parties became more and more severe, and the relationship between Silimbani and Rahn more and more tense, it was decided to hold a conference of senior Italian and German government and military officials in Rome, "to discuss the problems of Tunisia." Discussed at the conference, which took place on 2 January 1943 and was chaired by Count Vitetti, were a long series of political and administrative subjects that had arisen from the new reality created in Tunisia following the presence of the Axis powers and the sudden and obvious weakening of the French regime in that country. Among these problems were the relationships with the bey, the French administration, and the French collaborators;[13] the date on which the "liberating" German-Arab unit would be transferred to Tunisia; the activity of the mufti of Jerusalem, Haj Amin el-Husseini, and the extent of his influence on the Muslims of North Africa; and the status of Habib Bourguiba and the pros and cons of returning him to Tunisia. Although the deliberations were lengthy, most of the decisions reached were in matters of secondary importance.[14] The resolution summarizing the conference, however, included a statement that "all of the most urgent problems were discussed . . . and solutions were found, in a spirit of most amicable cooperation."[15]

Yet, among the multitude of subjects discussed, and so fully and amicably agreed upon, there was only the barest whisper—in the words of the German delegate Moellhausen[16]—of the real reason for the weakness of the Italian position in Tunisia (and the entire area): their policy goals were not accepted by any segment of the population, or by any one of the political factors operating on the scene (except for the members of the Italian colony itself). They were opposed by the French, Gaullists and Vichy supporters alike, who remained united in their aim to preserve the "Frenchness" of the country; the Muslims, who desired true independence for their country, rather than the mere replacement of one colonial regime by another; and the Jews, who surely had no interest in supporting a racist, antisemitic government allied with Nazi Germany. There may have been more than a grain of truth in the Italian allegation that the German diplomats and military personnel in Tunisia acted with arrogance and condescension, as if they owned the territory; it is probable that they did indeed make trouble for their ally and refused to cooperate. Nonetheless, it was the short-sightedness of the Italian leadership, as well as its unrealistic policy, that forced Italy's representatives in Tunisia into this embarrassing situation, which afforded them no way out and no chance of success.

Under these circumstances, the results of Italy's efforts to protect its Jewish citizens constituted a commendable political achievement—one of the few for which it could claim credit at that time.

By contrast to the situation that had prevailed before the landing of the Axis troops, negotiations on the status and destiny of those Tunisian Jews holding Italian citizenship, following that landing, were mostly conducted with the German representatives, whether in Tunisia itself or in Rome and Berlin. The Vichy government was no longer involved in the matter (and, in fact, had ceased to be any more than the shadow of a sovereign government with the entry of the German armed forces into its territory). As for the French authorities in the protectorate, they had no control over the steps taken by the Germans against the Jews; at most, they could intervene on behalf of a few individuals, by virtue of their high social or economic status or of their special rights vis-à-vis France.

The first German action against the Jews of Tunisia, and Italy's first diplomatic appeal on behalf of its Jewish citizens, took place simultaneously and apparently with no circumstantial relationship between them, some two weeks after the Axis landing. On 23 November 1942, the Germans arrested several leading members of the Jewish community in Tunis: the chairman of the community, Moïse Borgel and his son-in-law; the former chairman, Felix Semama and his brother-in-law; and Jacques Cittanova, the Finnish consul in the city.[17]

The first report after the landing, dispatched by Consul Silimbani to the Foreign Office on 30 November 1942, indicates the arrest, at about the same time, of an Italian citizen, Dr. Ugo Ben Sasson, a familiar face in consular circles.[18] Ben Sasson had been in charge of medical services in the Italian schools and had volunteered to serve in the Italian armed forces in the Ethiopian campaign; according to Silimbani's slick definition, "he had consistently maintained correct political behavior, even following the publication of the race laws in Italy."[19] Silimbani intervened with Rahn on his behalf and obtained his release, even though he was fully aware that

Dr. Ben Sasson's two sons were among the main activists of the local Communist party.[20] The arrest of the remaining Jews puzzled Silimbani, as he considered them to be "harmless persons"; he therefore raised the possibility that the list bearing their names had been drawn up by the French authorities to shelter "more prominent elements" or even to enable their escape. In fact, Admiral Estéva intervened on behalf of the arrested Jews in a forceful and dignified letter,[21] and they were released after several days of investigation. The chairman of the Jewish community, Moïse Borgel, was obligated to present himself at the German military headquarters each morning to report on the activities of his community and to receive instructions, so that "if necessary, he will be able to take upon himself the responsibility for hostile actions, if any, against the Occupation armies."[22]

In the same period, Marquis d'Ajeta instructed the Italian Embassy in Berlin:

> to direct the attention of the German Government to the need to give the German military headquarters in Tunisia instructions to ensure that contact is maintained with our civilian representative in Tunis, in all matters concerning the protection of the non-Aryan Italian citizens dwelling there, and the behavior toward them. The special nature of this Italian colony, represented in the upper [social] strata by non-Aryan elements, obligates us to note again that we have a special political interest in delaying the implementation of any steps of a racist nature against these citizens.[23]

In fact, on 24 November 1942, the advisor to the Italian Embassy in Berlin, Count Carlo Fecia di Cossato, conveyed the content of that message to the German Foreign Ministry.

Thus, yet again, the senior German officials found themselves torn between their desire not to damage their relationship with their Italian allies—especially in the matter of Tunisia, a country concerning which the Italians were so sensitive—and their aim not to interfere with the orderly operation of the German security forces, especially in an area as important to them as the "solution of the Jewish problem." For this reason, the phrasing of their reply was discussed at various levels and amended several times.[24] Finally, on 8 December 1942, the supreme command of the German armed forces notified its staff in Tunisia of the Italian message and stated: "The Italians' request should be complied with, as long as it remains in line with military needs. If, for military reasons, the need should arise to take measures against Jews holding Italian citizenship, the commander in Tunisia will have to coordinate the matter with the Italian Consul-General and with Representative Rahn."[25]

Three days later, the advisor to the German Embassy in Rome, Prince Otto von Bismarck, notified the Italian Foreign Ministry of the German instructions. The formulation of that notification has not come down to us; it was, however, apparently general and not binding. Nevertheless, it was received with satisfaction by the Italian Foreign Ministry; on the same day, 11 December, Ciano advised Silimbani that the German Embassy in Rome had announced the transmission of clear instructions to Rahn "to assit you as far as possible in the fulfilling of your duties, in all matters concerning the protection of the Italian colony—including the non-Aryan [citizens]— and the management of civilian administrative affairs in the area occupied by the Axis military forces."[26] Ciano himself signed the cable—even the copy kept in the Foreign Ministry files in Rome bears Ciano's actual signature—and this apparently indicates the special importance ascribed by Italian diplomatic circles to this message. In fact, developments in subsequent months proved that their evaluation of its importance was correct. It was that very message, along with the statement published on 14 December 1942 by von Ribbentrop concerning the willingness of the German government to "take into consideration" the preferred status of the Italians in the area that finally (and favorably) settled the situation of the Tunisian Jews holding Italian citizenship.[27] During the five months that passed before the Liberation, those Jews enjoyed preferential treatment and were protected from harassment and exempted from the decrees imposed on the rest of the Jewish community.[28]

On 6 December 1942, General Nehring ordered the recruiting of 3,000 Jews to work on fortifications in northern and southern Tunisia and in the Bizerte area. According to those orders, the Jewish community was responsible for arranging the recruiting and for providing the requisite equipment and supplies. In addition, its representatives were required to accompany the groups of workers, in order to maintain ongoing contact with the local German staffs, to ensure the implementation of their instructions, and to bear responsibility for any failure that might be discovered.[29] On the same day, the SS commander in Tunisia, Colonel Rauff, summoned the chairman and the chief rabbi of the Jewish community and informed them of the contents of the order. In his generosity, Rauff raised the number of recruits to between 3,000 and 4,000 and demanded that 2,000 of them report for work the very next morning. He also announced that the recruits would wear a large yellow star on their backs, "so that they may be identified from a distance and shot if they attempt to escape."[30]

This order, which the Jews tried in vain to have repealed or restricted,[31] was initially accompanied by acts of violence and terror on the part of German army and SS units: arrest of hostages; indiscriminate snatching of Jews from street corners and private homes; storming into the synagogue, hitting worshipers, and firing into the air. The Jews went so far as to establish a special committee, the Comité de Recrutement de la Main-d'Œuvre Juive, in charge of implementing the recruiting.[32] The quota was finally filled, and nearly 3,000 Jews were sent to various labor sites. Some of these were near Tunis, enabling the recruits to return home every evening; others were in distant areas, and the Jews sent there were lodged in temporary camps, deserted farms, or tents—in many cases, under the most difficult conditions.[33]

In the months to come, the number of recruited Jews changed several times. During late December and early January, additional groups of workers were added to the first group of nearly 3,000, bringing the total figure to something like 4,500. After that, the number began to drop rapidly. As the military position of the Axis forces in Tunisia became more difficult, discipline declined among the Italian and German troops, as did both the need and the desire to invest work and effort in the construction of fortifications and military facilities. Many Jews were therefore able to free themselves from their labor assignments by various means (bribery, false medical certificates, etc.) or simply to escape from their posts. By mid-February 1943, there were no more than 2,500 Jews on forced labor.[34] It has been estimated that about 100 Jews perished during the entire period of recruitment: some were murdered in cold blood by their German guards; others died of disease or following unaccustomed physical effort; and still others (the majority of the victims, especially those posted to or near the port of Bizerte) were killed in aerial bombardments.[35]

General Nehring's recruitment order, dated 6 December 1942, referred to the enlistment of "male Jews," without distinguishing between Italian citizens, French citizens, and subjects of the bey. The poster printed by the Jewish Recruiting Committee was similarly addressed to "the Jewish population of Tunis" in general.[36] At the same time, there can be no doubt that Jews holding Italian citizenship were not affected by the recruitment order; those few included in the hostage list and arrested by the Germans in the first days of terror were immediately released.[37] Admittedly, in April

1943—that is, about a month before the Liberation—a few dozen Italian Jews were recruited for labor. This operation, however, was implemented in quite another framework. On 10 April 1943, the *resident général* ordered the recruitment for labor of all (non-Jewish) French youths born between 1920 and 1922; on 20 April, this was expanded to include those born between 1917 and 1919. The leading members of the Italian colony decided that their young people should also give their share to the joint effort; in that framework, the Italian Jewish community was asked to supply a few dozen volunteers for work within the city of Tunis. Concerning that group, we have only the most meagre information; we do not even know whether its members were put to work at all, and if so, for how many days.[38]

This policy of preferential treatment enjoyed by Italian Jews displeased the German authorities in Tunisia, who, though forced to implement it by the unbreakable orders they had received, did not hide their disappointment. On 10 December 1942, as the first Jews were sent out on forced labor assignments (two days after the Supreme German Command had ordered that no steps be taken against Jews holding Italian citizenship without prior coordination with the local Italian Consul), Rahn reported to the embassy in Paris that "the labor service of the Jews has begun. The Italian Consulate General has objected to the imposition of this measure on the Italian Jews, and they are therefore exempt."[39] Two weeks later, in a report to Berlin dated 24 December, Rahn—the subtle diplomat, the representative of the "moderate and liberal" school in the German Foreign Ministry—complained that the concentration of the Axis forces in Tunisia within a small and crowded area, a sort of unfortified fortress, was extremely limiting to their activity in various political and propaganda areas. Nor did the establishment of armed units from among the citizens supporting the Axis significantly change matters. "Encouraging the looting of Jewish shops, while turning demonstrations into pogroms and so forth, is impossible, as long as our forces have not at least reached the Algerian border."[40] Fortunately for the Tunisian Jews, the military campaign developed in another direction.

An additional disappointment, worse than its precursors because of its effect on the entire Jewish community, was incurred by Rauff, Rahn, and their cronies concerning the wearing of the badge. On 17 March 1943, the official in charge of the police in the French administration reported to Admiral Estéva that Colonel Rauff had called his attention to the fact that "the Jews of Tunisia should be obliged to wear the yellow star" and that this instruction should be coordinated with General von Arnim's head-quarters. As for the Italian Jews, added Rauff, they were "subject to a special order of the Supreme Command"—meaning that the German authorities in Tunisia were not empowered to impose this obligation on them. Estéva requested the opinion of the administration's legal advisors, who did draw up a draft order to that effect but, at the same time, expressed the opinion that there would be no possibility of exempting the Italian Jews. Not only would the bey consider such an exemption a discrimination against his subjects; the definition of the term *Jew* had clearly and explicitly been set forth in the Tunisian law of 12 March 1942 (art. 2). There was thus no legal possibility of relating to the Jewish community, nor of imposing obligations or decrees on it other than in accordance with that definition, which "included all the Jews, of whatever nationality."[41] Rauff apparently believed that, given the overall collapse of the entire Axis military array in Tunisia, the time was not right for negotiations with the Italians in this matter. Accordingly, the Germans imposed the wearing of the badge on Jews residing in peripheral locations where no Italian Jewish community existed, such as Sousse and Kairouan,[42] whereas all the Jews of Tunis (and most of the Jews in Tunisia) were exempt from this order.

Another matter, which has hardly been discussed in the professional literature to date, concerns the labor camps administered by the Italian armed forces in Tunisia, in which about 1,000 Jews were interned during the initial period. No information on these camps has as yet been found in the Italian documentation;[43] we therefore have no alternative but to content ourselves with published material, especially the testimony given by Jews who had been released from the camps following the Liberation. In fact, the consensus of this testimony is unequivocal and constitutes a nearly universal commendation of the Italians.[44]

It appears from this testimony that the Italians were in charge of a series of labor camps (many of which consisted of a building or two and a handful of tents), from La Goulette near Tunis to Enfidaville in the south, about halfway between Tunis and Sousse. A large group of Jews, some 350, worked in the Zaghouan area. Smaller groups served in Sainte-Marie-du-Zit, Kairouan, Sbikha, Djelloula, and other places. The main difficulties were revealed in the first days of recruitment and resulted from logistical disorganization (lack of equipment, delays in supply convoys, etc.) and from the extremely primitive living and sanitary conditions. These conditions later improved (although they never became really good), and life in the labor camps became more or less regular. Three Jews (Jules Taïeb, Henry Sfez, and S. Baranes) were appointed by the recruiting committee to take charge of liaison with the Italian authorities. They were provided with a small Citroën automobile, in which they drove from place to place, noted the special problems in each camp, and attempted to solve them with the aid of the nearest Jewish community or that of Tunis. The guarding of the camps—or, more precisely, of the forced laborers—was given over to army reservists, many of them old and exhausted by the protracted military campaign. The relations between the guards and the Jews were generally correct; at times, barter and trade relations (primarily involving cigarettes and food supplies) sprang up between the two groups.[45] Of course, there were also arrogant and rude guards, and even some petty thieves, who helped themselves to the supplies intended for the Jews.

Toward the end of the winter, the number of interned Jews began to decrease. By March, the Italians were responsible for no more than 150 to 200 Jews,[46] the remainder having been set free or simply having escaped (or been allowed to escape). Borgel, in his book, mentions the names of several Italian military personnel outstanding in their assistance to the Jews, including Captain Corsi and Sergeant Gallese. The latter was also court-martialed for having aided the Jews and was sentenced to reduction in rank.

On 29 January 1943, following a campaign that had begun at El Alamein and continued for three months, units of the British Eighth Army under Field Marshal Montgomery crossed the Libyan-Tunisian border. Two weeks later, they reached the Matmata-Mareth fortification line, or "Maginot Line of the desert," as its French planners called it. This was a miserable, outmoded fortification line, built by the French before the war in order to ward off any eventual Italian attack from Libya. Now the tables had been turned, and the line (which had been mostly dismantled in accordance with the June 1940 armistice agreements, at the initiative and under the supervision of the Italians, and partially rehabilitated following the Axis landing in November 1942 at the initiative of the same Italians) was occupied by Axis forces trying to hold back the Allied offensive from Libya.

In Rome, various political and military circles followed the development of events with great concern. It was clear that what hung in the balance this time was not only the fate of a military campaign but the future of fascist Italy's imperialist vision—that is, of its role as successor to the mighty Roman Empire. On 13 March, under ever-increasing military pressure, Mussolini once more approached Hitler with a request for urgent assistance in order to defend the last bit of Africa still under Axis control. Tunisia, he claimed, was "an essential factor of the [Axis] strategic array . . . and should be defended at all costs."[47] Hitler agreed with him, but only outwardly. In fact, he had never recognized the importance of the military campaign in North Africa, which had been forced on him by his Italian allies, and was not entirely convinced of its necessity. In any event, he was certainly incapable—with the Red Army offensive on the eastern front in full swing—of providing the additional armored reinforcements that Italy had requested and that he himself had promised several months before. Instead of troops and equipment, he dispatched Marshal Albert Kesserling to Tunisia on 16 April, bearing an unequivocal order from the Führer: "Tunisia is to be defended at all costs." This time, however, words proved of no avail.

On the evening of 7 May 1943, the first units of the British Seventh Division entered Tunis. At the same time, the U.S. Ninth Division conquered the port of Bizerte. Four days later, on 11 May, General von Arnim signed the surrender agreement of the German armed forces; Italy followed suit on 13 May. After nearly three years of stubborn fighting and seven campaigns by the two armies, back and forth between Egypt and Libya, the military struggle for North Africa had ended; the curtain was now to rise on a new campaign that would continue for two years on Italian soil.

For the Jews of Tunisia, the day of liberation was like waking from a nightmare. For years, they had been subject to the shameful and discriminatory policy of the Vichy government; for months, they had suffered violence and persecution at the hands of the German armed forces. Like their coreligionists in the occupied countries of Europe, the Jews of Tunisia had hovered on the brink of extinction, unable to guess the extent of the disaster that so nearly overcame them. Most fortunately for them, they were saved from that horror at the very last second. The small community of Jews holding Italian citizenship had enjoyed preferential treatment throughout the entire period—in practice, if not in principle—thanks to the protection granted them by the Italian authorities, primarily out of concern for their own political interests in the area. We cannot know, and probably should not even conjecture, how those same authorities would have acted under different circumstances.

In Tunisia, as had been the case in Algeria and Morocco, the Liberation did not solve the problems that the Jews faced as a small national minority in a foreign land—more precisely, in a land whose population had begun to struggle for its own national independence. In the area of legal and civil rights alone, the Jews of Tunisia had to wait three whole months, until 8 August 1943, for the repeal of the Statut des Juifs, which had set the legal basis for their discrimination, and of the laws and orders resulting from that statute. Even this was a real achievement by comparison to the situation in Algeria, where the antisemitic French administration—which continued the Vichy policy under Darlan and Giraud with the backing of the U.S. armed forces—prevented the restoration of civil rights to Jews for quite a while.[48]

Nor could the Jews, especially those who had been brought up in an atmosphere of French culture, easily forget the fact that, throughout those long and ugly years, there had existed "another" France, a France that had betrayed them, persecuted them, and refused to recognize their long-standing loyalty. "I had rejected the Orient," wrote Albert Memmi in the conclusion of his autobiography, "and the Occident rejected me."[49] Slowly but surely, many Jews began to believe—and, in time, to be certain—that Tunisia was no longer a place for Jews to live and that each individual Tunisian Jew now had to plan his or her own way for the future, in accordance with his or her personal and national views and the possibilities at his or her disposal. Now more than ever, the various segments of the Tunisian Jewish community began to share a common destiny with the rest of the Jewish people and to take part in the dilemmas, the hopes, and the disappointments of postwar Jewry as a whole.

# CONCLUSIONS

The behavior of the Italian authorities toward the Jews in the territories under their occupation in France and Tunisia—as well as in Croatia and Greece—was linked first and foremost with the complex political and economic factors directing Italian policy in those days. Clear evidence of this may be found both in the statements made by those concerned and in their actions, which, as has been described, were always aimed at attaining these political and economic objectives. However, this episode also touches on ideological and moral issues that only rarely and covertly find expression in diplomatic maneuvers and negotiations. It seems appropriate to consider these, too, even if only briefly.

These issues are on different planes. At the internal Italian level, is the matter of the general attitude of Italian fascism to the Jews in Italy and abroad—that is, in accordance with its own original conceptual position, irrespective of changing circumstances and passing political pressures. At the human level in general is the issue of individuals and national groups facing moral decisions whose implications are far more profound and far-reaching even than those of political decisions made by nations and politicians in times of crisis.

There is widespread agreement among scholars, writers, and thinkers that Italy was a country (or even "the only country") where "antisemitism did not strike roots,"[1] either in the liberal era—the first period in its history as a unified state—or in the days of the fascist regime. According to this view the legislation "for the defense of the race" that the fascist government enacted at the end of 1938 was fundamentally foreign to the social and cultural fabric of Italy, the direct or indirect effect of the pact with Nazi Germany that was taking shape in those years. This also explains the lack of response by Italian diplomats and military personnel when asked to assist their allies in implementing the arrest and deportation of Jews living in the regions they occupied.

Despite the evidence that supports this view, it is far from reflecting the problem in all its complexity, and it represents only a partial—and to a large degree even unbalanced—picture of events and motives. It is therefore appropriate to reexamine these assumptions from several aspects and to introduce some reservations in order to provide the proper explanation for the attitude of Italian fascism toward the Jews, with all the real and apparent reversals that took place and the reactions it aroused among different strata of the nation.

From the establishment of the united national state in 1861 until the start of the "race campaign"[2] in 1938 Italy did not have a "Jewish problem," or a problem of hatred for Jews, either as a popular phenomenon or as a factor of social or political significance. The small number of Jews in the country (around one in 1,000 of the total population) and their high degree of integration over many generations in local culture explain why emancipation of the Jews—the equality of civil rights that the Jews acquired in the second half of the nineteenth century—was chiefly a recognition in retrospect of the situation that had been in existence for many years.[3] The liberal secular state—which had arisen in a stubborn struggle against the temporal rule of the church—favored this process: in fact it allowed the Jews to become integrated in the society as well as the economy, and, in several cases, some even advanced to senior leadership positions. This happened despite the fact that not all were in agreement, even in the liberal camp,[4] and that prejudices originating in ancient Christian tradition toward the figure of the Jew and his character, occupation, and beliefs had certainly not disappeared among the population, especially in regions where the Jewish presence was more prominent. In the long run, however, it was not these factors that determined the position of the Jews and their continually improving social position in the new state.

A certain change took place at the end of the nineteenth century and in the first years of the twentieth century, when the new ideas of modern antisemitism with its nationalist and racist foundations originating in Germany, Austro-Hungary, and France penetrated even Italy. These ideas were at first accepted mainly among Catholic circles, in particular among those close to the Jesuit Order and its organ, *La Civiltà Cattolica*, who considered the time ripe for an attempt to graft something of the new antisemitism onto the ancient stem of Christian hatred for the Jews.[5] What is more important, however, was that these new conceptual currents affected the views of the nationalist circles, who arose in Italy during this period and merged at the end of 1910 to form a political movement. In the public writings and in literary works by some of their members, the image of the Jew did in fact appear more than once in the repellent stereotypes of a man ugly in appearance, greedy, lukewarm in his patriotic feelings, and indifferent to all those ideals of military glory and imperial greatness that were so fervently desired by the nationalists—a kind of symbol of democratic and pacifist bourgeoisie that they hated intensely and wanted to remove from the face of the earth.[6]

It is true that in those days this phenomenon remained mainly literary and had only little bearing on social or political reality. The Nationalist movement, which was principally an elitist movement, a weakly linked conglomerate of intellectual circles, never succeeded in expanding its influence among the masses (even though the nationalists also included personalities from the world of literature and art). On the other hand, it had some ideological influence on many of the founding members of the fascist movement during its early years,[7] at a time when fascism was still a militant, revolutionary anti-bourgeois body, extremist and violent, that attracted an increasing number of people (among whom there were in fact very few intellectuals).[8] In March 1923, the two movements finally joined forces in a single party, based on their shared views concerning the rejection of liberalism and democracy on the one hand, and of all streams of socialism on the other. From that time onward, many of the personalities originally from the Nationalist movement became a part of the new party, and some of them even advanced to leader positions in the regime (even if they never gained any decisive influence).

The union of the two movements, only a few months after the Fascist party seized control over the government, opened the roads for the nationalists to operational posts for the first time since their appearance on the political stage; and it seemingly gave them the opportunity to implement the principles of their doctrine, which until then they had merely been exhaustively debating theoretically. It was to be expected that they would wish to give some expression to the negative attitude toward the Jews that some of their members had expressed in their literary creations, even more so as on this subject the nationalist intellectuals had found influential allies among the ranks of the Fascist party itself, mainly among the founding members. Although the latter had not been engaged in creating Jewish negative characters in literary works, they combined their revolutionary anti-bourgeois and antidemocratic fervor with hostile propaganda against Jews that was verbally violent and possessed both nationalist and racist overtones.

Their most prominent representative was Roberto Farinacci, a longtime member of the Fascist party and one of the leaders of the "punitive squads" in northern Italy. At various periods Farinacci had filled central positions in the party and the state—despite his critical attitude to Mussolini, whose policies on internal and external affairs were too compromising for his taste.[9] As the most prominent representative of irrational "intransigent" fascism,[10] Farinacci during all those years stood at the head of the most extreme antisemitic faction within the Fascist party and the national institutions, going so far as to fully identify with the policies of Nazi Germany, including the Jewish topic. In the middle of the 1920s, when Farinacci held the position of party secretary, he became closely associated with a one-time priest, Giovanni Preziosi, a journalist editing the periodical *La Vita Italiana*, member of the Nationalist movement and, following the union, of the Fascist party. Preziosi had for a long time been engaged in the publication and distribution of antisemitic literature—including the well-known antisemitic libel *The Protocols of the Elders of Zion* in Italian—and was during the twenty years of the fascist regime the leading theoretician and propagandist in Italy of the most extreme, irrational, and racist antisemitism.[11]

This combination of elements from such different backgrounds—but to a large extent mutually complementary—was sufficient to arouse the fear (or from the nationalists' expectations) that in the new regime a significant change for the worse would sooner or later take place in the social and perhaps also in the legal status of the Jews. Warning voices on this note were in fact heard at that time from various Jewish personalities, particularly within the Zionist camp.[12] Although events seemed at first to have allayed the fears of all those who had anticipated an imminent change for the worse, reality in the long run showed that these fears had not been groundless.

Despite the opposition it initially aroused, the Fascist party seized power and held onto it, among other things thanks to its success in attracting all the forces of the antidemocratic right in the country. It gained support from those wishing to make an anti-bourgeois revolution, who dreamt of building "a new world order" and "a new civilization" upon its ruins, making use of violence according the principles of Sorel's doctrine. It also attracted Catholic and conservative circles of the old school, whose one objective was to prevent revolutions, restore the old order, and preserve everything as it was then. Fascism on the eve of its rise to power thus appeared in a number of forms, some seemingly contradictory, yet all equally were its true face. However, after the Fascist party came to power (and after it had silenced its opponents in parliament on the one hand and had removed its most militant and radical supporters from the reins of government on the other), from 1925 onward it established a totalitarian and antidemocratic regime, conservative and bourgeois in domestic policies, rational and realistic abroad. Of the original militancy of the "Fascist revolution" the regime had retained just the external mannerisms—the verbose extremist outbursts, the uniforms, the popular mass rallies, and the rattling of swords flourished from time to time to inflame the masses at home and cast sand in the eyes of politicians and opinion makers abroad.

The man who chose the course for the party after its rise to power and determined the nature of the regime was of course the Duce, Benito Mussolini, a man with two souls: that of the Sorelian syndicalist, the anti-bourgeois revolutionary, the nationalist dreaming of restoring the grandeur of Imperial Rome, alongside that of a realistic politician, cynical, opportunistic, familiar with the importance of international factors, and careful to avoid any head-on collision with them. These two souls, these two "fascisms," found clear expression in the various trends that characterized Mussolini's policies during the two periods into which the days of his regime may be divided: that between 1925 and 1936,[13] distinguished by the conduct of a rational conservative policy, and that between 1937 and 1943 that began after the establishment of the empire in Africa and ended with Mussolini's downfall. During this second period he strove to return to the irrational revolutionary roots of his movement, with all that this implied for the policies of his government in domestic affairs (among others the introduction of the racial laws) and foreign policy (first and foremost, the establishment of the Axis with Nazi Germany).[14]

The same intricate and apparent contradictions that could be discerned in Mussolini's general policy may also be found during the years of his rule in his policy toward Jews, in Italy and abroad. From both an emotional and an ideological point of view, Mussolini's personal attitude to the Jews and Judaism had always been negative, tinged with suspicion and intolerance. He rejected outright any attempt to grant Jews any political or even simply organizational expression beyond the narrow limits of their religious and communal institutions. He believed in the tremendous power of "international Judaism" and in its ability to influence far-reaching political moves, overtly and covertly, by means of international monetary circles in democratic countries, in the Soviet Union, and among the left-wing movements in every single country.[15] Acting as both prime minister and foreign minister, Mussolini was in the habit of taking a constant, almost obsessive interest in events within the "Jewish World." He kept himself informed—by regularly reading newspapers, including internal Jewish ones, by requesting reports from the Italian diplomatic delegations, or even by means of secret special envoys—of the smallest details of events and topics involving Jewish communities in Europe and America, including Zionist congresses, rabbinical councils, political trends, and cultural disputes.[16] Yet, just because of this excessive and unrealistic esteem for the power of Judaism, Mussolini took care to avoid confrontations with it as long as he was conducting a realistic and rational policy; on several occasions, he even tried to make use of Jewish communities outside Italy and of the World Zionist movement to raise loans from international banks or to further Italian interests in Mediterranean countries.[17]

This policy changed sharply in 1937–1938 and went to the other extreme, following the general changes that were taking place during those years in Mussolini's policies and in his views concerning the character of the regime and its ideological and political tendencies. The enactment of the racial laws and the introduction of the policy of social discrimination and economic dispossession of the Jews, on which the Fascist Grand Council had decided on 6 October 1938, were therefore not, as is often stated, the direct or indirect outcomes of the pact with Nazi Germany; rather, they were a political decision and an independent fascist ideological choice. To be more precise, it was a political decision conforming with the ideological sources of the Fascist party, or at least with those sources that Mussolini wanted to revive and on which he wanted to focus his political activity. The antisemitic policy of fascism was therefore not a foreign phenomenon that suddenly rushed onto the stage of Italian history, exploiting a moment of weakness that supposedly overcame the country's leadership. It was no casual accident on the road taken by the regime either. It was an irrational decision that matched the irrational and reckless trends in fascist policy of that period; a decision that gave political expression to ideological and literary sources that had long been hidden among some of the strands of the fascist movement and in the nationalist and Catholic circles that accompanied it or were absorbed within it. The antisemitic policy of the fascist regime was not a mere replica of what was happening north of the Alps, from the birth of modern antisemitic movements until the rise to power of the Nazi party, even though it developed alongside these movements and in their shadow—and more than once received from them its inspiration and some of its ideological foundations and external trappings.[18]

The change Mussolini made in his policy during 1937–1938 was to have catastrophic consequences for him and his regime, not to mention the Jews of Italy. For the first time since the fascist movement had been consolidated into a broadly based party, Mussolini with his own hands caused a breach in the consensus among the various factions of the antidemocratic right, a consensus on which he had relied over the years for his principal power. Broad sectors of the population which until then had supported the regime now began to draw away from him, either because they could no longer identify with him on matters of principle or because they feared his new policy would sooner or later lead to a deterioration in their own social standing and the loss of their economic achievements. The myths of creating "a new civilization" and of establishing "a new world order" did not captivate those whose principal object had always been the prevention of social revolutions and preservation of the status quo. The pact with Nazi Germany—which from the outset many had regarded as a step liable to lead to a dangerous military escapade—and the acceptance of the annexation of Austria to the Great Reich, which was one of the first and most embarrassing results of that pact, created a breach even within the fascist leadership. In June 1940, only five years after he had reached the pinnacle of his popularity following the foundation of the empire, Mussolini decided to throw his country into the military contest, although most of the nation was opposed to this step and many even within his own camp questioned his decision.[19]

The broad front of opposition aroused by Mussolini's policies of 1937–1938 did not disregard the measures against the Jews. Moreover, as indicated, the hatred of Jews was not widespread in modern Italy, even less so in its racist guise as Mussolini tried to impose it, which for historical and ethnic reasons was totally foreign to most Italians. Even within the fascist camp, many were therefore wondering about the meaning of these measures; finding no answers they dissociated themselves from the racial polices.[20] Others regarded the steps against the Jews as the beginnings of a move that was eventually liable to harm the whole stratum of the bourgeoisie to which they belonged, and so they opposed it from the outset, from a desire to protect themselves, just as there were some who believed in the myths of the "Fascist revolution" and the need for the pursuit of a policy of "defending the race" as a stage on the road to their implementation. In general, however, the steps against the Jews did not meet with the approval of society, just as the policy of the regime in those days did not enjoy broad public support. For the most part, people regarded them as distorted expressions of a mistaken policy.

Against the background of this complex situation, at the end of 1942 the Italian Army appeared as conqueror in several regions of southern France and in Tunisia—and before that also in Croatia and in Greece—and the question quickly arose of the fate of the Jews living in these areas. The German security authorities and their local camp-followers were insisting that these Jews be surrendered into their hands in order to implement their policy toward all of European Jewry, whereas the large majority of Italian diplomats and military personnel responsible for operations in these regions displayed a lack of readiness or even clearly opposed compliance with these demands and any collaboration with their allies on this matter.

As has already been indicated, the prime motives for adopting this attitude were connected with weighty political and economic considerations: some were of a generally strategic nature, arising from Italy's standing within the Axis camp, others were tactical and arose from the special conditions in each country. However, the question of the fate of the Jews in the countries occupied by the Italian Army did not remain in a vacuum in the eyes of those who were dealing with the matter; rather, it formed a part of the complex of problems confronting them during those years, following the change in policy of the regime. The position they adopted on the question of the Jews was therefore to some degree or other the outcome of the position they had adopted toward this policy as a whole and on all that derived from it—such as the pact with Nazi Germany and the race policy. Admittedly, there is no doubt that during the 1920s and 1930s most of the Italian diplomats and the military were among the supporters of the regime, whether out of ideology or for social status. Their inclinations, however, were for the most part toward the conservative rational fascism of the decade 1926–1936, not toward the anti-bourgeois trend of the late 1930s. Just as in 1938 their opposition to the new direction of Mussolini policy had been expressed among other things by their reservation concerning the introduction of the race laws, so during the war years this opposition directly and logically gave rise to their unwillingness to collaborate on the "Jewish question" with the German security forces in the occupied countries outside their own borders.

It must also be said that after details became known on the nature of the steps the Germans were taking toward the Jewish population in the countries they occupied (and quite detailed and precise information on this had already reached the Italians at the end of 1941 and the beginning of 1942 and had been fully understood), most Italian diplomats and military personnel expressed their deep revulsion and their unwillingness to be partners to this despicable crime.

The humane and sometimes even sympathetic attitude that many Italians displayed toward Jews in the Italian-occupied zones during World War II is not an act that may be credited to fascism—as has been written more than once (and not just by those writing its history with the prior intention of embellishing its actions). The reverse is true. It was mainly a further expression of the failure of fascism to generate a change in its policies and establish a regime that was to its own liking (or at least to the liking of those guiding its actions during those years). This was indeed the one and only ray of light for many Jews in southern France, Croatia, and Greece in the continuing darkness that engulfed their miserable lives in those days. This beam of light, however, did not arise from fascism. Rather, it sprang from people's dissent from fascism and from the policies it represented and was implementing in that period.

As for the individuals who participated in this operation, thanks to which were saved the lives of thousands of human beings, they surely proved to themselves and to their consciences that basic ethical norms are binding at all times, even in times of crisis—in such times more than ever—even when the majority of mankind disregards them; and devotion to these norms needs no apology.

# NOTES

## Abbreviations

*Archivio Storico, Ministero Affari Esteri*, ASMAE (Archives of the Italian Foreign Ministry), Affari Politici, AP (Political Affairs section), Rome.

*Archivio Storico, Stato Maggiore Esercito*, ASSME (Archives of the Italian Army, Ground Forces), *Commissione Italiana di Armistizio con la Francia*, CIAF (Armistice Commission with France), Rome.

*Centre de Documentation Juive Contemporaine*, CDJC (Jewish Documentation Center), Paris.

United Restitution Organisation, URO, Frankfurt am Main.

## Introduction (pp. 1–15)

1. At the time of the signing of the Steel Pact on 22 May 1939, von Ribbentrop declared to the Italian foreign minister, G. Ciano, that it was in Germany's interest and its intention to ensure a long period of peace "at least for three years" (G. Ciano, *Diario, 1937–1943*, Milan, 1980, p. 299).
2. The *Gran Consiglio del Fascismo*, the higher body of the Fascist party, was recognized by law after the fascists came to power as a national consultative body.
3. Ministero degli Affari Esteri, *I documenti diplomatici italiani*, nona serie: 1939–1943, vol. 3, Rome, 1959, p. 578. Mussolini explains there that the goals of the parallel war were to remove the bars and knock down the walls enclosing the "Mediterranean jail" in which Italy is incarcerated. The bars and walls to which he refers are Corsica, Bizerte, Malta, Gibraltar, and Suez.
4. R. Graziani, *Ho difeso la patria*, Milan, 1947, p. 202.
5. See on that G. Rochat and G. Massobrio, *Breve storia dell'esercito italiano dal 1861 al 1943*, Turin, 1978, pp. 270–275.
6. According to Ciano, Mussolini was indignant when he learned on 12 October 1940 of the German-Romanian pact that, among other things, allowed the German Army to pass through and encamp on Romanian soil. Mussolini declared to him: "Hitler always faces me with a *fait accompli*. This time I am going to pay him back in his own coin. He will find out from the papers that I have occupied" (*Diario*, p. 470).
7. Ciano, *Diario*, p. 443.
8. On these policy trends, as well as the differences of opinion concerning their implementation among the German leadership, see books written by two diplomats who were among those chiefly responsible for the implementation of Ger-

man foreign policy toward Vichy France, see O. Abetz, *Histoire d'une politique franco-allemande, 1930–1950. Mémoires d'un ambassadeur*, Paris, 1953; R. Rahn, *Un diplomate dans la tourmente*, Paris, 1980. See also E. Jäckel *La France dans l'Europe de Hitler*, Paris, 1968, particularly pp. 148–153, 228–258.

9. On the day of the signing of the armistice agreement, Ciano noted in his journal (*Diario*, p. 446): "I am not altogether certain that the Pétain government can succeed in imposing its will, especially on the Empire and on the Navy." Four months later, after the Montoire talks between Hitler, Pétain, and Laval, Ciano wrote that in his conversation with von Ribbentrop he did not conceal his doubts and suspicions regarding the Vichy government and that in any case "it is essential that the inclusion of France in the Axis camp shall not be to our detriment" (pp. 472–473). The Italian position against the policy of collaboration with France and doubts as to its benefit are reflected in many internal sources. Perhaps the most conspicuous among these are the protocols of the nine talks between Mussolini and the chairman of the Italian-French Armistice Commission, General Arturo Vacca Maggiolini, between 12 July 1941 and 12 February 1943 (ASSME, CIAF, various records).

10. The *zone occupée*, the Occupied Zone, was subordinated to the German military commander in France (Militärbefehlshaber in Frankreich). It included 55 percent of the area of France, 67 percent of the population, and 80 percent of its economic resources. Some northern districts of France were subordinated to the German Army staff in Belgium. Alsace and Lorraine were, in effect, annexed to the Reich.

11. On the period of Italian rule there, see J. L. Panicacci, "L'occupazione italiana di Mentone (giugno 1940–settembre 1943)," *Notiziario dell'Istituto Storico della Resistenza in Cuneo e Provincia*, 24 (1983), pp. 3–18.

12. Commissione Italiana di Armistizio con la Francia, CIAF. The position of chairman of that commission was occupied successively by General P. Pintor (27 June–7 December 1940), General C. Grossi (7 December 1940–16 June 1941), and General A. Vacca Maggiolini (16 June 1941–8 September 1943). Throughout most of its existence, the central figure of the CIAF was its secretary general, General F. Gelich (27 June 1940–20 December 1942), succeeded by Colonel E. Fioravanti (20 December 1942–8 September 1943). Operating beside the CIAF was a French representative body subordinate to the Vichy Ministry of War, the Délégation Française auprès de la Commission Italienne d'Armistice (DFCIA), commanded by Admiral E. Duplat. On its activity, see J. B. Duroselle, "Le gouvernement de Vichy face à l'Italie," in J. B. Duroselle and E. Serra (eds.), *Italia e Francia (1939–1945)*, 1, Milan, 1984, pp. 83–96.

13. According to the testimony of Ciano (*Diario*, p. 444) Mussolini made this a condition in relinquishing (until the peace negotiations) his remaining economic and territorial claims.

14. These were called R. Delegazione per il Rimpatrio e Assistenza Italiani all'Estero (Royal Delegations for Repatriation and Assistance to Italians Abroad) and were subordinate to the Foreign Ministry department in charge of affairs for

"Italians Abroad" (Direzione Generale degli Italiani all'Estero). Similarly, in Tunisia the Italians also returned their consular delegates under the guise of members of the Armistice Commission. See Chapter 9.

15. As a rule, the Germans were most meticulous about closing the foreign diplomatic delegations in the countries they occupied. However, they were not always able to resist the pressure of their allies who were interested in maintaining these delegations. The Italians were in fact prevented from maintaining their representative in Warsaw (but they had a delegate at the General Government in Cracow, the legal adviser Cesare Vernarecci di Fossombrone), but succeeded in keeping their delegations in Western Europe: in Oslo, the Hague, Brussels, and Paris. In the middle of 1941, the Germans demanded that these delegations also be closed. The matter was discussed at the highest level, during Mussolini's visit to the Führer's headquarters in East Prussia (August 1941). Following these talks, the German Foreign Ministry announced to the Italian Embassy in Berlin that "the Reich Government no longer insisted on their demand to close the Italian consular delegations in the occupied countries, in Norway, Holland, Belgium, and France." See report by the Italian ambassador in Berlin to the Foreign Ministry, 31 August 1941 (ASMAE, *Germania*, busta 73).

16. From Consul General Quinto Mazzolini to the Foreign Ministry, 22 March 1943 (ASMAE, AP, *Francia*, busta 68). Summary of his activity in Nice. On Consul Mazzolini, see also Chapter 1, note 26.

17. "Justice and Liberty," an antifascist movement of a social-democratic flavor founded in 1929 among the Italian intellectuals who had found refuge in France.

18. The literature on the subject is very extensive. See A. Garosci, "La concentrazione antifascista a Parigi," in C. Lupo (ed.) *Terzo programma. Trent'anni di storia politica italiana (1915–1945)*, Rome, 1962, pp. 185–196; P. Guillen, "La question des 'Fuorusciti' et les relations franco-italiennes (1925–1935)," in Duroselle and Serra (eds.), *Italia e Francia dal 1919 al 1939*, pp. 21–38; L. Valiani, "L'émigration antifasciste et la deuxième guerre mondiale," in Duroselle and Serra (eds.), *Italia e Francia (1939–1945)*, 1, pp. 285–294.

19. This evaluation is found in many documents issued by the Italian Consulate. See, for example, the report of Vice-Consul Pasquinelli of 23 September 1942 (CDJC, XLVIII-28); an internal note of the consulate of 28 January 1943; and a letter from Orlandini to the embassy in Paris of 29 January 1943 (CDJC, XLVIII-1, no. A.71.I).

20. According to a communication from the General Commissariat for Jewish Affairs of the Vichy Government to the Italian Consulate in Paris dated 18 December 1941, there were in the Seine Department 499 Italian Jews, 464 of them in Paris and 35 in the surroundings (CDJC, XLVIII-28).

21. Many of them had received the citizenship of the Grand Duchy of Tuscany in the days of the regime of Capitulations because of their commercial ties with the Jews of Livorno. After the unification of Italy (1860), they automatically became Italian citizens.

22. On Carlo Rosselli, see the monograph by A. Garosci, who of all the Italian antifascists in France was closest to him (*La vita di Carlo Rosselli*, Florence, 1945). On his brother Nello, see G. Belardelli, *Nello Rosselli, uno storico antifascista*, Florence, 1982. On both, see A. Levi, *Ricordi dei fratelli Rosselli*, Florence, 1947.

23. Chayim Enzo Sereni (born in Rome in 1905) was an outstanding leader of the Zionist-Socialist party in Palestine. After the outbreak of World War II he joined the British Army. He was parachuted into Italy still under German occupation, captured by German soldiers, and shot to death in Dachau concentration camp 18 November 1944.

24. Literature on the subject is very extensive. See E. Decleva, "L'unità d'azione alla prova: I socialisti italiani e il fronte popolare francese, 1934–1939," in Duroselle and Serra (eds.), *Italia e Francia dal 1919 al 1939*, pp. 303–339; idem, "Le delusioni di una democrazia: Carlo Rosselli e la Francia, 1929–1937," ibid., pp. 39–84.

25. See E. Serra, "Il confine meridionale della Libia e gli accordi Mussolini-Laval," in Duroselle and Serra (eds.), *Italia e Francia dal 1919 al 1939*, pp. 125–218; P. Milza, "Le voyage de Pierre Laval à Rome en janvier 1935," ibid., pp. 219–243.

26. See on the subject P. Milza, *L'Italie fasciste devant l'opinion française, 1920–1940*, Paris, 1967.

27. H. Michel, "Les relations franco-italiennes (de l'armistice de juin 1940 à l'armistice de septembre 1943)," in *La guerre en Méditerranée, 1939–1945*, Paris, 1971, p. 491; Duroselle, "Le gouvernement de Vichy," pp. 83–89.

28. See also Chapter 1, note 30.

29. In effect, until November 1942, in the meetings of the Italian-French Armistice Commission the subject of the situation of the Jews residing in the Unoccupied Zone was never brought up, neither in general terms nor on an individual level, despite the fact that the commission met on average once a week and often discussed individual cases in detail.

30. One case of this kind reported the Italian delegation in Nice to the embassy in Paris, 19 March 1942 (ASMAE, AP, *Francia*, busta 64/8, no. 51/38500/5922).

31. In those days, various antisemitic French sources published extremely inflated estimates of the number of Jews in France. The daily *Le Matin*, in a series of articles on 3, 4, and 5 June 1942, stated that their number was 1,200,000, of whom "over 350,000 had been absorbed in Paris and its vicinity." (The articles were published again in Ph. Ganier Raymond, *Une certaine France*, Paris, 1975, p. 73.) According to a report from the Italian Embassy in Paris of 15 August 1942, "a person from the General Commissariat for Jewish Affairs [had announced that], according to the latest census, out of 1,200,000 Jews residing on French territory only 150,000 were living in the Occupied Zone" (ASMAE, AP, *Francia*, busta 64/8, n. 2534/1311). The first general commissioner for Jewish affairs, Xavier Vallat, announced on 1 April 1941 that the Jews represented 2.4 percent of the total population of France. (This was 48 million souls, so in

this report Vallat repeated the estimate of 1,200,000 Jews.) In his well-known memorandum of 1 July 1941, the adviser (*Referent*) for Jewish affairs in France, T. Dannecker, estimated the number of Jews within the territory of the Vichy government as "between 400,000 and 800,000" (URO, *Dokümente über die Verantwortlichkeit des Reiches für die Judenmassnahmen im besetzten und unbesetzten Frankreich, insbesondere auch in Algerien, Marokko, Tunis*, Frankfurt am Main, 1959, p. 41). Most probably, the estimate of 700,000 Jews within the Unoccupied Zone, which is included in the protocol of the Wannsee Conference, arose out of these fanciful figures. See D. Carpi, "The Number of Jews in France according to the Wannsee Conference Protocol (January 1942)—Fantasy and Reality," *Massuah*, 13 (1985), pp. 129–132; D. Michman, "Historical Accuracy," *Yalkut Moreshet*, 45 (1988), pp. 197–200; A. Cohen, "L'échec de la propagande du Commissariat Général face aux questions juives en France," in *Idéologie et propagande en France*, Paris, 1987, pp. 206–207.

32. On 27 September 1940, when life in France was beginning to return to normal and after the signing of the armistice agreement, the German Military Government published an order forbidding Jews who had fled to southern France to return to their homes in the Occupied Zone (CDJC, *Les juifs sous l'occupation. Recueil des textes français et allemands, 1940–1944*, Paris, 1945, pp. 18–19). See also Chapter 1.

33. Ibid., p. 53.

34. This estimate is found in many sources. See, among others, the memorandum from Dannecker of 28 February 1941 (URO, *Judenverfolgung in Frankreich*, p. 24).

35. Several scholars have expressed the opinion that not all Jews were included in the census figures. See S. Klarsfeld, *Vichy-Auschwitz. Le rôle de Vichy dans la solution finale de la question juive en France 1942*, 1, Paris, 1983, p. 24; L. Lazar, *La résistance juive en France*, Paris, 1987, p. 49. However, this assertion is by no means certain.

## 1: Social Discrimination and Economic Restrictions (pp. 19 – 38)

1. *Verordnung über Massnahmen gegen Juden*. In all, the German Military Government in France published nine orders against the Jews (27 September 1940– 8 July 1942). These orders were effective in the Occupied Zone only, but the laws of the Vichy government were valid in both zones. Both the orders of the German Military Government and the laws of the Vichy government were published by the Centre de Documentation Juive Contemporaine (CDJC, *Recueil des textes*).

2. CDJC, *Recueil des textes*, p. 25. The German source reads "komissarischer Verwalter." The official French translation in one place reads "commissaire administrateur," and in another "administrateur provisoire." In the laws published later, they were also called "commissaires-gérants."

3. CDJC, *Recueil des textes*, pp. 27–29.

4. He was considered one of the moderates in the German officer corps in his relations to the civilian population and was replaced in February 1942 by his cousin Karl Heinrich von Stülpnagel. The instructions of 12 November 1940, signed by him, were issued by the Economic Department of the Military Government (Verwaltungsstab, Abteilung Wirtschaft) headed by Dr. Elmar Michal. On the activities of Dr. Michal in the years he held this position in France, from 13 July 1940 till 17 August 1944, see his evidence in Hoover Institution, *France during the German Occupation, 1940–1944*, 3, Paris, 1959, pp. 1622–1635. The man in charge of Jewish affairs in this department was Dr. Haut Blanke.

5. CDJC, *Recueil des textes*, pp. 29–30.

6. C. Browning, *The Final Solution and the German Foreign Office*, New York-London, 1978, pp. 49–50.

7. He served in the consulate in Paris from August 1936 to September 1943. In the summer of 1940 he was still vice-consul. Was later appointed consul general.

8. From Consul Orlandini to the Foreign Ministry, 6 October 1940 (CDJC, XLVIII-28, no. 1060/606).

9. One of the senior officials at the ministry, he served in this capacity from October 1937.

10. From the head of the Department for Italians Abroad to the Italian Consulate in Paris, 29 November 1940 (CDJC, XLVII-28, no. 37616/2262; ASMAE, AP, *Francia*, busta 66).

11. From Dr. Michal to the Italian Consulate in Paris, 14 January 1941, summary of the conversations (CDJC, XLVIII-28, Abt. Wi. I/5277/41).

12. See also Chapter 10, note 8.

13. From Consul Orlandini to the Foreign Ministry, Department for Italians Abroad, 18 January 1941 (CDJC, XLVIII-28, no. 494/385).

14. From the head of the Department for Italians Abroad to the Italian Consulate in Paris, 1 February 1941 (CDJC, XLVIII-28, no. 9630).

15. From Consul Orlandini to the Foreign Ministry, 28 February 1941 (CDJC, XLVIII-28, no. 1501/1091).

16. The reply telegram, signed by de Cicco, was sent for some reason by way of the Delegation of the Armistice Commission in Lyon, and they transmitted it to Paris on 3 May 1941 (CDJC, XLVIII-28, no. 14755).

17. From the consulate in Paris to the Foreign Ministry, Department for Italians Abroad, 14 May 1941 (CDJC, XLVIII-28, no. 3669/275).

18. From the consul general in Vienna, Roschira, to the Italian Embassy in Berlin, 7 March 1941 (CDJC, XLVIII-28, no. 1879).

19. This office (from 1937 Ministero della Cultura Popolare) was notorious for the pedantic—at times senseless—supervision that it imposed on the activities of the media and also in the various spheres of art and culture. On 25 July 1943, Alfieri participated in the meeting of the Fascist Grand Council and voted for the proposal to dismiss Mussolini. For that, he was condemned to death in his absence (January 1944). After the war he published his memoirs: *Deux dictateurs face à face. Rome-Berlin, 1939–1943*, Paris, 1948. On his activi-

ties in Berlin, see also the uncomplimentary words published after the war by one of his assistants, L. Simoni, *Berlino, Ambasciata d'Italia, 1939–1943*, Rome, 1946.

20. From the Italian ambassador in Berlin to the Foreign Ministry in Rome, 31 March 1941 (CDJC, XLVIII-28, no. 04082/896).

21. From Leonardo Vitetti to the Italian Embassy in Berlin, 11 May 1941 (CDJC, XLVIII-28, no. 34/R/4948/38). Vitetti, one of the senior Italian diplomats, stood at the head of the Political Department (Direzione Generale Affari Generali, AG) from September 1936 until the beginning of January 1942. Afterward, he was director of the Department for Affairs of Europe and the Mediterranean (Affari Europa e Mediterraneo, AEM), and on the strength of this position he was also in charge of the affairs of France. After the war he was ambassador in Washington and Paris. See E. Serra, "Leonardo Vitetti e una sua testimonianza," *Nuova Antologia*, 519 (1973), pp. 487–501.

22. From the Italian Embassy in Berlin to twenty-two consulates subordinate to them (CDJC, XLVIII-28, no. 5643).

23. From the Italian Consulate in Paris (CDJC, XLVIII-28). The copy of the letter has no date, it appears to be from the last week in May 1941.

24. CDJC, *Recueil des textes*, pp. 47–49.

25. See the exchange of letters between Consul Orlandini (or Advocate Indelli) and the head of the Economic Department of the Military Government, Dr. Michal (or his assistant Dr. Blanke), of 18 and 26 June and 25 July 1941 (CDJC, XLVIII-28, Abt. Wi. I/2, Az. 7719/41; no. 4611).

26. On Consul Mazzolini, his personality, and some of his activities, see: J.R. Molho, "Documents for Holocaust Research in the Community of Greece and the Efforts for Rescue," *Otzar Yehude Sefarad*, 4 (1961), pp. 155–163; Idem, "Count Quinto Mazzolini, One of the Saviours of the Jews of Rhodes," *Otzar Yehude Sefarad*, 5 (1962), pp. 155–157; H. M. Franco, *Les Martyrs Juifs de Rhodes et des Cos*, Elisabethville, 1952, pp. 29–74.

27. From Consul Mazzolini to the Foreign Ministry, 12 June 1941 (CDJC, XLVIII-28, no. 19/R).

28. In fact, in a report he presented on 22 March 1943, on completion of his service in Nice, Mazzolini could state with satisfaction that the assistance that the delegation had extended to all the Jews who were in that place—Italians, French, and even refugees from occupied countries—was of immediate service to the Italian authorities and improved their image in the eyes of all the local population (ASMAE, AP, *Francia*, busta 68).

29. From the head of the Department for Italians Abroad to the Italian Consulate in Paris (copy to the consulate in Nice), 28 June 1941 (CDJC, XLVIII-28, no. 51/52663/1359). To be precise, in Italy there also was a lack of consistency in the application of the racial laws to foreigners, and holders of American and Turkish nationality were exempt from most of the restrictions.

30. See Duroselle, "Le gouvernement de Vichy," pp. 83–89, 92–93; Ciano, *Diario*, pp. 520, 523, 564–565. On 5 September 1941, on his return from a visit to Hitler

on the eastern front, Mussolini already informed General Vacca Maggiolini, head of the Armistice Commission with France, that "the time was not yet ripe for negotiating with France on agreements between the two countries" (ASSME, CIAF, racc. 51/1). The only achievement that Darlan obtained in this sphere, his meeting with Ciano in Turin on 10 December 1941 (one day before Italy declared war on the United States!) became a ceremonial event without purpose.

31. The agreement dealt with three main subjects: (1) transporting equipment and supplies via the harbor of Bizerte to the Axis forces in North Africa; (2) placing bases in West Africa at the disposal of the German submarine fleet; (3) placing bases in Syria at the disposal of Axis forces operating in, or about to be sent to Iraq. See Abetz, *Mémoires*, pp. 200–215; Jäckel, *La France*, pp. 235–251.

32. Memorandum extending over dozens of pages, from SS-Obersturmführer Theodor Dannecker of 1 July 1941. Excerpts from it were published in URO, *Judenverfolgung in Frankreich*, pp. 37–42. Dannecker served for two years, till the end of July 1942 in the capacity of adviser for Jewish affairs (Juden-referent) in France. In the course of his service, he was promoted to the rank of SS-Hauptsturmführer. Later on, he served in the same capacity in Bulgaria, Hungary, and Italy. It should be pointed out that the words of Dannecker were written thirty days before the dispatch of the letter from Göhring to Heydrich, in which he ordered him to begin the necessary preparation for carrying out "the solution to the Jewish question in European territories under German in-fluence" (J. Robinson and H. Sachs, *The Holocaust. The Nuremberg Evidence*, Jerusalem, 1976, p. 136, no. 2014).

33. Although this organization (Union Générale des Israélites de France, UGIF) was established in November 1941, the discussions concerning its creation began a few months before that. See R. J. Cohen, *The Burden of Conscience, French Jewry's Response to the Holocaust*, Bloomington and Indianopolis, 1987.

34. URO, *Judenverfolgung in Frankreich*, p. 44. SS-Sturmbannführer Dr. Helmut Knochen served in the Security Police and the SD in France for four years, until August 1944. In the first two years, he was subordinate to the commander of the Security Police in Belgium and in France. In March 1942, he was promoted to the rank of SS-Standartenführer, and in May 1942, after General C. A. Oberg came to France, he was appointed commander of the Security Police and the SD (Befehlshaber der Sipo und des S.D.) in France. On his activity in France, see also his testimony, Hoover Institution, *France during the German Occu-pation*, 3, pp. 1635–1644. The announcement by Knochen precedes, by three months, the orders sent in the name of Himmler to the commander of the Security Police in Belgium and France, on 23 October 1941 (CDJC, XXV b-7). Actually Heydrich's office had already issued instructions on 20 May 1941 to halt the emigration from France and Belgium (URO, *Dokumentsammlung über die Judenverfolgung in Rumanien*, 1, Frankfurt am Main, 1959, pp. 131–133). The first reason given for this prohibition was that emigration from France

and Belgium was liable to reduce the prospects of emigration of the Jews of Germany, in which there was special interest. In its later part, however, the document says that the prohibition was made "in consideration of the Final Solution of the Jewish Problem, which no doubt is imminent." In other words, both trends coexisted.

35. On these two camps, see H. Bulawko and D. Diamant, *Pithiviers et Beaune-la-Roland*, Paris, 1951; J. Weill, *Contribution à l'histoire des camps d'internement dans l'anti-France*, Paris, 1946.

36. The Drancy camp was opened on 20 August 1941 to receive the thousands of Jews arrested that day. See the detailed bibliography published by S. Klarsfeld, *Vichy-Auschwitz*, 1, p. 533. See also M. Marrus and R. Paxton, *Vichy France and the Jews*, New York, 1981, pp. 241–255.

37. Report from the commander of the Paris police of 21 August 1941 that quotes from the operation orders given him on 18 August 1941 (Klarsfeld, *Vichy-Auschwitz*, 1, pp. 26–27).

38. In 1947, in the course of the trial against him, Xavier Vallat declared that "for diplomatic and political reasons" Jews having citizenship of several countries—Romania, Turkey, Bulgaria, and Hungary—were not arrested in that manhunt (*Le procès de Xavier Vallat présenté par ses amis*, Paris, 1948, p. 123). But this does not agree with the text of the order issued and certainly does not agree with the facts.

39. From Consul Orlandini to the German Embassy in Paris, 22 August 1941 (CDJC, XLVIII-4/5).

40. Luciolli served first in the consulate in Lyon, was vice-consul in Paris from the beginning of August 1941 until the beginning of June 1942, and was later transferred to Munich. During the time of his stay in Paris he dealt with the affairs of Italian Jews.

41. From the German Military Government to the Italian Consulate in Paris, 9 December 1941 (CDJC, XLVIII-28, Abt. Verw., Az. 285/01/797/41). To be precise, the German announcement included the names of twelve Jews, of whom eleven were included in the list of the Italians, and one more, Mr. Oppenheimer, who until then had not been mentioned in any list. The two Jews who were not released were Elia Levi and Samuele Hemsi. They apparently did not succeed in proving that they had Italian citizenship.

42. From the German Military Government to the Italian Consulate in Paris, 20 January 1942 (CDJC, XLVIII-28, Abt. Verw., Az. V pol. 285/01).

43. CDJC, XLVIII-11. This letter, like all the letters from the detainees at Drancy and like most of those from their families, was written in French. After the war, Nissim Calef published his memoirs (*Campo di rappresaglia*, Rome, 1946).

44. The correspondence on matters connected with the confiscation of Jewish property and the appointment of trustees over it is very extensive, both during October and November 1941 and in the first half of 1942. Participating in it beside people from the consulate and from the German Military Government are also French authorities objecting to the granting of a special status to the Ital-

ian Consulate, as well as representatives of Italian economic organizations in France (Federazione delle Associazioni Economiche Italiane in Francia) who were trying to get their hands on a part of the Jewish property.

45. From Vice-Consul Giovanni Luciolli to the Foreign Ministry, 4 September 1941 (CDJC, XLVIII-28, no. 6144/5126). Report on the "Treatment of the Italian Jews in France." The German order concerning the confiscation of radio receivers was published in CDJC, *Recueil des textes*, p. 72.

46. From Vice-Consul Luciolli to the Foreign Ministry, 16 October 1941 (CDJC, XLVIII-28, no. 7213/6101).

47. From Consul Orlandini to the Foreign Ministry, 13 December 1941 (CDJC, XLVIII-28, no. 8772/7515). Clearly the first suggestion on the matter, signed by Luciolli, was sent with the knowledge of Orlandini (and may have been sent according to his direct instructions).

48. The report of the *prefetto* of Turin from 23 March 1942 was brought to the attention of the Italian Consulate in Paris on 24 May 1942 by the head of Ciano's cabinet, Marquis Blasco Lanza d'Ajeta (CDJC, XLVIII-28, no. 34 R/5158). The *prefetto* mentions in great detail the case of two Jews stuck at Bardonecchia, Nissim Calef and Vittorio Pardo-Roquez, both released from Drancy. The writer did not specify to what "instructions" he was referring. The law "for the protection of the race" of 17 November 1938 (art. 24) stated that all foreign Jews who entered the country after 1 January 1919 would have to leave the territory of the state by 12 March 1939. However, there was no clause "encouraging" the emigration of Italian Jews. Apparently the Ministry of the Interior had issued internal instructions to the *prefetti* whose aims were to encourage emigration.

49. From Ambassador Gino Buti to the Foreign Ministry, 30 May 1942 (CDJC, XLVIII-28, no. 1383/754). Buti was one of the senior Italian diplomats. He stood at the head of the Department for the Affairs of Europe and the Mediterranean (AEM) from 1936 until January 1942 when he was named ambassador in Paris.

50. From Consul Orlandini to the Foreign Ministry, 10 June 1942 (CDJC, XLVIII-28, no. 4080/3385).

51. From Marquis Blasco Lanza d'Ajeta to the Italian Consulate in Paris, 25 June 1942 (CDJC, XLVIII-28, no. 34/R/6327/37). D'Ajeta indicates that a circular on the matter had been sent out by the Department for Italians Abroad on 11 November 1941 to all the Italian delegations. This circular was thus issued a short time after receipt of Luciolli's proposal (which was dated 16 October 1941), and it is not impossible that there was a connection between the two and that the purpose was to foil the initiative of the consulate in Paris.

52. CDJC, *Recueil des textes*, pp. 107–108.

53. From Consul Orlandini to the Foreign Ministry, 18 December 1941 (CDJC, XLVIII-28). On 10 December, Darlan, who was then acting as deputy prime minister, announced that all the foreign Jews who had entered France after 1 January 1936 would be recruited into special labor battalions, but the text

of the resolution that the Ministry of the Interior published on 2 January 1942 stated clearly that "Jews enjoying the protection of their country of origin" were exempt from this duty (CDJC, *Recueil des textes*, p. 129). Hence, the Italian citizens were from the start exempt from this obligation.

54. It was established at the end of March 1941 with the goal of dealing all the aspects of the Vichy government's anti-Jewish policy. From 29 March 1941 until 6 May 1942, the veteran antisemite Xavier Vallat headed the Commissariat, followed by Louis Darquier de Pellepoix. See J. Billig, *Le Commissariat Général aux Question Juives, 1941–1944*, vols. 1–3, Paris, 1955–1960. Vallat published his memoirs after the war (*Le nez de Cléopâtre. Souvenirs d'un homme de droit, 1919–1944*, Paris, 1957) and testimony on his wartime activities (Hoover Institution, *France during the German Occupation*, 2, pp. 626–647). See also the book published by his friends, *Le procès de Xavier Vallat*. See also Marrus and Paxton, *Vichy France*, pp. 96–112; and R. Millman, *La question juive entre les deux guerres*, Paris, 1992, according to index. On Darquier de Pellepoix, see Chapter 2, note 2.

55. See the extensive correspondence between the three bodies: the consulate, the General Commission for Jewish Affairs, and the Military Government (CDJC, XLVIII-28).

56. Protocol of the meeting, from 27 June 1942, probably signed by Vice-Consul Pasquinelli (CDJC, XLVIII-28). On 7 July 1942, Consul Orlandini sent a detailed summary of these decisions to the Foreign Ministry (ibid., no. 4867/4036). Missing in this summary—surely not by accident—is the last paragraph, concerning the transfer of money in evasion of the German prohibition. Also stated in this summary was the consulate's proposition that the bank accounts would, from the outset, be in their name. On 21 August 1942, the ministry approved the consulate's proposals (ibid., no. 34/R/8334/308). It should be noted that from the end of May 1941, Aryan French (and, of course, also Aryan Italians) had been allowed to transfer sums of money from one zone to the other.

57. CDJC, *Recueil des textes*, p. 155. From the start, the Germans had wanted the Vichy authorities to publish an order for this, so that the obligation would apply to the Jews in both zones. When they did not succeed, they published their own "Order Number Eight," which of course only applied to Jews of the Occupied Zone. On the whole episode, see L. Poliakov, *L'étoile jaune*, Paris, 1949, pp. 21–42.

58. From Ambassador Buti to the Foreign Ministry, 20 May 1942 (ASMAE, *Francia*, busta 64/8). See also the letter from the ambassador to the Italian consulates in Bordeaux, Dijon, Le Havre, Nantes, Reims, and Nancy of 1 June 1942 (CDJC, XLVIII-28, no. 1428). This "achievement" on which the Italians very much prided themselves was in fact quite modest, for after considerable hesitation and even before they published the order, the Germans had decided that it would not apply to the citizens of countries where this obligation was not current (Poliakov, *L'étoile jaune*, pp. 36–38).

## 2: The Massive Manhunts and the Deportation to the East (pp. 39–61)

1. On his activities in that period see also his evidence, written in 1945 while he was in prison, and where, of course, he stressed his part "in the protection of the Jews" (Hoover Institution, *France during the German Occupation*, 1, pp. 526–533).

2. Head of the Rassemblement Anti-Juif de France. See Klarsfeld, *Vichy-Auschwitz*, 1, pp. 50–51; J. Laloum, *La France antisémite de Darquier de Pellepoix*, Paris, 1979.

3. On his activities in France since May 1942, see S. Klarsfeld, "Notices biographiques des principaux responsables de la 'Solution Finale' en France," in J. Billig, *La Solution Finale de la question juive*, Paris, 1977, pp. 198–201. Heydrich himself came to Paris (and stayed there between 5 and 12 May 1942) in order to demonstrate by his presence the importance he accorded the entry of Oberg to the position. In the course of his visit, Heydrich met Darquier, who had just been appointed to his new post. According to Italian sources, on leaving the meeting Darquier had declared that "severe and tough steps" would be taken against the Jews in order to purify France from the "spirit of Judaism" that was threatening to "emasculate and bastardize the spirit of the French people forever" (Commissione Italiana di Armistizio con la Francia, *Notiziario Quindicinale relativo ai territori francesi sotto controllo armistiziale*, 35 [May 1942], p. 37).

4. He replaced Theodor Dannecker toward the end of July 1942. On his activities in France in the course of two years see Klarsfeld, *Vichy-Auschwitz*, 1, according to index; Marrus and Paxton, *Vichy France*, according to index.

5. Memorandum signed by Dannecker, 15 June 1942 (URO, *Judenverfolgung in Frankreich*, pp. 75–76).

6. Report from SS-Sturmbannführer Herbert-Martin Hagen of 4 July 1942 (Klarsfeld, *Vichy-Auschwitz*, 1, pp. 227–232); report from Dannecker of 6 July 1942 (ibid., pp. 235–236; URO, *Judenverfolgung in Frankreich*, pp. 86–87).

7. On 30 May, Ambassador Buti had already reported to the Foreign Ministry that "according to available information new measures will shortly be taken against the Jews in the Occupied Zone. Among these measures there will apparently be: the obligation to wear the yellow star, further deterioration in the economic sphere and more severe measures concerning the deportations" (ASMAE, AP, *Francia*, busta 64/8, no. 3731 R.).

8. On this, see D. Carpi, "The Rescue of Jews in the Italian Zone of Occupied Croatia," *Rescue Attempts during the Holocaust*, Jerusalem, 1977, pp. 470–476, 508–511; Idem, "The Italian Diplomat Luca Pietromarchi and His Activities on Behalf of the Jews of Croatia and Greece," *Yalkut Moreshet*, 33 (1982), pp. 145–152; M. Shelah, *History of Holocaust. Yugoslavia*, Jerusalem, 1990, pp. 227–276.

9. From d'Ajeta to the Italian Embassy in Paris, 25 June 1942 (CDJC, XLVIII-28, no. 34/R/6327/37). This telegram was preceded by another, of 28 May, signed by the foreign minister himself, that dealt with the matter of protecting the

Jews of Italian nationality in Tunisia, based on reasons very similar to those detailed here (see Chapter 10). It is clear, therefore, that the telegram signed by d'Ajeta was sent with the approval and in accordance with the foreign minister's instructions.

10. See Chapter 1, note 10.

11. After the war he published his memoirs, in which he attempted to stress the "moderate stance" he had taken there toward Jews at the time of his service as ambassador in Paris (*D'une prison*, Paris, 1949, pp. 165–168, 268–279).

12. URO, *Judenverfolgung in Italien, den italienisch besetzten Gebieten und in Nordafrika*, Frankfurt am Main, 1962, p. 47.

13. See Introduction, note 12.

14. From General Gelich to the chairman of the Armistice Commission, 4 July 1942 (ASSME, CIAF, racc. 3/3, doc. 76, pp. 9–10). On this conversation, see Chapter 10, note 58.

15. From Ambassador Abetz to the Foreign Ministry, 4 July 1942 (Doc. NG 133, photocopy in *Yad Vashem* archives, Jerusalem, JM 2013).

16. He served in this capacity from the beginning of May 1940 until the beginning of April 1943, when he was dismissed from his post and placed under arrest in Sachsenhausen camp. The Third Office (Referat III) of the German Department was in charge of Jewish affairs. On the activities of this office and the man heading it, see Browning, *The German Foreign Office*, according to index and in particular pp. 23–28.

17. He served in this capacity from 1 July 1938 until the end of July 1943. From the beginning of August 1943, he served as German ambassador to the Vatican and was linked with the silencing action that was performed at the Holy See during the days of the manhunt after the Jews of Rome (16–17 October 1943). After the war, he published his *Erinnerungen*, Munich, 1950. On his activities in Berlin until July 1943, see also Browning, *The German Foreign Office*, according to index.

18. URO, *Judenverfolgung in Italien*, pp. 58–59.

19. From Ambassador Buti to the Foreign Ministry, 16 July 1942 (ASMAE, AP, *Francia*, busta 64/8, no. 22145 PR).

20. He replaced Giovanni Luciolli in June 1942 and was in charge of day-to-day handling of the affairs of Italian Jews in the Occupied Zone.

21. From Consul Orlandini to the command of the German Security Police and SD, 4 August 1942 (CDJC, XLVIII-28, no. 5516). Translation into French in L. Poliakov, *La condition des Juifs en France sous l'occupation italienne*, Paris, 1946, p. 49. The translation of the document mistakenly stated that the meeting had taken place on 21 July (instead of 31 July), and hence the mistake slipped into many other publications. This book has been translated into Italian, English, and Yiddish. But the Italian and German documents have been translated in these three languages from the French translation and the result is often quite erroneous. I prefer therefore to quote the French edition, with a few exceptions, which are always pointed out.

22. From Röthke to the German Embassy in Paris, 21 August 1942 (photocopy

of the document *Yad Vashem* archives, Jerusalem, TR-3, 720; Poliakov, *La condition des juifs*, p. 50).

23. Five days later, Röthke transmitted a note—no less indignant in style—on the same subject to the participants of a working meeting about to take place in Berlin at the IVB4 Department of the Reich Security Main Office. He repeated his accusations against the officials of the Italian Consulate in Paris and his decision not to have any dealings with them in the future. He also expressed the opinion (that at that meeting was represented by his assistant, SS-Untersturmführer Horst Ahrent) that the exemption from wearing the badge that had been granted to the citizens of a number of countries should be canceled, or at least should in the first stage be canceled for the citizens of European countries. Röthke explained that if this was done, it would be possible to include these Jews with the other candidates for deportation. See note by Röthke of 26 August (Klarsfeld, *Vichy-Auschwitz*, I, pp. 365–366). Röthke's proposal was discussed at a meeting that took place in Berlin on 28 August and on which Ahrent reported on 1 September 1942 (ibid., pp. 392–393). Eichmann agreed in principle to the proposal but declared that the matter was in the hands of the Foreign Ministry and that no satisfactory solution had yet been found.

24. From Ambassador Buti to the Foreign Ministry, 4 August 1942 (ASMAE, AP, *Francia*, busta 64/8, no. 8326). On 24 August 1942 the Political Department sent a copy of the Ambassador's letter to the Department for Italians Abroad (ibid., no. 2378/1248), so that this department would also be aware of the agreement that had supposedly been reached.

25. From Ambassador Buti to the Italian consulates in France, 15 September 1942 (CDJC, XLVIII-28, no. 3048).

26. Klarsfeld, *Vichy-Auschwitz*, I, pp. 484, 487–493. In view of this development, the meaning of the obscure sentence in Röthke's memorandum of 30 October 1942 becomes clear: "As the German Embassy in Paris has informed us, from now on it is also possible to deport the Jews of Greek nationality" (ibid., p. 484). Until then, the German security forces in France had for political or diplomatic reasons been restrained from including the Greek Jews in the deportation operation; now this restraining factor had been removed.

27. Browning, *The German Foreign Office*, p. 104; Klarsfeld, *Vichy-Auschwitz*, I, pp. 447, 451–454, 473.

28. Klarsfeld, *Vichy-Auschwitz*, I, pp. 365–366, 393, 420, 429, 473, 484.

29. Memorandum of 6 October 1942 from M. Luther, in which are quoted the words spoken by Döme Sztójay, the ambassador of Hungary in Berlin, in a conversation held on 11 August 1942 (*Trials of War Criminals before the Nuremberg Military Tribunals*, XIII, Washington, 1952, pp. 259–261).

30. Note by Röthke of 26 August 1942 (Klarsfeld, *Vichy-Auschwitz*, I, pp. 365–366).

31. Memorandum of 21 August 1942 (URO, *Judenverfolgung in Italien*, pp. 61–66, particularly pp. 64–65). See also *Trials of War Criminals*, pp. 243–249.

32. See D. Carpi, "Notes on the History of the Jews of Greece during the Holocaust Period," *Festschrift in Honor of Dr. George S. Wise*, Tel Aviv, 1981, pp. 31–32; idem, *Jews in Croatia*, pp. 472–477.

33. From Luther to the German Embassy in Rome, 17 September 1942 (URO, *Judenverfolgung in Italien*, pp. 79–80).

34. The note of von Bismarck for some reason was not preserved in the *France* files of the Foreign Ministry's archives. But two copies of the document, completely identical in content, are to be found in other sections: one in the *Yugoslavia* files of the political department of the Ministry (ASMAE, AP, *Jugoslavia*, busta 138/8), and one in the files of the Italian Consulate in Paris (CDJC, XLVIII-28). Prince Otto von Bismarck, grandson of the chancellor, served in various diplomatic capacities in the German Foreign Ministry from the mid-1920s. From April 1940 until August 1943 he was first secretary in the German Embassy in Rome.

35. Carpi, *Jews in Croatia*, pp. 475, 512; idem, "The Italian Diplomat Luca Pietromarchi and His Activities on Behalf of the Jews in Croatia and Greece," *Yalkut Moreshet*, 33 (1982), pp. 145–152 (in Hebrew). Count Pietromarchi in his diary interpreted these words simply: "per distruggerli" (for their destruction).

36. Hinting at laws against Jews, published in Tunisia at the instigation of the Vichy government. Although these were intended to harm the Jews, the whole Italian community, in which the Jews occupied important economic and social positions, was liable to be harmed because of them. On this, see Chapter 10.

37. ASMAE, AP, *Jugoslavia*, busta 138/8.

38. It should be emphasized that despite the fact that Mussolini agreed to the Germans' demands, the officials of the Foreign Office and officers of the Italian Army in fact prevented the surrender of the Jewish refugees from Croatia. See Carpi, *Jews in Croatia*.

39. CDJC, XLVIII-28, no. 34/R-110117/297. Ambassador Buti sent a copy of this document to the consulates in Paris and Vichy on 3 November 1942 (no. 3859).

40. URO, *Judenverfolgung in Italien*, pp. 100–103.

41. The *Gabinetto, Armistizio e Pace*, GABAP was set up in the spring of 1941, a short time after the invasion by the Axis forces of Yugoslavia and Greece. Its task was to handle all the political matters connected with these countries and to prepare the peace treaties with them.

42. Carpi, "Pietromarchi," p. 149. The fact that this note is from 10 December 1942 cannot raise any uncertainty as to whether the writer was referring to another decision of the Duce. Pietromarchi was in the habit of recording daily in his diary the events of the day, and from time to time to expand the entry, bringing examples and estimations from similar or parallel occurrences that had happened in the past or in some other place. Thus, in the entry for 10 December 1942, Pietromarchi discussed the situation of the Jews in Croatia and Greece and incidentally mentions what had happened in the recent past concerning the Jews of France.

43. Ciano, *Diario*, p. 655.

44. H. Krausnick, "Himmler über seinen Besuch bei Mussolini vom 11–14 Oktober 1942," *Vierteljahrshefte für Zeitgeschichte*, 4 (1956), pp. 423–426. The purpose of Himmler's visit to Rome was to test the truth of the rumors that had reached Berlin concerning the undermining of the popularity of the fascist regime among the Italian people and the spread of opposition to the continued participation in the war. Himmler provided Hitler with a very optimistic report that was far from reflecting the truth. He also mentioned that the Jewish question had been very extensively discussed in his conversation with Mussolini.

45. See also Chapter 6.

46. See note 19.

47. These two letters have not been preserved. They are quoted extensively in a memorandum that the Italian Consulate sent on 12 September 1942 (see note 56).

48. In fact, this obligation did not apply to Italian citizens, but it appears that she had received French citizenship on her marriage. The letter of 25 August 1942 is preserved in the German documentation (CDJC, XXVa-211). The other letters are quoted in the memorandum of the Italian Consulate of 12 September 1942 (footnote 56).

49. Letter of 3 September 1942 (CDJC, XXVa-214).

50. Letter of 9 September 1942 (CDJC, XXVa-212).

51. The two letters concerning A. Hassan and S. Levi are quoted in the memorandum of 12 September 1942 (note 56).

52. Letter of 11 September 1942 (CDJC, XXVa-230).

53. Letter of 5 September 1942 (CDJC, XXVa-221). From this, we can assume that the nephew was not only an Italian citizen but was also considered Aryan according to the Italian racial laws.

54. See especially CDJC, XXVa-211, 212, 214, 221, 223, 231, 232, 340.

55. See note 22.

56. From Consul Orlandini to the command of the German Security Police in France, 12 September 1942 (CDJC, XLVIII-28).

57. From Consul Orlandini to SS-Obersturmführer Röthke, 16 September 1942 (the original in the German documentation: CDJC, XXVa-233; copy in the Consulate files: CDJC, XLVIII-28).

58. In the margin of the letter from Orlandini, Röthke wrote in his own hand (beside a few language corrections): "Please bring to the attention of Obersturmbannführer Lischka. Since we have rejected direct relations with the Italian Consulate General, I shall be unable to receive the Vice-Consul. Do I have to direct him by phone to the German delegation? 17/9/42" (CDJC, XXVa-233). On Kurt Lischka and the positions he held at the German Embassy in France in those years, see Klarsfeld, "Notices biographiques," pp. 197–198.

59. During the period of 28 days, between 2 and 30 September 1942, thirteen trains of deportees left France, one from Pithiviers, and twelve from Drancy. See Klarsfeld, *Vichy-Auschwitz*, I, p. 191.

60. On Dr. Karl-Theodor Zeitschel and Dr. Ernst Achenbach, see Klarsfeld,

"Notices biographiques," pp. 189–190, 201; Idem, *Vichy-Auschwitz*, 1, according to index. On the positions held by Zeitschel in the German Embassy and on his part in the treatment of the Jewish problem, see also Abetz, *D'une prison*, pp. 165–168, 221–223, 268–279. On the activity of Achenbach in that period, see also his evidence in Hoover Institution, 3, pp. 1619–1622.

61. Report from Vice-Consul Pasquinelli, 26 September 1942 (CDJC, XLVIII-28, no. A.71.I). The quotations are from this document.

62. From the rest of his words, that altogether there remained a total of 60,000 Jews who were due to be deported, one may learn that at that stage Zeitschel was referring just to the Occupied Zone. And, in fact, in a further conversation between the two, which took place a few days later, he said this explicitly and even expressed the hope that it would soon be possible to persuade the Vichy government "to take the same road" (see note 63). According to Zeitschel, "Laval had already given his consent to this, but there is still resistance on the part of Petain."

63. Report from Vice-Consul Pasquinelli, 26 September 1942 (see footnote 61). The three Jews—in fact, three Jewesses—on whose deportation the Italians had been informed were Giovanna Levy Piperno, Luisa Andjel, and Lucia Danon Cohen. The last had been detained at the Pithiviers camp and had been deported with her two children. The Italians also protested for the deportation of Abraham Hasson. See memorandum of 25 September 1942 signed by Orlandini, which Pasquinelli handed to Zeitschel at the start of the meeting with him (CDJC, XLVIII-28, no. A.71.I).

64. From the consul general in Paris to the consul in Metz, 29 September 1942 (CDJC, XLVIII-28, no. A.71.I).

65. From the consul in Metz, F. Campanella, to the consulate general in Breslau (and copy to the consulate general in Paris), 6 October 1942 (CDJC, XLVIII-28, no. 12.246).

66. Pasquinelli signed the three letters in the name of Consul General Orlandini. The letter of 17 September 1942 concerns the matter of Esther Amon Gulbas (originally an Italian citizen who had married a Lithuanian); the letter of 19 September concerns the matter of Giovanna Levy Piperno (who as indicated was deported a few days later on 23 September); the letter of 22 September contains the personal data of nine Jews with Italian citizenship and of three women whose citizenship was still being clarified. Originals of the letter were preserved in the German documentation (CDJC, XXVa-217, 211, 232). A copy of the third letter is also preserved in the consulate files (CDJC, XLVIII-28, n. Q. 222). The list of names of the Jews was also given to Zeitschel (on 22 September) and to Achenbach (on 20 October) with slight changes.

67. CDJC, XXVa-215. The letter had been addressed to "Mme. Louise Levy V.ve Andjel, Bloc 4, Esc. 13, Ch. 3, Drancy."

68. March by members of the fascist movement toward the capital of Italy, which was intended to seize power. At the time the fascists regarded whomever had participated in it as patriots with special credit.

69. The three deportees mentioned by name were Renata Gabbai Mizrachi, Giovanna Levy Piperno, and Giuseppe Catarivas. Not mentioned this time were two women, L. Levy Andjel and L. Danon Cohen, on whose deportation Vice-Consul Pasquinelli had protested in his second conversation with Zeitschel. This was apparently because, at the time of the deportation, their right to Italian citizenship had not been determined. On the other hand, two Jews were mentioned, whose deportation had become known in those days.

70. From Consul General Orlandini to the Italian Embassy in Paris (CDJC, XLVIII-28, no. 7161). The draft of the memorandum is from 9 October 1942, and written on the final copy of the memorandum is the date 29 October 1942. If one of the two dates is not mistaken, twenty days had passed between writing the draft and dispatching the final version.

71. See note 39.

## 3: The Last Days of Italy's Axis Partnership (pp. 62–66)

1. The fact that the last train for 1942 had left on the same day that the Germans invaded southern France is a mere coincidence. The Germans had long since planned an intermission in the deportations during the months of winter 1942–1943. (Zeitschel also pointed this out in his talks with Pasquinelli in September.)

2. See Part II.

3. From Consul Orlandini to the Foreign Ministry, 30 November 1942 (CDJC, XLVIII-28, no. 8322/6860). The letter was addressed to both the Political Department and the Department for Italians Abroad, a fact that indicates the considerable importance the writer had attributed to the subject. Attached to the draft for the letter in the consulate files was a handwritten list that contained the names of twenty detainees. Beside some of the names, a note was added later on what had happened to them. It appears that by 9 February 1943 another five detainees were released, two were deported, and there was no change in the situation of the remaining six.

4. ASMAE, AP, *Francia*, busta 64/8, no. 4283/P.R. The embassy transmitted a copy of this telegram to the consulate in Paris on 16 December 1943 (CDJC, XLVIII-28, n. 4530).

5. See Chapter 2, note 38, and Part II.

6. From Foreign Minister von Ribbentrop to the German Embassy in Rome, 13 January 1943 (URO, *Judenverfolgung in Italien*, pp. 126–127).

7. From the German ambassador in Rome to the Foreign Ministry in Rome, 16 January 1943. Klarsfeld, *Vichy-Auschwitz*, 2, pp. 199–200.

8. URO, *Judenverfolgung in Italien*, p. 135.

9. A copy of the telegram (no. 3602/O P.R.) is in the files of both the Foreign Ministry (ASMAE, AP, *Francia*, busta 80/7) and the consulate in Paris (CDJC, XLVIIIa-1).

10. From Consul Orlandini to the Ministry of the Interior, 14 November 1942 (CDJC, XLVIII-28, no. 7961/6593). Approach by the consul in Paris to the

Ministry of the Interior, not by way of the Foreign Ministry (but with a copy to the latter), was an unconventional step that testifies to the urgency the consulate attributed to the matter.

11. From the Ministry of the Interior, Inspectorate of Police, to the Italian Consulate in Paris, 10 December 1942 (CDJC, XLVIII-28, no. 105501).

12. From Deputy Foreign Minister G. Bastianini to the Italian embassies in Berlin and in Paris, to the consulate in Prague and the delegations in The Hague, Brussels, and Oslo, 15 February 1943 (CDJC, XLVIIIa-1). Bastianini had been appointed as deputy foreign minister only five days before. About him and his activities, see Chapter 6, note 23. The transfer of Jewish property to Italy did not escape German notice. On 30 April 1943, Eberhard von Thadden, of the Inland II bureau at the German Foreign Ministry, announced to the German Embassy in Paris that steps must be taken to prevent the "repatriation" of this property (CDJC, XXVa-291). But there is no information on any practical steps taken to implement this order.

13. Ambassador Buti to the Italian delegations and consulates in France, 13 August 1943 (CDJC, XLVIIIa-1, no. 109).

14. A. Morelli, "Les diplomates italiens en Belgique et la 'question juive' 1938–1943," *Bulletin de l'Institut Historique Belge de Rome*, 53–54 (1983–1984), pp. 381–383, 398–399.

15. From Consul Orlandini to the Italian Embassy in Paris, 15 March 1943 (CDJC, XLVIIIa, no. A.71.I).

16. CDJC, XXa, 207–235.


## 4: The Unoccupied Zone (pp. 69 – 78)

1. CDJC, *Recueil des textes*, pp. 19–21.

2. The Italian basic racial law of 17 November 1938 (R. Decreto-Legge no. 1728, *Gazzetta Ufficiale*, no. 264, 19 November 1938) stated that would be considered as a Jew: (1) anyone born to parents of the Jewish race, even if that person was not Jewish by religion; (2) anyone born to one parent of the Jewish race and one parent of foreign nationality; (3) anyone born to a mother of the Jewish race and an unknown father; (4) anyone who belongs to the Jewish religion, born to parents who were both Italian, even if only one was Jewish.

3. CDJC, *Recueil des textes*, pp. 29–30.

4. Ibid., pp. 49–52. On Xavier Vallat, see Chapter 1, note 54.

5. CDJC, *Recueil des textes*, pp. 62–66, 98. Most of the laws intended to establish the principle of numerus clausus were published in 1941: 16 June (lawyers), 21 June (university students), 11 August (doctors), 24 September (architects), and 26 December (pharmacists).

6. CDJC, *Recueil des textes*, p. 53. This last law, which in fact applied the obligation imposed by the German Military Government in the "First Order" of 27 September 1940 to the Vichy zone, caused a certain amount of confusion among the Italian officials in Paris, particularly as the Spanish Consulate had

instructed its citizens not to register and even obtained the consent of the Military Government to this step. The Foreign Ministry, however, was not impressed by this precedent and ordered that the Italian Jews residing in France not exempt themselves from this obligation. The communication of this decision is quoted in a letter from Foreign Minister Ciano to the consul general in Rabat, 11 October 1941 (ASMAE, AP, *Marocco*, busta 20/3, no. 40121/19).

7. Introduction, pp. 11–13.

8. Here are a number of examples: The consul general in Nice announced on 10 December 1941 that the Vichy government had published a law under which all foreign Jews who had entered the country after 1 January 1936 would be interned (ASMAE, AP, *Francia*, busta 50/11). The ambassador in Paris on 18 March 1942 reported a meeting that had taken place in Nice between "seven delegates" from the Commissariat Général aux Questions Juives in the Unoccupied Zone and General Commissioner Xavier Vallat, at which future steps to be taken against the Jews were discussed (ASMAE, AP, *Francia*, busta 64/8, no. 458/240). The ambassador further reported on 27 March 1942 on the publication of a law forbidding Jews to change their name to another (ASMAE, AP, *Francia*, busta 64/8, no. 552/297). In the middle of June 1942, the Armistice Commission reported disturbances of an antisemitic nature that had occurred in Nice on 6, 7, and 8 June 1942, in the course of which Jews were beaten by gangs of Doriot's supporters (CIAF, *Notiziario Quindicinale*, issue no. 36 [mid-June 1942], p. 30). In the middle of July 1942 the same source reported that within Vichy government circles the possibility was discussed of also forcing the Jews within their borders to wear the yellow star (Ibid., issue No. 40 [mid-July 1942]).

9. This catch phrase attributed to the painter Jean-Gabriel Domergue is mentioned in many places. Among others, it was repeated by Marc Augier in *La Gerbe* of 24 October 1940 (H. Amouroux, *La grande histoire des Français sous l'occupation. Vol. 2. Quarante millions de pétainistes*, Paris, 1977, p. 494).

10. About him and his work, see Chapter 5, note 50.

11. From the consul general in Nice, Silvio Camerani, to the Armistice Commission in Turin, 29 July 1940. Copy to the Foreign Ministry of 30 August 1940 (ASMAE, AP, *Italia*, busta 71). At the end of the 1930s, Camerani had served as consul in Alexandria in Egypt, and from there he also sent outspokenly antisemitic reports. See A. Scarantino, "La Comunità ebraica in Egitto fra le due guerre mondiali," *Storia Contemporanea*, XVII (1986), no. 6, p. 1040. Luckily for the Jews, at the end of 1940, Camerani was transferred from Nice to Barcelona.

12. Copy of the report of 23 November 1940 that was sent to the Foreign Ministry (ASMAE, AP, *Italia*, busta 71).

13. The survey was supplied to the Foreign Ministry (or carried out on its initiative) and distributed without the name of its author at the beginning of 1942 (ASMAE, AP, *Francia*, busta 65/1).

14. From Ambassador Buti to the Foreign Ministry, 16 July 1942 (ASMAE, AP, *Francia*, busta 64/8, no. 22145 P.R.).

15. From Ambassador Buti to the Foreign Ministry, 24 July 1942 (ASMAE, AP, *Francia*, busta 64/8, no. 4949 R).
16. See note 3.
17. From SS-Hauptsturmführer Theodor Dannecker to his superiors in Berlin, 21 July 1942 (Klarsfeld, *Vichy-Auschwitz*, 1, p. 279). Report of his conversations with the *secrétaire général* of the French police, René Bousquet.
18. The report from Lyon of 27 August 1942 was published in a brochure published by the Foreign Ministry at the end of the war (Ministero degli Affari Esteri, *Relazione sull'opera svolta dal Ministero degli Affari Esteri per la tutela delle comunità ebraiche [1939–1943]*, n.d., n.p. [Rome, 1945?], p. 24). The two reports from Nice, of 29 and 31 August 1942 are included in a dispatch of 21 September 1942 from the Foreign Ministry to the Direzione Generale Demografia e Razza (Head Office for Demography and Race) at the Ministry of the Interior (ASMAE, AP, *Francia*, busta 64/8, no. 34/R 9323). The report from Chambéry is also copied (without giving the original date) in a dispatch to the Head Office for Demography and Race of 14 September 1942 (ASMAE, AP, *Francia*, busta 64/8, no. 34/R 9151). The report from Marseilles is from 2 September 1942 (ASMAE, AP, *Francia*, busta 64/8, no. 5747 R). On the manhunts carried out in the summer of 1942 in southern France, see also H. Saulnier, "Nizza occupata," *Les langues néo-latines*, 79 (1985), no. 253, p. 52; D. F. Ryan, *Vichy and the Jews: The Example of Marseilles, 1939–1944*, Ann Arbor, 1988, pp. 225–260; F. Fauck, "Judenverfolgung in Nizza 1942/43," *Gutachten des Instituts für Zeitgeschichte*, Stuttgart, 1966, 2, pp. 43–46; J. L. Panicacci, "Les juifs et la question juive dans les Alpes-Maritimes de 1939 à 1945," *Recherches Régionales Côte d'Azur et Contrées Limitrophes*, 3 (1983), pp. 254–259.
19. In the original, *la dissidenza*, that is, what the Italians called the French Resistance movement, because the latter did not accept the authority of the legal French government.
20. After the failure of the landing operation by the British Army on the coast of Dieppe.
21. Issue no. 42 (end of August 1942), pp. 12–13. Detailed descriptions of the arrests made in various places in the Unoccupied Zone are given there, pp. 47–48, 55–56, 61–62.
22. From Ambassador Buti to the Foreign Ministry, reports of 8, 17, 24, and 29 September and of 8 October and end of October 1942 (exact date is missing). All preserved in ASMAE, AP, *Francia*, busta 64/8.
23. Issue no. 43 (mid-September 1942); issue no. 44 (end of September 1942); issue no. 45 (mid-October 1942); issue no. 46 (end of October 1942).
24. The pastoral letter from Mgr. Saliège was read out in Toulouse on Sunday 23 August 1942 and in some of the places within the bishopric on Sunday 30 August 1942; the letter from Mgr. Théas was read out in Montauban on Sunday 30 August 1942; the words of Cardinal Gerlier were read out in Lyon on Sunday 6 September 1942, and that same day the words of Mgr. Delay were read out in Marseilles. See J. Duquesne, *Les catholiques français sous l'occupation*,

Paris, 1966, pp. 250–272; A. Rhodes, *The Vatican in the Age of the Dictators, 1922–1945*, London-Toronto, 1973, pp. 317–318; J. M. Mayeur, "Les églises devant la persécution des Juifs en France," in G. Wellers, A. Kaspi, S. Klarsfeld (eds.), *La France et la question juive, 1940/1944*, Paris, 1981, pp. 147–170; R. Rémond, "Les églises et la persécution des Juifs pendant la seconde guerre mondiale," in Ecole des Hautes Etudes en Sciences Sociales, *L'Allemagne et le génocide Juif*, Paris, 1985, pp. 396–398; H. de Lubac, *Résistance chrétienne à l'antisémitisme. Souvenirs 1940–1944*, Paris, 1988, pp. 159–203; A. Cohen, "Immigrant Jews, Christians and French Jews," in Y. Bauer et al. (eds.), *Remembering for the Future*, 1, Oxford, 1989, pp. 223–232. See also the words of the Italian socialist leader Pietro Nenni, who during those days was under house arrest in southern France. He wrote in his diary for 9 September 1942, "the calls of the bishops against the race persecutions is one of the effective subjects of propaganda in these days against the puppets of Vichy" (*Vingt ans de fascismes. De Rome à Vichy*, Paris, 1960, pp. 214–215).

25. CIAF, *Notiziario Quindicinale*, issue no. 44 (end of September 1942), pp. 30–31. See also the report from Ambassador Buti of 24 September 1942 (ASMAE, AP, *Francia*, busta 64/8, no. 3236/1623).

26. Issue no. 45 (mid-October 1942), p. 22. See also the detailed report from Ambassador Buti of 8 October 1942 (ASMAE, AP, *Francia*, busta 64/8, no. 3449/1719).

27. Issue no. 46 (end of October 1942), p. 15. The two cardinals were accompanied by the apostolic nuncio in Vichy, Mgr. Valerio Valeri and Léon Bérard, the Vichy ambassador to the Vatican. The two cardinals were received for an interview with Pétain, dined with him, and even attended a military parade. Thereby, they publicly demonstrated their support for Marshal Pétain, his regime, and his policy.

28. Copy of the report transmitted by the Foreign Ministry to the Italian Embassy at the Holy See on 9 October 1942 (ASMAE, AP, *Francia*, busta 64/8, no. 000735).

29. From Ambassador Buti to the Foreign Ministry, 8 September 1942 (ASMAE, AP, *Francia*, busta 64/8, no. 2900/1475). On 24 August 1942, Nuncio Valeri reported to the secretary of state of the Vatican, Cardinal Luigi Maglione, on the meeting he had with Laval two days earlier. According to him, during the course of the conversation he had arrived at the conclusion "that any debate will be useless, and that at a time like the present it is at most possible to try and save a few individuals, as I have done in the past with some success." Valeri also reported that Laval had told him he was determined to surrender the foreign Jews to the Germans and that he "was waiting for the moment when he would be rid of them, since they were to a large degree the cause for the situation in which France found herself" (Saint-Siège, *Actes et documents du Saint-Siège relatifs à la seconde guerre mondiale. Vol. 8. Le Saint-Siège et les victimes de la guerre, janvier 1941–décembre 1942*, Vatican City, 1974, p. 624). These words—written at the time of the events and by a man who cer-

tainly was not hostile to the Vichy government—make nonsense of Bousquet's testimony given after the war, according to which Laval "had sent Rochat (the secretary general of the Foreign Ministry) to see the foreign legations in order to obtain their protest" against the deportation of the Jews from France and that he, Laval, "had personally seen the Papal Ambassador" on this matter (Hoover Institution, *France during the German Occupation*, 3, pp. 1456–1457).

30. See note 29; Klarsfeld, *Vichy-Auschwitz*, 1, pp. 375, 443.

31. Consul Zoppi reported on this conversation to the embassy in Paris, and from the embassy the report was sent to the Foreign Ministry in Rome. From there, it was transmitted on 4 November 1942 to the Italian Embassy at the Holy See, without indication of the original date (ASMAE, AP, *Francia*, busta 64/8, no. 34/R 11100). Count Zoppi served as consul general in Vichy until mid-May 1943, when he was appointed deputy director of the Department for European and Mediterranean Affairs (AEM). About him and his activities in Vichy, see E. Terracini, "Vittorio Zoppi, ambasciatore piemontese," *L'Osservatore Politico Letterario*, 21 (April 1975), pp. 61–68. On his activities on behalf of the Jews of Tunisia, see Chapter 10, note 49. On the conversation between Laval and Deputy Nuncio Mgr. Rocco, see Klarsfeld, *Vichy-Auschwitz*, 1, pp. 369–370.

32. From the Italian Embassy in Lisbon to the Foreign Ministry, 7 September 1942 (ASMAE, AP, *Francia*, busta 64/8, no. 5744/R).

33. Issue no. 43 (mid-September 1942), p. 15. According to German sources, in the course of a meeting that took place between Tuck and Laval at the end of August 1942 (Klarsfeld, *Vichy-Auschwitz*, 1, p. 382), Tuck had expressed "his personal objection" to the deportation of the Jews from the Unoccupied Zone. Tuck, who served as deputy ambassador from May 1942 until November when the embassy was closed, was from the outset very pessimistic over the possibility of helping the Jews by means of protests toward the Vichy government. See his remarks to the representative of the "Joint" at the beginning of August, quoted in M. Moch and A. Michel, *L'étoile et la francisque*, Paris, 1990, pp. 209–210.

34. Issue no. 43 (mid-September 1942), p. 20. On the stand adopted by the U.S. government, see H. L. Feingold, *The Politics of Rescue. The Roosevelt Administration and the Holocaust, 1938–1945*, New Brunswick, New Jersey, 1970, pp. 165–166; D. S. Wyman, *The Abandonment of the Jews. America and the Holocaust, 1941–1945*, New York, 1984, pp. 36–38.

35. See note 31. On the plans for the transfer of Jewish orphans from France to the United States, see R. I. Cohen, *The Burden of Conscience*, pp. 122–123; Marrus and Paxton, *Vichy France*, pp. 263–269; J. Bauer, *American Jewry and the Holocaust*, Detroit, 1981, pp. 259–263; Feingold, *Politics of Rescue*, pp. 154–155.

36. Furthermore, the terrible distress in which the Jews of France found themselves drove them to seek shelter by illegally crossing the borders into the neighboring countries. In consequence of this, the Swiss delegation in Vichy published

an announcement on 30 September 1942 saying that the Swiss government was no longer able to accept people seeking shelter on their soil. Instructions had been given to return anyone trying to cross the border without a valid visa. The Swiss announcement was delivered for the attention of the Italian Embassy in Berlin, from where it was sent to Rome on 6 October 1942 (ASMAE, AP, *Francia*, busta 64/8, no. 34/R 10510). See also Klarsfeld, *Vichy-Auschwitz*, 1, p. 457.

37. The head of the foreign minister's cabinet, the Marquis Lanza d'Ajeta, sent explicit instructions on 16 October 1942 concerning this to the Italian Embassy in Paris (ASMAE, AP, *Francia*, busta 64/8, no. 32402/294 R). The German authorities in Paris heard of the existence of these instructions from an undisclosed informer in their service inside the Italian Embassy in Paris (CDJC, XXVa–252a). It appears this man had seen the original cable, for he informed the Germans that instructions had been received from the Foreign Ministry to make sure "that the arrests and deportation [of Italian Jews] would not recur." In the German document, it says "sich nicht wiederholen," which is an accurate translation of the Italian source "non abbiano a ripetersi." According to the testimony of Hélène Saulnier who was in Nice on the night of the manhunt for foreign Jews (25 August 1942), Italian officers who were members of the Armistice Commission were called out, and in the middle of the night they opened the commission offices in the Hotel Continental "in order to try and protect whole families" from among the Italian Jews ("Nizza occupata," p. 52). There is no hint of this detail in the documentary sources.

## 5: The Italian Occupation Zone: The First Days (pp. 79 – 101)

1. See Introduction, note 9.

2. The decision to invade the Unoccupied Zone of France was made at a meeting held in Munich on 10–11 November 1942 between Hitler, von Ribbentrop, and Ciano. Laval had also been invited to this meeting, but of course he did not participate in the discussions of the invasion and was faced with a fait accompli. See the somewhat picturesque description by Ciano (*Diario*, pp. 665–666).

3. H. Umbreit, *Der Militärbefehlshaber in Frankreich, 1940–1944*, Boppard am Rhein, 1968, pp. 77–78.

4. See Italian General Staff map for the region under Italian control: *Francia occupata. Zona ad est del Rodano* (Scale 1:500,000).

5. The Italian zone also included portions of the Bouches-du-Rhône Department; but these were small areas, a kind of frontier correction. In accordance with the agreement made between the parties, the existence of a demarcation line did not deprive the parties of the possibility of acting, to a limited extent, within the borders of the other side. In fact, the Germans kept officials on the Italian side, dealing mainly with police and security matters, and the Italian Army also opened a liaison office in Marseilles, with the main task of locating French military equipment and of confiscating it.

6. *Diario*, pp. 690–691.

7. Ibid.
8. After Italy's capitulation and the German invasion in September 1943, General Alessandro Trabucchi was one of the senior commanders among the partisan units operating in the Piedmont region. After the war he published a book of memoirs (*I vinti hanno sempre torto*, Turin, 1947) in which he briefly mentions the subject of the Jews in the Italian Occupation Zone in southern France (pp. 14–25). Lieutenant Colonel (Tenente Colonnello) Duran was in charge of the First Department (Ufficio I) at the Fourth Army Command and in that capacity was responsible for the subject of the Jews in the Italian Occupation Zone.
9. With the invasion of southern France, the two armistice commissions became in fact devoid of content. The two Axis powers, therefore, sent military missions to Vichy to represent their respective general staffs to the French authorities and negotiate with them on everything concerning the presence of the two armies on French soil. Simultaneously, the two diplomatic delegations who represented the foreign ministries continued to deal with political matters. Heading the Italian military mission—which in the documents of the period was referred to as COLFRAN (i.e., Collegamento Francia)—was General Carlo Avarna di Gualtieri, and General von Neubronn led the Germans. General Avarna, who assumed his position on 15 January 1943, published two short testimonies on his activities in Vichy. See "Una missione presso il Governo di Vichy," *Nuova Antologia* (January–April 1958), pp. 79–88; "Gli ebrei e l'occupazione italiana in Francia (1942–43)," *Nuova Antologia* (January 1962), pp. 245–248. The impression arising from the documentation and from Avarna's testimonies is that the functions of the Italian mission in Vichy were quite limited and that most of the decision at the local level were made at the Fourth Army Command.
10. H. Michel, "Les relations franco-italiennes," p. 504; C. Levy, "La 4ª Armata italiana in Francia (11 novembre 1942–8 settembre 1943)," in Istituto Storico della Resistenza, *8 settembre. Lo sfacelo della quarta armata*, Turin, 1979, pp. 38–39; J. L. Panicacci, "L'occupazione italiana della Alpi Marittime," *Notiziario dell'Istituto Storico della Resistenza in Cuneo e Provincia*, 13 (1978), pp. 17–18.
11. As, for example, the socialist leader Pietro Nenni, who at that time was living in a small village in the German zone. After lengthy negotiations, Nenni was extradited in February 1943 into the hands of the Italians who interned him on the island of Ponza. He was released from there after the fall of Mussolini at the end of July 1943.
12. He was later made commander of the security services in the Marseilles district. See also Chapter 7, note 65.
13. From the Delegation of the Armistice Commission in Lyon (Deleciaf) to the Foreign Ministry, 1 December 1942 (ASMAE, AP, *Francia*, busta 64/13, no. 7592).
14. ASMAE, AP, *Francia*, busta 64/13, no. 43114. Also mentioned in this dispatch are cables that arrived at the Foreign Ministry, apparently on the same subject, from Marseilles (3 December) and from Paris (8 December); these have not been preserved.

15. This notification is known from several German sources (CDJC, 1–33; CXXVIa–16), because copies of it were sent to the Foreign Ministry in Berlin, the German embassies in Rome and Paris, as well as the security services and army staffs in France. All these copies are translations into German, and the Italian original version has not been found. The document was published in French, from the German translation, by Poliakoff, *La condition des Juifs en France*, p. 52; M. Mazor, "Les Juifs dans la clandestinité sous l'occupation italienne en France," *Le Monde Juif*, no. 59 (1970), p. 24. This document is also mentioned in several publications and sources. See among others Klarsfeld, *Vichy-Auschwitz*, 2, pp. 203, 214; Browning, *The German Foreign Office*, p. 165; URO, *Judenverfolgung in Frankreich*, p. 134; M. Michaelis, *Mussolini and the Jews*, Oxford, 1978, p. 305 (Michaelis apparently understood this document to be an announcement that the German had delivered to the fascist government and describes further events accordingly).

16. In the original, "procedere all'internamento degli ebrei." This proposed solution to the problem of the Jewish refugees in the Italian Occupation Zone in southern France was no different in its character from the methods that had been employed in Italy itself since the beginning of the war, with refugees, foreigners, and all the nonconforming elements as a whole. There were different kinds of *internamento* (internment), and the differences between this measure and *residenza forzata* (enforced residence) were at times very fine (see note 63).

17. From d'Ajeta to the Italian Embassy in Berlin, 19 December 1942 (ASMAE, AP, *Francia*, busta 64/8, no. 43770 P.R.).

18. The final report of 23 January 1943—sent by Rudolf Schleier, the first counselor at the German Embassy in Paris, to the German Department (Deutschland Abteilung) of the Foreign Ministry—did, in fact, clearly state that, during the course of December, it had been agreed between the SD Command in France and the Vichy authorities that the latter would evacuate all the Jews from the departments on the coast. The foreign Jews among them would be concentrated in camps "for the purpose of deportation later on to the East," but the holders of French citizenship and also foreigners who were "exempt" from the restrictions would be detained in regular places of residence (URO, *Judenverfolgung in Italien*, p. 133). On this report, see also Chapter 6, note 6. Schleier was attached to the German Embassy in Paris in June 1940 with the rank of consul general and was later appointed first counselor. He returned to the Foreign Ministry in Berlin at the end of November 1943 (according to him, under pressure from the Gestapo). See his evidence in Hoover Institution, *France during the German Occupation*, 3, pp. 1611–1619.

19. The circular of 6 December 1942 from the Vichy authorities and the order of 20 December from the prefect of the Alpes-Maritimes Department, Marcel Ribière, are mentioned in several places. See Poliakoff, *La condition des Juifs en France*, pp. 20–22, 57–58; Michel, "Les relations franco-italiennes," p. 505; Klarsfeld, *Vichy-Auschwitz*, 2, pp. 197–199. Ribière, one-time Poincaré's *chef*

*de cabinet*, was one of the faithful followers of the Vichy regime; he always took care to the best of his ability to implement the measures against the Jews in the most severe way. (Despite that, he testified after the war that he had had nothing to do with the implementation of these measures. See Panicacci, "Les juifs dans les Alpes-Maritimes," p. 253). For French nationalist reasons, Ribière adopted a most hostile attitude toward the Italians, and he was in fact removed from his post in the spring of 1943 at their demand. Appointed in his place was Jean Chaigneau, a man close to the French Resistance, who revealed a more favorable attitude toward the Jews. See his testimony in Hoover Institution, *France during the German Occupation*, 1, pp. 433–437. See also Poliakoff, ibid., p. 28; Panicacci, ibid., p. 253; Klarsfeld, ibid., 2, p. 91; Lazar, *La résistance juive*, pp. 250, 253; Marrus and Paxton, *Vichy France*, pp. 134, 170, 320. These scholars stated that the change of prefects took place in July, but according to the Italian sources the Vichy authorities decided in April to dismiss Ribière, and, in fact, Chaigneau took up his post on 11 May 1943. So also A. Cavaglion, *Nella notte straniera, Gli ebrei di S. Martin Vésubie e il campo di Borgo S. Dalmazzo*, Cuneo, 1981, p. 30.

20. From Consul Calisse to the Foreign Ministry, 24 December 1942 (ASMAE, AP, *Francia*, busta 64/8, no. 8103 [8123?] R). Calisse wrote about the "Department" (in the singular) to which the expelled Jews would be transferred and emphasized that it was in the German Occupation Zone. This phrasing does not accurately reflect the text of the instructions of the Vichy government, and possibly this was no accident. Some scholars mention a dispatch that Calisse supposedly sent to Rome on 22 December 1942, but this information is apparently erroneous. On the approach of Calisse to Ribière concerning those holding Italian citizenship, we learn from the memorandum from Ribière to his superiors in Vichy of 14 January 1943 (Klarsfeld, *Vichy-Auschwitz*, 2, p. 197). Calisse was serving as consul general in Nice from July 1942 to the beginning of May 1943, and his activities were greatly valued by the Jews.

21. Ministero Affari Esteri, *Relazione*, pp. 25–26. The words, coming from General Trabucchi, were addressed to the General Staff in Rome. From there, they were leaked to the Foreign Ministry through Baron Michele Scammacca, an official of the Foreign Ministry in charge of the contacts with the General Staff.

22. From Inspector Barranco to Consul Calisse, 6 January 1943 (ASMAE, AP, *Francia*, busta 80/7, no. 027).

23. From d'Ajeta to Count Bonarelli di Castelbompiano, head of the *liaison office* of the Foreign Ministry with the Fourth Army, 29 December 1942 (ASMAE, AP, *Francia*, busta 64/8, no. 34/R 12825). Copies were sent to the Italian representatives in Paris, Vichy, Nice, and Lyon as well as to the General Staff, Military Intelligence (SIM), and the Police Head Branch of the Ministry of the Interior. Excerpts from this document were published by Poliakoff, *La condition des Juifs en France*, p. 21.

24. ASSME, *Stato Maggiore—Ufficio Informazioni*, no. 4849/I. Portions of the document were published in Ministero Affari Esteri, *Relazione*, p. 26. In this

publication the date of the document is said to be 1 December 1942. But that is evidently wrong, because the instructions from Vichy are dated 6 December, and the order of the department prefect is from 20 December. The mistake apparently occurred because on the original document the date was preceded by the Military Post number (P.M. 1) and the number indicating the day of the month in the copy in the archives is very blurred (i.e., the head of the letter reads: "P.M. 1—dicembre 1942"). In German documents from the beginning of 1943, this order is mentioned frequently (and, of course, not in a complimentary tone) and it is always mentioned as dated 30 December.

25. This document, translated into German, has been preserved among the documents of the German security services in France (CDJC, I-34). It has been published several times translated into French (based on the German translation). See Ministero Affari Esteri, *Relazione*, p. 63 (here too there was a mistake in the date); Poliakoff, *La condition des Juifs en France*, p. 53; Mazor, "Les Juifs dans la clandestinité," p. 24. As may have been expected, the paragraph speaking of the possibility of using military force to avoid the implementation of the Vichy order was not included in the notification to Colonel Bonnet.

26. Klarsfeld, *Vichy-Auschwitz*, 2, p. 197.

27. From Consul Calisse to the Foreign Ministry, Minister's Cabinet, 6 January 1943 (ASMAE, AP, *Francia*, busta 80/7, no. 3 R). The first part of this letter was published by Poliakoff, *La condition des Juifs en France*, p. 22. In this publication there also is a mistake in the date.

28. Klarsfeld, *Vichy-Auschwitz*, 2, pp. 197–198; Poliakoff, *La condition des Juifs en France*, pp. 58–59.

29. CDJC, *Recueil des textes*, p. 172.

30. Several examples: the embassy in Paris to the Foreign Ministry, 8 December 1942 (ASMAE, AP, *Francia*, busta 64/8, no. 12711); the consul in Toulouse, O. Gloria, to the Foreign Ministry, 22 December 1942, quoted in an additional letter of 13 January 1943 (ASMAE, AP, *Francia*, busta 80/7, no. 565/97); the vice-consul in Nice, Giovanni Ludovico Borromeo, to the embassy in Paris, 1 January 1943 (CDJC, XLVIIIa-1); the consul in Lyon, Silvio Delich, to the Foreign Ministry, 12 January 1943 (ASMAE, AP, *Francia*, busta 80/7, no. 212).

31. From Ciano to Count Bonarelli, 2 January 1943 (ASMAE, AP, *Francia*, busta 80/7, no. 12936). Copies were sent to the Italian representatives in Paris, Vichy, Nice, and Lyon as well as the General Staff, Army Intelligence (SIM), and the Police Head Branch at the Ministry of the Interior.

32. Klarsfeld, *Vichy-Auschwitz*, 2, p. 198.

33. Ibid., p. 199. According to Ribière, he did in fact bring up this suggestion before both an Italian general, whose name he does not mention, and the consul general in Nice (i.e., Calisse). Both, however, rejected it outright.

34. From the Italian Embassy in Paris, signed by Count Zoppi to the consulate general in Vichy, 14 January 1943 (ASMAE, AP, *Francia*, busta 80/7, no. 207/78). See Ministero Affari Esteri, *Relazione*, pp. 27–28; Poliakoff, *La condition des juifs en France*, pp. 23–24.

35. See among many sources P. Erlanger, *La France sans étoile*, Paris 1974, pp. 246–247; Saulnier, "Nizza occupata," p. 53.

36. It appears that similar feelings were widespread also among the French population, many of whom regarded the Italian occupation as the lesser evil. See Ceva, "4ᵃ armata e occupazione italiana della Francia. Problemi militari," pp. 98–99; J. L. Panicacci, "L'8 settembre nel Nizzardo," in *8 settembre. Lo sfacelo della quarta armata*, Turin, 1979, p. 107.

37. In the first half of December, Italian sources in Nice reported that the Jews on the whole were accepting the Italian occupation with a feeling of relief, supported it, and hoped also to enjoy its protection in the future. According to this source, "Jewish welfare organizations in Marseilles" wanted to know whether they would be allowed to transfer their place of residence to the Italian Occupation Zone and, if so, to which place. From Consul Calisse to the Foreign Ministry, 15 December 1942 (ASMAE, AP, *Francia*, busta 64/8, no. 2525 R). See also R. I. Cohen, *The Burden of Conscience*, pp. 123–124.

38. Issue no. 51 (beginning of January 1943), pp. 14–15.

39. Issue no. 52 (mid-January 1943), p. 3.

40. This movement was in fact a roof organization of the Zionist youth movements. It was established in May 1942 at a conference held at Montpellier, on the initiative and under the leadership of Shimeon Levitt (Lazar, *La résistance juive*, pp. 78–93). It maintained close ties with the Eclaireurs Israélites de France (Jewish scout movement) under the leadership of Robert Gamzon (Castor) and Shimeon Hammel (Chameau). See J. Ariel, "Jewish Self-defense and Revolt in the Days of the Holocaust in France," *Gesher*, 9 (1963), pp. 176–179; idem, "Jewish Self-defense and Resistance in France during World War II," *Yad Vashem Studies*, 6 (1967), pp. 237–238; Lazar, *La résistance juive*, pp. 67–69; R. I. Cohen, *The Burden of Conscience*, pp. 149–152; F. C. Hammel, *Souviens-toi d'Amalek, témoignage sur la lutte des juifs en France (1938–1944)*, Paris, 1982, pp. 179–181; R. Gamzon, *Les eaux claires. Journal, 1940–1944*, Paris, 1982; A. Michel, *Les Eclaireurs Israélites de France pendant la seconde guerre mondiale*, Paris, 1984. Both movements were later active in the Jewish Fighting Organization, the Armée Juive.

41. Lazar, *La résistance juive*, pp. 246–248; Hammel, *Témoignage*, pp. 169, 424–425.

42. Testimony of Angelo Donati (on him and his testimony see the rest of the chapter and note 50). On these concentrations of refugees, see also Chapter 7.

43. Some of the refugees had arrived in the city in June 1940 during the mass flight from the North, some in the summer of 1942, after the great manhunt of 16 July, but most of them had come in the winter of 1942–1943, after the rumor had spread of the accommodating attitude of the local Italian authorities.

44. It is not clear when the committee began its activities. Most of the researchers state that it was founded after the beginning of the Italian occupation, but it seems that at that time it was already in existence, even if only on a more limited scale. See about it Lazar, *La résistance juive*, pp. 248–251; Saulnier,

"Nizza occupata," pp. 52–54; Panicacci, "Les juifs dans les Alpes-Maritimes," pp. 262–263; Erlanger, *Souvenirs*, pp. 255–256; D. Knout, *Contribution à l'histoire de la résistance juive en France*, 1940–1944, Paris, 1947, pp. 38–39; A. Latour, *La résistance juive en France (1940–1944)*, Paris, 1970, pp. 141–142; A. Rutkowski, *La lutte de's juifs en France à l'époque de l'occupation*, Paris, 1975, pp. 315–317; T. R. P. Marie-Benoît, "Resumé de mon activité en faveur des Juifs persécutés (1940–1944)," in *Livre d'or des congrégations françaises*, Paris, 1948, pp. 306–309.

45. Some of Fink's papers, among them his final testimony, are preserved as photocopies by Dr. Lucien Lazar in Jerusalem, who graciously placed them at my disposal and for which I wish to express my thanks. These papers are referred to below as the Fink Documents. The other members of the committee included Dr. Vidal Modiano, Georges Weinstein, Max Blasberg, Wolf Toronczyk, Claude Kelman, the Stern brothers, Kriegel, Schendler, and Wachtel. The last three, as well as one of the Stern brothers were arrested by the Germans and died in deportation. At a certain stage, the committee set up two commissions, a "social" one headed by Topiol, and a "political" one headed by Joseph Fischer (Ariel). Fischer had served for years as chairman of the Jewish National Fund (*Keren Kayemet leIsrael*) in France, and during the war he was one of the active members of the Organization Juive de Combat (Jewish Fighting Organization). See Ariel, "Jewish Self-defence," pp. 205–206; Lazar, *La résistance juive*, by index. After the war Fischer acted as Israel's ambassador to Belgium. The testimony of Toronczyk, preserved in the Centre de Documentation Juive (CDJC, CCXVI-61), has been published with several omissions by Rutkowski, *La lutte des Juifs*, pp. 315–317.

46. Fink Documents, testimony, pp. 6–7. According to Fink, Donati came one day on his own initiative to the offices of the Dubouchage Committee and offered his assistance. That was in the middle of December 1942. From then on, Fink and Topiol used to visit him every morning in his office in order to make plans with him and take his advice on whatever had to be done among the Jews and in particular in contacts with the Italians.

47. In this connection it should be mentioned that the certificate of appreciation that the Jews of Nice presented to Consul Calisse on 10 May 1943 (Chapter 7) was signed by Doubinsky as *presidente della Comunità degli ebrei stranieri di Nizza* (chairman of the Congregation of Foreign Jews in Nice) and by Donati as *fiduciario delle opere di assistenza ebraica* (trustee for the Jewish Welfare Institutions). A photostat of the certificate is preserved among the "Donati Documents" (see note 50). It was published by Klarsfeld, *Vichy-Auschwitz*, 2.

48. Two examples of this form are preserved in the Yivo Archives in New York (Coll. 116, D. 35). They were photographed by Dr. Lucien Lazar from Jerusalem, who graciously placed them at my disposal.

49. At the same time, from the beginning of 1943 the consulate itself had been issuing a certificate to Jews of Italian nationality, stating that the bearer, "despite being considered by his national law [that is to say, by the law in his country of

origin] as belonging to the Israelite race, enjoys all the rights granted to Italian citizens residing in France. Therefore, just because of the fact that he is a member of the Israelite race, he cannot be the object of steps that would be liable to restrict his liberty, both personal and in the conduct of his affairs, without the formal prior consent of this civil Delegation" (CDJC, XXa-317; XLIIIa-7). A copy of this certificate is preserved with the Donati Documents (see note 50).

50. Remnants of the papers of Angelo Donati on his activities in southern France, including the testimony he gave in 1944 when he was already in Switzerland, are today in the keeping of Serge Klarsfeld in Paris, who was kind enough to let me have photostats of them, and for that I wish to express my gratitude. These documents are referred to as the Donati Documents.

51. L. Carpi, "Lettere di Jabotinski," in D. Carpi (ed.), *Scritti in Memoria di Leone Carpi*, Jerusalem, 1967, pp. 43–45.

52. On 25 July 1943, the day Mussolini was ousted, Donati was in Rome. There, together with Father Pierre Marie-Benoît, he was trying to organize the transfer of the Jewish refugees from southern France to North Africa. On his activities in this period, see the rest of the chapter. After the Italian capitulation, Donati found asylum in Switzerland. At the end of 1944, he returned to Paris, where he died in December 1960.

53. Copies of the two letters, from Q. Mazzolini of 30 March 1942 (original mark: n. 724), and from A. Calisse of 17 September 1942 (original mark: n. 2195 R), both addressed to the deputy head of the Italian police, Salvatore Rosa, are preserved among the Donati Documents. On Count Quinto Mazzolini and some of his activities, see also Chapter 1, note 26.

54. Donati Documents, testimony.

55. Ibid., p. 1.

56. See, for example, Cavaglion, *Nella notte straniera*, pp. 26–27; R. De Felice, *Storia degli ebrei italiani sotto il fascismo*, 4th ed., Turin, 1988, p. 445.

57. See, for example, Poliakoff, *La condition des Juifs en France*, pp. 20–21.

58. Donati's belief "that the reply [of the Foreign Ministry] had been drafted by Mussolini," (Donati Documents, testimony, p. 1) has no support in the sources and is undoubtedly groundless.

59. See note 20.

60. On the news of the massacre of Jews, which reached the Italian Foreign Ministry during November 1942, and on the use of gas for this purpose, see Carpi, "Pietromarchi," p. 148.

61. A copy of the memorandum from Barranco was appended to the letter of 6 January 1943 from Consul Calisse to the Foreign Ministry (ASMAE, AP, *Francia*, busta 80/7, no. 3 R). Therefore, the memorandum was composed, delivered to the consul, and sent to the Foreign Ministry in one day.

62. Apparently, in addition to his first position, which as indicated was that of coordinator of police operations with the German security services in Lyon. In Nice, Barranco made his home in the seat of the consulate and not at the Fourth Army headquarters, because he belonged to the civil police, subordinate to the

Ministry of the Interior, and not to the army. However, for operational matters he could have the support of the Carabinieri regiment stationed there (which was subordinate to the Army Staff).

63. The method of "enforced residence" (*residenza forzata*) in remote villages had been customary in fascist Italy for years against opponents of the regime (see also note 16). From the start of the war, the authorities also used this method for foreigners, refugees, and the like. Many memoirs have been published since the end of the war by people who were among those who had been sentenced to a period of "enforced residence." See among these the well-known book by Carlo Levi, *Cristo si è fermato a Eboli*, Turin, 1945.

64. The word *comodamente* (conveniently) here refers to the Italian authorities (i.e., it would be easy for them to supply a place to sleep and food for those transferred).

65. In his memorandum of 6 March 1943, Röthke indicates that on 16 February 1943 the commander of the Fourth Army had announced to the German commander-in-chief in the West that "the operation of concentrating the dangerous Jewish elements was under way" and that the operation of transferring the remaining Jews would begin on 20 February. Nevertheless, Röthke claimed that until that day "nothing had been done" (Yad Vashem Archives, Jerusalem, TR-3, 249; URO, *Judenverfolgung in Italien*, p. 159; Klarsfeld, *Vichy-Auschwitz*, 2, pp. 231–233). See also the reports of 4, 5, and 6 March 1943 from the German consul general in Marseilles claiming that the evacuation operations of the Jews in the Italian zone had not yet begun (CDJC, XXVa-279). See also the reports of SS-Obersturmbannführer Kurt Lischka of 9 and 13 March 1943 (Klarsfeld, *Vichy-Auschwitz*, 2, pp. 243, 240; S. Klarsfeld, *Die Endlösung der Judenfrage in Frankreich*, Paris, 1977, pp. 110, 184). From the Italian documentation, however, it appears that during the second half of February the first stage of the operation had already begun.

66. On 23 February 1943 Consul Calisse informed Count Bonarelli, the liaison officer with the Fourth Army headquarters, that "in Nice a committee had been established among the Jews that would be ready to attend to the livelihood of their needy coreligionists." He wanted to know the number of Jews "to be put on enforced residence" so that the committee could be able to prepare for the task (ASMAE, AP, *Francia*, busta 68 [fasc. Nizza], no. 159 R). Two days later, Bonarelli replied that in his estimation the number of those Jews would be some 1,200 (ASMAE, AP, *Francia*, busta 80/7, no. 277/c).

### 6: The Struggle over the Fate of the Jewish Refugees in the Italian Occupation Zone (pp. 102–135)

1. A note from General C. A. Oberg of 9 January 1943 (CDJC, XXVa-253, 318). Several unsigned copies of this note have been preserved, one of them bears the stamp *Der Höhere SS und Polizeiführer im Bereich des Militärbefehlshabers in*

*Frankreich.* The document has been published by Klarsfeld, *Vichy-Auschwitz*, 2, pp. 195–196.

2. A French official very close to Bousquet, he ended this office at the end of 1943 and was appointed *préfet* of one of the departments. About him and his activities, see Hoover Institution, *France during the German Occupation*, 3, pp. 1155–1159; Klarsfeld, "Notices biographiques," p. 196.

3. "und bittet um entsprechende Unterstützung," according to Knochen's version of the conversation (see also note 5).

4. See Chapter 1.

5. From SS-Standartenführer H. Knochen to SS-Gruppenführer Heinrich Müller, 13 January 1943 (CDJC, XLVIIIa-12; Yad Vashem Archives, Jerusalem, TR-3, 815; Poliakoff, *La condition des Juifs en France*, pp. 54–55; Ministero Affari Esteri, *Relazione*, p. 64; Klarsfeld, *Die Endlösung*, p. 168; idem, *Vichy-Auschwitz*, 2, pp. 196–197). This document does not mention the day on which the meeting between Leguay and Knochen took place. It was probably close to the date on which Knochen's report was composed.

6. From Schleier to the Foreign Ministry, 23 January 1943 (Yad Vashem Archives, Jerusalem, TR-3, 726; URO, *Judenverfolgung in Italien*, pp. 133–134). An earlier draft of the document, bearing the date 22 January 1943, is preserved in the archives of the *Centre de Documentation Juive* in Paris (CDJC, XXVa-254). Concerning the notification of the Italians, see Chapter 2, note 15.

7. For example, on 21 January 1943, a detailed report was published in *The Times* of London by a correspondent of the paper "who was staying on the French border" (that is, on the Spanish side of the Pyrénées) concerning the opposition of the Italian General Staff to the Vichy government order concerning the wearing of the badge. The whole piece was copied in the original language by the German Espionage Service and is preserved among the papers of the SD staff in Paris (CDJC, XXVa-339).

8. The excerpt is quoted in the letter from SS-Gruppenführer Müller to the Foreign Ministry of 25 February 1943 (Klarsfeld, *Vichy-Auschwitz*, 2, p. 226). See also Browning, *The German Foreign Office*, p. 166.

9. The two dispatches were sent on 31 January 1943 but were written on 27 January (URO, *Judenverfolgung in Italien*, pp. 136–139). A copy of the cable to Paris is preserved in the Centre de Documentation Juive in Paris (CDJC, XXVa-257a).

10. Ministero Affari Esteri, *Relazione*, pp. 28–29. The memorandum presented by Bismarck carries the date 3 February 1943, but Bismarck's report on the conversation itself is from February 4 (see note 11). Therefore, the conversation possibly took place on 4 February, not 3. Count Luigi Vidau was one of the senior Italian diplomats. He served as deputy director of the Department for European and Mediterranean Affairs (Affari Europa e Mediterraneo, AEM) until 17 January 1942, when he was appointed director of the political department (Affari Generali, AG). In this post he did a great deal for the Jews of southern France and Tunisia (see Part III, especially Chapter 10, note 62). In his talk with the Italian diplomats, von Bismarck mentioned among other things

the article published in *The Times* (see note 7) and brought it as proof that the Italian stand was liable to harm the Axis.

11. From von Bismarck to the Foreign Ministry in Berlin, 4 February 1943. The Foreign Ministry sent a copy of this report to the German Embassy in Paris, which on 8 February sent a copy of it to the head of the Security Police and the SD in France (CDJC, XLVIIIa-13; I-37; Yad Vashem Archives, Jerusalem, TR-3, 407; URO, *Judenverfolgung in Italien*, pp. 143–144; Poliakoff, *La condition des Juifs en France*, pp. 63–65; Klarsfeld, *Vichy-Auschwitz*, 2, pp. 214–215; Mazor, "Les Juifs dans la clandestinité," p. 25). According to von Bismarck, his host was Marquis d'Ajeta, but according to the Ministero Affari Esteri, *Relazione*, it was Luigi Vidau. There is not necessarily any contradiction between the two versions because it is possible and also logical that both of them participated in the conversation. If this is not so, then von Bismarck's version is preferable, having been written the day of the meeting (or the following day).

12. See Chapter 3.

13. The memorandum, which was sent directly to the Italian foreign minister and classified as secret, was published by De Felice, *Storia degli Ebrei Italiani*, pp. 602–605. On Ambassador Dino Alfieri, who held a position of the first rank in the fascist leadership and was a one-time minister of propaganda, see Chapter 1, note 19. Evidence of the repercussions raised at the time by Alfieri's memorandum, even outside the Foreign Ministry, shows in the fact that it is also mentioned in a record by the industrialist Alberto Pirelli of 22–23 April 1943 (*Taccuini 1922/1943*, Bologna, 1984, p. 430).

14. In brackets in the original.

15. CDJC, XVIIIa-19; Poliakoff, *La condition des Juifs en France*, p. 62; Klarsfeld, *Vichy-Auschwitz*, 2, pp. 202–203.

16. CDJC, XXVa-260; Klarsfeld, *Vichy-Auschwitz*, 2, pp. 205–206. On 7 February 1943, General G. Blumentritt informed Knochen that the Supreme Command-West was unable to decide on the question of the treatment of the Jews in the Unoccupied Zone of France "as long as it seems the Italian government has different views on the matter." The general therefore proposed to clarify first the matter at the political levels in the two countries (CDJC, XXVa-266).

17. CDJC, XXVa-261a; Klarsfeld, *Vichy-Auschwitz*, 2, pp. 204–205.

18. CDJC, XXVa-262; Klarsfeld, *Vichy-Auschwitz*, 2, pp. 211–212.

19. CDJC, XXVa-259; Klarsfeld, *Vichy-Auschwitz*, 2, p. 203.

20. CDJC, XXVa-261; Klarsfeld, *Die Endlösung*, p. 170; idem, *Vichy-Auschwitz*, 2, pp. 212–213.

21. Carpi, "Pietromarchi," p. 149, entry for 2 February 1943.

22. Dismissed together with Ciano was his head of cabinet, the Marquis d'Ajeta, and he too was transferred to the Italian Embassy to the Holy See. Appointed in place of d'Ajeta was the diplomat Francesco Babuscio Rizzo.

23. Before that, Bastianini had served as ambassador in Poland (1932–1936), as deputy foreign minister (1936–1939), as ambassador in Great Britain (1939–1940), and as governor of Dalmatia (1941–1943). He was a veteran in the fascist

movement and a member of the Fascist Grand Council. Nevertheless, on the night of 25 July 1943 he was among the majority who voted for the dismissal of Mussolini. Because of that, following the creation of the Republic of Salò, he was sentenced to death in absentia (1944). After the war, he published his memoirs: *Uomine, cose, fatti. Memorie di un ambasciatore*, Milan, 1959. On his nomination as deputy minister in February 1943, Bastianini appointed Egidio Ortona as director of his secretariat. Ortona, who then was a junior diplomat, has published parts of the diary he kept in those days: "Il 1943 da Palazzo Chigi. Note di Diario," *Storia Contemporanea*, XIV (1983), pp. 1076–1147.

24. See Carpi "Jews in Croatia," pp. 465–507; M. Shelah, *History of the Holocaust: Yugoslavia*, Jerusalem, 1990.

25. Browning, *The German Foreign Office*, pp. 23–34, 147–154. On Horst Wagner and Eberhard von Thadden, see Browning, ibid., by index. Within the framework of the reorganization carried out at the German Foreign Ministry in those days, the functions of the Deutschland Department were transferred to the Inland II Department.

26. Klarsfeld, *Vichy-Auschwitz*, 2, pp. 215, 217, 220–221, 228–229, 231, 246, 254, 393.

27. From Knochen to SS-Gruppenführer Müller, 12 February 1943 (CDJC, I-38); Poliakoff, *La condition des Juifs en France*, pp. 66–70; Klarsfeld, *Die Endlösung*, pp. 172–175; idem, *Vichy-Auschwitz*, 2, pp. 218–220; Ministero Affari Esteri, *Relazione*, pp. 66–68).

28. Ministero Affari Esteri, *Relazione*, p. 28. The author of this publication relies on a memorandum written on 10 February 1943 in the course of the conversation; today it is not in the appropriate file in the Foreign Ministry archives.

29. From the Supreme Command-West to the Head of the Security Policy in France, 17 February 1943 (Poliakoff, *La condition des Juifs en France*, p. 72). The writer quotes an announcement from the Fourth Army headquarters of 16 February 1943. See also the memorandum by Röthke of 6 March 1943 (see Chapter 5, note 65). The Italian Foreign Ministry also delivered a similar note to the German Embassy in Rome (Poliakoff, ibid., p. 73).

30. From the German Embassy in Rome to the Foreign Ministry, 25 February 1943 (ASMAE, AP, *Jugoslavia*, busta 138/8). The Italians were also asked to retract their announcement to the Vichy authorities concerning the measures they were planning. On this, see also the dispatches from the German embassies in Rome and Paris on 19 February 1943 (Browning, *The German Foreign Office*, p. 166).

31. From the embassy counselor, Dr. Ernst Achenbach, to the head of the Security Policy in France, for the attention of SS-Obersturmführer Röthke, 11 February 1943 (CDJC, XXVa-267; Klarsfeld, *Die Endlösung*, p. 171; idem, *Vichy-Auschwitz*, 2, p. 218).

32. CIAF, *Notiziario Quindicinale*, issue 54 (end of February 1943), p. 22. On 10 February the Fourth Army headquarters had already informed the Italian consul general in Vichy that "there were signs" that the Germans were prepar-

ing manhunt operations in Lyon like those recently carried out in Marseilles. Ambassador Buti reported on this to the Foreign Ministry on 16 February 1943 (ASMAE, AP, *Francia*, busta 68 [fasc. Lione], no. 687/258). However, this report does not state that the operation was liable to spread into the Italian zone. The German Foreign Ministry notified the Italian Embassy in Berlin in advance on "the intention of the Reich to conduct a purge in the recently occupied French territory, its main purpose being the removal from the coastal region of the disloyal elements, particularly all the Jews." These arrests were intended to be carried out by the French police. The German Foreign Ministry requested of the Italian authorities to cooperate and prevent the escape of the "wanted elements" into the Italian zone. It is not known on what day the Germans delivered this announcement. Ambassador Alfieri reported on it to the Foreign Ministry on 19 February 1943, but for some reason his dispatch only reached Rome on the 21 (ASMAE, AP, *Francia*, busta 65/6, no. 5509 P.R.). Even if the Italian Foreign Ministry had informed its delegations the following day on what was about to take place—and there is no evidence of this—this warning would no longer have been able to influence events in the field.

33. Quoted in a cable from the SS unit in Lyon to the head of the Security Police in Paris, 20 February 1943 (CDJC, XXVa-272).

34. From General Vercellino to the General Staff, 22 February 1943 (ASSME, *Diario Storico Comando 4ᵃ Armata*, racc. 1127, all. 56). See also Ministero Affari Esteri, *Relazione*, p. 29.

35. See detailed reports of the Italian consular representatives in Grenoble, of 25 February 1943 (ASMAE, AP, *Francia*, busta 68 [fasc. Savoia], no. 1282/179), and in Chambéry, of 24, 27, and 28 February 1943 (no. 0296-R, no. 0317-R, no. 0326-R). See also the German documentation: CDJC, XXVa-274, 274a, 277, 282, 282a, 286; Klarsfeld, *Die Endlösung*, pp. 179, 184, 186–187; idem, *Vichy-Auschwitz*, 2, pp. 36, 222, 225, 226, 240–242. Concerning the Drôme Department, see reports from the department prefect, quoted by Levy, "La 4ᵃ Armata," pp. 45–46.

36. CIAF, *Notiziario Quindicinale*, issue 54 (end of February 1943), p. 23. The Italian consul in Grenoble (who generally did not reveal great sympathy for the Jewish cause) indicates that on 24 February a "Jewish delegation" had come to his office for the purpose of thanking him for the actions of the army authorities. According to him, he had replied that the action had been taken because of the desire of the occupying power to retain in its own hands "the control of elements who could be dangerous to the peace of the public and the security of the troops" (see note 35).

37. From Knochen to the Reich Security Main Office, Bureau IVB4, for the attention of SS-Gruppenführer Müller, on 22 February 1943 (CDJC, 1-38; Poliakoff, *La condition des Juifs en France*, pp. 74–76; Ministero Affari Esteri, *Relazione*, pp. 69–70; Klarsfeld, *Vichy-Auschwitz*, 2, pp. 223–224).

38. Ortona, "Diario," p. 1083; Simoni, *Ambasciata d'Italia*, p. 316.

39. Browning, *The German Foreign Office*, p. 166; URO, *Judenverfolgung in Ita-*

*lien*, p. 153. The text, which includes the Jews of Italy among those whose fate had to be discussed—something unusual in those times—was found this time in all the German documents connected with von Ribbentrop's visit in Rome and dealing with the Jewish topic (see notes 40–43).

40. Ministero Affari Esteri, *Relazione*, p. 34.

41. URO, *Judenverfolgung in Italien*, pp. 152–153.

42. Browning, *The German Foreign Office*, p. 166.

43. From von Hahn to the Reich Security Main Office for the attention of SS-Obersturmführer A. Eichmann, 25 February 1943 (Yad Vashem Archives, Jerusalem, TR-3, 961; URO, *Judenverfolgung in Italien*, p. 154). Fritz-Gebhardt von Hahn had since December 1942 been in the Third Department (Referat DIII) of the Deutschland Department at the Foreign Ministry, which was responsible for Jewish affairs (see about him in Browning, *The German Foreign Office*, by index).

44. From *SS-Gruppenführer* Müller to the Foreign Minister, 25 February 1943, (Yad Vashem Archives, Jerusalem, TR-3, 962; Klarsfeld, *Vichy-Auschwitz*, 2, pp. 225–227). In the document it is said that the memorandum had been composed from material supplied by Eichmann. One day later, Eichmann informed Knochen that the subject would be discussed in the talks being conducted in Rome between the foreign minister and the Duce (CDJC, XXVa-328/9; Poliakoff, *La condition des Juifs en France*, p. 77).

45. See F. W. Deakin, *The Brutal Friendship: Mussolini, Hitler and the Fall of Italian Fascism*, London, 1966, pp. 205–223. On the tête-à-tête meeting no record of any kind and no information have been preserved, except for the brief reference in Ortona's diary (see note 48).

46. Report of 27 February 1943 on the meeting of the 25th. The section concerning the Jews was published by URO, *Judenverfolgung in Italien*, pp. 155–156; Klarsfeld, *Vichy-Auschwitz*, 2, p. 228; Office of the U.S. Chief Counsel for the Prosecution of Axis Criminality, *Nazi Conspiracy and Aggression*, Washington, 1946, 7, pp. 188–190. The part of the section mentioning the Jews of Trieste was published only by URO.

47. Colonel Vincenzo Carla testified after the war that he had heard from his commanding officer, General Mario Robotti, commander of the Eleventh Army stationed in Croatia, that Mussolini had told him that in the course of his talks with von Ribbentrop the latter had raised the question of surrendering the Yugoslav Jews. See Poliakoff, *La condition des Juifs en France*, pp. 152–153 (in the Italian edition), pp. 147–148 (in the English edition); Carpi, "Jews in Croatia," pp. 496–497. Apparently, Mussolini was referring to von Ribbentrop's general remarks concerning "the Jews in the Italian Occupied Zones," and naturally, in a conversation with the commander of the Italian troops in Croatia, he concentrated on the Jews in that country.

48. Ortona, "Diario," pp. 1085–1086. According to Ortona, Mussolini had told Bastianini that in the tête-à-tête conversation von Ribbentrop had wanted to know the real reasons for Ciano's dismissal (p. 1086). Bastianini himself ex-

tensively discusses von Ribbentrop's visit in his book of memoirs (*Memorie*, pp. 272–275), but he does not mention a discussion of the Jewish topic.

49. The diary of Count Luca Pietromarchi has not yet been published. The two excerpts quoted below are from the manuscript of the diary kept by his son, Ambassador Antonello Pietromarchi. The sections concerning the Jews of Croatia were published in Hebrew (Carpi, "Pietromarchi").

50. Here the author was not accurate. Von Ribbentrop spoke about all the Jews, in Italy and the countries occupied by the Italians, not about the Italian citizens outside the borders of Italy. As indicated, at this stage the Italians had already decided to repatriate the Jews holding Italian citizenship.

51. Clearly the reference is to the dispatch from Ambassador Alfieri of 3 February 1943 (see note 13).

52. This is what Pietromarchi habitually calls the *Magen David* (literally, "shield of David"; in Italian, "star of David").

53. See note 44. In fact, in their reply the Italians refer to the German approach "of 25 February," the date of the memorandum from the Reich Security Head Office, but the note of von Ribbentrop was delivered on the 26th.

54. See note 34.

55. See notes 44 and 53.

56. See note 34.

57. *Collegamento Francia*. Liaison unit for the General Staff with the Vichy government (see Chapter 5, note 9).

58. ASSME, *Diario Storico Comando 4ª Armata*, racc. 1428, all. 4. A copy of the cable was sent to the operations branch of the General Staff (ibid., racc. 1218) and to the Foreign Ministry (ASMAE, AP, *Francia*, busta 80/7, no. 6581 P.R.).

59. Copy to the Foreign Ministry of the dispatch from the General Staff to COLFRAN (ASMAE, AP, *Francia*, busta 80/7, no. 6582 P.R.).

60. One of Laval's faithful followers. In April 1942 he was appointed to the position of *secrétaire d'état auprès du chef du gouvernement* (deputy minister at the prime minister's office).

61. The reference is probably to the eight Jews who immediately after their arrest were transferred to the Gurs camp. This camp was in the Pyrénées Department in the zone under German control. On this camp, see H. Schram and B. Vormeier, *Vivre à Gurs*, Paris, 1979; A. Rutkowski, "Le camp d'internement de Gurs," *Le Monde Juif*, 100 (1980), pp. 128–146; 101 (1981), pp. 13–32; R. Adler Cohen, "Le Camp de Gurs—une étape historique essentielle de 1940 à 1942," in K. Bartosek, R. Galissot, O. Peschanski (eds.), *Réfugiés et immigrés d'Europe Centrale dans le mouvement antifasciste et la Résistance en France (1933–1945)*, Paris, 1986, pp. 1–12.

62. Poliakoff, *La condition des Juifs en France*, pp. 91–92; Mazor, "Les Juifs dans la clandestinité," pp. 27–28; Klarsfeld, *Vichy-Auschwitz*, 2, p. 229. The first two publications are translations into French of the translation into German that Knochen had sent to Müller on 24 May 1943 (CDJC, XXVa-280). The third publication is a translation into French from the translation into German

that Schleier had sent, apparently to Oberg, on 4 March 1943 (Klarsfeld, ibid., p. 230). The Italians also published the document in French (Ministero Affari Esteri, *Relazione*, p. 71), but even in this case it is not certain that this was the original text. Either way, the variations between the versions are only stylistic and make no difference. In the publication of the Italian Foreign Ministry there was a mistake in the date of the document, which, as indicated, was 2 March.

63. According to a short note in the army archives, by which there is the remark that "the document itself has been lost" (ASSME, *Stralcio dal Diario Storico del Comando Supremo*, racc. 1443, all. 14). The contents are confirmed from the text of the memorandum (*Promemoria*) written at the General Staff on 3 April 1943 (ASSME, *Diario Storico del Comando Supremo*, racc. 1492, allegato tra 216 e 217). On this memorandum, which has been published in French by Klarsfeld (*Vichy-Auschwitz*, 2, pp. 260–263), see the rest of the chapter.

64. Klarsfeld, *Vichy-Auschwitz*, 2, p. 230.

65. Ministero Affari Esteri, *Relazione*, p. 30. That same day, 5 March 1943, Deputy Foreign Minister Bastianini dealt with the matter exhaustively in a cable to the Italian Embassy in Berlin. In summing up, the deputy minister stated: "as for the Jews, French or foreign, in our zones of occupation, the decision that measures in relation to them may be taken only and exclusively by our military authorities remains indisputably in force" (ASMAE, AP, *Francia*, busta 80/7, no. 7807/269 P.R.).

66. This hint seemingly made the required impression. For instance, the memorandum from the General Staff of 3 April (see note 63), opens by basing itself on "the instructions from the Duce" that had been given to the Foreign Ministry.

67. From Deputy Minister Bastianini to General Rossi, 7 March 1943 (ASMAE, AP, *Francia*, busta 80/7, no. 8129 P.R.). This document was first published in Ministero Affari Esteri, *Relazione*, pp. 29–30. This essay was published (without a date) immediately after the war, and the documents included with it were published sometimes with changes and omissions, in accordance with the general feelings of the time and for the needs of the hour. This document was in fact published with the omission of the writer's name (Bastianini had a rich history within the Fascist party, and they did not want to credit him with an operation with which the Foreign Ministry wished to pride itself). Also omitted was the word "French" (printed was: "the Government should be approached," instead of "the French Government"), probably to avoid unpleasantness with a country that once again was part of the victorious camp and with which relations in those days were quite tense. The document, with the same omissions, was later published by Klarsfeld, *Vichy-Auschwitz*, 2, p. 233.

68. From General Ambrosio to the Fourth Army Command, 8 March 1943 (ASMAE, AP, *Francia*, busta 80/7, no. 1500 R; Klarsfeld, *Vichy-Auschwitz*, 2, pp. 233–234).

69. The question of sentencing the Jews accused of criminal acts was discussed on different occasions and at several levels, for frequently Jews who had been

sentenced for trivial offenses in French courts were handed over to the Germans. Therefore, the commander of the Fourth Army already ordered that in no case were Jewish prisoners to be delivered to the Germans (apparently, the reference is to Jews holding Italian citizenship). The head of the Italian police remarked that this order contravened the conditions of the agreement made between the two police forces on 1 April 1936, according to which the latter were permitted to carry out extraditions "without the need for diplomatic proceedings." On 9 March 1943, the Foreign Ministry was asked to decide on the matter. On 2 April 1943, Bastianini replied that "an agreement between the two police forces, which in itself is an unconventional act, cannot be applied to the occupied territories" (ASSME, *Diario Storico del Comando Supremo*, racc. 1492, all. 110).

70. From General Ambrosio to General Avarna, 8 March 1943 (ASMAE, AP, *Francia*, busta 80/7, no. 1499 R).

71. See notes 44 and 53.

72. Today the document is not found in the *Francia* files, but a copy of it is appended to the note of 14 March 1943 from Count Vitetti, preserved in one of the *Jugoslavia* files (ASMAE, AP, *Jugoslavia*, busta 138/8). On 13 March Deputy Minister Bastianini sent a very detailed summary of the document to the General Staff, to Military Intelligence (SIM), and to the Police Head Branch of the Ministry of the Interior and a copy to the Italian Embassy in Paris, the liaison unit of the Foreign Ministry with the Fourth Army headquarters, and the consulate general in Vichy (ASMAE, AP, *Francia*, busta 80/7, no. 34/R. 2815). This summary was also copied almost word for word in the memorandum of 3 April 1943 from the General Staff (see note 63).

73. As submitted in Schleier's report of 4 March 1943 (Klarsfeld, *Vichy-Auschwitz*, 2, p. 230).

74. From von Ribbentrop to Ambassador von Mackensen, 9 March 1943 (Klarsfeld, *Die Endlösung*, p. 182; idem, *Vichy-Auschwitz*, 2, pp. 235–237). This dispatch is based on the reports that reached Berlin in those days, among them the reports from Schleier of 4 March 1943 (Klarsfeld, *Vichy-Auschwitz*, 2, p. 230) and from Röthke of 6 March 1943 (see Chapter 5, note 65).

75. That is, of course, not so in relation to the units of the MVSN (Milizia Volontaria Sicurezza Nazionale), the armed force of the Fascist party under its direct control.

76. Ortona, "Diario," p. 1088.

77. Deakin, *Mussolini-Hitler*, pp. 233–234; Ortona, "Diario," p. 1088. According to Deakin the meeting took place on 8 March 1943 and according to Ortona on the 9th. It seems that Ortona's version is preferable.

78. Although as indicated this note bears the date 9 February 1943, it appears from the words of von Ribbentrop (see note 79) that it was delivered to the German Embassy in Rome only on 11 February.

79. From von Ribbentrop to the German Ambassador in Rome, 13 March 1943 (Klarsfeld, *Die Endlösung*, p. 184; idem, *Vichy-Auschwitz*, 2, pp. 238–240).

80. As for the date of the meeting, there is a discrepancy between two documents, even though they are both of the same period and both are from von Mackensen. In his first report of 18 March 1943, the ambassador said that he was meeting Mussolini "this evening" (see note 81). On the other hand, in the second report of 20 March, he said that he had been called for an interview with Bastianini "on the Duce's instructions, following the meeting with him of the 17th of this month" (see note 99). It would seem preferable to favor the first version, which had, after all, been written on the day of the meeting. That, in fact, is what was done by R. Kempner (*Eichmann und Komplizen*, Zurich, 1961, p. 325). Kempner also took care to note that the (first) report by von Mackensen had been sent off "that very evening, at 21:25 hours." This statement, however, cannot be reconciled with the feverish activity that took place in Rome on 18 March in order to change Mussolini's decision. Furthermore, on examining the photostat of the original German document preserved in the Yad Vashem Archives, I realized that it clearly stated that the dispatch had been sent from Rome "on 18 March 1943 at 09:25" (and not "at 21:25, as Kempner wrote). That means that von Mackensen's report was sent from Rome in the morning of 18 March (at 09:25) and not in the evening of that day, and hence it could only refer to a meeting that had taken place the previous evening. The report was therefore composed on the evening on which the meeting took place (17 March) and was sent off the following morning (18 March). For some reason, in all the collections of documents in which this particular item has been published (see note 81) the hour the dispatch had been sent from Rome and the hour it was received in Berlin have been omitted.

81. From Ambassador von Mackensen to the Reich Foreign Minister, 18 March 1943 (Yad Vashem Archives, Jerusalem, TR-3, 456; URO, *Judenverfolgung in Italien*, pp. 163–164; Klarsfeld, *Vichy-Auschwitz*, 2, pp. 245–246; Poliakoff, *La condition des Juifs en France*, pp. 68–70 [English edition], pp. 63–65 [Italian edition]; Kempner, *Eichmann und Komplizen*, pp. 325–326).

82. Carmine Senise served as *capo della polizia* (chief of police) from December 1940. He was not popular with the Germans and the pro-German wing within the Fascist party and was dismissed from his post in April 1943. He was active in the plot formed to depose Mussolini, and after the latter's fall on 25 July 1943 he was reinstated as chief of police. On 23 September 1943 he was arrested by the Germans, sent to the concentration camp of Dachau, and held in captivity until the end of the war. After the war, he published his memoirs (*Quando ero capo della polizia, 1940–1943*, Rome, 1946).

83. Bastianini, *Memorie*, pp. 86–88. See also Pirelli, *Taccuini*, p. 430.

84. According to several sources a conversation also took place between Mussolini and General Ambrosio at the beginning of the morning, in the course of which Ambrosio tried unsuccessfully to change the Duce's decision, but it is not certain that this information is correct.

85. Memorandum from the General Staff of 3 April 1943 (see note 63). See also Pietromarchi diary, entry for 31 March 1943 ("Frammenti delle memorie

dell'ambasciatore Luca Pietromarchi. La difesa degli ebrei nel '43," *Nuova Antologia*, fasc. 2161 [January–March 1987], pp. 245–247).

86. Senise, *Capo della polizia*, p. 103.

87. Ortona, "Diario," p. 1091. In fact, the date of the meeting between the two leaders was postponed because of the start of the British offensive in Tunisia. As an expert on the "Jewish problem" in the occupied countries, Count Vidau had been attached to the Italian delegation for the meeting that eventually took place on 7–10 April 1943, (Ortona, ibid., p. 1096), but there is no evidence that this subject was actually discussed.

88. Note from Mgr. Giovanni Battista Montini for Mgr. Ambrosio Marchioni, 18 March 1943 (*Documents du Saint-Siège*, 9, p. 196). See there, in footnote, the reply of the nuncio on 19 March 1943. See also R. A. Graham, "Il Vaticano e gli ebrei profughi in Italia durante la guerra," *La Civiltà Cattolica*, no. 3281 (1987), pp. 435–439. A similar step was also taken in those days on behalf of the Jewish refugees in the Italian Occupation Zone in Croatia (*Documents du Saint-Siège*, 9, p. 183).

89. Pietromarchi, "Frammenti delle memorie," pp. 245–247 (entry for 31 March 1943).

90. Bastianini, *Memorie*, p. 88.

91. See Chapter 2, pp. 51–54.

92. In connection with this, it is of interest to quote an episode mentioned by Ortona in his diary (p. 1130). On 24 July 1943, several hours before the meeting in the course of which Mussolini was ousted, Ortona approached Dino Grandi, who was serving as president of the Senate and was the initiator of the ouster to inform him of Bastianini's support. Ortona took the opportunity to ask Grandi whether he did not fear for his life and that of his colleagues, as a detachment of "blackshirts" was permanently stationed in the vicinity of the place where the meeting was due to take place. Grandi, who among the fascist leaders was perhaps the man who knew Mussolini better than anyone else, replied without hesitation: "Nothing of that kind you fear will happen. He is afraid of blood!"

93. According to Senise's memoirs, General Castellano represented the General Staff at a meeting held at the beginning of 1943 in the Foreign Ministry, in which was decided not to agree to the German demand about the surrender of the Jews in southern France (*Capo della polizia*, p. 104).

94. From Mussolini to General Vercellino and to the head of the Armistice Commission with France, 19 March 1943. The dispatch is appended to the memorandum of 3 April 1943 from the General Staff (see note 63), and it is marked: "Allegato 1 al foglio n. 1352."

95. Memorandum from the General Staff of 3 April 1943 (see note 63).

96. The rank of *ispettore generale* was a high rank in the Italian police. It was not the rank of chief of police (*capo della polizia*), as may be interpreted. The statement that it was Mussolini who chose Lospinoso from four candidates who had been proposed to him, is based on the words of Bastianini to von Mackensen (see note 99). After the war, Lospinoso himself claimed that

Senise had proposed four names and that it was General Vercellino who had chosen among them (V. Statera, "L'ex questore Lospinoso ci racconta come aiutò quarantamila israeliti," *La Stampa*, 5 May 1961). But that is only one of many attempts made by Lospinoso to minimize his connections with the Duce and the fascist leadership. His words cannot be reconciled with the sources, and we cannot accept them. On the contrary, Mussolini's opening words to Lospinoso prove clearly that he, Mussolini, had chosen him and had done so on the basis of personal acquaintance. On the personality of Inspector General Lospinoso and his activities in southern France, see Chapter 7.

97. What follows is based mainly on the testimony that Lospinoso gave after the war. This was published, together with some of his other papers, by Rochlitz, *Documents*, pp. 49, 59, 65. Lospinoso repeated this evidence, briefly and with some changes, in an interview he gave to a daily paper following the Eichmann trial (Statera, "L'ex questore Lospinoso").

98. The date of this meeting is not absolutely certain. According to the report from von Mackensen to von Ribbentrop of 20 March 1943 (below, note 99), he had met Bastianini during the morning of that same day. On the other hand, according to Bastianini and also Pietromarchi the meeting took place the day the nuncio had received the "reassuring information," namely, on 19 March. It seems that in this case there is no reason not to accept the statement in the ambassador's report.

99. From Ambassador von Mackensen to the Reich foreign minister, 20 March 1943 (URO, *Judenverfolgung in Italien*, pp. 166–167; Poliakoff, *La condition des Juifs en France*, pp. 70–72 [in the English edition], pp. 65–68 [in the Italian edition]; Klarsfeld, *Vichy-Auschwitz*, 2, pp. 245–246).

100. Pietromarchi, "Frammenti delle memorie," pp. 245–247 (entry for 31 March 1943).

## 7: The Italian "Race Police" in Nice (pp. 136–163)

1. Most scholars are full of praise for the man's initiative, and there are even some who find an explanation for Lospinoso's actions in that he himself was of Jewish origin, a descendant of the Marannos! See for example, Latour, *La Résistance juive*, p. 142. All these assumptions, however, are groundless.

2. See also Chapter 5, note 8.

3. The description of the meeting at the Fourth Army headquarters is based on the memorandum of 3 April 1943 from the General Staff (see Chapter 6, note 63). Lospinoso does not mention at all this meeting in his testimony, and this fact is puzzling enough.

4. Lospinoso testimony (Rochlitz, *Documents*, p. 49). To be precise, Lospinoso wrote that he had arrived in Nice "the following day"—meaning the day following that of his interview with Mussolini, but that apparently is a slip of the pen. According to other sources, Lospinoso reached Nice only a few weeks later,

but perhaps this had been a rumor deliberately spread to mislead the Germans.

5. Several sources mention the activities on behalf of the Jews of the commander of the Carabinieri regiment attached to the Fourth Army, Colonel Giuseppe Borla, the commander of the Carabinieri unit stationed in Nice, Lieutenant Colonel Mario Bodo, and one of their officers, Captain Salvi. After the capitulation of Italy Salvi joined the Italian resistance movement, was taken prisoner and executed—apparently by fascists of the Salò Republic. About him see also Chapter 8, note 21.

6. The following is based principally on his evidence, published in the *Livre d'or des congrégations françaises* ("Résumé de mon activité," pp. 306–309). This evidence is the most detailed and accurate of all those that he published after the war. See also "Una lettera di Padre Benedetto," *La Voce della Comunità Israelitica* (July, 1955); "Pagine di storia, Angelo Donati," *Israel*, 46 (13 April 1961), p. 3; CDJC, *La France et la question juive, 1940–1944*, Paris, 1981, pp. 253–254. See also the testimonies of Lospinoso (Rochlitz, *Documents*, pp. 49, 65).

7. This courageous action that he undertook with total disregard for his safety did not make him forget his Christian duty, as he saw it. In a memorandum that he presented on 15 July 1943 to Pope Pius XII to ask for his intervention on behalf of the Jews of France, he notes with satisfaction that in the period when he was living in Nice he had succeeded in baptizing fifty-one Jews (*Documents du Saint-Siège*, 9, p. 393).

8. Testimony of Father Marie-Benoît ("Résumé de mon activité," p. 308).

9. In fact, all scholars, except for Father R. Graham who mentions the "cunning" of Lospinoso ("Il Vaticano e gli ebrei," p. 437).

10. Lospinoso testimony (Rochlitz, *Documents*, pp. 49, 65).

11. On the intelligence activity of Lospinoso during the years he served in the Italian Consulate of Nice (1928–1940), see interesting details in R. Schor, "Il fascismo italiano nelle Alpes-Maritimes 1922–1939," *Notiziario dell'Istituto Storico della Resistenza in Cuneo e Provincia*, 26 (1984), pp. 48–49.

12. CIAF, *Notiziario Quindicinale*, 57 (mid-April 1943), p. 15. The number of Jewish refugees there had grown, particularly after the manhunts conducted in Marseilles on 22–24 January 1943. See on this Ryan, *Marseilles 1939–1944*, pp. 344–365; G. Guicheteau, *Marseilles 1943: La fin du Vieux Port*, Marseilles, 1973.

13. It seems that these figures were very close to the reality of those days. It would perhaps be correct to say that the total number of Jews in the Italian Occupation Zone was between 25,000 and 30,000 souls.

14. It seems reasonable that Lospinoso reached this decision after consulting with Consul Calisse and particularly after he realized that the Jews whom Inspector Barranco had begun to intern some two months earlier had also been transferred to the Haute-Savoie Department. But as usual for him, Lospinoso in his testimony does not mention the part played by others, and it is not known whether he had consulted them.

15. Fink Documents (see Chapter 5, note 45), testimony, p. 5.

16. On the part of the Jewish organizations in financing the operation, see CDJC,

*Activité des organisations juives en France sous l'occupation*, Paris, 1947, pp. 18, 83, 143.

17. On the educational activity, see H. Gorgiel-Sercaz, "Memoirs of a Jewish Girl," *Yalkut Moreshet*, 50 (1991), pp. 175–195.

18. See testimonies of Lospinoso (Rochlitz, *Documents*, pp. 50, 58, 66), Fink Documents, pp. 6–7, (see Chapter 5, note 45), and Donati Documents (see Chapter 5, note 50).

19. B. Halpern, *A Ray of Light in the Darkness*, Jerusalem, 1967, p. 55. On the fate of the Jewish refugees in St. Martin after the capitulation of Italy, see A. Cavaglion, *Nella notte straniera*, Cuneo, 1981.

20. According to a report from the end of May 1943 of the *Union Générale des Israélites de France* (UGIF), quoted by Klarsfeld, *Vichy-Auschwitz*, 2, p. 51.

21. The estimates on the number of these Jews varies between 4,500 and 6,000, but it is doubtful that there were many more than 4,500.

22. In the Italian version the document says: "To / ALBERTO CALISSE / Consul General of Italy / who, in accordance with the instructions of his Government, concerning the Jews resident and refugee in the Italian zone of occupation, France, gave high noble demonstration of humanity and justice. / With respects for eternal gratitude. / Nice, 10 May 1943." The certificate is signed by six rabbis (the two rabbis of Paris, as well as the rabbis of Metz, Dresden, Charleroi, and Czestochova), by I. Doubinsky as "Chairman of the Congregation of Foreign Jews in Nice," and A. Donati as "Trustee for the Jewish Welfare Institutions." Calisse was returned to the Foreign Ministry, where he was appointed to a senior post in the Political Department of the Ministry. Sent to Nice in his place was Consul Augusto Spechel, who took up his post in the middle of May 1943.

23. Donati Documents; Rochlitz, *Documents*, p. 106.

24. Ortona, "Diario," p. 1091.

25. From SS-Obergruppenführer Müller to the commander of the Security Police and the SD in Paris, 2 April 1943 (CDJC, I-43; Yad Vashem Archives, Jerusalem, TR-3, 820; URO, *Judenverfolgung in Italien*, p. 168; Poliakoff, *La condition des Juifs en France*, p. 79; Klarsfeld, *Vichy-Auschwitz*, 2, p. 259).

26. Klarsfeld, *Vichy-Auschwitz*, 2, p. 259. On the meeting between Mussolini and Müller, see also Senise (*Capo della polizia*, p. 103). Senise wrongly wrote there that Mussolini had entrusted the mission in southern France to Lospinoso that same morning. As indicated, this had occurred nine days earlier.

27. "File note—secret" of 3 April 1943 signed by SS-Hauptsturmführer Nosek (CDJC, XXVa-237). After the war Baron Francesco Malfatti di Montetretto served in the Foreign Ministry in a number of senior diplomatic posts and ended his career with the rank of *segretario generale* of the ministry.

28. From Knochen to the Reich Security Main Office, Bureau IV, for the attention of SS-Gruppenführer Müller, 5 April 1943 (Yad Vashem Archives, Jerusalem, TR-3, 821; Poliakoff, *La condition des Juifs en France*, p. 80). See also note 34.

29. From Ambassador Buti to the Foreign Ministry, 5 April 1943 (ASMAE, AP, *Francia*, busta 80/7, no. 10620).

30. From Babuscio-Rizzo to the Italian Embassy in Paris, 7 April 1943 (ASMAE,

AP, *Francia*, busta 80/7, no. 11751/210 P.R.). On the dispatch of 13 March 1943, see Chapter 6, note 72.

31. From Müller to Knochen, 7 April 1943 (CDJC, XXVa-330; Poliakoff, *La condition des Juifs en France*, p. 82; Klarsfeld, *Vichy-Auschwitz*, 2, p. 265).

32. Copy to Knochen of the report from Hagen to Oberg, 7 April 1943 (CDJC, XXVa-238).

33. From Röthke to Knochen, 8 April 1943 (CDJC, XXVa-239).

34. From Knochen to the Reich Security Main Office, Bureau IVB4, 7 April 1943 (CDJC, XXVa-288; Klarsfeld, *Vichy-Auschwitz*, 2, p. 264).

35. From Knochen to the Reich Security Main Office, for the attention of Müller, 8 April 1943. The original draft of the cable, containing corrections in Knochen's handwriting is preserved at the *Centre de Documentation Juive Contemporaine* in Paris (CDJC, XXVa-330). See also Poliakoff, *La condition des Juifs en France*, p. 83; Klarsfeld, *Vichy-Auschwitz*, 2, p. 265).

36. From Müller to the commander of the Security Police and the SD in Paris, 9 April 1943 (CDJC, I-45; Yad Vashem Archives, Jerusalem, TR-3, 822; URO, *Judenverfolgung in Italien*, p. 169; Poliakoff, *La condition des Juifs en France*, p. 85; Klarsfeld, *Vichy-Auschwitz*, 2, p. 226).

37. Ortona, "Diario," p. 1100.

38. Renzo Chierici did in fact warn Mussolini of the plot against him, but on the night of 25 July he did nothing to prevent the Duce's ouster (he was also not ordered to do so by the latter). After the German invasion in September 1943, he was imprisoned by the fascists in the Verona prison, and in December 1943 a bomb exploded in his cell, putting an end to his life.

39. From von Thadden to the Reich Security Main Office, for the attention of Eichmann, 6 May 1943 (Yad Vashem Archives, Jerusalem, TR-3, 196; CDJC, *Le Dossier Eichmann et "La solution finale de la question juive,"* Paris, 1960, pp. 181–182).

40. From von Thadden to the Reich Security Main Office, for the attention of Eichmann, 10 May 1943 (Klarsfeld, *Vichy-Auschwitz*, 2, pp. 277–278).

41. From Knochen to the Reich Security Main Office, for the attention of Müller, 24 May 1943 (CDJC, XXVa-23, I-47; Yad Vashem Archives, Jerusalem, TR-3, 826; Poliakoff, *La condition des Juifs en France*, pp. 90–91; Klarsfeld, *Vichy-Auschwitz*, 2, pp. 280–281). Knochen added that he had sent one of his people to ask for details at the Italian Embassy in Paris, but he had been told that Lospinoso had not yet arrived [in Paris] and that they knew nothing about his planned journey. Thereby, Knochen found additional confirmation of his opinion that "certain Italian services were not, to put it mildly, showing any interest in the solution of the Jewish problem in France." He therefore asked to find out from the Italian government whether the visit from Lospinoso was still on the agenda, and if so when it would take place. The first part of Knochen's report is based on the information he had received that day from Röthke, concerning the meeting that had taken place at the Italian Embassy between SS-Obersturmführer Gudekunst and Malfatti (CDJC, XXVa-246; Yad Vashem Archives, Jerusalem, TR-3, 825; Poliakoff, ibid., p. 89).

42. From Röthke to the commanders of the Security Police and the SD in Dijon, Lyon, and Marseilles, 12 May 1943 (CDJC, I-46, Yad Vashem Archives, Jerusalem, TR-3, 824; Poliakoff, *La condition des Juifs en France*, p. 86).

43. From SS-Obersturmführer Klaus Barbie to the Security Police headquarters in Paris, 15 May 1943 (CDJC, XXVa-331/332; Poliakoff, *La condition des Juifs en France*, pp. 87–88; Mazor, "Les Juifs dans la clandestinité," p. 23). On Barbie, see Klarsfeld, "Notices biographiques," p. 190.

44. From SS-Obersturmführer August Moritz to the Security Police headquarters in Paris, for the attention of Röthke, 26 May 1943 (CDJC, I-50; Klarsfeld, *Die Endlösung*, p. 199; Poliakoff, *La condition des Juifs en France*, pp. 99–100). Moritz belonged to the Reich Security Main Office. During the war he served in command positions in the Security Police units in Orleans, Lyon, Marseilles, and Nice. He distinguished himself by his enthusiasm for action in the deportation of the Jews and the suppression of the French Resistance movement. After the war, he served a number of years in the management of an organization based in Hamburg for victims of the Nazis (!). See Klarsfeld, "Notices biographiques," p. 198; Ryan, *Marseilles 1939–1944*, p. 346.

45. CDJC, I-51; Poliakoff, *La condition des Juifs en France*, pp. 101–105; Ministero Affari Esteri, *Relazione*, pp. 77–80.

46. On the Police aux Questions Juives, see Marrus and Paxton, *Vichy France*, pp. 135–137.

47. See Chapter 5, note 9.

48. See Chapter 6, note 62.

49. See Chapter 6, note 63.

50. From General Ambrosio to the Fourth Army headquarters, 8 March 1943, copy to the Foreign Ministry, Department AG (ASMAE, AP, *Francia*, busta 80/7, no. 1500 R.; Ministero Affari Esteri, *Relazione*, pp. 30–31; Klarsfeld, *Vichy-Auschwitz*, 2, pp. 233–234).

51. Report from SS-Obersturmführer Lischka to the Reich Security Main Office, Bureau IVB4, 15 March 1943. In this report, Lischka quotes the indicated order from Colonel Giovanelli, based on a memorandum that he, Lischka, had received from the director of the Department for Investigation and Control of the Commissariat Général aux Questions Juives (CDJC, XXVa-282a; Klarsfeld, *Die Endlösung*, pp. 186–187; idem, *Vichy-Auschwitz*, 2, pp. 240–242). On Kurt Lischka and his activities in France from November 1940 until November 1943, see Klarsfeld, "Notices biographiques," pp. 197–198.

52. Klarsfeld, *Vichy-Auschwitz*, 2, p. 242.

53. From General Avarna to Admiral Bourrague, 29 March 1943 (CDJC, I-47; Yad Vashem Archives, Jerusalem, TR-3, 826; Poliakoff, *La condition des Juifs en France*, pp. 93–94; Ministero Affari Esteri, *Relazione*, p. 72; Klarsfeld, *Vichy-Auschwitz*, 2, p. 258).

54. From General Avarna to General Bridoux, 27 April 1943 (CDJC, XXVa-241; Poliakoff, *La condition des Juifs en France*, pp. 94–95; Ministero Affari Esteri, *Relazione*, p. 74; Klarsfeld, *Vichy-Auschwitz*, 2, pp. 275–276).

55. Report from General Avarna to the General Staff, 29 March 1943, in which he

summarizes the claims of the French (ASSME, *Diario Storico del Comando Supremo*, Allegato n. 2225.); and a report of that day from the General Staff to the Foreign Ministry (Ministero Affari Esteri, *Relazione*, p. 31).

56. A note from Röthke, a copy of which was sent to Lischka and to Hagen, 23 March 1943 (CDJC, XXVc-228; Klarsfeld, *Vichy-Auschwitz*, 2, pp. 247–249). In fact, the French police did participate in the deportation of Jews (many of them French) carried out on 23 and 25 March 1943.

57. Klarsfeld, *Vichy-Auschwitz*, 2, pp. 247–248.

58. The excerpt is quoted in the note of 25 March 1943 signed by Hagen (CDJC, XXVc-232; Klarsfeld, *Vichy-Auschwitz*, 2, p. 255). In speaking of "the latest declaration of the Führer," Oberg was probably referring to the speech Hitler had made a short time before at a ceremony in memory of "the heroic fallen," in which he repeated the need to solve the Jewish problem "with a radical solution."

59. From Knochen to the Reich Security Main Office, Bureau IVB4, 29 March 1943 (CDJC, XXVc-235; Klarsfeld, *Vichy-Auschwitz*, 2, p. 259).

60. Lospinoso testimony (Rochlitz, *Documents*, pp. 49–67).

61. Ibid., pp. 50–51.

62. Summary by Hagen of 29 June 1943 on the conversation that had taken place between him and Bousquet on 23 June 1943 (CDJC, XXVa-333; Poliakoff, *La condition des Juifs en France*, pp. 110–111). Bousquet does not mention what day Lospinoso had visited him; it was probably a short time previously. Some pieces of information on the opposition of the Vichy authorities to the transfer of Jews to Megève have been preserved. The reason given was that the township of Megève was intended to receive evacuees from the regions under aerial bombardment in the north of the country (and in fact about 1,000 evacuee children had been sent to Megève a short time before the arrival of the Jews). This official opposition was also frequently accompanied by an expressly antisemitic note. See, for example, *Au Pilori* on 1 July 1943 (CDJC, XXVa-305).

63. From Knochen to the commander of the Security Police and SD, SS-Obergruppenführer Kaltenbrunner and to Bureau IV of the Reich Security Main Office for the attention of SS-Gruppenführer Müller, 23 June 1943 (CDJC, I-52; URO, *Judenverfolgung in Italien*, pp. 182–183; Poliakoff, *La condition des Juifs en France*, pp. 108–109; Mazor, "Les Juifs dans le clandestinité," pp. 28–29; Klarsfeld, *Vichy-Auschwitz*, 2, p. 296). See also the report of 1 July 1943 from Oberg to Himmler and to Kaltenbrunner (CDJC, XXVII-22; Klarsfeld, ibid., 2, pp. 299–300).

64. See Marrus and Paxton, *Vichy France*, pp. 321–329; Klarsfeld, *Vichy-Auschwitz*, 2, pp. 89, 315–316, 320–328.

65. From SS-Sturmbannführer Mühler to the commander of the Security Police in Paris, 10 July 1943 (CDJC, XXVa-324/325; Poliakoff, *La condition des Juifs en France*, pp. 112–114; Klarsfeld, *Vichy-Auschwitz*, 2, p. 302). On Mühler, see also Chapter 5, note 12. The report from Mühler is not sufficiently specific concerning the place and date of the meeting. In any case, it is clear that it had

taken place between 7 and 10 of July (the conversation with Barranco had taken place on 7 July, and on 10 July Mühler reported that the conversation had taken place).

66. Possibly, Luceri was referring to the estimate made by the Armistice Commission.

67. See note 65.

68. On 2 August 1943 a copy of the report of the meeting, which had taken place on 21 July 1943 between Lospinoso and the *directeur de la Section d'Enquête et de Controle du Commissariat Général aux Questions Juives pour la Zone Sud* (director of the Inquiry and Control Section of the Commissariat for Jewish Affairs for the Southern Zone), was delivered to Röthke by the heads of the Commissariat (CDJC, I-53; Poliakoff, *La condition des Juifs en France,* pp. 119–123; Klarsfeld, *Vichy-Auschwitz,* 2, pp. 311–313). This meeting is not mentioned at all in Lospinoso's evidences.

69. Thus, explicitly in the words of the document. Actually, it might have been expected that it would be Lospinoso who would have been asked to present the list to the French. On this subject see also Chapter 8, note 53.

## 8: The Forty-five Days of the Badoglio Government (pp. 164–192)

1. On this, see also Part III.

2. Report on the strikes, delivered by Chief of Police Chierici to Mussolini (Deakin, *Mussolini-Hitler,* p. 251).

3. R. Cruccu, "La 4ª armata e l'armistizio," in Istituto Storico della Resistenza in Cuneo e Provincia, *8 settembre. Lo sfacelo della quarta armata,* Turin, 1979, p. 69.

4. Saulnier, "Nizza occupata," p. 55. See also Levy, "La 4ª Armata," pp. 58–59; Trabucchi, *I vinti,* p. 14; J. B. Duroselle and E. Serra, *Italia e Francia (1939–1945), Vol. 2. La diplomazia italiana e la ripresa dei rapporti con la Francia (1943–1945),* Milan, 1984, pp. 22–30. To be precise, Saulnier writes that the festivities were "on 25 July 1943." But that is surely a mistake. The announcement concerning Mussolini's "resignation" was first broadcast in Italy on 25 July at 22:45 and in France the next day. On the reaction of the French population, Ambassador Buti reported on 28 July 1943, saying: "The great majority of the French people received the events in Italy with evident satisfaction. Especially since they assumed that the change of government preludes to the withdrawal of Italy from the war, which in turn was likely to shorten it greatly and eventually improve the future standing of France." (Quoted by E. Serra, "Cade Mussolini, resiste Vichy," *La Stampa,* 7 October 1981).

5. CIAF, *Notiziario Quindicinale,* issue no. 64 (end of July 1943), p. 15.

6. CIAF, *Notiziario Quindicinale,* issue no. 65 (mid-August 1943), p. 16. These tendencies were described in almost identical words in the memoirs of one of the officers in the Fourth Army, Mario Brocchi. This is what he said: "The panic

among the Jews was growing. The Army headquarters [in Nice] are under a proper siege. Like it also are the other Italian institutions—the Consulate and the Delegation of the Armistice Commission. The Jews in their masses asked for passports to cross the border and escape from the approaching Teutonic persecution" (R. De Felice, "Un nuovo documento sulla condizione degli ebrei nella zona d'occupazione italiana in Francia durante la seconda guerra mondiale," in F. Del Canuto (ed.), *Israel, "Un decennio," 1974–1984*, Rome, 1984, p. 182).

7. According to the evidence quoted in Lazar, *La résistance juive*, p. 251. And in fact on receipt of the news of the capitulation of Italy, a number of convoys of refugees left the township of St. Martin and crossed the border through the alpine passes into Italy.

8. From Consul Spechel to the Foreign Ministry, 31 July 1943 (ASMAE, AP, *Francia*, busta 80/7, no. 21831 P.R.).

9. From Consul Spechel to the Foreign Ministry—"Most urgent. Personal, for Minister Vidau only"—31 July 1943 (ASMAE, AP, *Francia*, busta 80/7, no. 5000). Spechel also indicates that in the absence of Donati from the town he had not succeeded in gathering all the details on the subject and that he would report on it soon in greater detail. See note 15 for his report of 7 August.

10. From Vidau to the Ministry of the Interior, 2 August 1943 (ASMAE, AP, *Francia*, busta 80/7, no. 4255).

11. From Senise to the Foreign Ministry (A.G.-Ufficio IV), 4 August 1943 (ASMAE, AP, *Francia*, busta 80/7, no. 12404/227800).

12. From Vidau to the delegations in Nice, Chambéry, Grenoble, Cannes, the Princedom of Monaco, to the embassy in Paris, and to the liaison office with the Fourth Army headquarters, 6 August 1943 (ASMAE, AP, *Francia*, busta 80/7, no. 24335/C P.R.).

13. From Giacomo Silimbani (in Vidau's name) to the Ministry of the Interior, Police Bureau, 7 August 1943 (ASMAE, AP, *Francia*, busta 80/7, no. 24508 P.R.). The communication from Spechel has not been preserved. It is quoted in the letter from the Ministry of the Interior to the Foreign Ministry. On Giacomo Silimbani, who earlier had been consul general in Tunis, see Part III.

14. From Senise to the Foreign Ministry (A.G.-Ufficio IV), 8 August 1943 (ASMAE, AP, *Francia*, busta 80/7, no. 5270 R).

15. From Consul Spechel to the Foreign Ministry, 7 August 1943 (ASMAE, AP, *Francia*, busta 80/7, no. 22702 P.R.).

16. There were at least two summaries of this meeting: one written by officials from the Department for European and Mediterranean Affairs (AEM) and presented to Foreign Minister Raffaele Guariglia on 11 August 1943 (ASMAE, AP, *Francia*, busta 66); and one written by the officials of the Department for General Affairs (AG). Today this second document is not in the *Francia* files in the archives. From excerpts published in Ministero Affari Esteri, *Relazione*, p. 35, we find that the second document was more detailed than the first, but Vidau's proposals are identical in both summaries. Guariglia was one of the senior Italian diplomats; during the 1930s he had been in close contact with several

Zionist leaders and knew the Jewish problem well. After the war he published his memoirs: *Ricordi*, Naples, 1948.

17. Vidau remarked that his proposal to transfer the Jewish refugees to Italy "would be a step giving rise to negative interpretations by the Reich government" (Ministero Affari Esteri, *Relazione*, p. 35).

18. Trabucchi, *I vinti*, p. 21; Cruccu, "La 4ª Armata," pp. 69–70. There is no support for Panicacci's conjecture that one of the considerations for making this decision was the desire "to protect the Jewish colony" in southern France ("L'occupazione Italiana," p. 31).

19. According to a memorandum that contained the decisions of the meeting and that has been preserved in the army archives (ASME, *Comando Supremo*). This document was published with several abridgments by Panicacci, "L'occupazione Italiana," p. 32. In Ministero Affari Esteri, *Relazione*, p. 35, the holding of the meeting is mentioned, with the names of the participants (which are not in the memorandum in the army archives), but for some reason, the decisions themselves were not published.

20. See also note 32. On 30 August 1943, Donati reported on these negotiations to Fink (Fink Documents, see Chapter 5, note 45); but there is no doubt that he had already informed him earlier, at least in general terms. On 31 August 1943 in a dispatch to the Foreign Ministry the vice-consul in Nice, Arrighi, mentioned "the instructions given me through Donati" and announced that he was awaiting their confirmation (ASMAE, AP, *Francia*, busta 80/7, no. 24271 P.R.). Many pieces of evidence have been preserved on the flooding of Jews into Nice and its surroundings. See among others the report of 8 September 1943 from the Alpes-Maritimes prefect, quoted in H. Amouroux, *La grande histoire des Français sous l'occupation. Vol. 5. Les passions et les haines*, Paris, 1981, pp. 306–307.

21. From Consul Spechel to the Foreign Ministry, "Confidential, personal for Vidau," 3 September 1943 (ASMAE, AP, *Francia*, busta 80/7, no. 6107 R). In a quite unconventional aside, Spechel noted in this dispatch that Captain Salvi "had shown himself as the most competent and the most effective organizer of the measures pertaining to the problem discussed."

22. From Malfatti to the Foreign Ministry, 3 September 1943 (ASMAE, AP, *Francia*, busta 80/7, no. 2).

23. From Vidau to the Delegation in Chambéry, 5 September 1943 (ASMAE, AP, *Francia*, busta 80/7, no. 27323/18 P.R.).

24. From A. Rosso to the General Staff, 6 September 1943 (ASMAE, AP, *Francia*, busta 80/7, no. 27477). See also notes 59–62.

25. From A. Rosso to the embassy in Paris, 6 September 1943 (ASMAE, AP, *Francia*, busta 80/7, no. 27449 P.R./469).

26. In testimony he published after the war (see Chapter 7, note 6) Father Marie-Benoît in his modesty played down his part in the operation. In a letter he published in the periodical of the Jewish community in Rome he even claimed that "the initiative and the credit belong to my dearest friend Angelo Donati."

But, Father Marie-Benoît was entitled to far greater credit than he himself was prepared to acknowledge.

27. Donati Documents (see Chapter 5, note 50), testimony, p. 3.

28. In his first and most important testimony, Father Marie-Benoît expressly says "in order to get pressure to be applied to Mussolini on this subject" ("Résumé de mon activité," p. 309). In the two other testimonies ("Una lettera di Padre Benedetto"; *La France et la question juive*), he uses the words "on the Italian government."

29. Testimony of Father Marie-Benoît in A. Wellers, A. Kaspi, S. Klarsfeld (eds.), *La France et la question juive*, p. 254.

30. Ibid.; *Documents du Saint-Siège*, 9, p. 401 and note 1.

31. *Documents du Saint-Siège*, 9, pp. 393–397. The memorandum from Father Marie-Benoît bears the date 15 July 1943. The appendices have not been published. The audience took place, as mentioned, on 16 July 1943, and Mgr. Tardini's note was written on the 18th.

32. These four vessels—the *Duilio, Giulio Cesare, Saturnia*, and *Vulcania*—had earlier served for the repatriation of Italian civilians from East Africa, with the consent and under the protection of the British. They were already painted with the colors of the Red Cross and on board there were crews who had already passed security screening by the British. See on this the letter from Donati to the "Joint" (footnote 39).

33. Donati Documents, testimony, p. 3.

34. Testimony of Father Marie-Benoît ("Résumé de mon activité," pp. 311–312). The contents of this testimony are fully corroborated by the testimony of Donati (even though the latter lacked some of the details). See also the words of Sir Francis Osborn himself in his report of 24 August 1943 to the Foreign Office: "I have had several visits from an Italian Jew, Donati . . . who has been doing excellent work at considerable personal risk and expense on behalf of refugee Jews . . . in Italy and more particularly that part of Southern France the occupation of which is now being turned over from the Italians to the Germans" (quoted in Michaelis, *Mussolini and the Jews*, pp. 342–343).

35. *Documents du Saint-Siège*, 9, pp. 401–402. The date on the original document is apparently incomplete, because it was completed by the editor: "[16] July 1943," but this conjecture is apparently incorrect. This date is not corroborated by the text of the document, which mentions the audience with the pope on 16 July as something in the past. The contents of the document also unquestionably indicate that it was written after the fall of Mussolini (25 July 1943). The words of Father Marie-Benoît, implying that the British government had at that time already "agreed in principle" to the plan were to some degree premature and seem to reflect his wishes.

36. Document No. 321, from the beginning of September 1943, which had been published in *Documents du Saint-Siège* (9, pp. 465–467), is a copy of the memorandum that Donati had transmitted to the representative of the "Joint"

in Lisbon. This document therefore does not testify to action taken by the Vatican, as the editor had thought, but it does indicate that the Vatican authorities would have reported such action. See also note 39.

37. See report by Sir Francis Osborn (quoted in note 34) ending with the following words: "Please give the proposal your personal and sympathetic consideration."

38. Fink Documents. Attached to this memorandum of 30 August 1943 is Donati's visiting card on which he wrote: "M. Fink, 24 Blvd. Dubouchage," but presumably these matters were intended for all the members of the committee. The document also says that the subject for negotiation was "about 30,000 Jews, living in Italy and in areas under Italian control."

39. This document was published at least three times: the first time by Father Marie-Benoît in French, in his testimony of 1948 ("Résumé de mon activité," pp. 312–314); a second time, again by Father Marie-Benoît, this time in Italian in 1961, in the words of eulogy for A. Donati (p. 3); and a third time, in French, in the *Documents du Saint-Siège* (9, pp. 465–467). Seemingly, Father Marie-Benoît took care to deliver a copy of the document at the time it was actually composed to the Congregazione for "Special Ecclesiastic Affairs" so they should be informed of what was being done.

40. Donati did not of course know that on 7 September 1943, a day before publication of the announcement of the capitulation of the Badoglio government, Osborn had still written to the British Foreign Office: "It is useless . . . to hope for large scale removal of refugees from Italy for a good time ahead; but why can't they stay in Italy?" (*Documents du Saint-Siège*, 9, p. 466, note 2).

41. In the original, "M.[onsieur] Jefrokin," apparently Dyka Jefroykin, "Joint" representative in France (Knout, *Résistance juive*, pp. 72, 105; R. I. Cohen, *The Burden of Conscience*, p. 114).

42. The same day, after publication of the announcement of the signing of an armistice agreement, Bonomi was forced to go underground until the liberation of Rome by the Allies. After the war he published his memoirs: *Diario di un anno: 2 giugno 1943–10 giugno 1944*, Milan, 1947.

43. *Documents du Saint-Siège*, 9, p. 466, note 2.

44. From the consul general in Geneva, Cortese, to the Foreign Ministry, 5 August 1943 (ASMAE, AP, *Francia*, busta 80/7, no. 5254 R). See also Serra, *La Diplomazia Italiana*, p. 20.

45. From the Italian minister in Bern to the Foreign Ministry, 12 August 1943 (ASMAE, AP, *Francia*, busta 80/7, no. 22948 P.R.). Magistrati indicates that he had also informed Consul Cortese in Geneva of this.

46. Report by Ambassador Buti to the Foreign Ministry, 28 July 1943, based on information received from the Italian delegation in Vichy (quoted by Serra, *La Diplomazia Italiana*, p. 23). Meaning that Laval's reaction was of 26 or 27 July, that is one or two days after Mussolini's deposition.

47. Ibid., pp. 24–25.

48. Cruccu, "La 4ª Armata," pp. 68–69; Trabucchi, *I vinti*, pp. 14–17; Panicacci, "L'occupazione Italiana," pp. 30–31; R. Zangrandi, *1943: L'8 settembre*, Milan, 1967, pp. 377–378.

49. Zangrandi, *L'8 settembre*, p. 378; Cruccu, "La 4ª Armata," p. 69.

50. Cruccu, "La 4ª Armata," pp. 71–72.

51. From Hagen to SS and Police Commander, 18 August 1943 (CDJC, XXVa-311; Klarsfeld, *Die Endlösung*, p. 214; idem, *Vichy-Auschwitz*, 2, p. 329).

52. Lospinoso testimony (Rochlitz, *Documents*, pp. 52–53, 60). As usual, he contradicts himself on many details, which it is pointless to enumerate in detail.

53. From SS-Sturmbannführer Mühler to the commander of security services in Paris, 19 August 1943 (CDJC, I-56; Poliakoff, *La condition des Juifs en France*, p. 126; Klarsfeld, *Vichy-Auschwitz*, 2, p. 330).

54. From Knochen to the Special Commando of the Security Police and SD in Marseilles, for the attention of SS-Sturmbannführer Mühler, 26 August 1943 (CDJC, I-56; Poliakoff, *La condition des Juifs en France*, p. 127; Klarsfeld, *Vichy-Auschwitz*, 2, p. 335).

55. From SS-Sturmbannführer Mühler to the Security Service in Paris, for the attention of Dr. Knochen, 28 August 1943 (CDJC, I-56; Poliakoff, *La condition des Juifs en France*, p. 128; Klarsfeld, *Vichy-Auschwitz*, 2, pp. 339–340).

56. From SS-Obersturmführer Dr. Schmidt to the Special Commando of the Security Police and SD in Marseilles, for the attention of Mühler, 1 September 1943 (CDJC, XLVIIIa-28; Poliakoff, *La condition des Juifs en France*, p. 129; Klarsfeld, *Vichy-Auschwitz*, 2, p. 340).

57. From Mühler to the Security Service Command in Paris, for the attention of Dr. Schmidt, 2 September 1943 (CDJC, XLVIIIa-28; Poliakoff, *La condition des Juifs en France*, p. 130; Klarsfeld, *Vichy-Auschwitz*, 2, p. 341).

58. Lospinoso testimony (Rochlitz, *Documents*, pp. 54, 58–62). According to Lospinoso's own testimony, at the beginning of 1946 he had been put on trial before the committee dealing with the acts of office holders in the fascist period and was accused of having "collaborated with the Fascist Republican government [i.e., the Salò government] and sworn allegiance to it." He was found guilty (at least on part of the charges) and reprimanded. The high commissioner for matters of "defascistization" entered an appeal against the light punishment to the Central Committee (the highest authority on those matters). We do not know whether the appeal was heard, but in general "light" cases such as that of Lospinoso were closed under the various amnesties granted in that period. At the beginning of March 1946, while the case was being heard at the first level, Angelo Donati visited Rome, and he submitted a brief written declaration in defense of Lospinoso, which among others stated: "The undersigned . . . is happy to be able to certify that being in Nice during the period of Italian Occupation, as Head of the Committee for the defense of the Jews, his coreligionists, . . . he enjoyed the greatest collaboration on the part of Inspector General of Police Guido Lospinoso. Inspector General Lospinoso, always in agreement with the undersigned, and in obedience to the instructions he has

received from the Italian Government, opposed the deportation of the foreign Jews, attended to their transfer to hotels in St. Martin-de-Vésubie, Megève, and St. Gervais—with the assistance of the Jewish Committee and under the protection of the Carabinieri. From the documents found in the Gestapo archives in France . . . it appears that Inspector General Lospinoso fulfilled his duties humanely, did not collaborate with the Germans, and never surrendered a single Jew into their hands." In the last paragraph of the declaration, Donati states that "after 8 September Inspector Lospinoso had burnt the lists and documents in his possession"; but that at best was hear-say evidence, as on 8 September Donati was no longer in Nice.

59. From the General Staff to the Foreign Ministry, 25 August 1943 (ASMAE, AP, *Francia*, busta 80/7, no. 23760 P.R.).

60. From Ambassador Buti to the Foreign Ministry, 28 August 1943 (ASMAE, AP, *Francia*, busta 80/7, no. 24348 P.R.). Marquis Cristoforo Fracassi Ratti was appointed in May 1943 to head the Italian delegation in Vichy, in place of Count Vittorio Zoppi.

61. The consulate general in Nice to the Foreign Ministry, 31 August 1943; Fourth Army headquarters to the Army Operations Branch, 1 September 1943; Army Operations Branch to the General Staff, 2 September 1943; idem, of 3 September 1943; General Staff, note on the announcement received over the telephone and transmission of instructions to the Fourth Army headquarters, 3 September 1943; General Staff to the Foreign Ministry, 3 September 1943 (ASMAE, AP, *Francia*, busta 80/7).

62. From Secretary General Rosso to the General Staff, 6 September 1943 (ASMAE, AP, *Francia*, busta 80/7, no. 27447 P.R.).

63. Cavaglion, *Nella notte straniera*, p. 31, quoting a document at the Centre de Documentation Juive Contemporaine in Paris (CDJC, XXXVII, appendix I/1).

64. Note signed by Röthke, also intended for the attention of SS-Sturmbannführer Hagen, 4 September 1943 (CDJC, XXVa-338; Poliakoff, *La condition des Juifs en France*, pp. 131–135; Klarsfeld, *Vichy-Auschwitz*, 2, pp. 341–343).

65. Klarsfeld, *Vichy-Auschwitz*, 2, pp. 116–119; Marrus and Paxton, *Vichy France*, pp. 320–321; Amouroux, *Les passions*, pp. 306–307. On Prefect Chaigneau see Chapter 5, note 19. On the activities of Alois Brunner in France, see Klarsfeld, ibid., by index; R. I. Cohen, *The Burden of Conscience*, pp. 89–90, 100. Spechel and his deputy, Borromeo, were arrested by the Germans a few days later and spent the rest of the war as prisoners of the Germans.

66. See note 58.

67. Klarsfeld, *Vichy-Auschwitz*, 2, pp. 124–125; A. Cohen, "Factors in the Rescue of Jews in France during the Holocaust," *Proceedings of the Tenth World Congress for Jewish Studies*, Jerusalem, 1990, p. 499.

68. Quoted by Amouroux, *Les passions*, p. 307.

69. See also Chapter 5, note 45.

70. See testimonies of Father Marie-Benoît, and also S. Sorani, *L'assistenza ai profughi ebrei in Italia (1933–1947). Contributo alla storia della "Delasem,"*

Rome, 1983, pp. 137–158, 288–290; M. Leone, *Le organizzazioni di soccorso ebraiche in età fascista*, Rome, 1983, pp. 249–250.

71. See Chapter 7, note 20.

72. Fink Documents, testimony, pp. 17–18. According to Fink, he was sent to welcome the arrivals and was an eyewitness to the arrest of the Jews by the bridge over the Var River. In contrast to this, according to the memoirs of Hélène Gorgiel-Sercarz who was in the convoy from St. Gervais she, together with her family and friends safely reached Nice ("Memories of a Jewish Girl," *Yalkut Moreshet*, 50 (1991), p. 182).

73. See footnote 7.

74. On this episode, see Cavaglion, *Nella notte straniera*, pp. 59–69; Halpern, *A Ray of Light*, pp. 55–69; idem., "Gli ebrei di St. Martin-de-Vésubie e lo sbandamento della 4ª armata," Istituto Storico della Resistenza in Cuneo e Provincia, *8 settembre. Lo sfacelo della quarta armata*, Turin, 1979, pp. 205–227.

75. The operation in Nice was first directed by Claude Gutmann and Jacques Weintraub, but the first was arrested on 23 September and the second on the 25th. See Lazar, *La résistance juive*, pp. 252–256. Also arrested a short time later was Donati's secretary, Mme. Gervaise Maier. See her "confession" of 20 September 1943 (CDJC, I-59; Rutkowski, *La lutte des Juifs*, pp. 198–201). The three were questioned, transferred to the Drancy camp, and from there were deported "to the East" and did not return. Among the heads of the Dubouchage Committee, apparently the most active during the underground period was Claude Kelman. See Fink Documents, pp. 12–13.

## 9: General Background (pp. 195–199)

1. F. Anfuso, *Roma-Berlino-Salò*, Milan, 1950, p. 162.

2. Concerning Tunisia's place in the fascist government's array of colonial demands, see J. Bessis, *La Méditerranée fasciste. L'Italie mussolinienne et la Tunisie*, Paris, 1981; idem, "La question tunisienne dans l'évolution des relations franco-italiennes de 1935 au 10 juin 1940," in Duroselle and Serra (eds.), *Italia e Francia dal 1919 al 1939*, pp. 245–255; R. H. Rainero, "La politique fasciste à l'égard de l'Afrique du Nord: L'épée de l'Islam et la revendication sur la Tunisie," *Revue Française d'Histoire d'Outre-Mer*, 46 (1977), pp. 498–514; idem., *La rivendicazione fascista sulla Tunisia*, Milan, 1978; N. Pasotti, *Italiani e Italia in Tunisia dalle origini al 1970*, Rome, 1971.

3. For a summary of the Munich talks from the Italian viewpoint, see G. Carboni, *Più che il dovere. Memorie segrete 1935–1948*, Florence, 1955, pp. 95–99. The stages of Mussolini's withdrawal from his original demands have not been sufficiently clarified. Even following his return from Munich, Mussolini gave his approval on 21 June 1940 to a document drawn up by Marshal Badoglio—then chief of staff—and General Roatta, stating that Corsica, Tunisia, French Somalia, and all the districts of France up to the Saône-Rhône rivers' line would be

occupied by Italy (ASSME, CIAF, racc. I/A). According to Roatta, Mussolini ordered this version to be changed only nine hours before the submission of the document to the French Delegation (*Otto milioni di baionette. L'esercito italiano in guerra dal 1940 al 1944*, Milan, 1946, pp. 100–104).

4. See Introduction, note 12.

5. The structure of the CIAF was rather complicated and changed every so often in accordance with the developments of the war. In North Africa, it originally had four subcommissions: one for the ground forces, one for the air force, one for the navy, and the fourth "for the control of the Libyan-Tunisian border." In May 1941, the Delegazione Generale per il Nord Africa (General Delegation for North Africa) was established as the unified representative of the Armistice Commission. Its offices were in Algiers, and it was originally headed by Admiral F. Farina followed by Admiral S. Salza (15 November 1941–10 November 1942). The three military subcommissions (the one controlling the Libyan-Tunisian border had meanwhile been abolished) were subordinate to the Delegazione Generale, which had extensions in most cities of Algeria and Tunisia: Algiers, Oran, Constantine, Biskra, Oudja, Philippeville, Bône, Tunis, Sfax, Sousse, Bizerte.

6. Jäckel, *La France*, pp. 156–157. Alongside the German delegation in Morocco operated an Italian representative, the Delegazione di Collegamento con l'Ispettorato Tedesco in Marocco.

7. Weygand's term of office in North Africa is reviewed in his book *Mémoires. Rappelé au service*, Paris, 1950, pp. 344–552. See also his evidence, "The Reconstruction of the Army of Africa, 1940–1941," in Hoover Institution, *France during the German Occupation*, 2, pp. 761–775.

8. Weygand wrote that German Ambassador in Paris, Otto Abetz, demanded his recall to France as early as September 1941 (*Mémoires*, pp. 524–525). Italian documentation, however, shows that the Italians were those who pressured the Germans to have him ousted, even at the cost of real concessions. Indeed, in exchange for Weygand's recall, Admiral Darlan obtained the release of more than 10,000 French soldiers who had been taken prisoner by the Germans, as well as Italy's agreement to transfer to North Africa (but not to Tunisia) the units that had been transferred from Syria to France following the British invasion. See the correspondence dated 21–23 November 1941 between the Italian and German representatives of the armistice commissions, as well as the report by General Vacca Maggiolini to the Italian Chief of Staff on 17 November 1941 (ASSME, CIAF, racc. 13/1, 51/1, 73/7). In a private conversation with General Vacca Maggiolini, Darlan added a request that the Italians should also dismiss the head of their *delegazione* in North Africa, Admiral Farina. General Vacca Maggiolini had no difficulty in acceding to this request, as, according to his testimony, he had signed an order for Farina's recall the day before, quite independently of those negotiations (ASSME, CIAF, racc. 51/1). See also Chapter 10, note 4.

9. *Mémoires*, p. 409.

10. Both figures appear to be exaggerated. It is possible that Weygand may have referred to all personnel of the Armistice Commission, in France and North

Africa, whose numbers totaled 583 in April 1942. In November of that year, there were 227 members of the Armistice Commission in Algeria (these were later taken prisoner by the U.S. armed forces), and 71 (including 15 civilians) in Tunisia.

11. Italian interests in Morocco were represented by the Portuguese Consulate. German interests in Tunisia were represented by the Swedish Consulate (until July 1942, when the German Consulate reopened in Algiers and was placed in charge of Tunisian affairs).

12. See also Introduction, notes 13–14.

13. Admiral Jean-Pierre Estéva commanded the fleet in Bizerte during the first months of the war; he was appointed *résident général* of Tunisia in July 1940, replacing M. Peyrouton. Both Estéva and Peyrouton had objected to the signing of the armistice agreement with Germany in June 1940 and had supported the continuation of the war from the Empire; nonetheless, both later became loyal supporters of the Vichy government. Concerning Peyrouton, see his memoirs, in which he also discussed his brief term of service in Tunisia (*Du service public à la prison commune*, Plon, 1950). On Estéva's position and activity as *résident général* of Tunisia, see also the protocols of his trial in March 1945, in which he was condemned to life imprisonment, G. London, *L'amiral Estéva et le général Dentz devant la Haute Cour de Justice*, Lyon, 1945.

14. From the Italian Embassy in Paris to the Foreign Ministry, 23 April 1943 (ASMAE, AP, *Tunisia*, busta 17, n. 2589 R). Additional details are given in a message sent by the Direzione Generale per gli Affari di Europa e del Mediterraneo, Ufficio III of the Foreign Ministry, to the Italian representation in Tunisia, 20 April 1943 (ASMAE, AP, *Tunisia*, busta 15, n. 1162 P.R.). This message is signed by the diplomat Alberto Mellini Ponce de Leon, at that time in charge of the "Arab desk" (Ufficio III) at the Direzione. Concerning Mellini and his activities in the war years, see his memoirs (*Guerra diplomatica a Salò*, Florence, 1950), and my article, "The Mufti of Jerusalem, Amin el Husseini, and His Diplomatic Activity during World War II (October 1941–July 1943)," *Studies in Zionism*, 7 (1983), pp. 101–131.

15. The only reservation was that the number of French included 16,633 former Italian citizens, who had received French citizenship a short time previously—some of them, according to Italian officials, under pressure by the French colonial authorities (ASMAE, AP, *Tunisia*, busta 11).

16. See, for example, ASMAE, AP, *Tunisia*, buste 11, 14/8, and 17.

17. On the Jews of Italian origin in Tunisia, see R. Darmon, *La situation des cultes en Tunisie*, Paris, 1930, pp. 78–80; A. Chouraqui, *Les juifs d'Afrique du Nord*, Paris, 1952, pp. 272–274; C. Z. Hirschberg, *History of the Jews in North Africa*, Jerusalem, 1965, 2, pp. 120–123; I. Abrami, "The 'Grana' Community in Tunis According to Its Minute-books," in M. Abitbol (ed.), *Judaisme d'Afrique du Nord aux xix<sup>e</sup>–xx<sup>e</sup> siecles*, Jerusalem, 1980, pp. 64–95.

18. J. L. Miege, *L'impérialisme colonial italien de 1870 à nos jours*, Paris, 1968; G. Rumi, *L'imperialismo fascista*, Milan, 1974; A. A. Mola, *L'imperialismo*

*italiano*, Rome, 1980; M. Palla, "L'imperialisme fasciste," *Revue d'Histoire de la deuxième guerre mondiale*, 139 (1985), pp. 25–46.

19. On this subject, see Bessis, *La Méditerranée fasciste*, pp. 344–352; Carpi, "The Mufti of Jerusalem," pp. 129–130.

### 10: In the Shadow of Vichy Government Policy (pp. 200–227)

1. London, *L'amiral Estéva*, p. 125.
2. From General Roberto Lerici in Tripoli to the headquarters of the Armistice Commission in Turin, 16 August 1940. Copy from the Armistice Commission to the Foreign Office, 26 August 1940 (ASMAE, AP, *Tunisia*, busta 12, n. 13043 AG).
3. From the Military Intelligence Service (SIM) to the Foreign Office, 1 September 1940 (ASMAE, AP, *Tunisia*, busta 11, n. Z/121849).
4. Copy from the Armistice Commission to Foreign Ministry, 7 March 1941 (ASMAE, AP, *Tunisia*, busta 12, n. 4344 AG). Farina was also frequently subject to "verbal intemperance" when speaking with or of the French. For this reason—and for other personal reasons that should not be listed here—the commander of the Armistice Commission saw fit to transfer him from his post as of 15 November 1941 (ASSME, CIAF, racc. 46).
5. In this connection, see Ciano's entry of 5 July 1941 (*Diario*, p. 531): "Meeting of the Council of Ministers . . . Silimbani gives an interesting exposition of the situation in Tunisia: even the stones there support De Gaulle, and 80 percent of the middle classes believe in a British victory. They hate the Germans but admire them; they simply despise us."
6. Several of Silimbani's reports were given to Mussolini for his perusal, even before he reinstated himself as foreign minister (February 1943). See, for example, reports dated 21 May and 20 June 1941, bearing the letter *M* in Mussolini's handwriting (ASMAE, AP, *Tunisia*, busta 12, n. 03336/1335, n. 04075/1586).
7. The antifascist circle of *mazziniani* included among its active members, alongside the non-Jewish veteran leader Giulio Barresi, two Jews: Dr. Guido Levi and Enrico Forti. Among the socialist activists was Alfonso Errera; the communists included the Ben Sasson brothers (see Chapter 11, note 20), the Gallico brothers, and Marco Vais. In 1939, Jews of Italian extraction, among them G. Montefiore, funded the publication of a daily—later weekly—antifascist paper, *Il Giornale*, edited by Giorgio Amendola (see also G. Amendola, *Lettere a Milano 1939–1945*, Rome, 1973, pp. 3–10). Among the members serving in the Political Department of the Tunisian Communist party were Maurizio Valenzi and Loris Gallico. In 1938, Valenzi founded a League against Racialism and published a booklet against the fascist racial policy (A. Mortara [=M. Valenzi], *Ebrei italiani di fronte al "razzismo,"* Tunis, 1938). After the war, Marco Vais edited the Communist party organ *L'Unità* in Turin, and Maurizio Valenzi became mayor of Naples.
8. These estimates are to be found in many documents. See, for example, ASMAE, AP, *Italia*, busta 87.

9. Ministero degli Affari Esteri, Direzione Generale degli Affari Generali, Ufficio Storico Diplomatico, *Tunisia—Situazione politica dell'anno XIX (29 ottobre 1940–28 ottobre 1941)*, Quaderno n. 23-E. Segreto, p. 21 (ASMAE, AP, *Tunisia,* busta 14/8).

10. In the draft of this document, which has also been preserved in Foreign Ministry files, appear several important details that were not included in the final version, apparently for reasons of prudence. The draft is entitled *La Tunisia sotto l'auspicato dominio italiano*; in the section dealing with the Jews, following the passage on their alleged subversiveness, appears the statement that "they are elements that must be removed from Tunisia, even if they have received French citizenship." The section on Italian Jews includes an additional paragraph, stating that "as for them, it will be possible to apply the Italian race laws with a certain tolerance, expanding the section on those eligible for exemption (*discriminazioni*), in such a way as to include rights acquired in Tunisia" (ASMAE, AP, *Tunisia,* busta 17, pp. 64–65).

11. See Chapter 4.

12. In both Statuts des Juifs appear paragraphs dealing with the implementation of the law "in Algeria, the colonies, and those countries in a trusteeship or mandate" (paragraph 9 of the Alibert Statute; paragraph 11 of the Vallat Statute). Similar paragraphs also appear in several of the other laws.

13. The situation in Algeria was different from that in Tunisia, in terms of both legal status (Algeria, with its three districts, was subordinate to the French Home Office, whereas Tunisia, as a protectorate, was subordinate to the Foreign Office) and the status of the Jews. On the other hand, there are some similarities between Tunisia and Morocco; these are reflected both in the antisemitic statutes and in the Italian response thereto.

14. Concerning the number of Jews in Tunisia, see the end of Chapter 9. The 1941 census in Algeria counted a total of 116,800 Jews (see M. Abitbol, *Les juifs d'Afrique du Nord sous Vichy*, Paris, 1983, p. 71, note 49). Various estimates have been made of the number of Jews in Morocco. According to the French census of 1931, they totaled 117,603. Italian intelligence sources in 1940 estimated their total number at 161,213 (ASSME, CIAF, racc. 73/2). A Jewish-Zionist source in 1946 estimated their number at 200,000 (M. Laskier, "The Evolution of Zionist Activity in the Jewish Communities of Morocco, Tunisia and Algeria: 1897–1947," *Studies in Zionism*, 8 [1983], p. 214).

15. The law was passed on 30 November 1940 and published in the *Journal Officiel Tunisien* on 3 December. We will henceforth refer to the initial dates on which the various laws were passed, as is customary in studies of this type.

16. The list of these laws and orders appears in J. Sabille, *Les juifs de Tunisie sous Vichy et l'occupation*, Paris, 1954, pp. 163–165.

17. "Art. 6 . . . Les Juifs peuvent exercer librement une profession artisanale ainsi que le commerce de détail" (*Journal Officiel Tunisien*, 14 March 1942).

18. See Sabille, *Les juifs de Tunisie*, pp. 24–26; Abitbol, *Les juifs d'Afrique du Nord*, p. 81. See also the testimony of Pierre de Font-Réaulx, the legal adviser

to the French administration in Tunisia (Hoover Institution, *France during the German Occupation*, 2, pp. 712–720).

19. Following the Liberation, Ghez published a diary describing his activity among the Jewish community under German occupation: P. Ghez, *Six mois sous la botte*, Tunis, 1943. See also Y. Zur, "The Jews of Tunisia under the German Occupation: A Divided Community in time of Crisis," *Contemporary Jewry*, 2 (1985), pp. 169–172 (Hebrew).

20. According to paragraph 11 of the Statut des Juifs, the bey was entitled to grant personal exemptions from all of the prohibitions and limitations imposed on the Jews, according to his own considerations, irrespective of those cases defined by law that were entitled to limited exemptions by virtue of their deeds.

21. This is repeatedly confirmed in the documentation of the Italian Foreign Ministry. Following are two examples: in an internal memorandum dated 28 November 1942, Alberto Mellini noted that "the Bey and the Tunisian nationalists are prepared to increase their cooperation with the Axis, whereas the Bey's brother Hussein has adopted a pro-British position" (ASMAE, AP, *Tunisia*, busta 14/1). On 11 December 1942, General Ambrosio forwarded to the Foreign Ministry a cable from General Lorenzelli, one of the Italian Army commanders in Tunisia, stating that "the Bey of Tunisia has declared that Italian blood flows in his veins and that he expects our forces to stand up for him openly. His son, Prince Raouf, comes to see me and pleads for Italian aid" (ibid., n. 4050). See also J. Schröder, "Les rapports des puissances de l'Axe avec le monde arabe," in Comité d'Histoire de la 2ᵉ Guerre Mondiale, *La guerre en Méditerranée 1939–1945*, Paris, 1971, pp. 607–626; Ch. R. Ageron, "Les mouvements nationalistes dans le Maghreb pendant la 2ᵉ guerre mondiale," ibid., pp. 627–631.

22. CIAF, *Notiziario Quindicinale*, no. 46 (second half of October 1942), p. 50.

23. On the antisemitic tendencies of that organization in France and North Africa, see Marrus and Paxton, *Vichy France*, pp. 126, 210–211. Heading the Tunisian branch at the time was a Vallat supporter named Malcor. He was apparently the one who signed the letter of 25 March 1942 to Admiral Estéva, in which the demand was raised for preferential treatment of French citizens in the distribution of property seized from the Jews of Tunisia (Sabille, *Les juifs de Tunisie*, pp. 167–169). Malcor was dismissed from his post on 15 December 1942 and replaced by G. Saint-Martin, who was trusted by the Germans.

24. CIAF, *Notiziario Quindicinale*, no. 45 (first half of October 1942), p. 50.

25. According to Marrus and Paxton (*Vichy France*, p. 364), "the Italians defended foreign Jews as well as Italian nationals, not only in their own country but also in France, Tunisia, Croatia, and Greece." Nonetheless, regarding Tunisia, this was apparently a slip of the pen.

26. From the Italian Consulate in Tunis to the Foreign Ministry, 3 December 1940 (ASMAE, AP, *Italia*, busta 87).

27. See on him Chapter 1, note 21.

28. ASMAE, AP, *Tunisia*, busta 12, n. 34.R/6831.

29. From Consul Silimbani to the Foreign Ministry, 21 May 1941 (ASMAE, AP,

*Tunisia*, busta 12, n. 03336/1335). The report, a dozen pages long, was submitted to Mussolini for his perusal and bears marginal notes in his handwriting designating the passages that especially interested him.

30. ASMAE, AP, *Tunisia*, busta 12, n. 4895 R. To date, nothing concerning this slaughter has been published. Silimbani's words are corroborated by the testimony of two former residents of Gabes, now living in Israel, Yair Rokach and Avner Degani (Boucobza). According to their testimony—preserved in the files of the Institute for the Study of the Zionist and Pioneer Movement in Oriental Countries, Yad Tabenkin, Israel—the names of those killed were Massoud Rekach, Assila Rekach, Moshe Hachmon, Mantina Hachmon (Moshe's wife), Mevorach Hajaji (the synagogue sexton), Albert Azer Ben-Attiye, and Bahariya Ben-Attiye (a sixteen-year-old girl).

31. The Italian Foreign Ministry apparently ascribed great importance to the Gabes incident; on 1 June 1941, it sent copies of Silimbani's second report to the Supreme Command, the three military ministries, war, naval, and air, the Colonial Office (*Africa Italiana*), the Armistice Commission, and the Italian representatives in Berlin, Algiers, Rabat, and Lyons. On 7 November 1941, Consul Silimbani notified the Foreign Ministry that the trial of the Arabs accused of that murder had been concluded and that four of them had been condemned to death.

32. ASMAE, AP, *Tunisia*, busta 12, n. 04075/1586.

33. Sabille, *Les juifs de Tunisie*, pp. 25–26.

34. From the vice-consul, Cesare Regard, to the Foreign Ministry, 5 September 1941 (ASMAE, AP, *Tunisia*, busta 12, n. 06369/2378, p. 4). See also the testimony given by Vallat's friends after the war—apparently on the basis of Vallat's own words: "Enfin, en Tunisie, il eut avec l'amiral Estéva des entretiens à la suite desquels un certain nombre de décisions ont été prises par l'autorité beylicale, calquées sur des textes de la métropole, et dont l'application paraît avoir été faite avec modération" (*Le procès Vallat*, p. 399).

35. From Vice-Consul Cesare Regard to the Foreign Ministry, 19 September 1941 (ASMAE, AP, *Tunisia*, busta 12, n. 06777/2498). The passage is also quoted in the document on the situation in Tunisia (see note 9), p. 22.

36. This passage is not sufficiently clear. The reference may have been to the various groups of Jews as defined in the statute or to the various professions and occupations practiced by the Jews.

37. ASMAE, AP, *Tunisia*, busta 12, n. 34.R/10731. An additional step was taken by the Foreign Office via the Italian diplomatic representation in Bern on 24 April 1942, regarding limitations imposed on the Jewish doctors in Tunisia. This is mentioned in a letter sent by Silimbani to the Foreign Office on 6 May 1942 (ASMAE, AP, *Tunisia*, busta 14/8, n. 14438 PR). See also: Ministero degli Affari Esteri, *Relazione*, p. 38.

38. All of the documentation concerning the Jews of Morocco between 9 August and 28 November 1941 is filed in ASMAE, AP, *Marocco*, busta 20/3.

39. From Consul Silimbani to the Foreign Ministry, 8 October 1941 (ASMAE, AP, *Tunisia*, busta 12, n. 07402/2716).

40. CIAF, *Notiziario Quindicinale*, no. 40 (second half of July 1942), p. 65; no. 41, (first half of August 1942), p. 72.
41. ASMAE, AP, *Tunisia*, busta 14/8, n. 03552/1315, p. 8. In his lengthy report, which takes up some twelve pages, Silimbani noted that "no less than 2,000 Aryan Italians are employed in Italian and Tunisian Jewish businesses." Should those businesses be closed down or turned over to the French, these Aryan Italians would be dismissed and replaced by French workers.
42. ASMAE, AP, *Tunisia*, busta 14/8, n. 03801/1340.
43. From Consul Silimbani to the Foreign Ministry, 27 May 1942 (ASMAE, AP, *Tunisia*, busta 14/8, n. 3635 R). Estéva went to Vichy on 26 May 1942. Silimbani reported, perhaps with a touch of exaggeration, that "first of all the question to be discussed is that relative to the Jewish question."
44. *Journal Officiel Tunisien*, 31 mars 1942. The order (*arrêté*) stated that the number of Jewish lawyers would not exceed 5 percent of the number of their non-Jewish colleagues (that is, in the city of Tunis, 5 percent of 105); and, as an exception, up to 1 January 1945, 5 percent of the total number of lawyers registered on the day of the order (that is, in the city of Tunis, 5 percent of 316). A prior order concerning lawyers had been given on 9 October 1941.
45. *Journal Officiel Tunisien*, 2 Mai 1942, "Réglementation de l'accès des Juifs à la propriété foncière" (*décret*); "Interdiction aux Juifs d'acquérir des fonds de commerce sans autorisation" (*décret*).
46. *Journal Officiel Tunisien*, 19 Mai 1942. The effective date of the limitations on insurance activity was set for 1 July 1942; that of the limitations on the stock exchange and banking, for 1 June 1942.
47. These lawyers were Giuseppe Morpurgo and Carlo Pariente, both of whom had distinguished themselves in their service in the Italian Army during World War I.
48. From Consul Silimbani to the Foreign Ministry, 23 April 1942 (ASMAE, AP, *Tunisia*, busta 14, n. 04803/1796). The lists of Jewish lawyers permitted to continue in their profession were published in early June. These included the names of 17 lawyers (14 from Tunis, 2 from Sousse, and 1 from Sfax), representing 5 percent of the total number of lawyers in Tunisia (344 in all). In addition, 13 Jews were permitted to continue in their profession due to their "special professional merits." All of these were from Tunis, and 3 of them held Italian citizenship (G. Morpurgo, C. Pariente, and G. Shalom).
49. See on him Chapter 4, note 31.
50. From Foreign Minister Ciano to the Italian Embassy in Paris, 28 May 1942. (ASMAE, AP, *Tunisia*, busta 14/8, n. 34/R 5294). The Italian appeal to the Vichy government is also briefly mentioned in CIAF, *Notiziario Quindicinale*, no. 36 (second half of May 1942), p. 46.
51. From Ambassador Buti to the Foreign Ministry, 4 June 1942 (ASMAE, AP, *Tunisia*, busta 14/8, n. 1459/800).
52. From Ambassador Buti to the Foreign Office, 13 June 1942 (ASMAE, AP, *Tunisia*, busta 14/8, n. 1611/884).
53. From Ambassador Buti to the Foreign Ministry (Department for Italians

Abroad), 16 May 1942 (ASMAE, AP, *Tunisia*, busta 14/8, n. 1201/654). Quoted in the report from Ambassador Buti to the Foreign Ministry, 4 June 1942 (ibid., n. 1459/800).

54. ASMAE, AP, *Tunisia*, busta 14/8, n. 1968/1050. Buti does not mention the date of the second meeting between Zoppi and Lagarde.

55. From Ambassador Buti to the Foreign Ministry, 31 July 1942 (ASMAE, AP, *Tunisia*, busta 14/8, n. 2287/1187). The words "di comune intesa" (out of a common intent) are emphasized in the original.

56. Concerning Tunisia, see, inter alia, R. S. Rainero, "Gli accordi di Torino tra la CIAF e il governo di Pétain sulla Tunisia (Natale 1941)," in Duroselle and Serra (eds.), *Italia e Francia (1939–1945)*, I, pp. 228–244.

57. Emphasized in the original.

58. From General Gelich to the chairman of Armistice Commission, General Vacca Maggiolini, 4 July 1942 (ASSME, CIAF, racc. 3/3, doc. 76, pp. 9–10).

59. From Ambassador Abetz to the German Foreign Ministry, 4 July 1942 (Doc. NG 133; photocopy in Yad Vashem Archives, Jerusalem, JM 2013).

60. URO, *Judenverfolgung in Italien*, pp. 58–59.

61. See d'Ajeta's cable to Silimbani of 16 June 1942 (ASMAE, AP, *Tunisia*, busta 14/8, n. 21069/121 P.R.) and Silimbani's reply of 1 July 1942 (ibid., n. 19954).

62. ASMAE, AP, *Tunisia*, busta 14/8, n. 34/R 7859, n. 27882/255–256. Naturally, we cannot know who actually wrote the text of these cables, which were sent out over the foreign minister's signature. It may have been the head of his cabinet, d'Ajeta; or it may have been Vitetti, who had been appointed to head the Department Affari Europa e Mediterraneo (AEM) on 7 January 1942. It is also possible—and there is even some evidence to this effect—that it may have been Luigi Vidau, who had been deputy head of the AEM until January and had been appointed to replace Vitetti as head of the Direzione Generale Affari Generali (AG) on 17 January 1942 (see Chapter 6, note 10).

63. To be precise, the French claimed that the nonimposition of these laws on the Italian Jews would undermine their entire antisemitic policy, which would cause the Germans to protest.

64. The order, published on 11 July 1942, resulted from the joint initiative of the local German headquarters and the Greek governor of Macedonia (Carpi, *Jews in Greece*, p. 30).

65. ASMAE, AP, *Tunisia*, busta 14/8. See also Silimbani's cable to the Foreign Office, 19 August 1942 (ibid., n. 25681 P.R.).

66. URO, *Judenverfolgung in Italien*, pp. 72–73.

67. Cable dated 7 September 1942 (ibid., pp. 74–75); and see also: URO, *Judenverfolgung in Frankreich*, pp. 123–124.

68. URO, *Judenverfolgung in Italien*, p. 78.

69. *Trials of War Criminals*, XIII, p. 253.

70. Sabille, *Les juifs de Tunisie*, p. 185.

71. Between 28 August and 4 September 1942, Admiral Estéva visited Vichy and met with Pétain, Laval, Bousquet, and Darlan; we do not know, however,

whether the Jewish question was discussed at that meeting (CIAF, *Notiziario Quindicinale*, no. 43 [first half of September 1942], p. 72).

## 11: Under the Heel of the Axis Army (pp. 228–240)

1. Abetz, *Pétain et les Allemands. Mémorandum d'Abetz sur les rapports Franco-Allemands*, Paris, 1948, p. 182. In his memoirs, published several years later, Abetz quoted the same document but omitted the words "émanant de cercles du Vatican" (*Mémoires*, p. 271).
2. See the memoirs of the island's former governor, A. Annet, *Aux heures troubles de l'Afrique Française, 1939–1943*, Paris, 1952.
3. From General Gelich to the chairman of Armistice Commission in Turin, 31 October 1942 (ASSME, CIAF, racc. 56/2A, pp. 8–9).
4. CIAF, *Notiziario Quindicinale*, no. 46 (second half of October 1942), p. 47. The same sources also mention another opinion: a *Paris-Soir* journalist named Paule Herfort, on her return from a tour of Morocco, expressed the opinion that, should there be a landing of forces in that country, "the army and the population would welcome the Anglo-Americans with open arms," and the army, supplied with modern armaments, would set out to fight the Axis forces in North Africa.
5. Among the works attesting to the confusion prevailing in those days are the memoirs of M. Lanza, a diplomat on the staff of the Italian Embassy in Berlin (Simoni, *Ambasciata d'Italia*, p. 285) and of Marshal U. Cavallero, chief of staff of the Italian armed forces (*Comando Supremo*, Rocca S. Casciano, 1948, pp. 367–376). On 7 November, General Gelich warned the commander of the Delegazione Generale in North Africa, Admiral Salza, that the landing would "probably" take place in French North Africa (ASSME, CIAF, racc. 73/8).
6. The French ground forces in Tunisia, some 12,000 in number, retreated toward the Algerian border on the order of their commander, General G. Barré, and joined the Allied camp on 20 November (Barré, *Tunisie 1942–1943*, Paris, 1950). The naval forces in Bizerte, under the command of Vice-Admiral Derrien, surrendered to the German ultimatum on 12 November and thus opened this important base to the Italian forces, which landed there on 14 November.
7. On his activity in Tunisia, see his book *Un diplomate*, pp. 247–273. Assisting Rahn was the diplomat Eitel Friedrich Moellhausen. In his memoirs (*Il giuoco è fatto!*, Florence, 1951), Moellhausen stresses the polite and civilized attitude—in his opinion—of the German soldiers and SS units toward Tunisian Jews during the Axis occupation (pp. 432–442). We did not deem necessary to point out the many inaccuracies and distortions that could be found in the book.
8. Walther Rauff was the commander of Department II/D in the Reich Security Main Office. On his activity in Tunisia, see J. Robinson-H. Sachs, *The Holocaust. The Nuremberg Evidence*, Jerusalem, 1976, nn. 1426, 1998, 2155, 2188. His senior assistant in Tunisia was SS-Hauptsturmführer Theo Saewecke. Also present in Tunisia for some time was SS-Sturmbannführer Dr. Karl-Theodor

Zeitschel, advisor for Jewish affairs in the German Embassy in Paris (see Chapter 2, note 62). See Silimbani's report to Mellini of 12 January 1943 (ASMAE, AP, *Tunisia*, busta 16, n. 00286), and Zeitschel's own report (Poliakov, *Jews under Italian Occupation*, pp. 191–192 [English translation]).

9. Following the landing of the Axis forces, five commissions (for general affairs, civil defense, municipal services, public works, and general security) were established in Tunisia at the initiative of Rahn to supervise the activities of the French administration. Each committee included three members, representatives of the local population (one Italian, one French, and one Muslim), as well as a German "observer." The "observers" serving on the first four committees were army officers; that of the fifth, an SS officer. The Italian diplomatic and military authorities in Tunisia had no part in these committees, which were extremely influential.

10. The role played by the Italians in the military campaign for Tunisia is discussed in General Messe's memoirs (*La mia armata in Tunisia. Come finì la guerra in Africa*, Milan, 1960). Prior to his service in Tunisia, General Messe commanded the Italian expeditionary forces in the Soviet Union (July 1941–November 1942).

11. From d'Ajeta to Bismarck, 11 December 1942; Bismarck's response to the Foreign Ministry, 14 December 1942 (ASMAE, AP, *Tunisia*, busta 14/1).

12. Silimbani's reports of November–December 1942 are full of examples of this kind. Silimbani especially complained that the Germans were accustomed to "treat us with an attitude of superiority" and to denigrate the importance of the Italian military contribution (ASMAE, AP, *Tunisia*, busta 16/1).

13. Following the landing of the Axis forces, several of the French officials most favorable to cooperating with the Germans were transferred to Tunisia, to force this line on Estéva's administration. Among these were Georges Guilbaud, founder of the Tunisian pro-Nazi organization Comité d'Unité d'Action Révolutionnaire and of an extremely pro-Nazi and antisemitic newspaper, *Tunis-Journal*. Rahn referred to Guilbaud in one of his letters as "our trusted friend" (Sabille, *Les juifs de Tunisie*, p. 183). Also sent to Tunisia was Colonel Sarton du Jonchay, another trusted ally of the Germans, who was appointed as Estéva's *chef de cabinet et préfet de police*. See Abitbol, *Les juifs d'Afrique du Nord*, p. 125; Rahn, *Un diplomate*, pp. 262–263; London, *L'amiral Estéva*, pp. 19, 21, 48, 97–98.

14. For example, the definition of Guilbaud's status and authority (the Italians wished these to be as limited as possible to reduce the extent of French influence); deferring the mufti's trip to Tunisia, and so on. On the other hand, nothing binding was determined concerning the important matter of Italian representation on the "supervisory" committees.

15. ASMAE, AP, *Tunisia*, busta 16/2. The complete protocol, some fourteen pages long, was summarized for Mussolini's perusal.

16. See pp. 6–7 of the protocol. See also the Moellhausen version (*Memorie*, pp. 425–426).

17. Ghez, *Six mois sous la botte*, pp. 13–15; R. Borgel, *Etoile jaune et croix gammée*, Tunis, 1944, pp. 21–30.

18. According to the copy of the report sent by the Foreign Ministry to the Supreme Command and to the Italian Embassy in Berlin, 10 December 1942 (ASMAE, AP, *Tunisia*, busta 14/1, n. 42660 P.R.). Silimbani left his place of residence in Tunis, along with all of the consulate staff, and returned to Italy on 17 November, when it began to appear to him that the Allied offensive from Algeria was about to succeed. He reported to Ciano that "the situation in Tunisia is hopeless, the Americans are advancing without encountering resistance, and the city is, in fact, in the hands of the Gaullists, who will rise up as soon as the American flag appears on the horizon" (Ciano, *Diario*, p. 668). After matters had calmed down and the front had stabilized following the Axis counteroffensive, he returned to Tunis. However, in January 1943, he was recalled to Rome for consultations (ibid., p. 690); initially appointed to replace him in early February was Enrico Bombieri, who had already been consul general in Tunis between 1929 and 1936. This time, he served for only three months in that position; in early May, at the conclusion of the military campaign, he was captured by Allied forces.

19. ASMAE, AP, *Tunisia*, busta 14/1.

20. Sources at the political secret police OVRA had announced, as early as the beginning of 1941, that "the mainstays of Communism in Tunisia were and are the Ben Sasson brothers." One of the brothers was even sentenced by a Tunisian court to two years' imprisonment for disseminating communist propaganda. According to that source, the Ben Sasson brothers strengthened their connections with the Communist party under the influence of the "passionaria tunisina," a nineteen-year-old beauty named Clelia Barresi, the daughter of a veteran antifascist (see Chapter 10, note 7) and "a leader of the local communist organizations and a fervent propagandist."

21. Published by Abitbol, *Les juifs d'Afrique du Nord*, pp. 194–195.

22. According to Silimbani's report (see note 18). Silimbani may well have heard these details from Rahn.

23. This document no longer exists in the *Tunisia* files, but a copy of it has been preserved in the *France* files (ASMAE, AP, *Francia*, busta 66). This copy is quite faded, and it is impossible to read the second digit of the date on which the cable was sent. In any event, the first digit is clearly 2. The date, then, could be 22 or 23 (?) November 1942.

24. URO, *Judenverfolgung in Italien*, pp. 121–125.

25. The document has been published in photographic form and in French translation by Sabille (*Les juifs de Tunisie*, Figure 14 [opposite p. 131] and p. 186). The translation includes a printer's error: the date of the message from the Foreign Office is 5 December, not 15, as erroneously stated.

26. ASMAE, AP, *Tunisia*, busta 14/1, n. 310 R./278.

27. Abitbol quotes a passage from a cable of 13 January, sent by von Ribbentrop to the German ambassador in Rome, instructing him to notify the Italian government that, after 31 March 1943, the Germans would consider themselves free to act against Jews holding Italian citizenship and choosing to remain in Germany (including the Bohemian and Moravian protectorate) and in the

countries occupied by Germany (Abitbol, *Les juifs d'Afrique du Nord*, pp. 128–129, and p. 144, note 74). Abitbol believed that this document also applied to the Jews of Tunisia; this, however, is not the case. The document refers to the occupied countries of Western Europe, in which Italy still had diplomatic representation, that is, France, Belgium, Holland, and Norway (in addition to Germany itself and the protectorate), and has nothing to do with Tunisia.

28. We do not know how the Tunisian Jews viewed this discrimination. It may be assumed to have aroused their jealousy, but I have not found clear evidence of this in any sources. The chairman of the community, M. Borgel, discusses this subject in a dry, factual manner (*Etoile jaune*, pp. 61, 173).

29. The document has been published in photographic form and in French translation by Sabille (*Les juifs de Tunisie*, Figure 4 [opposite p. 43] and p. 182). Rahn reported on the same day that the instruction had been given in coordination with the French administration (ibid., p. 183).

30. Borgel, *Etoile jaune*, pp. 31–36.

31. The chairman of the community asked Admiral Estéva to intervene, but the latter was only able to obtain a deferment of twelve hours; in return for this "concession," Rauff demanded that the first group of workers be composed of 3,000 men (Borgel, *Etoile jaune*, pp. 39–40).

32. Hereinafter Recruiting Committee. This affair is further discussed in Y. Zur, "The Jews of Tunisia," pp. 169–172 (Hebrew).

33. Testimony on one of those camps has been given by author Albert Memmi, himself among the recruits, whose writing provides an artful description of the overall atmosphere (though admittedly not entirely accurate). See *La statue de sel*, Paris, 1966, pp. 291–339.

34. Borgel, *Etoile jaune*, p. 60, note 1; Abitbol, *Les juifs d'Afrique du Nord*, p. 141; Ghez, *Six mois sous la botte*, pp. 84–98. At that time, those working on fortifications in Tunisia also included several thousand hired Arabs from Libya.

35. Gaston Guez, *Nos martyrs sous la botte allemande, ou les ex-travailleurs juifs de Tunisie racontent leur souffrances*, Tunis, 1943; R. Attal, "Les Juifs de Tunisie sous l'occupation nazie d'après les témoignages oraux," *Le Monde Juif*, 21 (1966), pp. 34–37.

36. Sabille, *Les juifs de Tunisie*, Figure 2 (opposite p. 39).

37. See note 28. See also C. Regard, "Anche in Tunisia aiutammo gli ebrei," *Il Tempo*, 14 July 1979, p. 20.

38. Borgel, *Etoile jaune*, p. 61, note 1; p. 194, note 1; Consul Bombieri in Tunis to the Foreign Ministry, 21 April 1943 (ASMAE, AP, *Tunisia*, busta 15).

39. From a report by Minister Schleier of the German Embassy in Paris to the Foreign Ministry, 12 December 1942 (URO, *Judenverfolgung in Frankreich*, p. 133).

40. The document was published in its entirety in URO (*Judenverfolgung in Frankreich*, pp. 129–131). The passage relevant to Tunisia was also published in French translation by Sabille (*Les juifs de Tunisie*, p. 184). A translation into English, submitted to the Nuremberg trials, was published by Abitbol (*Les juifs d'Afrique du Nord*, pp. 192–193).

41. From the French administration's legal advisor to Admiral Estéva, 20 March 1943 (Sabille, *Les juifs de Tunisie*, pp. 179–181). See also the evidence of the legal adviser to the French administration, Pierre de Font-Réaulx (Hoover Institution, *France during the German Occupation*, 2, p. 719).

42. The obligation to wear the badge may have been imposed in a few places at the initiative of junior SS commanders or even of local pro-Nazi French (members of the Service d'Ordre Légionnaire, SOL). See Borgel, *Etoile jaune*, p. 179.

43. In the Foreign Ministry files that have been made available to scholars for their perusal (not all of the files still exist), there is no mention of these camps. This may be because the camps were administered by the army, or because their inmates did not include holders of Italian citizenship. The files of the Armistice Commission offer nearly no material on Tunisia following the Axis landing (because the general delegation in North Africa was intended to supervise the implementation of the June 1940 armistice agreements, which lost all relevance after the landing). It may be assumed that interesting material on this subject was recorded in the logs of army units active on the Tunisian front.

44. Even Borgel—who, as a French patriot, should certainly not be suspected of sympathy for the Italians (and, in any event, not in 1944)—writes: "The Italians, it must be admitted, behaved toward our people with humanity. With them it was possible to express opinions, and from time to time, they were prepared to admit the legitimacy of our arguments" (*Etoile jaune*, p. 122). Borgel also mentions that the intervention of the Italian Army headquarters in Tunisia made it possible for the Jews to bake ritual unleavened bread for Passover of 1943 (ibid., p. 185).

45. See mainly Borgel, *Etoile jaune*, pp. 119–127.

46. Ghez, *Six mois*, pp. 97–98.

47. Simoni, *Ambasciata d'Italia*, p. 321.

48. Abitbol, *Les juifs d'Afrique du Nord*, pp. 149–174. See also Giraud's writings, in which he justifies his position with astonishing cynicism (*Un seul but, la victoire, Alger 1942–1944*, Paris, 1949, pp. 29–31, 118–124).

49. Memmi, *La statue*, pp. 352–353.

## Conclusions (pp. 241–249)

1. See among many Ch. Weizmann, *Trial and Error*, London, 1949, pp. 356–357; F. Chabod, *L'Italia contemporanea (1918–1948)*, 3rd ed., Turin, 1961, p. 96; A. Gramsci, *Lettere dal carcere*, 5th ed., Turin, 1947, p. 144.

2. *Campagna della razza*, according to the expression current in those days.

3. See also my article "The Origin and Development of Fascist anti-Semitism in Italy (1922–1945)," in Y. Gutman and L. Rothkirchen (eds.), *The Catastrophe of European Jewry*, Jerusalem, 1976, pp. 288–298.

4. During the first years of the Italian unified state, the candidacy of Jews to the office of Minister of Finance was foiled on two occasions: in the first case, following Christian religious arguments, in the second case because of the opposition

of a liberal-secular member of parliament who argued that Jews were disqualified from serving in the office of minister because of their "adherence to two nationalities." See the summary of these incidents by Delio Cantimori in his introduction to the first edition of the book by De Felice, *Storia degli ebrei italiani*, Turin, 1962, pp. xxii–xxvi.

5. Among many others, see articles published in *La Civiltà Cattolica*: "Della questione giudaica in Europa: 1. Le cause," fasc. 967 (22 September 1890), pp. 5–20; "2. Gli effetti," fasc. 970 (4 November 1890); pp. 385–407; "3. I rimedi," fasc. 972 (9 December 1890), pp. 641–655. These articles were reprinted in a separate booklet under the same title (Prato, 1891) that was distributed in a large edition.

6. For a short bibliography of publications of a racist nature that appeared during this period, see G. Landra-G. Cogni, *Piccola bibliografia razziale*, Rome, 1939. Two collections of these works were published by R. Mazzetti (*Orientamenti antiebraici della vita e della cultura italiana. Saggi di storia religiosa, politica e letteraria*, Modena, 1939; *L'antiebraismo nella cultura italiana dal 1700 al 1900*, Modena, 1939). On the Italian nationalists and their racist tendencies, Benedetto Croce already wrote in 1927 that "there were also among the nationalists those who, recalling Prussian ideas of the State, or under the influence of Pan-Germanism, tried to introduce in Italy a 'religion of the State,' a dark and terrible idol, fantastically remote from human life and seeking to challenge and override it, or a 'religion of race,' such as had for some time past boasted apostles and priests in various parts of Europe and the world" (*A History of Italy, 1871–1915*, 1, New York, 1963, p. 249).

7. On other aspects of this influence, see R. De Felice, *Intellettuali di fronte al fascismo*, Rome, 1985.

8. On the "anti-intellectual" character of fascism see G. Gentile, "The Philosophical Basis of Fascism," *Foreign Affairs*, 6 (1927–1928), pp. 290–304; idem, *Origini e dottrina del fascismo*, Roma, 1929 (particularly, Chapter 10, "Pensiero e azione").

9. Among other posts Roberto Farinacci served from February 1925 to March 1926 as party secretary, at the time when Mussolini needed a man to lead his party on a line of violence and with a heavy hand against the extensive opposition that had arisen in the country after the murder of Matteotti. Farinacci was a member of the Fascist Grand Council from its establishment (December 1922). Early in 1939, he was appointed chairman of the Legislative Committee in La Camera dei Fasci e delle Corporazioni (the fascist parliament). On 9 December 1939, at the meeting of the Fascist Grand Council, Farinacci voted against the government decision concerning nonbelligerence and for the immediate entry of Italy into the war alongside Germany. In July 1943, after the collapse of the fascist regime he fled to Germany. He returned to Italy after the Germans took over the country and in April 1945 was executed by partisans. See on him H. Fornary, *Mussolini's Gadfly*, Nashville, 1971.

10. *Intransigente*, according the current definition of those days.

11. Giovanni Preziosi also fled to Germany after Mussolini was ousted. He returned

to Italy in the wake of the German Army and in March 1944 was appointed head of a new racial office (Ispettorato Generale per la razza) attached to the presidency of the Council of Ministers in the Salò Republic. The Ispettorato was responsible for the policy toward the Jews. In this capacity, Preziosi advocated implementation of extreme measures for "an integral solution for the Jewish Problem." Together with his wife he committed suicide in Milan on 25 April 1945, on the eve of the liberation of the city. On his journalistic activity from the beginning of the 1920s—against the parliamentary opposition, against the antifascist emigrés, and, first and foremost, against the Freemasons and the "International Jewry"—see De Felice, *Intellettuali*, pp. 128–189; M. T. Pichetto, *Alle radici dell'odio, Preziosi e Benigni antisemiti*, Milan, 1983.

12. See the quotations in my article "The Jewish Problem in Italian Policy between Two World Wars," *Molad*, 166/167 (1962), pp. 188–189.

13. In the years 1922–1924, even after the rise to power of the Fascist party, most of the democratic institutions were still operating. The beginning of the totalitarian rule of fascism is usually set on 3 January 1925, when constitutional legality was terminated.

14. On Mussolini's policy in this period, see De Felice, *Mussolini il duce*, pp. 254–330.

15. This may also be deduced from Mussolini's own words, from 1919 onward, and from the evidence of his close associates. See, for example, the words of two officials of the Italian Foreign Ministry who, in the course of their duties, became closely familiar with the subject (and who certainly had no intention of blackening Mussolini's name): Raffaele Guariglia, who for years was in charge of liaison with the Zionist Movement (*Ricordi*, pp. 143, 182), and Luigi Villari, who was considered the ministry expert on the United States and American Jewry (*Italian Foreign Policy under Mussolini*, New York, 1956, pp. 197–200).

16. Anyone browsing through the files of the Italian Foreign Office will find that Mussolini had viewed an astounding number of documents concerning Jews, including reports dealing with quite trivial and incidental matters (such as a dispute over kosher slaughtering between orthodox rabbis and neologists in Hungary, or the distribution of liturgic books among the Jews of Rhodes). Mussolini read them, marked with his blue or red pencil the paragraphs that interested him most, sometimes wrote short instructions and signed them with his well-known *M*.

17. Mussolini himself explained some of the motives and goals of this policy in a message he sent to Hitler on the eve of the declaration of the "one-day boycott" in Germany. The document was first published in the appendix to my article: "Weizmann's Political Activity in Italy from 1923 to 1934," in D. Carpi and G. Yogev (eds.), *Zionism. Studies in the History of the Zionist Movement and of the Jewish Community in Palestine*, Tel Aviv, 1975, pp. 237–239. On this episode, see also Vittorio Cerruti, the Italian ambassador in Berlin at that time (URO, *Judenverfolgung in Italien*, pp. xvi–xvii).

18. On the other hand, De Felice attributes the decision to introduce the racial

policy to external factors only, namely, the influence of the pact with Nazi Germany (*Mussolini l'alleato, 1940–1945. Vol. 1. L'Italia in guerra*, Turin, 1990, pp. 312–318). It seems there is room to differ with him on this point. Michaelis, too, basically follows the De Felice's thesis. See his book (*Mussolini and the Jews*, pp. 118–191) and his paper on "The Holocaust in Italy and Its Representation in Italian Post-War Literature" (*Remembering for the Future*, 1, Oxford, 1989, pp. 254–265), in which he summarizes his view: "The Duce's decision to break with the Jews was due, not to any irresistible foreign pressure, but to his recognition of Italy's changed alignment in Europe and more particularly to his desire to cement the German-Italian alliance by eliminating any strident contrast in the policy of the two Fascist Powers" (p. 255). It seems to me, however, that the crucial problem is not whether there were, or were not, direct German demands to introduce a racial policy, because everybody understands that in the 1930s the German leadership could not allow itself to make such demands. The problem is whether from the beginning there were inside the fascist movement ideological principles and political forces that pushed toward the implementation of a policy of social discrimination and economic dispossession of the Jews in Italy because of their own internal logic and without any connection to changes in foreign policy.

19. See among others Rochat and Massobrio, *L'esercito italiano*, pp. 268–270; N. Gallerano, "Il fronte interno attraverso i rapporti delle autorità. 1942–43," *Il Movimento di Liberazione in Italia*, 109 (1972), pp. 4–32; N. Ravelli, *La strada del davai*, Turin, 1966.

20. Bastianini testifies, perhaps with a touch of exaggeration, that "in Italy no one understood the meaning of these race laws" (*Memorie*, p. 54).

# BIBLIOGRAPHY

Abetz, Otto. *D'une prison*, Paris, 1949.

———. *Histoire d'une politique franco-allemande, 1930–1950. Mémoires d'un ambassador*, Paris, 1953.

———. *Pétain et les Allemands. Mémorandum d'Abetz sur les rapports Franco-Allemands*, Paris, 1948.

Abitbol, Michel. *Les juifs d'Afrique du Nord sous Vichy*, Paris, 1983.

Abrami, Isaac. "The 'Grana' Community in Tunis According to Its Minute-books," in M. Abitbol (ed.), *Judaisme d'Afrique du Nord aux XIXᵉ–XXᵉ siècles*, Jerusalem, 1980, pp. 64–95 (Hebrew).

Adler-Cohen, Raya. "Le Camp de Gurs—une étape historique essentielle de 1940 à 1942," in K. Bartosek, R. Gallisot, D. Peschanski (eds.), *Réfugiés et immigrés d'Europe Centrale dans le mouvement antifasciste et la Résistance en France (1933–1945)*, Paris, 1986, pp. 1–12.

Ageron, Charles-Robert. "Les mouvements nationalistes dans le Magreb pendant la 2ᵉ guerre mondiale," in Comité d'Historie de la 2ᵉ Guerre Mondiale, *La guerre en Méditerranée, 1939–1945*, Paris, 1971, pp. 626–641.

Alfieri, Dino. *Deux dictateurs face à face. Rome-Berlin, 1939–1943*, Paris, 1948.

Amendola, Giorgio. *Lettere a Milano, 1939–1945*, Rome, 1973.

Amouroux, Henri. *La grande histoire des Français sous l'occupation. Vol. 2. Quarante millions de pétainistes*, Paris, 1977; *Vol. 5. Les passions et les haines*, Paris, 1981.

Anfuso, Filippo. *Roma-Berlino-Salò*, Milan, 1950.

Annet, Armand. *Aux heures troubles de l'Afrique Française, 1939–1943*, Paris, 1952.

Ariel, Joseph. "Jewish Self-defence and Resistance in France during World War II," *Yad Vashem Studies*, 6 (1967), pp. 221–250.

———. "Jewish Self-defence and Revolt in the Days of the Holocaust in France," *Gesher*, 9 (1963), pp. 170–183 (Hebrew).

Attal, Robert. "Les Juifs de Tunisie sous l'occupation nazie d'après des témoignances oraux," *Le Monde Juif*, 21 (1966), pp. 34–37.

Avarna di Gualtieri, Carlo. "Gli ebrei e l'occupazione italiana in Francia," *Nuova Antologia* (January 1962), pp. 245–248.

———. "Una missione presso il Governo di Vichy," *Nuova Antologia* (January–April 1958), pp. 79–88.

Barré, Georges. *Tunisie, 1942–1943*, Paris, 1950.

Bastianini, Giuseppe. *Uomini, cose, fatti. Memorie di un ambasciatore*, Milan, 1959.

Bauer, Yehuda. *American Jewry and the Holocaust*, Detroit, 1981.

Belardelli, Giovanni. *Nello Rosselli, uno storico antifascista*, Florence, 1982.

Bessis, Juliette. *La Méditerranée fasciste. L'Italie mussolinienne et la Tunisie*, Paris, 1981.

————. "La question tunisienne dans l'évolution des relations franco-italiennes de 1935 au 10 juin 1940," in J. B. Duroselle and E. Serra (eds.), *Italia e Francia dal 1919 al 1939*, Milan, 1981, pp. 245–255.

Billig, Joseph. *Le Commissariat Général aux Questions Juives, 1941–1944*, vols. 1–3, Paris, 1955–1960.

————. "La condition des Juifs en France (juillet 1940–août 1944)," *Revue d'Histoire de la Deuxième Guerre Mondiale*, 6 (1956), pp. 22–55.

————. *La Solution Finale de la question juive*, Paris, 1977.

Bonomi, Ivanoe. *Diario di un anno: 2 giugno 1943–10 giugno 1944*, Milan, 1947.

Borgel, Robert M. *Etoile jaune et croix gammée. Récit d'une servitude*, Tunis, 1944.

Browning, Christopher. *The Final Solution and the German Foreign Office*, New York, London, 1978.

Bulawko, Henri, and Diamant David. *Pithiviers et Beaune-la-Rolande*, Paris, 1951.

Calef, Nissim. *Campo di rappresaglia*, Rome, 1946.

Carboni, Giacomo. *Più che il dovere. Memorie segrete, 1935–1948*, Florence, 1955.

Carpi, Daniel. "The Italian Diplomat Luca Pietromarchi and His Activities on Behalf of the Jews in Croatia and Greece," *Yalkut Moreshet*, 33 (1982), pp. 145–152 (Hebrew).

————. "The Italian Government and the Jews of Northern France, 1942–1943," *Zion*, 54 (1989), pp. 179–204 (Hebrew).

————. "The Italian Government and the Jews of Tunisia in the Second World War (June 1940–May 1943)," *Zion*, 52 (1987), pp. 57–106 (Hebrew).

————. "The Mufti of Jerusalem, Amin el-Husseini, and His Diplomatic Activity during World War II (October 1941–July 1943)," *Studies in Zionism*, 7 (1983), pp. 101–131.

————. "Notes on the History of the Jews in Greece during the Holocaust Period. The Attitude of the Italians (1941–1943)," in H. Ben-Shahar et al. (eds.), *Festschrift in Honor of Dr. George S. Wise*, Tel Aviv, 1981, pp. 25–62.

————. "The Number of the Jews in France according to the Wannsee Conference Protocol (January 1942)," *Massuah*, 13 (1985), pp. 129–132 (Hebrew).

————. "The Origin and Development of Fascist Antisemitism in Italy (1922–1945)," in Y. Gutman and L. Rothkirchen (eds.), *The Catastrophe of European Jewry*, Jerusalem, 1976, pp. 288–298.

————. "The Rescue of Jews in the Italian Zone of Occupied Croatia," in Y. Gutman and E. Zuroff (eds.), *Rescue Attempts during the Holocaust*, Jerusalem, 1977, pp. 465–525.

————. "Weizmann's Political Activity in Italy from 1923 to 1934," in D. Carpi and G. Yogev (eds.), *Zionism. Studies in the History of the Zionist Movement and of the Jewish Community in Palestine*, Tel Aviv, 1975, pp. 193–242.

Carpi, Leone. "Lettere di Jabotinsky," in D. Carpi et al. (eds.), *Scritti in memoria di Leone Carpi*, Jerusalem, 1967, pp. 32–56.

Castellano, Giuseppe. *Come firmai l'armistizio di Cassibile*, Milan, 1945.
Cavaglion, Alberto. "Gli Ebrei di St. Martin-de-Vésubie e lo sbandamento della 4ª armata," in Istituto Storico della Resistenza in Cuneo e Provincia, *8 settembre. Lo sfacelo della quarta armata*, Turin, 1979, pp. 205–227.
———. *Nella notte straniera. Gli ebrei di S. Martin Vésubie e il campo di Borgo S. Dalmazzo*, Cuneo, 1981.
Cavallero, Ugo. *Comando Supremo*, Rocca S. Casciano, 1948.
Centre de Documentation Juive Contemporaine (CDJC). *Activité des organisations juives en France sous l'occupation*, Paris, 1947.
———. *Le Dossier Eichmann et "la solution finale de la question juive*," Paris, 1960.
———. *La France et la question juive, 1940/1944*, Paris, 1981.
———. *Les juifs sous l'occupation. Recueil des textes français et allemands. 1940–1944*, Paris, 1945.
Ceva, Lucio. "4ª armata e occupazione italiana della Francia. Problemi militari," in Istituto Storico della Resistenza in Cuneo e Provincia, *8 settembre. Lo sfacelo della quarta armata*, Turin, 1979, pp. 93–105.
Chabod, Federico. *L'Italia contemporanea (1918–1948)*, 3rd ed., Turin, 1961.
Chouraqui, André. *Marche vers l'Occident. Les Juifs d'Afrique du Nord*, Paris, 1952.
Ciano, Galeazzo. *Diario, 1937–1943*, Milan, 1980.
*La Civiltà Cattolica.* "Della questione giudaica in Europa: 1. Le cause," fasc. 967 (22 September 1890), pp. 5–20; "2. Gli effetti," fasc. 970 (4 November 1890), pp. 385–407; "3. I rimedi," fasc. 972 (9 December 1890), pp. 641–655.
Cohen, Asher. "L'échec de la propagande du Commissariat Général face aux questions juives en France," in *Idéologie et propagande en France*, Paris, 1987, pp. 201–219.
———. "Factors in the Rescue of Jews in France during the Holocaust," *Proceedings of the Tenth World Congress for Jewish Studies*, Jerusalem, 1990, pp. 495–500 (Hebrew).
———. "Immigrant Jews, Christians and French Jews," in Y. Bauer et al. (eds.), *Remembering for the Future*, 1, Oxford, 1989, pp. 223–232.
Cohen, Richard I. *The Burden of Conscience, French Jewry's Response to the Holocaust*, Bloomington and Indianapolis, 1987.
Comité d'Histoire de la 2ᵉ Guerre Mondiale, *La guerre en Méditerranée, 1939–1945*, Paris, 1971.
Commissione Italiana di Armistizio con la Francia (CIAF), *Notiziario Quindicinale relativo ai territori francesi sotto controllo armistiziale*, biweekly bulletins, Turin.
Croce, Benedetto. *A History of Italy, 1871–1915*, vols. 1–2, New York, 1963.
Cruccu, Rinaldo. "La 4ª armata e l'armistizio," in Istituto Storico della Resistenza in Cuneo e Provincia, *8 settembre. Lo sfacelo della quarta armata*, Turin, 1979, pp. 65–91.
Darmon, Raul. *La situation des cultes en Tunisie*, Paris, 1930.

Deakin, F. William. *The Brutal Friendship: Mussolini, Hitler, and the Fall of Italian Fascism*, London, 1966.

Decleva, Enrico. "Le delusioni di una democrazia: Carlo Rosselli e la Francia 1929–1937," in J. B. Duroselle and E. Serra (eds.), *Italia e Francia dal 1919 al 1939*, Milan, 1981, pp. 39–84.

——. "L'unità d'azione alla prova: I socialisti italiani e il fronte popolare francese 1934–1939," in J. B. Duroselle and E. Serra (eds.), *Italia e Francia dal 1919 al 1939*, Milan, 1981, pp. 303–339.

De Felice, Renzo. *Intellettuali di fronte al fascismo*, Rome, 1985.

——. *Mussolini il duce. Vol. 2. Lo Stato totalitario, 1936–1940*, Turin, 1981.

——. *Mussolini l'alleato, 1940–1945. Vol. 1. L'Italia in guerra, 1940–1943*, Turin, 1990.

——. "Un nuovo documento sulla condizione degli ebrei nella zona d'occupazione italiana in Francia durante la seconda guerra mondiale," in F. Del Canuto (ed.), *Israel "Un decennio" 1974–1984*, Rome, 1984, pp. 179–184.

——. *Storia degli ebrei italiani sotto il fascismo*, 1st ed., Turin, 1962 (4th ed., revised and amplified, Turin, 1988).

Duquesne, Jacques. *Les catholiques français sous l'occupation*, Paris, 1966.

Duroselle, Jean-Baptiste. "Le gouvernement de Vichy face à l'Italie (juillet 1940–septembre 1943)," in J. B. Duroselle and E. Serra (eds.), *Italia e Francia (1939–1945)*, vol. 1, Milan, 1984, pp. 83–96.

Duroselle, Jean-Baptiste, and Enrico Serra (eds.). *Italia e Francia dal 1919 al 1939*, Milan, 1981.

——. *Italia e Francia (1939–1945)*, vols. 1–2, Milan, 1984.

Ecole des Hautes Etudes, *L'Allemagne Nazie et le génocide juif*, Paris, 1985.

Erlanger, Philippe. *La France sans étoile. Souvenirs de l'avant-guerre et du temps de l'occupation*, Paris, 1974.

Fauck, F. "Judenverfolgung in Nizza, 1942/43," *Gutachten des Instituts für Zeitgeschichte*, 2 (1966), pp. 43–46.

Feingold, Henry L. *The Politics of Rescue. The Roosevelt Administration and the Holocaust, 1938–1945*, New Brunswick, New Jersey, 1970.

*Foreign Relations of the United States. Diplomatic Papers 1943*, vol. 1, Washington, D.C., 1963.

Franco, Hizkia M. *Les martyrs juifs de Rhodes et de Cos*, Elisabethville, 1952.

Gallerano, Nicola. "Il fronte interno attraverso i rapporti delle autorità, 1942–43," *Il Movimento di Liberazione in Italia*, 109 (1972), pp. 4–32.

Gamzon, Robert. *Les eaux claires. Journal 1938–1944*, Paris, 1982.

Ganier Raymond, Philippe. *Une certaine France: l'antisémitisme 1940–1944*, Paris, 1975.

Garosci, Aldo. "La concentrazione antifascista a Parigi," in C. Lupo (ed.), *Terzo programma. Trent'anni di storia politica italiana (1915–1945)*, Rome, 1962, pp. 185–196.

——. *La vita di Carlo Rosselli*, Florence, 1945.

Gentile, Giovanni. *Origini e dottrina del fascismo*, Rome, 1929.

Ghez, Paul. *Six mois sous la botte*, Tunis, 1943.

Giraud, Henri. *Un seul but, la victoire. Alger, 1942–1944*, Paris, 1949.

Gorgiel-Sercaz, Hélène. "Memories of a Jewish Girl," *Yalkut Moreshet*, 50 (1991), pp. 175–195 (Hebrew).

Graham, Robert A. "Il Vaticano e gli ebrei profughi in Italia durante la guerra," *La Civiltà Cattolica*, fasc. 3281 (1987), pp. 429–443.

Gramsci, Antonio. *Lettere dal carcere*, 5th ed., Turin, 1947.

Grandi, Dino. *25 Iuglio. Quarant'anni dopo*, Bologna, 1983.

Graziani, Rodolfo. *Ho difeso la patria*, Milan, 1947.

Guariglia, Raffaele. *Ricordi*, Naples, 1948.

Guez, Gaston. *Nos martyrs sous la botte allemande, ou les ex-travailleurs juifs de Tunisie racontent leurs souffrances*, Tunis, 1943(?).

Guicheteau, Gérard. *Marseille 1943: La fin du Vieux Port*, Marseilles, 1973.

Guillen, Pierre. "La question des 'Fuorusciti' et les relations franco-italiennes (1925–1935)," in J. B. Duroselle and E. Serra (eds.). *Italia e Francia dal 1919 al 1939*, Milan, 1981, pp. 21–38.

Halpern, Bronka. *A Ray of Light in the Darkness*, Jerusalem, 1967 (Hebrew).

Hammel, Frederic Ch. *Souviens-toi d'Amalek. Témoignage sur la lutte des Juifs en France (1938–1944)*, Paris, 1982.

Hirschberg, Chajim Zeev. *History of the Jews in North Africa*, Jerusalem, 1965 (Hebrew).

Hoover Institution, Stanford University. *France during the German Occupation, 1940–1944*, vols. 1–3, Paris, 1958–1959.

Istituto Storico della Resistenza in Cuneo e Provincia. *8 settembre. Lo sfacelo della quarta armata*, Turin, 1979.

Jäckel, Eberhard. *La France dans l'Europe de Hitler*, Paris, 1968.

Kempner, Robert Max W. *Eichmann und Komplizen*, Zurich, 1961.

Klarsfeld, Serge. *Die Endlösung der Judenfrage in Frankreich*, Paris, 1977.

———. "Notices biographiques des principaux responsables de la 'Solution Finale' en France," in J. Billig, *La Solution Finale de la question juive*, Paris, 1977, pp. 189–201.

———. *Vichy-Auschwitz. Le rôle de Vichy dans la solution finale de la question juive en France*, vols. 1–2, Paris, 1983–1985.

Knout, David. *Contribution à l'histoire de la Résistance Juive en France (1940–1944)*, Paris, 1947.

Krausnick, Helmut. "Himmler über seinen Besuch bei Mussolini vom 11–14 Oktober 1942," *Vierteljahrshefte für Zeitgeschichte*, 4 (1956), pp. 423–426.

Laloum, Jean. *La France antisémite de Darquier de Pellepoix*, Paris, 1977.

Landra, Guido, and Giulio Cogni. *Piccola bibliografia razziale*, Rome, 1939.

Laskier, Michael. "The Evolution of Zionist Activity in the Jewish Communities of Morocco, Tunisia and Algeria: 1897–1947," *Studies in Zionism*, 8 (1983), pp. 205–236.

Latour, Anny. *La Résistance juive en France (1940–1944)*, Paris, 1970.

Lazar, Lucien. *La résistance juive en France*, Paris, 1987.

Leone, Massimo, *Le organizzazioni di soccorso ebraiche in età fascista*, Rome, 1983.

Levi, Alessandro. *Ricordi dei fratelli Rosselli*, Florence, 1947.

Levi, Carlo. *Cristo si é fermato a Eboli*, Turin, 1945.

Levy, Claude. "La 4ª armata italiana in Francia (11 novembre 1942–8 settembre 1943)," in Istituto Storico della Resistenza in Cuneo e Provincia, *8 settembre. Lo sfacelo della quarta armata*, Turin, 1979, pp. 35–61.

London, Geo. *L'amiral Estéva et le général Dentz devant la Haute Cour de Justice*, Lyon, 1945.

Lubac, Henri de. *Résistance chrétienne à l'antisémitisme. Souvenirs, 1940–1944*, Paris, 1988.

Lubetzki, J. *La condition des juifs en France sous l'occupation allemande, 1940–1944. La législation raciale*, Paris, 1945.

Marie-Benoît, T. R. P. "Una lettera di Padre Benedetto," *La Voce della Comunità Israelitica*, July 1955.

———. "Pagine di storia. Angelo Donati," *Israel*, 46 (13 April 1961), p. 3.

———. "Résumé de mon activité en faveur des Juifs persécutés (1940–1944)," in *Livre d'or des congrégations françaises, 1939–1945*, Paris, 1948, pp. 305–330.

———. In G. Wellers, A. Kaspi, S. Klarsfeld (eds.), *La France et la question juive, 1940/44*, Paris, 1981, pp. 253–256.

Marrus, Michael, and Robert Paxton. *Vichy France and the Jews*, New York, 1981.

Mayeur, Jean-Marie. "Les églises devant la pérsecution des Juifs en France," in G. Wellers, A. Kaspi, S. Klarsfeld (eds.), *La France et la question juive. 1940/1944*, Paris, 1981, pp. 147–170.

Mazor, Michel. "Les juifs dans la clandestinité sous l'occupation italienne en France," *Le Monde Juif*, 59 (1970), pp. 21–31.

Mazzetti, Roberto. *L'antiebraismo nella cultura italiana dal 1700 al 1900*, Modena, 1939.

———. *Orientamenti antiebraici della vita e della cultura italiana. Saggi di storia religiosa, politica e letteraria*, Modena, 1939.

Mellini Ponce de Leon, Alberto. *Guerra diplomatica a Salò*, Florence, 1950.

Memmi, Albert, *La statue de sel*, Paris, 1966.

Messe, Giovanni. *La mia armata in Tunisia. Come finì la guerra in Africa*, Milan, 1960.

Michaelis, Meir. "The Holocaust in Italy and Its Representation in Italian Post-War Literature," Y. Bauer et al. (eds.), *Remembering for the Future*, 1, Oxford, 1989, pp. 254–265.

———. *Mussolini and the Jews*, Oxford, 1978.

Michel, Alain. *Les Eclaireurs Israélites de France pendant la seconde guerre mondiale*, Paris, 1984.

Michel, Henri. "Les relations franco-italienne (de l'armistice de juin 1940 à l'armistice de septembre 1943)," in Comité d'Histoire de la 2ᵉ Guerre Mondiale. *La guerre en Méditerraneé, 1939–1945*, Paris, 1971, pp. 485–511.

Michmann, Dan. "Historical Accuracy," *Yalkut Moreshet*, 45 (1988), pp. 197–200 (Hebrew).

Miege, Jean-Louis. *L'impérialisme colonial italien de 1870 à nos jours*, Paris, 1968.

Millman, Richard. *La question juive entre les deux guerres*, Paris, 1992.

Milza, Pierre. *L'Italie fasciste devant l'opinion française, 1920–1940*, Paris, 1967.

———. "Le voyage de Pierre Laval à Rome en janvier 1935," in J. B. Duroselle and E. Serra (eds.), *Italia e Francia dal 1919 al 1939*, Milan, 1981, pp. 219–243.

Ministero degli Affari Esteri, *I Documenti Diplomatici Italiani* nona serie: 1939–1943, vol. 3, Rome, 1959; vol. 4, Rome, 1960.

Ministero degli Affari Esteri, *Relazione sull'opera svolta dal Ministero degli Affari Esteri per la tutela delle comunità ebraiche (1938–1943)*, n.d., n.p. (Rome, 1945?).

Moch, Maurice, and Alain Michel. *L'étoile et la francisque*, Paris, 1990.

Moellhausen, Eitel Friedrich. *ll giuoco è fatto!*, Florence, 1951.

Mola, Alessandro Aldo. *L'imperialismo italiano*, Rome, 1980.

Molho, Isaac R. "Count Quinto Mazzolini, One of the Saviours of the Jews of Rhodes," *Otzar Yehude Sefarad*, 5 (1962), pp. 155–157 (Hebrew).

———. "Documents for Holocaust Research in the Community of Greece and the Efforts for Rescue," *Otzar Yehude Sefarad*, 4 (1961), pp. 155–163 (Hebrew).

Monneray Henri, *La persécution des Juifs en France et dans les autres pays de l'Europe de l'Ouest*, Paris, 1949.

Morelli, Anne. "Les diplomates italiens en Belgique et la 'question juive,' 1938–1943," *Bulletin de l'Institut Historique Belge de Rome*, 53–54 (1983–1984), pp. 357–407.

Mortara, Andrea (Maurizio Valenzi). *Ebrei italiani di fronte al "razzismo,"* Tunis, 1938.

Nenni, Pietro. *Vingt ans de fascismes. De Rome à Vichy*, Paris, 1960.

Office of U.S. Chief Counsel for the Prosecution of Axis Criminality. *Nazi Conspiracy and Aggression*, vol. 7, Washington, D.C., 1946.

Ortona, Egidio. "Il 1943 da Palazzo Chigi. Note di Diario," *Storia Contemporanea*, 14 (1983), pp. 1076–1147.

Palla, Marco. "L'imperialisme fasciste," *Revue d'Histoire de la deuxième guerre mondiale*, 139 (1985), pp. 25–46.

Panicacci, Jean-Louis. *Les Alpes-Maritimes de 1939 à 1945. Un département dans la tourmente*, Nice, 1989.

———. "Les juifs et la question juive dans les Alpes-Maritimes de 1939 à 1945," *Recherches Régionales Côte d'Azur et Contrées Limitrophes*, 3 (1983), pp. 239–327.

———. "L'8 settembre nel Nizzardo," in Istituto Storico della Resistenza in Cuneo e Provincia, *8 settembre. Lo sfacelo della quarta armata*, Turin, 1979, pp. 107–117.

———. "L'occupazione italiana delle Alpi Marittime," *Notiziario dell'Istituto Storico della Resistenza in Cuneo e Provincia*, 13 (1978), pp. 7–34.

————. "L'occupazione italiana di Mentone (giugno 1940–settembre 1943)," *Notiziario dell'Istituto Storico della Resistenza in Cuneo e Provincia*, 24 (1983), pp. 3–18.

Pasotti, Nullo. *Italiani e Italia in Tunisia dalle origini al 1970*, Rome, 1971.

Peyrouton, Marcel. *Du service public à la prison commune*, Paris, 1950.

Pichetto, Maria Teresa. *Alle radici dell'odio, Preziosi e Benigni antisemiti*, Milan, 1983.

Pietromarchi, Luca. "Frammenti delle memorie dell'ambasciatore Luca Pietromarchi. La difesa degli ebrei nel '43," *Nuova Antologia*, fasc. 2161 (January–March 1987), pp. 241–247.

Pirelli, Alberto. *Taccuini 1922/1943*, Bologna, 1984.

Poliakov, Leon. *La condition des juifs en France sous l'occupation italienne*, Paris, 1946 (English translation: *Jews under the Italian Occupation*, Paris, 1955; Italian translation: *Gli ebrei sotto l'occupazione italiana*, Milan, 1956).

————. *L'étoile jaune*, Paris, 1949.

*Le procés de Xavier Vallat présenté par ses amis*, Paris, 1948.

Rahn, Rudolf. *Un diplomate dans la tourmente*, Paris, 1980.

Rainero, Romain. "Gli accordi di Torino tra la CIAF e il governo di Pétain sulla Tunisia (Natale 1941)," in J. B. Duroselle and E. Serra (eds.), *Italia e Francia (1939–1945)*, vol. 1, Milan, 1984, pp. 228–244.

————. "La politique fasciste à l'égard de l'Afrique du Nord: L'epeé de l'Islam et la revendication sur la Tunisie," *Revue Française d'Histoire d'Outre-Mer*, 64 (1977), pp. 498–514.

————. *La rivendicazione fascista sulla Tunisia*, Milan, 1978.

Ravelli, Nuto. *La strada del davai*, Turin, 1966.

Regard, Cesare. "Anche in Tunisia aiutammo gli ebrei," *Il Tempo*, 14 July 1979, p. 20.

Rémond, René. "Les églises et la persécution des Juifs pendant la Seconde Guerre Mondiale," in Ecole des Hautes Etudes en sciences sociales, *L'Allemagne nazie et le génocide Juif*, Paris, 1985, pp. 375–403.

Rhodes, Antony. *The Vatican in the Age of the Dictators, 1922–1945*, London, Toronto, 1973.

Roatta, Mario. *Otto milioni di baionette. L'esercito italiano in guerra dal 1940 al 1944*, Milan, 1946.

Robinson, Jacob, and Henry Sachs. *The Holocaust. The Nuremberg Evidence*, Jerusalem, 1976.

Rochat, Giorgio, and Giulio Massobrio. *Breve storia dell'esercito italiano dal 1861 al 1943*, Turin, 1978.

Rochlitz, Joseph (ed.). *The Righteous Enemy. Document Collection*, Rome, 1988.

Rumi, Giorgio, *L'imperialismo italiano*, Rome, 1980.

Rutkowski, Adam. "Le camp d'internement de Gurs," *Le Monde Juif*, 100 (1980), pp. 128–146; 101 (1981), pp. 13–32.

————. *La lutte des juifs en France à l'époque de l'occupation*, Paris, 1975.

Ryan, Donna Frances. *Vichy and the Jews: The Example of Marseille, 1939–1944*, Ann Arbor, 1988.

Sabille, Jacques. *Les juifs de Tunisie sous Vichy et l'occupation*, Paris, 1954.

Saint-Siège, *Actes et documents du Saint-Siège relatifs à la seconde guerre mondiale. Vol. 8. La Saint-Siège et les victimes de la guerre, janvier 1941–décembre 1942*, Vatican City, 1974; *Vol. 9. janvier–décembre 1943*, Vatican City, 1975.

Saulnier, Hélène. "Nizza occupata," *Les langues néo-latines*, 253, 79ᵉ année (1985), pp. 49–58.

Scarantino, Anna. "La Comunità ebraica in Egitto tra le due guerre mondiali," *Storia Contemporanea*, 17 (1986), 6, pp. 1033–1082.

Schor, Ralph. "Il fascismo italiano nelle Alpes-Maritimes, 1922–1939," *Notiziario dell'Istituto Storico della Resistenza in Cuneo e Provincia*, 26 (1984), pp. 21–56.

Schramm, Hanna, and Barbara Vormeier. *Vivre à Gurs*, Paris, 1979.

Schröder, Joseph. "Les rapports des puissances de l'Axe avec le monde arabe," in Comité d'Histoire de la 2ᵉ Guerre Mondiale, *La guerre en Méditerranée, 1939–1945*, Paris, 1971, pp. 607–626.

Senise, Carmine. *Quando ero capo della polizia, 1940–1943*, Rome, 1946.

Serra, Enrico. "Cade Mussolini, resiste Vichy," *La Stampa*, 7 October 1981.

———. "Il confine meridionale della Libia e gli accordi Mussolini-Laval," in J. B. Duroselle and E. Serra (eds.), *Italia e Francia dal 1919 al 1939*, Milan, 1981, pp. 125–218.

———. *Italia e Francia 1939–1945. Vol. 2. La diplomazia italiana e la ripresa dei rapporti con la Francia (1943–1945)*, Milan, 1984.

———. "Leonardo Vitetti e una sua testimoninza," *Nuova Antologia*, 519 (1973), pp. 487–501.

Shelah, Menahem. *History of the Holocaust. Yugoslavia*, Jerusalem, 1990 (Hebrew).

Simoni, Leonardo (Michele Lanza). *Berlino. Ambasciata d'Italia, 1939–1943*, Rome, 1946.

Sorani, Settimio. *L'assistenza ai profughi ebrei in Italia (1933–1947). Contributo alla storia della "Delasem,"* Rome, 1983.

Statera, Vittorio. "L'ex questore Lospinoso ci racconta come aiutò quarantamila israeliti," *La Stampa*, 5 April 1961.

Terracini, Enrico. "Vittorio Zoppi, ambasciatore piemontese," *L'Osservatore Politico Letterario*, 21 (April 1975), 4, pp. 61–68.

Trabucchi, Alessandro. *I vinti hanno sempre torto*, Turin, 1947.

*Trials of War Criminals before the Nuremberg Military Tribunals*, vol. 13, Washington, D.C., 1952.

Umbreit, Hans. *Der Militärbefehlshaber in Frankreich, 1940–1944*, Boppard am Rhein, 1968.

United Restitution Organisation (URO), *Dokumentsammlung über die Judenverfolgung in Rumanien*, vol. 1, Frankfurt am Main, 1959.

———. *Dokumente über die Verantwortlichkeit des Reiches für die Judenmassnah-*

men im imbesetzten und unbesetzten Frankreich, insbesondere auch in Algerien, Marokko, Tunis, Frankfurt am Main, 1959.

————. Judenverfolgung in Italien, den italienisch besetzten Gebieten und in Nordafrika, Dokumentensammlung. Frankfurt am Main, 1962.

Valiani, Leo. "L'émigration antifasciste et la deuxième guerre mondiale," in J. B. Duroselle and E. Serra (eds.), Italia e Francia (1939–1945), vol. 1, Milan, 1984, pp. 285–294.

Vallat, Xavier. Le nez de Cléopâtre. Souvenirs d'un homme de droit, 1919–1944, Paris, 1957.

Villari, Luigi. Italian Foreign Policy under Mussolini, New York, 1956.

Weill, Joseph. Contribution à l'histoire des camps d'internement dans l'anti-France, Paris, 1946.

Weizmann, Chaim. Trial and Error, London, 1949.

Weizsäcker, Ernst von. Erinnerungen, Munich, 1950.

Weygand, Maxime. Mémoires. Rappelé au service, Paris, 1950.

Wyman, David S. The Abandonment of the Jews. America and the Holocaust, 1941–1945, New York, 1984.

Zangrandi, Ruggero. 1943: L'8 settembre, Milan, 1967.

Zur, Yaron. "The Jews of Tunisia under the German Occupation: A Divided Community in Time of Crisis," Contemporary Jewry, 2 (1985), pp. 169–172.

# INDEX

German racial policy, 11–12, 15, 33–34, 40–41, 45, 48–50, 52–54, 60, 66, 72, 98, 107, 191–192, 248–249, 261n.56; attitude toward Germany, 2–3, 9, 65, 85, 170; attitude toward the Italian Jews under Nazi rule, 3, 15, 21–22, 24–25, 28, 34–36, 49–51, 64–66, 78, 106, 262–263n.9, 270n.6, 274n.37; attitude toward Vichy government, 4, 10–11, 29, 79, 83, 92, 99, 130, 252n.9, 258n.30; disputes with the Germans about the fate of Jews, 41–64, 85–87, 100–101, 103–109, 112, 114–121, 125–129, 134–135, 146–154, 157, 161–162, 183–185, 225–227, 232–234, 296n.41; disputes with Vichy government about the fate of Jews, 89–92, 102–104, 122–124, 154–156, 160, 185–186, 218–227, 273n.33; evacuation of Jewish citizens from Nazi zones of occupation, 11, 34–35, 42, 48–49, 57, 60, 63–66, 91, 106–107, 125, 167–168, 173, 191; foreign Jews, 50, 276n.16; Foreign Ministry, 12, 21, 23–25, 35, 48–49, 51, 54, 57, 59–60, 63–65, 86–87, 105, 107, 109–110, 116, 120, 124–125, 129, 168, 174, 210–211, 217, 252–253n.14, 257n.21, 260n.51, 262n.9, 264n.24, 265n.38, 269n.10, 271n.18, 273n.31, 277n.21, 289n.67, 312n.31; Fourth Army, 12, 82, 88–89, 106, 112–114, 124, 131, 133, 136–138, 142, 147, 149, 155, 166, 169, 170–172, 174, 182–183, 188, 275n.8, 275n.9, 282n.62; General Staff, 12, 54, 82, 86, 104–105, 108–110, 118, 121, 124, 129, 133–134, 265n.38, 277n.21, 283n.7; Jews, 163, 242, 287n.39; "law for the protection of the race", the, 8, 11–12, 21, 25, 28, 44, 49–50, 57, 66, 69, 90, 168, 203, 241, 245–248, 257n.29, 260n.48, 269n.2; Ministry of Interior, 34, 36, 64, 148, 168–169, 175, 260n.48, 269n.10, 271n.18; police, 126, 129–131, 133–135, 137, 146, 148, 150, 153, 160, 162–163, 168, 172, 283n.7, 292n.96; Propaganda Ministry, 25, 256n.19; World War II, 2–3, 6, 60–63, 66, 80, 127, 162, 164–165, 174, 211

Jabotinsky, Zeev, 96
Japan, 39

Jefroykin, Dyka Jules, 179, 303n.41
Jerusalem, 27
Jewish star, the, 37–38, 45–46, 48–49, 51–52, 55, 60, 111, 121, 224, 235–237, 261n.58, 262n.7, 264n.23, 270n.8, 283n.7
"Joint", 143–144, 179
Jonchay, Sarton du, 316n.13
"Justice and Liberty", 7, 253n.17

Kairouan, 237
Kelman, Claude, 280n.45, 306n.75
Kesserling, Albert, 239
Knochen, Helmut, 31, 103–104, 108, 114–115, 147–149, 152–153, 157, 160–161, 258n.34, 296n.41
Kriegel, 280n.45

La Grave, 94
Lagarde, 219–220
La Goulette, 237
Lanza, Michele, 315n.5
Lanza d'Ajeta, Blasco, 36, 41, 64, 86–87, 89, 106, 217, 225, 233, 260nn.48, 51, 274n.37, 284nn.11, 21, 314n.62
Laurencie, Benoît-Léon de la, 20
Laval, Pierre, 9, 29, 39, 91–92, 103, 123, 126, 182, 186, 217, 220, 226–227, 267n.62, 274n.2, 272–273n.29, 314n.71
Légion Française des Combattants, 208, 311n.23
Leguay, Jean, 103, 156–157, 283n.2
Le Havre, 46
Lerici, Roberto, 309n.2
Lerins, 75
Les Milles, 94
Levi, Elia, 259n.41
Levi, Guido, 309n.7
Levi, Vittoria, 55
Levitt, Shimeon, 279n.40
Levy Andjel, Luisa, 59, 267n.63, 268n.69
Levy Piperno, Giovanna, 55, 267nn.63, 66, 268n.69
Levy, Sara, 55
Liberia, 228
Libya, 119, 127, 164; refugees, 201, 215–216
Lisbon, 77
Lischka, Kurt, 266n.58, 282n.65, 297n.51
Livorno, 253n.21

UNIVERSITY PRESS OF NEW ENGLAND publishes books under its own imprint and is the publisher for Brandeis University Press, Brown University Press, University of Connecticut, Dartmouth College, Middlebury College Press, University of New Hampshire, University of Rhode Island, Tufts University, University of Vermont, Wesleyan University Press and Salzburg Seminar.

LIBRARY OF CONGRESS CATALOGING-IN-PUBLICATION DATA

Carpi, Daniel.
    Between Mussolini and Hitler : the Jews and the Italian
authorities in France and Tunisia / Daniel Carpi.
       p.   cm. – (The Tauber Institute for the Study of European
Jewry series ; 17)
    Includes bibliographical references and index.
    ISBN 0-87451-662-5
    1. Jews—France—Persecutions.  2. Holocaust, Jewish (1939–1945)—
France.  3. France—History—Italian occupation, 1942–1943.
4. Jews—Tunisia—Persecutions.  5. France—Ethnic relations.
6. Tunisia—Ethnic relations.  I. Title.  II. Series.
DS135.F83C37  1994
944'.004924—dc20
  &#8734;                                     93-36810